THE AFFECT EFFECT

→ The Question of Political Ideology
expand on UCS
Role of Neuroscience & Psycho...
& Culture in the chapter
as parties as groups.

Leege & Wald.

The Affect Effect

DYNAMICS OF EMOTION IN
POLITICAL THINKING AND BEHAVIOR

Edited by W. Russell Neuman, George E. Marcus,
Ann N. Crigler, and Michael MacKuen

THE UNIVERSITY OF CHICAGO PRESS   Chicago and London

W. RUSSELL NEUMAN is the John Derby Evans Professor of Media Technology at the University of Michigan and the coauthor of *The Gordian Knot: Political Gridlock on the Information Highway* and *Affective Intelligence and Political Judgment*, the latter published by the University of Chicago Press.

GEORGE E. MARCUS is professor of political science at Williams College and the co-author of *Political Tolerance and American Democracy* and *Affective Intelligence and Political Judgment*, the latter published by the University of Chicago Press.

ANN N. CRIGLER is professor and chair of the Department of Political Science at the University of Southern California and the coedtitor of *Rethinking the Vote: The Politics and Prospects of Election Reform*.

MICHAEL MACKUEN is the Burton Craige Professor of Political Science at the University of North Carolina, Chapel Hill, and the coauthor of *Affective Intelligence and Political Judgment*, published by the University of Chicago Press, and *The Macro Polity*.

The University of Chicago Press, Chicago 60637
The University of Chicago Press, Ltd., London
© 2007 by The University of Chicago
All rights reserved. Published 2007
Printed in the United States of America

16 15 14 13 12 11 10 09 08 07   1 2 3 4 5

ISBN-13: 978-0-226-57441-7 (cloth)
ISBN-13: 978-0-226-57442-4 (paper)
ISBN-10: 0-226-57441-5 (cloth)
ISBN-10: 0-226-57442-3 (paper)

Library of Congress Cataloging-in-Publication Data

The affect effect : dynamics of emotion in political thinking and behavior / edited by W. Russell Neuman . . . [et al.].
    p. cm.
  Includes bibliographical references and index.
  ISBN-13: 978-0-226-57441-7 (cloth : alk. paper)
  ISBN-10: 0-226-57441-5 (cloth : alk. paper)
  ISBN-13: 978-0-226-57442-4 (pbk. : alk. paper)
  ISBN-10: 0-226-57442-3 (pbk. : alk.paper) 1. Political psychology. 2. Emotions. I. Neuman, W. Russell.
  JA74.5.A35 2007
  320.01'9—dc22

                2007009524

CONTENTS

CHAPTER ONE

Theorizing Affect's Effects

W. RUSSELL NEUMAN, GEORGE E. MARCUS,
ANN N. CRIGLER, AND MICHAEL MACKUEN

This book responds to a resurgent interest in the way emotion[1] interacts with thinking about politics and, as a result, the way citizens engage in or withdraw from political activity. We have come to conclude that there is indeed an *affect effect*, actually, numerous, diverse, and significant effects. Our explicit goal in this work is to draw focused attention to what had been a relatively neglected area in the study of mass political behavior.

We organize this introductory discussion around five spanning topics. The first is the varying *centrality* of emotional concepts in theorizing about political behavior. The second is the character of the phenomenon of emotion itself—in particular, the question of its *structure*. Third, and perhaps most important, is *functionality*—what role do human emotions play in a theory of political thinking and behavior, and how are affect and cognition structurally linked? Fourth, how is this phenomenon to be assessed—what are the available *methodologies*? And finally, we discuss *praxis*—a brief review of how what we know thus far of the dynamics of political affect might be applied in political practice and perhaps public policy.

It will become evident to even a casual reader of this book we have not yet converged on a singular theory of the role that emotions play in political thinking and behavior. In Part IV Lupia and Menning constructively chide us about the conceptual vagaries and inexplicit rules of scientific inference in this literature. They hold up the field of game theory as an instructive model of relative conceptual and inferential clarity. Some might question whether the phenomena at hand lend themselves to that sort

---

1. In this chapter we use the terms *emotion* and *affect* interchangeably, although some scholars attempt to make distinctions among those terms as well as the term *mood* (White 1993).

TABLE 1.1: Key theories of affect-cognition interaction

Key concept	Exemplary source	Relevant chapters	Brief definition
Theories of cognitive primacy:			
Appraisal theory	Lazarus 1991	2, 4, 6, 8, 9, 10, 15, 16	Emotions are elicited and differentiated on the basis of a person's subjective evaluation of the personal significance of a situation, object, or event. Thus, primary cognitive appraisal of threat or goal achievement precedes emotional state. A secondary cognitive appraisal of coping capacity modifies the level of significance and emotional reaction to a stimulus.
Social construction of emotion	Harre 1987	1, 2	Posits interpretations as intervening variables between stimulus and response. Since human interpretation relies on concepts, and concepts are social products that vary across social position, time, and culture, emotions will depend on such social variation. Thus, the triggering conditions for various emotions, at least, are socially dependent.
Selective attention/ Selective exposure	Sears 1967	4, 5	Posits that individuals are more likely to attend to information and information sources they judge to be familiar than to challenge existing beliefs and preferences
Theories of affective primacy:			
Affect-as-information	Forgas 1995	14	General affective state or mood substitutes for detailed information in heuristic appraisal of low-salience stimuli
Affect infusion model	Forgas 1995	4, 5	Affectively loaded information exerts an influence on and becomes incorporated into the judgmental process, entering into the judge's deliberations and eventually coloring judgment. Most likely to occur in the course of constructive processing that involves the substantial transformation rather than mere reproduction of existing cognitive representations; such processing requires a relatively open information search strategy and a significant degree of generative elaboration of the available stimulus details.

Concept	Citation	Refs	Description
Affective intelligence	Marcus et al. 2000	2, 3, 4, 5, 6, 7, 8, 9, 10, 11, 12, 13, 16	There are two systems that are responsible both for how we react to novel situations and how we use habitual behaviors. The *dispositional* system monitors habit, or scripts, and allows us to perform tasks without consciously considering them. When expectations are not challenged by new information, we can safely rely on habitual responses to incoming stimuli. The central emotions of the dispositional system are enthusiasm and aversion, the former for rewarding actions and the latter for punishing actions. From the perspective of affective intelligence, then, even the simplest of habits relies on affective processing. The *surveillance* system is activated when something unexpected is encountered, producing anxiety in such novel situations. Anxiety then drives conscious attention to a problem that in turn promotes learning. Thus, when new information is incongruent with habitual response or habitual response produces outcomes inconsistent with expectations, control is shifted to conscious awareness.
Affective primacy	Zajonc 1980	5, 7	The first response to the environment is affective. Affect is always part of cognition, whereas the converse is not true. An individual can like something or be afraid of it before he or she knows precisely what it is and perhaps without knowing what it is.
Affective priming	Bargh et al. 1996	5, 8	Affect influences the encoding, retrieval, and selective use of information in the constructive process of social judgment.
Elaboration likelihood model	Petty and Cacioppo 1986	4, 8	Emphasizing two distinctive patterns of information processing, the posited central route engages high levels of thinking and cognitive elaboration. The posited peripheral route, on the other hand, uses less thought and elaboration and is characterized by a reliance on peripheral and situational cues for evaluative judgments.
Symbolic politics	Sears 1993	5, 6, 8, 14, 16	In early life people acquire standing predispositions that influence their adult perceptions and attitudes. In adulthood, then, they respond in a highly affective way to symbols that resemble the attitude objects to which similar emotional responses were conditioned or associated in earlier life.

Key concept	Exemplary source	Relevant chapters	Brief definition
Linkage models:			
Affective tag	James 1884	5	A positive or negative affective linkage or tag associated with stimuli in the environment
Hot cognition	Abelson 1963	4, 5	Information about social objects is inevitably charged with affect, and the object cannot be activated without also activating this tag.
Symbolic psychologic	Abelson	1	Early provocative model that posited an affective logic along the lines of Heider's Balance Model which paralleled formal mathematical 'cognitive' logic
Subliminal linkage models:			
Automaticity of affect	Fazio 2001	4, 5, 6	Presentation of an attitude object has been shown to automatically activate from memory the evaluation that an individual associates with the object.
Dual process model	Deutsch and Gerard 1955	4, 14	A dichotomy between controlled and automatic mental processing. Dual-process models hypothesize two distinct cognitive and neural systems mediating, on one hand, the top-down, goal-directed, or endogenous control of thought and activity, and, on the other, mental processing that is bottom-up or automatic or exogenous (not controlled).
Heuristic/systemic model	Chaiken 1980	5	Holds that individuals will use one or both modes of information processing when attempting to evaluate information in order to arrive at a judgment that squares with relevant facts. Systematic processing is a high-involvement mode in which an individual actively seeks information and evaluates it in an effortful and structured manner. Heuristic processing is a more casual mode in which the individual relies on current knowledge or experience and utilizes mental shortcuts to evaluate information.
Mere exposure effect	Zajonc 1968	5	The propensity for individuals to judge familiar objects positively

Online processing	Anderson and Hubert 1963	5	Individuals use the affective content of information processed about a political figure to update the affective vector attached to the candidate and then forget the information at an exponential rate. Thus, when the individuals are asked their opinion of the political figure, the most readily accessible information is their emotional response. When asked the reasons for their opinions, they simply make use of whatever affectively congruent considerations are most accessible.
Recurrent multilevel appraisal model	Spezio and Adolfs (this volume)	4, 9	Emotional processing begins as the outcome of initial low-level evaluative processing in terms of autonormative outcomes, resulting in the activation of a set of automatic and sensorimotor processes in the body, such as the heart rate, pupillary dilation, changes in skeletal muscle tone, and the representations in the brain that mediate these activations. Emotional responses first influence downstream processing in the domains of selective attention, memory encoding and retrieval, associative learning, action planning, and thought. Second, they influence the evaluative processing functions due to changes in attention, memory, imagery, and semantic processing.
Somatic marker theory	James 1884	4, 9, 16	Emotional processing is prior to and contributes to the appraisal of events within decision making. Emotion is elicited by first categorizing an event and then activating a link between the event category and emotional signals. Both the categorization of the event and the activation of the appropriate acquired association between the event and the elicited emotion can and usually do take place outside of conscious awareness.

Models of functional form:

Negativity bias	Cacioppo and Berntson 1994	1	The human brain has a greater sensitivity to negative or unpleasant information or stimuli.
Positivity offset	Cacioppo and Gardner 1999	1	Humans exhibit a positivity offset in which they are likely to interpret neutral surroundings as positive and encourages exploration of new environments.
Yerkes-Dodson model	Yerkes and Dodson 1908	4, 14, 16	The relationship of the emotion and behavioral performance depends on the level of emotion—often defined as arousal—such that performance is low at very low and very high levels of emotion and optimal somewhere in between.

of scientific precision and parsimony. Indeed, the complexities of mass political behavior are not likely to yield to a notion as straightforward as a singular, well-understood payoff matrix. But the challenge Lupia and Menning put before us is about clarifying the nature of the phenomena, the character of causal relations, and the principles of inference from data. This is not an inappropriate challenge but merely a difficult one.

Most of the contributors have known each other and have been reading each other's work for years now. We exchanged chapter drafts and commentaries electronically and met for a weekend workshop in Ann Arbor in the fall of 2004 to compare notes and, as much as possible, integrate our analyses for this book. But there is still much work to be done in clearing out the theoretical underbrush and clarifying the central ideas. By our count, there are 23 named theories, models, or central concepts used to explicate the interaction of affect and cognition at various points in this work, as summarized in table 1.1. Part of the terminological pluralism results from the different forms of empirical investigation and contexts of analysis undertaken. Part of it results from the fact that we are still early in the game, pre-paradigmatic, as Thomas Kuhn would characterize it. The contributors agree that, politically speaking, affects do indeed have effects. Bear with us as we try to work out exactly how and when. If we meet partial success in closing off some of the dead ends and clarifying a few urban myths, we will take it as evidence of the very important role that multiauthor volumes can play in moving scholarship forward.

THE CENTRALITY OF AFFECT IN THEORIES OF POLITICAL THOUGHT AND BEHAVIOR

There have been numerous studies of the cyclical nature of attention and inattention to the emotional side of the human condition. In the broader sweep of history the alternation between an emphasis on the natural expression of human yearnings and the need to constrain, redirect, or simply repress such appetites by religious or civil authority is a familiar theme. Norbert Elias's classic and influential *History of Manners* (in the original German: *The Process of Civilization*, 1939) is one prominent exemplar. Of course, fashions of scholarship usually trail these alternating cultural emphases, occasionally bucking the trend—one thinks, of course of Freud's response to Viennese Victorianism. Recently Peter Stearns (2004) has reviewed the extensive historical literature in this domain. Many comprehensive studies and textbooks about the psychology of emotion take note of such predictable cycles (Izard 1971; Damasio 1994;

Lazarus 1994; Goleman 1995; Cornelius 1996). A closer look, however, reveals some interesting insights into these patterns of public thought.

First, an increase or decrease in intellectual attention may or may not be associated with the corresponding cycle of the vilification and glorification of the emotional domain. Some analysts with long lists of the evils of emotional excess trailing behind them nevertheless argue that attention is due and that we must better understand this side of the human character. This is the school of emotionality and pathology, with particularly prominent examples in the nineteenth century of associating such human weakness with the feminine gender (Marcus 2002). Others (à la Elias) would argue that such topics are simply inappropriate for discussion in civilized company.

Second, changing definitions of what exactly an emotion is and what it is not complicate any attempts to trace the intellectual history of the concept. Michael Neblo's chapter in this volume does an excellent job of tracking these complexities, and each chapter addresses the interaction of emotion and cognition. As in the history of this literature, when two ideas are characterized as deeply intertwined, to talk of relative emphasis on one or the other is not very meaningful, but, until we develop a more sophisticated model of these complex physiological dynamics, it is probably unavoidable.

The cycles of attention to emotion in the study of politics also have been the subject of detailed inquiry. Marcus, Neuman, and MacKuen (2000) review these issues in a chapter titled "Human Affect in the Western Tradition." As in the broader literature of human psychology, the emphasis is on pathology and the potential role of human affect in distracting from, distorting, or simply overloading the cognitive capacities of the citizen faced with difficult choices about personal and public interests. Marcus (2002) picks up and develops the historical analysis, raising the centrally important point that concerns about citizen irrationality are intimately intertwined with judgments about democratic practice itself. If citizens are easily distracted or their judgments distorted, it is better to turn to a philosopher king, or at least an elite-oriented form of representative government that insulates policy from the undulating passions of the madding crowd.

Two scholars have attempted to model the waxing and waning of attention to the political psychology of emotion in modern political scholarship. Bill McGuire (1990) posits three distinct stages. First, McGuire characterizes research in the 1940s and 1950s as dominated by the concept of personality and psychoanalytic approaches focusing on, for example, the authoritarian personality and the psychohistories of notable political leaders. In the second stage, during the 1960s and 1970s, research focused on survey-based studies of voting behavior and spatial modeling of interest maximization. In McGuire's third stage, the 1980s and 1990s, scholars turned more to the attempt to understand the structure of political cognition, drawing on concepts of schema, belief systems, and ideology. Notably, theories of emotion played a major role in the first but only a minor supporting role the latter two stages of scholarship. This view is reinforced by Don Kinder's essay "Reason and Emotion in American Political Life" (1994). Kinder, however, adds two elements to what might be an emerging theory of cycles of attention to political affect. First, in his view, the early psychotheorists overreached a bit in explaining behavior on the basis of childhood experiences, the projections of personal feelings on public objects and, most famously, the rather grand pronouncements of *The Authoritarian Personality* (1950). Overextended and overtaxed theoretical constructions, unfortunately, may have driven younger scholars to look elsewhere for key explanatory variables instead of refining and reining in the predominant theory of the day. Second, Kinder notes that exciting new models stimulated by Anthony Downs's economically oriented work, focusing on rational choice and spatial modeling, became a magnet for scholarly attention. Some early critics believed this development to be an unfortunate "cognitive imperialism," but Kinder demurs and urges patience. There is no reason to diminish exciting new work because of its independent intellectual provenance. Let us see how far it can take us. When the limitations and incompleteness of rational choice modeling become increasingly evident, the importance of bringing the psychology of human affect back into the model will be abundantly clear. And, happily, Kinder asserts, that time has come. Indeed, Kinder (1994, 279) draws on a rather unusual word to characterize the current state of theory development as he asserts: "Theories of emotion are proliferating, and at a horrifying rate." Horrifying? (Graduate students, be forewarned.) Well, yes, there may be some danger of excess exuberance, as was evident with the F-scale, but perhaps we should simply relish the return of energy and attention to this neglected domain. We do agree, for example, that the existence of 23 independently named theories of affect effects represents undue terminological enthusiasm. But the underlying concepts are fewer in number, and the vocabulary and the direction of the findings are converging. The hard work of hammering out that integration, albeit only in part, is the essence of edited volumes such as this.

We may draw some encouragement from the broader literatures that track scholarly processes through history. Randall Collins's recent masterwork *The Sociology of Philosophies* (1998), for example, offers an intriguing dynamic model that may assuage Kinder's unease. His work literally maps the rise and decline of hundreds of schools of philosophy and theology around the world from its early Hellenistic manifestations to modern philosophical scholarship. One of his major notions is the idea of a limited *attention space*. Scholarship, he argues, thrives on controversy, but a community of scholars can only manage a limited set of controversies at a time—he terms it "the law of small numbers." As the naturally limited scholarly attention space is taken up by new issues, old ones are ignored or, much better, incorporated into existing theories by means of simplification and reorganization. We strive for the latter—less controversy, no less attention. Collins comes up with an average of 4 to 6 major schools of thought per scholarly generation. Interestingly, such a number is not very far from Miller's now-iconic 7 ± 2 (1956). Our analysis, of course, is at a much finer-grained level of scholarly attention than entire schools of philosophy, but we may at least have stumbled onto a useful and possibly achievable goal: to move from 23 to 6 or 7 key concepts and models that attempt to capture the essence of the interaction of political passion and cognition.

THE STRUCTURE OF AFFECT

In the following two sections we struggle with what affect is and with how affect interacts with other elements of human behavior. Our focal point is political behavior, but, in both cases, we draw on the related broader literatures that attempt to make sense of the dimensionality of human emotion and the critical interactions of emotion and cognition.

What is affect? Modern definitions make it difficult to imagine why it had been so long vilified and ignored. *Affect* is the evolved cognitive and physiological response to the detection of personal significance. Scherer (2005, 314) puts it a little more formally: affect is "an episode of massive synchronous recruitment of mental and somatic resources to adapt to and cope with a stimulus event that is subjectively appraised as being highly pertinent to needs, goals and values of the individual." It would seem to follow that students of political behavior should pay particular attention to the ways in which citizens, through a mixture of impulse and calculation, reckon what is politically significant to them. This perspective is frequently demonstrated in this volume, in particular, the essays in part II and Doris Graber's chapter in part III.

With a working definition in hand, we turn to the issue of structure. Psychology has traditionally identified three dimensions of mind: cognition, affect, and conation, cognition focusing on perception, storage,

and processing of information, affect focusing on the evaluation of information, and conation on the interaction of cognition, affect, and actual
behavior. The literatures of psychology and politics are replete with typologies, lists, catalogs, and models that attempt to capture the dimensional
structure of each and its linkages the others. We focus first on the dimensionality of the domain of affect.. The basic analysis has been developed
in more detail in Marcus, Neuman and MacKuen (2000 appendix A) and
Marcus (2003).

We identify three schools of thought in characterizing the dimensionality of affect: discrete models, valence models, and multidimensional
models. As the terminology implies, discrete approaches tend to identify a set of reliably identifiable emotional responses to unique circumstances without much attention their interconnection or dimensionality.
Valence models focus on a single positive-negative dimension on which
emotional states can be arrayed, frequently associated with the fundamental behaviors of approach and avoidance. Multidimensional models,
which are more recent, represent an extension and reinterpretation of a
valence model into multidimensional structure, sometimes identified as
a circumplex.

Discrete models have the longest literary pedigree and represent perhaps the most commonsensical approach. The work of Descartes, Darwin, and James has influenced the thinking of generations about the
diversity of emotional states. But most adults (and surely children as
well) from virtually any culture in the world, if asked to list a dozen different emotional states, could probably do so quickly and without significant effort, such a list representing a naturally evolved component of
most of the world's cultural and linguistic toolkits. The commonly used
terms that describe discrete emotions in English number in the hundreds
(Marcus 2003). Roseman's structural model of emotional responses to
different circumstances of success and failure has been particularly influential. (See table 1.2.) He demonstrates that appraisals of unexpectedness (not unexpected/unexpected), situational state (motive-inconsistent/
motive-consistent), motivational state (aversive/appetitive), probability
(uncertain/certain), control potential (low/high), problem source (non-
characterological/characterological), and agency (circumstances/other
person/self) differentiate a large number of widely discussed emotions
(Roseman 1984; Roseman, Antoniou, and Jose 1996). Lazarus's typology
of goal satisfaction and frustration and the similar and widely influential OCC model (Lazarus 1991; Ortony, Clore, and Collins 1988) encourage thinking in terms of discrete emotions (table 1.3, figure 1.1). More
recently, Paul Ekman's (1992) analysis of universally recognized facial

TABLE 1.2: An example of Roseman's structural model of discrete emotions

	Positive emotions Motive-consistent		Negative emotions Motive-inconsistent		
Circumstance-caused:	Appetitive	Aversive	Appetitive	Aversive	
Unknown	Surprise				
Uncertain	Hope		Fear		Weak
Certain	Joy	Relief	Sadness	Distress, disgust	
Uncertain	Hope		Frustration		Strong
Certain	Joy	Relief			
Other-caused: Uncertain Certain	Liking		Dislike		Weak
Uncertain Certain			Anger		Strong
Self-caused: Uncertain Certain	Pride		Shame, guilt		Weak
Uncertain Certain			Regret		Strong

Source: Roseman 1984; Roseman et al. 1991.

expressions has reenergized the study of discrete models. Several decades' worth of cross-cultural research converged on consistent evidence for the universal recognition of six emotions: anger, fear, disgust, sadness, happiness, and surprise. Some more recent analysis (Ekman and Rosenberg 2005) has suggested the possible additions of contempt and shame to this list.

The work of Don Kinder and Bob Abelson and colleagues on self-descriptive emotional reactions to political candidates has been particularly influential in emphasizing a discrete approach in political science. The early work assessed the discrete terms *hope, pride, sympathy, disgust, anger, fear,* and *uneasiness,* and those analytic concepts have become part of the National Election Studies tradition (Kinder, Abelson and Fisk 1979; Abelson et al. 1982).

TABLE 1.3: Richard Lazarus's appraisal model of six basic emotions

Emotion	Core relational theme	Important appraisal components
Anger	Other-blame	Motivationally relevant Motivationally incongruent Other-accountability
Guilt	Self-blame	Motivationally relevant Motivationally incongruent Self-accountability
Fear–anxiety	Danger–threat	Motivationally relevant Motivationally incongruent Low or uncertain (emotion- focused) coping potential
Sadness	Irrevocable loss, Helplessness about harm or loss	Motivationally relevant Motivationally incongruent Low (problem-focused) coping potential Negative future expectations
Hope–challenge	Effortful optimism, Potential for success	Motivationally relevant Motivationally incongruent High (problem-focused) coping potential Positive future expectations
Happiness	Success	Motivationally relevant Motivationally congruent

Source: Smith et al. 1993.

Valence models avoid some of the complexity of the structural-discrete models by focusing on a single bipolar dimension—positivity/negativity (approach/avoidance). The deep intellectual roots of this dimension in evolutionary theory and its cultural reinforcement in the demonstrated generality of the semantic differential, in addition to its simplicity, may reinforce its appeal.

But more recent empirical analyses have demonstrated that a multi-dimensional analytic structure more accurately captures the dynamics of human emotional response. Early work by Plutchik, Russell, and others dubbed this Cartesian space a "circumplex," given the convenient capacity to organize emotional states in a meaningful circular structure. The extensive literature concerning this structure is reviewed in Marcus, Neuman, and MacKuen (2000) and in Marcus (2003). In one version

FIGURE 1.1: OCC MODEL OF EMOTIONAL STRUCTURE

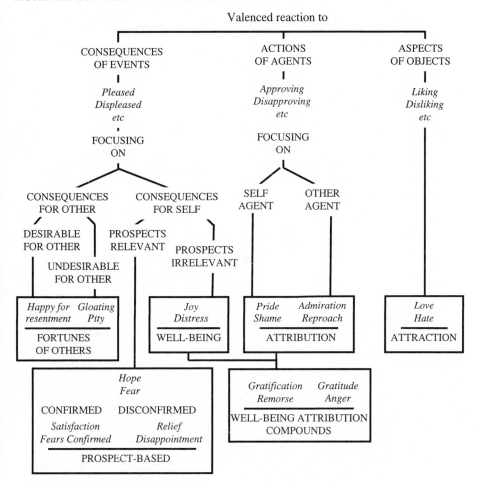

Source: Ortony, Clore, and Collins 1988.

of the two-dimensional scheme, one dimension is positivity-negativity, and the other represents level of arousal. In another variant positivity and negativity are defined as orthogonal dimensions, each varying in intensity. But each can simply be understood as a rotation of the defining orthogonal dimensions of the circumplex space. (See figure 1.2.)

We have reviewed three alternative approaches to organizing our thinking about different emotional states: (1) discrete emotions—sometimes a simple list with little structure, sometimes complicated structured models of emotional responses to success or frustration under different conditions; (2) valence models, which array emotional states along a

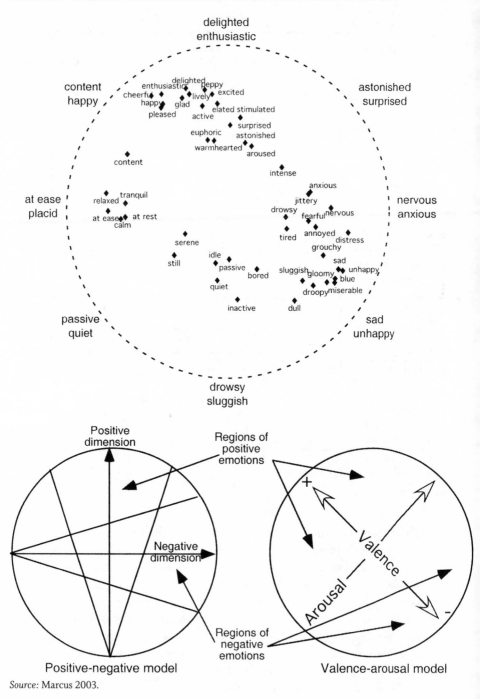

Source: Marcus 2003.

single bipolar dimension of positivity and negativity; and (3) the circumplex model, which extends the valence model into multidimensional spaces. The positivity-negativity distinction is a staple of all three approaches. Each approach continues to have its champions. It is probably not the case that the true character of human emotion is akin to the famous case of light in quantum physics, possessing the characteristics of a particle and of a wave. It may simply be that the discrete, valence, and dimensional approaches are not entirely mutually exclusive and that an ongoing competition to determine which of the three leads to the most productive science is the optimal path. The contributors to this volume draw loosely on all three conceptions. Perhaps in time a convergence of the three or a synthetic fourth model will prove most productive. Notwithstanding that prospect, we can anticipate that as the field matures, the structure of affect, in its preconscious and conscious guises, will be a continuing focus of research. An additional challenge, most clearly raised in the chapter by Huddy, Feldman, and Cassese, is that the structure of affect is likely to be dynamic (that is, of changing dimensional structure and of changing interdimensional dynamics, more or less orthogonal as circumstances change). This brings us to the functions of affect.

THE FUNCTIONS OF AFFECT AND COGNITION

The role of affect in human behavior has been informed by the medical study of brain injuries and pathologies (for example, Damasio 1994) and by more general inference from evolutionary biology (Lazarus 1991; Cosmides and Tooby 2004). Two themes arise from this complex and rich literature. The first is the role of affect as the engine of behavior—the motivating, directing, prioritizing function of the brain. The second is the complex interaction of affect and cognition—the alternative conditions under which affective states may diminish or stimulate the capacity for deliberation. It is indisputable that several million years of differential survival in the grasslands and jungles has influenced the ways the human brain responds to its environment. Such issues of mind and body have engaged theologians, philosophers, and scientists for ages, and we will not rehearse the continuing drama again here. Interested readers are referred to Damasio (1994), Cornelius (1996), and LeDoux (1996) for particularly persuasive and accessible reviews of this tradition. How well genetic optimization for a life of hunting and gathering in small communities has prepared us for the era of instantaneously televised global economics, politics, and warfare is a difficult question. Indeed, it lends urgency to the scholarly challenge ahead of us.

We have advanced since Hippocrates and Galen's theory of the four humors that govern personality and physiology: the sanguine (associated with blood), the phlegmatic (associated with phlegm), the choleric (associated with yellow bile), and the melancholic (associated with black bile). But it is humbling to acknowledge that we are only a little more than a century beyond the practice of bloodletting in an effort to rebalance fluids for emotional and physical health.

Table 1.1 presents an informal list of the theories and models utilized by this volume's various authors with brief descriptions and chapter cross-references. It is not a battle of paradigms, exactly, but more a variation in emphasis on causal primacy and, of course, the usual terminological pandemonium. The models are grouped under five headings that describe different types of interaction between affect and cognition. Theories of cognitive primacy are those that emphasize a direction of influence from cognition to affective state, most notably the various appraisal theories, which posit an initial evaluation of threat or goal achievement followed by a corresponding affective response. The appraisal school of thought includes many complex, multilevel, and dynamic theories of cognitive-affective interaction and should not be characterized as a simplistic one-way causal model. Theories of affective primacy such as affective intelligence theory, in contrast, emphasize the critical importance of the affective state on the level and character of subsequent attentiveness to various stimuli. These labels, of course, represent a tip of the hat to the legendary Zajonc-Lazarus debate about the relative primacy of cognition and affect (Zajonc 1982; Lazarus 1999). Although, at the time, it was (incorrectly) defined by many as a great debate about the relative importance of cognition and affect, it was really about the different character of cognitive and affective processes, a concern that occupies virtually all of the authors of this volume. The categories "linkage models" and "subliminal linkage models" capture models that posit various mechanisms for interaction between cognition and affect without implying a particular primacy for one or the other. Finally Models of functional form include theories that emphasize asymmetries and nonlinearity in models of interaction.

Table 1.1 may reveal that we have a fair distance to go in terminological and theoretical integration. A few of the concepts are used by a majority of the chapters, but on average the number of concepts used per chapter is only 2.5. In a few cases different authors are using different terms that mean pretty much the same thing. The affective tag and the somatic maker are virtually identical, for example. And some authors cite the heuristic/systematic model and others its close offspring, the elaboration likelihood model. But a close examination of the table's apples and oranges should motivate further integrative and metatheoretic efforts such as this book.

METHODOLOGICAL ISSUES

Social scientists are fond of drawing analogies from the physical sciences; a famous example is Thomas Kuhn's work on paradigms and scientific revolutions. Without the technical improvements in telescopic optics (read: methodology), we would have been long delayed in our transition from a geocentric to a heliocentric paradigm of the solar system. As the chapters by Spezio and Adolphs and by Schreiber demonstrate, neuroscience contributes a powerful and evolving array of methodologies for studying the brain in action. Yet as exciting as this new research and the promise it offers are, new means of measuring the activities of the human brain, even at the level of the individual neuron, present daunting measurement and theoretical challenges. The research reported in this volume covers an array of analysis ranging from the single neuron to adult populations numbering in the hundreds of millions. At one end of the spectrum, some of this research is concerned with describing the activity of individual cells, at the other, the political behaviors of very large groups of people (for example, partisan and social groups). In addition, the time scale of the various contributions in this volume ranges from milliseconds to many decades. And discussions located at various points along these temporal and spatial dimensions often do not meet at common points of reference.

Among the wide array of methodological strategies are aggregate studies such as those by Leege and Wald and by Nardulli and Kuklinski. These studies, conducted at the grandest temporal and spatial levels, have no direct measures of affect but rely instead on micro-models of affect to derive testable hypotheses to account for the historical dynamics they observe. Survey sampling studies (Huddy, Feldman, and Cassese; MacKuen, Marcus, Neuman, and Keele; and Just, Crigler and Belt) can generate large quantities of data with explicit measures of emotion. Such approaches most often rely on subjective measures of emotion, that is, they rely on the subject's ability to be introspective and accurately report on whatever emotional state is of interest to the researcher and respond to whatever stimulus object the researcher specifies. Doris Graber's use of content analysis provides another approach to determining the affect component, in this case that of major news stories, though the challenge remains, as with all methods, to ensure that the reactions of expert coders mimic the responses of diverse populations. Experimenters such as Brader and Valentino can choose from a variety of methods to assess

and validate emotional response; others use dynamic tracing of information gathering and decision making (Redlawsk, Civettini, and Lau). But
there is a wider array of methodologies, from reaction time (Cassino and
Lodge) to facial electromyographics, skin reactance, subjective response
to affect scales, and even fMRI and measurement of evoked potential
(Schreiber), and, we might add, some of the other techniques may make
use of split brain subjects and subjects who have suffered some injury
or illness that limits some neurological capacity. Although case studies
can use any of these methodologies, they are also capable of using contemporary and historical documents, an approach seen in Blight's (1990)
study of the role of emotion in accounting for American leaders' decision
making during the Cuban missile crisis and Doris Graber's study of news
stories. The research that adequately cross-validates each and all of these
approaches has yet to be done.

But the challenge of measurement is not, perhaps, itself the greatest challenge. Measurements, even those with established reliability and
validity, do not generate the theoretical account that connects concepts
of thinking, feeling, and acting (at the individual and aggregate levels).
Political psychologists who are interested in emotion have a rich array of
theoretical sources including, as Neblo persuasively argues, the rich classical and modern philosophic traditions. But the long-standing interest
in linear models (and the ubiquitous reliance on linear regression) may
miss most of the important relationships.[2] If, as neuroscientists are increasingly asserting, brain activity is interactive and compensatory, then
simple causal models will be inadequate. Linear models simply cannot
describe brain behavior that is due to inhibitory processes as well as to
excitatory ones, nor neural activity in one region (or module) that results
in cascading consequences, with both feed-forward and feed-backward
tuning (as when a sudden light not only shifts attention, a forward consequence, but also changes the visual focus, a backward consequence).
To be fully specified models, these iterative brain functions will almost
certainly require researchers to identify complex network and interactive
functions to be described. And that will be necessary simply to model the
complex neurological interdependencies that are already apparent.

Developing a macro-micro model that is provisionally adequate and
then scaling it up to the temporal and spatial dimensions of individual
action, group interactions, and the actions of large aggregations of people

2. Insofar as social scientists use nonlinear models, it is most commonly a decision
resulting from the categorical quality of a dependent variable and the probit and logit modeling, rather than a theoretically driven choice.

(including leader and follower linkages) over sweeping periods of time is a challenge that will consume the energies of researchers in this field for many years to come. More likely, in the interim, is the development of more limited middle-range theories. We already have an array of theories that are parsed at different levels of analysis: neurological, personal, interpersonal, and societal. A parsimonious yet comprehensive theory of affect and politics will require measurement and theory that can account for and link biological actions at very intimate levels of brain function and the actions of leaders and followers as they engage with each other and with other populations in settings both pacific and antagonistic. We hope, however, that the rich sampling of contemporary work presented in this volume suggests the value of the enterprise.

PRAXIS

The chapters in part IV, "Next Steps in Research and Outreach," most directly in address the question of praxis: How would one put these insights into human psychology to work in executing successful efforts at political communication, in promoting democratic institutions around the world, and in adjusting political institutions and practices to take the changing technologies of communication into account?

The authors of a very long line of previous scholarship have also turned (usually also in their concluding paragraphs) to the issue of practical application. As before, the connection is not an easy one to make. There are, however, five relatively new developments that give these discussions a fresh energy and magnetism.

First, scholarship of more recent generations is not burdened by the need to first apologize for the human condition before addressing the difficult challenge of trying to understand it. No apologies are expected, and none are offered. There is no need to justify attention to the significant interaction of emotion and cognition. The case has been made and the argument won.

Second, when systematic effects or distortions in human judgments are made evident, there is no need to sermonize. Patriotic, civic, and perhaps religious exhortations for citizens to be more deliberative and attentive to the political world are welcome, of course, but no longer need be intertwined with the scholarly literature. The effort to understand the conditions under which one or another predictable emotional state interacts systematically with cognition need not lead to homily. Zajonc (1980) asserted that preferences require no inferences. We would add: scientific inferences require no exhortations.

Third, the new methodologies, especially those associated with brain functioning and convergent findings from multiple methodologies, add new gravitas and perhaps urgency to theory building and testing in this domain. We are still in the early stages of convergence, but the evidence and momentum are accumulating.

Fourth, an important nonacademic audience for this work (whose interests are captured in part in Schnur's chapter) is the practitioner. This should be a two-way street as real-world applications and systematic testing of alternative institutional designs provide further data for analysis and reflection. The work reported in this volume does not, for example, include a systematic analysis of alternative electoral systems drawing on what we know about the psychology of political information flow and citizen engagement. But that is exactly the sort of analysis that McDermott's chapter calls for.

Fifth, a new audience is the citizenry itself. Higher education and the popular press take pride from time to time in providing their respective audiences with critical thinking skills and the "inside scoop" to help them respond to the inevitable flow of persuasive messages and images in the public sphere. Ultimately, the citizenry may represent the most important and, in time, the most appropriately concerned audience for this research enterprise.

Part I, "Putting the Affect Effect in Perspective," introduces major concepts and methodological alternatives and puts them in historical perspective. The main body of the book, as indicated above, focuses first on micro and then on macro analytic tools, in most cases in the context of American electoral politics. The book concludes with three forward-looking essays on praxis and next steps for the communities of researchers, political professionals, and, lest we forget, citizens.

PART I

Putting the Affect Effect
in Perspective

The three chapters in this section provide philosophical and neuroscientific foundations for the study of emotions and politics. From very different research traditions, they document the interrelatedness of emotion and rationality and demonstrate why political judgments and behavior require both. There are many challenges in joining together these distinct disciplinary approaches. Concepts are defined differently across disciplines and over time. Levels of analysis and measurement cover the whole range—from the cellular level to the cross-cultural dimension. Research methodologies vary widely. Theoretical assumptions about the underlying processes of human understanding are contested. But, as we shall see, the various contributors turn these challenges into opportunities by clarifying definitions, articulating the underlying theoretical assumptions, and testing hypotheses on a wide range of data. By carrying on conversations across research traditions, we can produce better science and further understanding of the processes underlying political judgment and behavior.

The chapter by Michael A. Neblo sets the theoretical stage by showing how three philosophers' thinking about the emotions continues to be relevant for political psychological research. Neblo takes a cognitive approach to argue that emotions were socially constructed for canonical thinkers who presented integrated theories of politics. Instead of applying psychological theories to politics, as is often done today, Neblo argues that philosophers such as Plato, Aristotle, and Hume were systematic thinkers who grounded their ethical and political theories in a descriptive psychology of human experience. Emotions are central to human experience and, thus, to each of their philosophies. By analyzing their major texts, Neblo shows how Plato offers a theory that interpenetrates emotion and reason and how emotions are key to political persuasion for Aristotle. He also argues that Hume gives priority to emotions in his writing about deliberations and human will. Neblo concludes the chapter with possible testable hypotheses for researchers in neuropolitics that are suggested by these early canonical thinkers.

Darren Schreiber begins chapter 3 with Aristotle's arguments about human nature and Machiavelli's thoughts about how human intelligence developed with the need to be more politically astute than one's rivals. On the basis of these ideas, and drawing on current scholarship in political psychology and neuroscience, Schreiber hypothesizes about the neural architecture needed by people to navigate everyday political life. He suggests that a dual processing model that distinguishes between reflective and reflexive thought processes is useful for explaining differences in political judgments between political novices and political sophisticates. This dual process model resonates with the disposition and surveillance systems of affective intelligence approaches. Using fMRI techniques to assess brain activity in response to viewing faces, Schreiber finds evidence to suggest that political sophisticates have a greater empathic connection to political figures than do political novices. It is this affective component that sets the former apart from the latter. These differences—rooted in affective processing—require political science to reconsider rational understandings of political judgment and behavior.

The chapter by Michael L. Spezio and Ralph Adolphs bridges political psychology and decision neuroscience by considering the challenges to the development of theory about the role of emotions in decision making. They argue that these challenges are rooted in the persistence of two dichotomies: those between controlled and automatic processing (what Schreiber calls reflective and reflexive processing) and between cognition and emotion. Disagreeing with Schreiber and others, Spezio and Adolphs find that brain activity is more integrated than these authors suggest. Dual processing models overlook the fact that automatic processing is necessary for human activity and that controlled processing often motivates and focuses automatic processing. The authors observe that the ironclad separation of cognition and emotion has yielded somewhat, but with research focusing on behavioral economics and rationality, emotions' adaptive functions are still frequently undervalued. Spezio and Adolphs advocate an iterative emotional processing model. Their recurrent multilevel appraisal model integrates more traditional appraisal theories (Lazarus 1994; Scherer, Schorr, and Johnstone 2001) and Damasio's somatic marker hypothesis (1994). The authors also argue strongly for the integration of multiple methodologies to provide convergent evidence for the study of the complex systems involved in political decision making. They note that this is increasingly important as neuroscientific research uncovers individual differences in brain functioning that overshadow commonalities across individuals and diminish the utility of normalized brain function studies.

CHAPTER TWO

Philosophical Psychology with Political Intent

MICHAEL A. NEBLO

Aristotle's approach to anger pointed the way to a modern, folk-centered, cognitive-motivational-relational theory of emotion. Indeed, Aristotle could be called the first cognitive theorist of the emotions, and his analysis makes implicit use of the ideas of relationship, appraisal, and action tendency.

RICHARD LAZARUS, *Emotion and Adaptation*

Let us therefore take it that the soul has its principal seat in the small gland located in the middle of the brain. From there it radiates through the rest of the body by means of the animal spirits, the nerves, and even the blood, which can take on the impressions of the spirits and carry them through the arteries to all the limbs. DESCARTES, *The Passions of the Soul*

INTRODUCTION

Descartes famously speculated that the nexus of the human mind and body centered on the pineal gland. Because our passions formed a crucial link between mind and body, they operated via the soul's influence on and receptivity to the "animal spirits" circulating through the pineal. Of course, we now know that Descartes was wrong in his conjectures about the pineal and the animal spirits. Moreover, few still think that his robust metaphysical dualism provides a satisfactory solution to the mind-body problem. As contemporary scientists, we are apt to look at Descartes's theory of the emotions with a kind of knowing smile of condescension.

I thank Ann Crigler, Michael MacKuen, George Marcus, Eileen McMahon, Russell Neuman, an anonymous reviewer, and especially John Parrish for helpful comments on this chapter.

In his defense, we might note that if we merely substitute the term *bio-electricity* or *hormones* for *animal spirits*, his theory sounds more prescient than silly. We might also add that no one since has provided a particularly compelling solution to the mind-body problem. But such apologetics miss the point. Modern, scientific psychology has demoted the pineal and supplanted talk of animal spirits just as surely as modern chemistry has done away with phlogiston, and physics with the ether.

So why should canonical thinkers, Descartes or Aristotle, for example, be of any more interest to the modern political psychologist than Ptolemy is to the modern astrophysicist? This is a reasonable question. Yet there are decisive disanalogies between the two cases that we ignore at the cost of retarding scientific progress and narrowing the relevance of the progress we do make.

The disanalogy begins with the fact that people can talk, whereas stars cannot. The maxim that every explanation is also an interpretation goes double when we endeavor to explain interpretive phenomena. In much social science, meaning is not merely something that we try to draw *from* an explanation; indeed, the key insight that makes the cognitive theory of the emotions superior to the behaviorist is that interpretations are *part of* any adequate explanation. Yet with regard to the hermeneutic and phenomenological analyses implied by this insight, we modern scholars have not developed anything like the kind of advantage over our predecessors that we enjoy in the realm of statistical and experimental technique. Indeed, we are more likely in relative deficit.

The key reason *why* historical thinkers spent so much time on the social and experiential facets of emotional phenomena is that they thought that they were hunting bigger game. Or, put differently, a philosopher's descriptive psychology had to serve as a logical base for his moral psychology, which served, in turn, to underwrite his ethical theory, and on to his political theory.[1] And moving in the other direction, his descriptive psychology had to be compatible with, and preferably entailed by, his epistemology, and in turn his metaphysics and ontology.[2] In short, these

1. I use the masculine throughout when referring to systematic, canonical philosophers before the twentieth century for accuracy and in order to acknowledge the potential bias that such a gender-exclusive legacy might induce in the context of their political psychologies. Wollstonecraft, de Staël, and dePizan, though not fully systematic or preeminent in the canon, might be partial exceptions.

2. None of this is to suggest that the authors literally worked out such relations in a temporal sequence, though some authors appear to have worked this way, and most present their expositions in this order. The point is that they had to integrate all the components coherently, whatever their order of development.

were *systematic* thinkers whose work spanned the practical, the scientific, and the philosophical. Thus, engaging their psychologies is also valuable because doing so provides a model for integrating modern psychological findings into broader contexts of academic and practical significance.

Thus, it should come as no surprise that Hobbes, for example, develops his psychology of the fear of violent death in the context of claiming that its burden makes anarchy intolerable and its universality makes sovereignty possible. His descriptive and prescriptive theories of politics are founded entirely on this interaction. Unlike much contemporary political psychology, therefore, the idea is not that we start from the concepts and findings of some completely separate, self-contained discipline, psychology, and see how they can be applied to politics. Rather, these historical theories were, from the beginning, *psychologies with political intent*.

Because they theorized in such an integrated way, historical thinkers were attentive to the social construction of emotion.[3] By *social construction* I mean nothing which implies that emotions are unreal or lack for a biological substrate. For the purposes of this argument, to say that the emotions are socially constructed is merely to point out that a cognitive theory of the emotions posits interpretations as intervening variables between stimulus and response.[4] Because human interpretation relies on concepts, and concepts are social products that vary across social position, time and culture, our emotions will depend on such social variation.[5] Thus the triggering conditions for various emotions, at least, are socially

3. I use this phrase with some hesitation, since it means many things to many people, some of them less helpful than others at the philosophical level (Hacking 1999; Griffiths 1997; Harre 1986). Nonetheless, I will be try to be clear about the points I want to make, and if the reader judges the term unhelpful, then it can be disregarded. It may seem comically false to attribute any kind of constructivism to, for example, Aquinas. Many canonical thinkers had a rather robust notion of human nature. Strangely, though, such abstract commitments did not seem to interfere with their highly contextualized first-order analyses.

4. Obviously, this specific point does not apply with the same force to noncognitive theories. For reasons that I cannot develop in this work, I happen to be a cognitivist about both the emotions and normative matters. There was significant variation concerning these matters in the canon, however, and contemporary political psychologists of both persuasions will find rich material on which to draw. Below, I try to develop ideas that apply to cognitive theories of the emotions (Plato and Aristotle) and to noncognitive theories (Hume).

5. Griffiths (1997) argues forcefully against the notion that concepts per se are of interest in the social construction of the emotions, preferring a social roles approach. For purposes of my brief exposition, I try to side-step this issue and fold social roles into *concept* broadly understood, in the sense that one has at least an implicit concept of one's social role and that that will affect one's notion of, say, shameful action for me.

dependent. To take an obvious example, a certain sexual behavior might, according to Victorian mores, may be an occasion for shame, whereas the same behavior in an American high school might trigger shame's inverse, a kind of prideful machismo.

Certain emotions appear to be biologically set "affect programs" (Ekman 1982), so for these only the triggering conditions can be socially constructed.[6] There is considerable evidence however, that the elements in our emotional repertoires beyond this common set actually vary (Harré 1987). That is, certain emotions are made available or unavailable to us depending on cultural forces and, more generally, the way we conceptualize the emotions affects the way we experience them. If the availability half of this claim seems far-fetched, one need only consider that it is merely an extension of the uncontroversial claim that triggering conditions are socially mediated. Presumably, in some cases, the triggering conditions could become so constricted as to eliminate occasion of the emotion.

Modern scientists typically do not attend to the interpretive and phenomenological issues surrounding the emotions with the same vigor as historical thinkers did. And to some extent the shift in emphasis is understandable. The scientific claim that emotions are dependent on antecedent psychological appraisals can be sustained and explored without understanding where those appraisals came from and what they feel like. But resting with this approach is a bit like some rational choice theorists' relegating preferences to the realm of the permanently exogenous. For some purposes it is interesting and justifiable, but past a certain point, it does not satisfy.

Thus we should not be surprised that, unlike Ptolemaic astronomy, the analytic framework of the Aristotelian psychology of the emotions has been revived and proved superior to the modern scientific psychology that reigned a mere twenty years ago. Indeed, despite his praise of Aristotle, Richard Lazarus understates just how much of a return modern cognitive theories represent. Aristotle did not merely make "implicit use of the ideas of relationship, appraisal, and action tendency." He made highly *explicit* use of them, employing Greek words that could be translated with the very same terms, serving nearly identical theoretical purposes, and generating similar predictions. As we shall see, there are many more examples of this phenomenon—that is, modern

6. Some triggering conditions also seem to be set programs—e.g., fear of loud noises. Moreover, all aspects of our emotional repertoires are biologically *delimited*, if not determined.

scientific psychology rediscovering ideas that canonical thinkers had described long ago.

Now, I do not want to push this argument to the point of absurdity by seeming to suggest that we could have forgone the past few decades' worth of justly celebrated research had we only dusted off old volumes of philosophy. Modern statistical and experimental techniques provide vastly more powerful warrants for believing that their systematic data support one theory rather than another. For the most part, canonical thinkers waged evidentiary warfare from their respective armchairs. Yet we are apt to mistakenly suppose that because a thinker's conception of science is pre-modern, his insights into psychology, politics, and the connection between them must also be antiquated. But it is a fallacy to suppose that theories and hypotheses that no one has adequately tested are therefore false or uninteresting. It is true that most such theories were not framed so as to be obvious grist for the operational rigors of contemporary science. Yet there is reason to believe that some of their insights are worthy of the best work today and that efforts to translate them into modern terms will yield greater fruit than doing science as if no one before the twentieth century had interesting thoughts about psychology or politics.[7] Indeed, such recent rediscoveries as the cognitive theory of the emotions warrant the belief that there are important insights that yet lay dormant on the shelves of intellectual history. We might say that canonical thinkers promise to be brilliant interlocutors in the context of discovery, if relatively mute company in the context of confirmation.

Embedding the psychology of the emotions, from the beginning, in a broader scientific and intellectual context also has important consequences for how we go about formulating concepts and the ontology that attends them—that is, what emotional phenomena we regard as real or basic. Consider an analogous example from biology: dolphins were once classified as fish, and in some ordinary language contexts, they still are. As evolutionary biology advanced, we discovered that cows, not sharks, are the dolphin's closest evolutionary cousins. So the category "fish" ceased to function as a useful scientific designation. This change represents a major advance in its field. Yet to some extent it also begs the question regarding the useful scope of that field's categories. Genetic descent is

---

7. Most people would acknowledge that canonical thinkers had interesting ideas about *normative* matters of politics. And a few scholars even acknowledge that pre-twentieth-century thinkers had interesting thoughts relating to the scientific aspects of psychology and politics. Yet such praise tends to be based on noticing similarity to modern theories after they have been developed.

not the only scientifically relevant way to categorize animal life because evolutionary biology is not the only relevant science. One can imagine ecologists making great use of the concept "marine predator" (sharks, dolphins, killer whales, but not baleen whales) while having no particular use for "marine mammal" (dolphins, all whales, but not sharks). Patterns of predatory behavior are no less real than patterns of genetic variation.[8]

In the same way, a truly *political* political psychology should not automatically presume that concepts that are central to psychologists or neuroscientists merit lexical priority over those that they might develop and deploy themselves. A broader range of explanatory concerns will alter the weight that we assign to different concepts in terms of their analytical cutting power. We should aspire to concepts that mesh as best they can with work from many fields and levels of analysis, but there is no a priori guarantee that they will slide cleanly into place to form a unified mosaic of science.

By juxtaposing two earlier points, we can appreciate the final reason why we political psychologists should attend to historical thinkers while our colleagues in physics can ignore Ptolemy: we should pay attention to these thinkers because they *continue* to influence the social construction of the emotions in the West via the way their theories of the emotions were sewn into their moral, political, and religious ideas. If the canon's scientific influence has waned, its legacy in normative, ordinary language and in institutional thinking still looms large. Thus, via social construction, the canon is actually part of the current causal story itself. For example, I attended Catholic high school and was taught about human nature, ethics, politics, and religion in a way that was still powerfully suffused with Thomism. Similarly, some contemporary notions of masculinity stubbornly refuse to shed the influence of their origins in Stoic psychology. And the founders of the United States were steeped in the entire Lockean system, so the institutions, rationales, and cultural traditions they initiated reflect conceptions of rights built from the psychological anthropology of his state of nature. Indeed, scientists studying the emotions today presume such a continuing influence when they complain that the weight of the Western tradition's hostility to the

---

8. This account is somewhat at odds with Griffiths's (1997) detailed discussion of similar issues. Though I cannot go into great detail, I would argue that a more thoroughly pragmatic theory of inquiry would not implicitly privilege molecular genetics over ecology merely because the latter cannot typically deal with closed systems. Indeed, scientific inquiry, though privileged, would not be the only arbiter of conceptual meaningfulness, because it is not the only way in which we go about navigating the world.

emotions impedes a proper understanding of the emotions, thus harming and distorting political practice.[9]

For all these reasons, then, political psychology could do well with a more intimate engagement with its past. Below, I consider three thinkers whose political and psychological theories informed each other in a way that is relevant to contemporary political psychology: Plato, Aristotle, and Hume. A full history of philosophical psychology with political intent is beyond the scope of this chapter. Indeed, a full analysis of these three thinkers is beyond its scope. Nevertheless, I hope to provide insights into all three, as well as illustrations of ways in which the canon and modern political psychology can interact fruitfully. I chose Plato, Aristotle, and Hume because they are relatively well known, represent very different views (for example, cognitive versus noncognitive), and connect well with some of the other contributions to this volume.[10] I try to show how these thinkers anticipated recent moves in contemporary psychology. In addition, though it may prove a fool's errand, I venture a few concrete suggestions about new theoretical moves and empirical hypotheses that might be derived from their ideas. Ultimately, though, it is hoped that they will spark the interest of practicing political psychologists.

PSYCHOLOGIES WITH POLITICAL INTENT

Plato

Isn't it quite necessary for us to agree that the very same forms and dispositions as are in the city are in each of us?   Republic 435b

Plato's analysis is the archetype of a psychology with political intent in that the whole argumentative trope of his *Republic* is organized around an analogy between the proper relationship among the elements of the human soul and the elements of the city. The soul is divided among the appetitive, the spirited, and the rational. The city is divided among the corresponding classes of producers (farmer, craftsmen, and so on),

---

9. Elsewhere, I argue that such claims about the canon's hostility to emotion are overstated, though doing so does not affect my point here.

10. A different sample of thinkers from the tradition might have highlighted different substantive issues in contemporary political psychology. But this does not change the main point about fruitful engagement between contemporary science and canonical thinkers. In future work I hope to provide a more thorough history of philosophical psychology with political intent.

the auxiliaries (soldiers), and the guardians (rulers). Plato's psychology and politics are so thoroughly intertwined that he defines regime types in terms of the modal emotional motivations of its rulers (who he thinks, in turn, are influenced by the nature of the regime).

In an aristocracy, Plato's preferred regime type, the rulers' motivations emerge from an erotic striving toward beauty, knowledge, and the good. The rational (but nonetheless emotional) parts of both the soul and the city harness and tutor the spirited and appetitive parts, integrating them into a healthy and cooperative whole. Such rulers tend to be firm but compassionate in their domestic policy and defensive realists in their foreign affairs. In a timocracy, the rulers are themselves ruled by the spirited part of the soul. They tend to be angry, contentious, and prideful in seeking glory and honor in an unreflective way. They are spartan and unsympathetic in their domestic policy and expansionist in their foreign policy. In an oligarchy, the rulers are ruled by the appetitive part of the soul in the service of a single appetite, namely, wealth. Thus, they are characterized by jealousy, vanity, pleasure seeking, and timidity with respect to threats. For Plato, such a commercialist oligarchy is intrinsically unstable and bad. Later thinkers, however, pick up on Plato's analysis to argue that such a regime is not intrinsically unstable and, though not ideal, it is a psychologically astute alternative to reckless timocracy, chaotic democracy, and absolutist tyranny.

In what Plato calls "democracy," the rulers are again ruled by the appetitive part of the soul, but it is in the service of a plethora of appetites, as expressed in their overweening passion for freedom (in the sense of license). Democrats are characterized by envy and resentment, as expressed in a reckless passion for false equality. Otherwise, they are not so much characterized by specific emotions as by a lack of order in emotional expression and object. Plato believed that democracy in this sense naturally degenerates into tyranny. The tyrant's master emotion is fear, in that all of his other emotions and behaviors are ruled by a compulsive desire to stay in power.

Plato's analysis of regime types (and their temporal dynamics) in terms of modal motivating emotions points toward a kind of comparative or historical political psychology. Most political psychology operates within a particular country or regime type (for example, advanced liberal democracies). However, analyzing the differential function of political emotion across different regime types, and between rulers and the ruled, would open up a relatively neglected zone of research. For example, anxiety will obviously take on differential functions in navigating the political landscape of a liberal democracy and an authoritarian theocracy, just as the modal emotional motivations of their leaders are likely to vary. Similarly, most political psychology investigates the present or the very recent past. But Plato's analysis suggests an approach to the development or decline of various regimes that could inform interesting historical work from a political-psychological perspective. As we shall see, Aristotle picks up on certain features of Plato's political psychology in this respect, but he modifies and extends them in several directions.

Plato's analysis of the soul-city relation has important implications for current debates within mainstream political psychology as well. Take, for example, his analysis of the structure of the emotions. For Plato, the important division was not between reason and emotion but, rather, among the appetitive, spirited, and rational parts of the soul. Now, to modern ears, his famous tripartite division of the soul might sound like a trivial variation on the traditional opposition between reason (the rational) and emotion (the spirited), merely spinning off the appetites from the emotions. Nonetheless, his theory is not so simple. What we would today categorize under the term *emotions* was distributed throughout all three portions of the soul. Indeed, several things that we would categorize under a *single* discreet emotional term, say, erotic love, he distributed throughout all three portions of the soul. For example, he argued that there was a powerfully erotic dimension to the rational part of the soul, informing its attention, motivations, and judgment. This insight alone is enough to refute the idea that Plato had a straightforwardly negative view of the emotions. Moreover, it indicates that he theorized a complex interpenetration of reason and the emotions.

Nor is eros the only example of the same nominal emotion taking on differential significance in different parts of the soul. Plato linked courage emanating from the spirited portion of the soul with mere true opinion. Courage rooted in the rational part of the soul involves "knowledge," which has a reflective aspect that requires a propositional cognitivism. The lower kind of courage only requires nonpropositional cognitivism, that is, accurate detection of signals of manageable danger, though not mindful or theoretically reflective. So animals, which have appetitive and spirited souls, share this lower kind of courage with us. In fact, Plato directly compares the spiritedness of a good dog with that of a virtuous but untutored youth (*Republic* 375b).

This move to contextualize the emotions by their origin in the structure of the soul has important implications for the way political psychologists might measure the emotions. For example, Plato thought that nearly all emotions were a kind of mixture of pleasure and pain. Only a few thinkers afterward followed him in this doctrine. Most substituted a good-evil or pleasure-pain dichotomy in their taxonomies. Recent psychological research suggests something in between these two views: positive and negative affect are often largely independent in that, for example, one can be both anxious and enthusiastic about the same object at the same time. Yet it is worth pausing to consider Plato's somewhat different point. He quotes Homer in support of his claim about dual valence: "Wrath that spurs on the wisest mind to rage; Sweeter by far than a stream of flowing honey" (*Philebus* 47e). He goes on to point out the combination of sorrow and pleasure we experience in tragic drama and even suggests that "lamentation and longing" both evince this kind of ambivalence. Nor does it seem right to explain away the phenomenon by saying that the situation eliciting the emotion merely has two different aspects that produce two different feelings. There is a sense in which the pleasure and the pain are fused into the same emotion or two distinct emotions that are internally related, as is often the case with hope and fear. Richard Lazarus is one of the few contemporary psychologists who takes a similar view: "It is common in the psychology of the emotions to distinguish sharply between negative and positively toned emotion and to treat them as if they were opposites . . . [but this] obscures their individual substantive qualities and the complex relational meanings inherent in each. . . . Not infrequently, the so-called positively toned emotions involve harms and threats, and even when they have largely positive valences they sometimes originate in frustrating or negative life conditions" (Lazarus 2001, 63).

Even if we believe that emotional bivalence is merely common, rather than ubiquitous, the phenomenon raises potentially important issues. For example, consider the nonlinear relation between fear and hope in their distinctly emotional senses.[11] Without a modicum of fear, there would typically be no occasion for hope. But past a point, overwhelming fear tends to be characterized by a lack of hope. More generally, the modestly negative correlation between negative emotional factors (such as anxiety) and positive ones (such as enthusiasm) could emerge from more complicated relations between subsets of their component items (for example, fear and hope) washing each other out. For some purposes in political psychology, then, standard factor analyses may be confounding our ability to trace out the real connections. Thus Plato's analyses suggest ways of

---

11. I say "distinctly emotional" because in ordinary language we can also use *fear* to designate probability rather than a powerful evaluative orientation, as in "I fear it might rain later." Similarly, *hope* can designate such slight evaluative orientations as "I hope you can make it to the party" rather than "I hope that the woman I love will accept my proposal of marriage [but fear that she may reject it, leaving me alone and miserable]."

extending the analysis by Huddy, Feldman, and Cassese (chapter 9 in this volume) of the structure of political affect.

Plato's approach to the soul-city metaphor had just as profound an effect on his political theory as it did on his political psychology. The normative superiority of aristocracy flows naturally from the way he sets up the metaphor. Note, however, that Plato's aristocracy is a very peculiar one given the modern connotation of that word. The guardian aristocrats in Plato's republic, though totalitarian in their discretion, have minimal and jointly held property. They live an austere life and receive astonishingly rigorous training. They really are there to serve the city as a whole, rather than to bias the functioning of the polis toward their own gain. Such strictures have led many commentators to suggest that Plato's city is utopian in the pejorative sense and, by association, his moral psychology as well. As we shall see, Aristotle seeks to work more cooperatively with human nature as he finds it in his psychology, and the consequence is that he countenances regimes that strike us as more plausible as well.

Aristotle

Clearly the student of politics must know somehow the facts about the soul, as the man who is to heal the eyes or the body as a whole must know about the eyes or the body; and all the more since politics is more prized and better than medicine.   Nichomachean Ethics 1102a

Many political psychologists will be surprised to learn that society values them more highly than it does physicians. Nevertheless, Aristotle's claim illustrates how thoroughly his psychology manifests political intent. Moreover, he frames it as a practical, therapeutic endeavor. Psychology is to politics as biology is to medicine. This is statecraft as soulcraft. If such terms seem too remote or lofty for modern purposes, we might substitute "political psychology as a policy science." Yet even with this formulation, we may want to beg off. Should not political psychology function as a basic science rather than risk the confusion of normative entanglements? But Aristotle thought that his normative commitments *advanced* his descriptive political psychology, rather than compromising it. And on this point we can learn something from him.

Modern political psychologists reasonably worry about maintaining scientific detachment. Ideological commitments certainly can interfere with good science and can do so all the more, because more subtly, in the social sciences. Yet ignoring or shunning the normative is seldom the best way to avoid such problems. Notice that the word *normative* has three distinct, though nested, meanings. Most generally, *normative* means simply "according to some standard," as in "a normative sample" for test scores. In some cases, standards carry an evaluative valence, as in "logic is the set of norms for valid reasoning." Thus, if my argument is illogical, it is a bad argument. Finally, some evaluative valences connote specifically moral judgment, as in "his normative transgressions make him a bad person."

Medicine is clearly normative in the first two senses that I have sketched and, in a limited way, the third as well. Doctors compare my heart's function to that of normal hearts. Mine might be diseased, and so function poorly. Moreover, we would typically regard this as a bad thing that, all things being equal, should be remedied (for example, via a right to basic medical care). Notice, first, that such normative entanglements do not compromise medical science as a science one whit. Indeed, they facilitate more rapid *scientific* progress on categories of special interest. We still would not understand the immunology of smallpox if we had waited for biology, unguided by medicine's normative conceptual apparatus, to stumble across a vaccine. For that matter, we probably would not have the concept "vaccine." Second, without medical science organizing itself around normative concepts in the first two senses, society would not be in a position to make a normative evaluation in the third sense. Now recall that Aristotle formulated his political psychology on an analogy to medicine. To understand a phenomenon, we must understand its purpose or function (εργον), which leads to an understanding of its excellence (αρετε).

Thus Aristotle considers each emotion *type* (for example, fear or anger) in virtue of the function that it serves and each *instance* of an emotion in terms of whether it conduces to adaptive behavior with respect to that function. Moreover, in the end, he glosses adaptivity as happiness. So far, his theory sounds much like modern accounts of "autonormative" behavior. For Aristotle, however, happiness is not a subjective hedonic state, and its normative standards are sociopolitical, not individual. From the perspective of modern science, there is no reason why sociopolitical standards cannot be rendered just as operationally concrete as autonormative standards. Indeed, in many cases they will be easier to measure because they rely on intersubjective criteria rather than indirect or circular inferences about what is in the subject's head. Moreover, if one is uncomfortable with a distinctively moral interpretation of these sociopolitical criteria, one can bracket it in the same way most rational choice theorists wisely bracket the implicit moral interpretation of their autonormative accounts (that is, ego-centered utilitarianism). Interpreted thus, Aristotle's notion of "virtue" would be akin to "rational," and "vice" would be like "irrational."

Aristotle thus calls patterns of adaptive behavior virtues and maladaptive behaviors vices. Each emotion has an attendant virtue and typically two vices, one of excess and one of deficiency.[12] So, for example, courage is merely a pattern of fear serving its function well—a tendency to correctly sort appropriate occasions for fight and flight. Cowardice might be understood as a kind of emotional disease. It is an overactive fear response causing us to fly when we should fight, just as rashness is an underactive fear response causing us to fight when we should fly.

It should be obvious from this discussion that Aristotle's normative approach to fear can be rendered just as scientific as modern accounts. He could (and to some extent did) give a scientifically serviceable, operational account of courage, cowardice, and rashness. One need not assent to the distinctly moral connotations of those categories to think that they designate scientifically interesting categories. Indeed, his criteria for cowardice are not all that different from those used for modern psychiatry's diagnosis of an anxiety disorder, especially as they shade into the subclinical realm.

So how might following Aristotle in formulating frankly normative concepts of excellence to accompany an analysis of function play out in the context of modern political psychology? Consider, for example, anxiety, one of the two key emotions for the affective intelligence research program in political psychology. MacKuen et al. (chapter 6 in this volume) do an excellent job of theorizing the function of anxiety (in Aristotle's sense) in political choice: "Increased anxiety tells us when we are entering the geography of uncertainty. Absence of anxiety tells us we are in the realm of the safe and familiar and that we can rely on past actions that will, as they have before, successfully manage our lives. And in such circumstances people display habituated choice as their decision strategy." They go on to provide overwhelming evidence that anxiety is active in the functional realm that they hypothesize for it—that is, anxiety has robust effects on whether habituated dispositions are deployed—and

---

12. Aristotle is slightly inconsistent about whether every emotion-action combination has an excellence. At 1107a he says, "There are some actions and emotions whose very names connote baseness, e.g., spite, shamelessness, envy." Yet later (1108b) he says, "Righteous indignation is the mean between envy and spite." But, presumably, righteous indignation and envy are similar in terms of emotional experience and are differentiated via a normative assessment of their appropriateness. Similarly, small conceptual issues surround his discussion of whether there are always two vices for every virtue.

they trace out the myriad behavioral and macrostructural ramifications of that finding. All of this constitutes a major advance.

Yet the affective intelligence research program never moves beyond its functional analysis to the second half of Aristotle's framework: a corresponding analysis of excellence. Stopping at a functional analysis cuts the program off from a huge line of complementary scientific research and greatly limits how it can speak to policy and political theory. MacKuen et al. seem to suggest that a functional analysis implies an analysis of excellence directly: "We resolve the conflict between an attractive normative macro theory—rational choice—and a seemingly more accurate but normatively disappointing micro theory . . . [that] sustains a normative portrait of democracy that is more encouraging than has previously been thought plausible."[13] But what does it mean to say that anxiety, for example, serves the function of managing novelty and threat? In a retrospective, evolutionary context, serving a function and serving it well begin to collapse into each other. If an evolved trait can be accurately explained in terms of some function, that is really just another way of saying that it served that function well enough to enhance survival. The notion of excellence is largely redundant to function.

Outside of a retrospective evolutionary context, however, some capacity can utterly fail to serve the function to which it is put. And making the leap from a neurobiological, evolutionary account of anxiety's function to the function it serves in a modern political context makes the question of excellence anything but redundant. An evolved trait's adaptivity for genomic reproduction in evolutionary time says almost nothing about its normative relevance for contemporary politics. Through a lack of anxiety, we *tell* ourselves that we are safe and can rely on familiar patterns. Whether, in fact, we *are* safe and can properly rely on the familiar is quite another thing. I see no direct evidence for the idea that the emotional mechanisms in question are even approximately utility-maximizing for the individuals involved, never mind for the macropolity.

Thus, we could think about anxiety's excellence from at least three distinct perspectives. First, the autonormative—is anxiety serving the

---

13. MacKuen et al. (chap. 6 in this volume) are relying on the normative analysis found in Marcus (2002). In my view, Marcus *does* establish an important normative claim, but the argument only works if we formulate it in conditional form. That is, *if* our emotional subsystems serve their information processing functions well, *then* some of the normative problems of low-information democracy will be attenuated. Yet we still need a normative conceptual analysis of what it would mean to serve those functions well, along with an empirical demonstration that they do.

individual citizen's immediate preferences, however she may see them? Second, the eudaimonistic—is anxiety serving the citizen's larger interests, free from psychopathology, manipulation, false consciousness, or akrasia? And third, the social—is anxiety advancing the citizen's responsibilities to the public and conducing to the health of the polity?

With such criteria in view, signally important questions for scientific political psychology, policy studies, and political theory begin to emerge that were not even formulable without them. With the rise of scientifically precise political communication strategies, it is truly an open question as to whether anxiety's function has become more a convenient lever of political manipulation than an adaptive mode for managing our political environment. It is not hard to imagine politicians inducing overwhelming amounts of systematic type I and II error in the public's surveillance systems. Indeed, Aristotle anticipated this general problem in the *Rhetoric* and the *Politics* (if not the scope it has come to occupy in applying modern scientific psychology to mass communication).

At first glance, it might seem strange that Aristotle's primary analysis of the emotions comes in the *Rhetoric*. However, rhetoric is about persuasion, and because Aristotle has rendered the emotions in cognitive terms, they are now subject to persuasion. He sharply distinguishes them from the appetites in that one cannot reason another out of being hungry in the same way that one might reason her out of being angry. If beliefs constitute an intrinsic component of emotions, and changing or inducing beliefs is the function of rhetoric, then changing or inducing emotions is also a function of rhetoric. And because the main object of rhetoric is political, the emotions play an enormous role in Aristotle's politics. For conceptions of the emotions as noncognitive, inducing or changing emotions is necessarily a kind of brute manipulation that could bear no relation to reasoned persuasion. For Aristotle, however, political rhetoric is at once emotional persuasion and rational persuasion—the two are internally related.

This internal relation may not be obvious at first. Aristotle sets up a seemingly stark distinction: "One element in the soul is irrational and one has a rational principle." But the Greek is ambiguous as to whether the first part of the soul is "irrational" or "arational." The former is used because it is a normal word in English. The latter is closer to Aristotle's meaning, however, because he thought that whether the two would be in conflict would be a contingent matter. Indeed, in the virtuous man, the two speak "on all matters, with the same voice" (1102b). Moreover, it is not clear whether they are able to be fully opposed even as a matter of contingency. He writes: "Whether these [two parts of the soul] are separated as the parts of the body . . . or are distinct by definition but by nature inseparable, like convex and concave in the circumference of a circle, does not affect the present question" (1102a). Thus, at the very least, they are like parts of the body, which may be divisible but which cooperate in symbiotic ways. And he countenances the idea that the two are only separable in a completely abstract sense—that is, they are merely two different facets of the very same phenomenon, as the idea of convex without concave is not really the idea of convex.

This strong connection between the emotional and the rational portions of the soul generates a crucial political ethics of rhetoric on both the sending end and the receiving end. Rhetoricians must practice their art in a way that respects the sense in which their attempts at persuasion aim to rationally motivate assent and action, even if the means are based in the emotions. And the virtuous listeners must have their sensibilities educated in such a way as to be persuaded and moved to action by the right kind of appeals whether they are aimed at prompting explicit rational consideration or the implicit rationality of a virtuous emotional disposition. Unlike Plato, with his unidirectional totalitarian aristocracy, then, Aristotle preferred a mixed regime that, like his theory of the soul, relied on communication and mutual influence between the various parts of the polity. Both Plato and Aristotle thus have a rather intra-individual analysis of the soul. Neither does much to explore how our political emotions interact with our political institutions. For that analysis, I turn to David Hume's unified account of the psychological, moral, and political sciences.

Hume

There is no question of importance, whose decision is not comprised in the science of man; and there is none, which can be decided with any certainty, before we become acquainted with that science. In pretending therefore to explain the principles of human nature, we in effect propose a complete system of the sciences.   Treatise of Human Nature

Ambition, avarice, self-love, vanity, friendship, generosity, public spirit: these passions, mixed in various degrees, and distributed through society, have been, from the beginning of the world, and still are, the source of all the actions and enterprises, which have ever been observed among mankind.
                    An Enquiry Concerning Human Understanding

Hume's entire philosophical system seems to have been motivated by a strangely genial hostility to religious dogmatism. Because God cannot underwrite our moral, political, or knowledge claims, we are thrown back on an analysis of how it is that we humans seem nonetheless to get about our business reasonably well. Psychology becomes the post-skeptical epistemology in both the theoretical realm and the practical realm. All the other domains of inquiry are based on it. Keep in mind, however, that this move to make psychology fundamental emerges from an even more fundamental act of theological-political protest against the dual dangers of superstition and what Hume came to call enthusiasm.

Many previous philosophical psychologies had emphasized reason more than emotion on quasi-religious grounds. In the great chain of being, humans were located between the divine (associated with reason) and the animal realm (associated with emotion). When Hume dispenses with the divine, he ends up ruthlessly inverting this traditional emphasis in psychology. Thus his famous dictum: "Reason is, and ought only to be, the slave of the passions" (Hume 2000/[1739], 415) Hume's newly naturalized account of psychology will have nothing of teleology. Rather than divine spark, reason is merely manual labor. Indeed, much of what goes under the name of reason is actually rooted in our emotional life. For example, when it appears that the mild voice of reason gets us to act from justice rather than our passionate personal desires, we are really only following the promptings of a different part of our emotional nature. To see how this is so, we need to consider Hume's innovative psychology in greater detail.

Hume reaches back to the Stoic theory of the emotions by starting with three basic taxonomic dimensions: positive versus negative, actual versus potential, and basic versus compounded. So, for example, fear is a basic emotion that arises in reaction to the potential of a negative event. Then he introduces two new dimensions. The first is calm versus violent emotions. He calls the latter the "passions" proper. The distinction is not merely dichotomizing a continuum for the sake of convenience. Contrary to most other interpreters, Hume intends the distinction to be one of kind, rather than merely degree: "We must, therefore, distinguish between a calm and weak passion; betwixt a violent and a strong one" (2000/[1739], 419). Each pair tends to track the other, but they are distinguishable in principle. Moreover, the violent passions are neither bad nor overwhelming with respect to deliberation and action: "'Tis evident passions influence not the will in proportion to their violence . . . but on the contrary, that when a passion has once become a settled principle of action . . . it commonly produces no longer any sensible agitation" (418). Powerful passions can become embedded as habits, at which point they continue to powerfully influence behavior without being experienced as powerful feelings.

Hume does not give the calm emotions names but rather describes them as having a kind of generalized aesthetic function that judges congruence, proportion, and the like. Yet they are of great interest to modern theorists of the emotions because in them we can see Hume anticipating the modern claim that there is a tremendous amount of background emotional processing that influences reason in ways that we often do not notice. Thus, according to Hume, we may not perceive the calm emotions as emotions: "Now 'tis certain there are certain calm desires and tendencies which though they be real passions produce little emotion in the mind, and are more known for their effect than by the immediate feeling or sensation" (2000/[1739], 417). He has in mind the kind of mild anxiety and enthusiasm that, modern research has shown, directs attention and influences our judgments in ways that are not obvious unless we are asked to thematize them. Moreover, we do not merely pass over these calm emotions without notice; rather, we mistake them for the operation of practical reason: "Reason, for instance, exerts itself without producing any sensible emotion. . . . Hence every action of the mind which operates with the same calmness and tranquility is confounded with reason" (ibid.). Yet for Hume, " 'Tis impossible that reason and passion can ever oppose each other, or dispute for the government of the will and actions" (416). So we are led to the conclusion that emotions play the decisive role in what we are accustomed to calling practical reason. We would do better, however, to rename this process "practical decision making" because its ubiquitous and decisive emotional content overshadows its specifically rational content. "Morals excite passions, and produce or prevent actions. Reason of itself is utterly impotent in this particular. The *rules* of morality, therefore, are not conclusions of our reason" (457). Thus, Hume urges an even more radical reclassification of emotional versus rational phenomena than contemporary psychologists have been willing to countenance.

In an important respect, Hume is merely extending an insight developed earlier by Thomas Hobbes. Hobbes rather radically reinterpreted the relations among reason, the emotions, deliberation, and the will. He inverted the long tradition that culminated in Thomism, declaring, "The definition of the will given commonly by the Schooles, that it is rational appetite, is not good" (Hobbes 1991/[1651], 44). Indeed, Hobbes does not merely give the emotions *priority* in deliberation and in determining the will. He makes emotions constitutive of deliberation and the will, as a pattern and species of the emotions, respectively: "Appetites, and aversions, hopes and fears concerning one and the same thing arise alternately. And diverse good and evil consequences of the doing or omitting the thing propounded come successively into our thoughts. . . . The whole sum of

desires, aversions, hopes, and fears . . . is that [which] we call deliberation. . . . [And] in deliberation, the last appetite or aversion immediately
adhering to the action, or to the omission thereof, is that [which] we
call the will" (ibid.). Deliberation is no longer conceived of as carefully
weighing evidence but, rather, merely a stir of the pot for our passions.

For Hobbes, this analysis of the emotive character of practical deliberation issues in a pessimistic political psychology, which in turn famously underwrites uncompromising absolutism in his political theory.
Unconstrained sovereignty is the only way to end the war of all against
all and therefore to secure commodious living. But Hume does not follow Hobbes down this road from emotivism to pessimism and finally to
absolutism. Hume ends up with a much more optimistic analysis that
comports more comfortably with the political sensibilities of modern democracies. To see why he is more optimistic, we need to link the previous
discussion to Hume's second novel distinction in the classification of the
emotions—that between direct and indirect passions.

The direct passions arise from pleasure and pain and map directly onto
the four basic Stoic emotions: joy for actual good, hope for potential good,
sorrow for actual evil, and fear for potential evil.[14] As with the direct passions, there are four fundamental indirect passions: pride and humility,
love and hatred. They are indirect because they are not predicated on
unmediated pleasure and pain. Rather, pride is a kind of positive feeling
toward the self that is mediated by a correlative positive association with
some object or action:

> If I compare, therefore, these two established properties of the passions,
> viz. their object, which is self, and their sensation, which is either pleas-
> ant or painful, to the two supposed properties of the causes, viz. their rela-
> tion to self, and their tendency to produce a pain or pleasure, independent
> of the passion; I immediately find that . . . the true system breaks in upon
> me with an irresistible evidence. That cause, which excites the passion,
> is related to the object, which nature has attributed to the passion; the
> sensation, which the cause separately produces, is related to the sensation
> of the passion: From this double relation of ideas and impressions, the
> passion is derived. The one idea is easily converted into its correlative;
> and the one impression into that, which resembles and corresponds to it.
> (2000/[1739], 418)

---

14. Hume actually divides the direct passions further along a third distinction, which
we might call the hedonic and the instinctive. Though interesting, the distinction is not
particularly relevant for present purposes.

Hume illustrates his theory with the example of a man who feels pride in his house. The beauty of the house, especially relative to other houses, produces the direct passion of joy in that it is good and that he has attained it. The indirect passion of pride, however, operates on a principle of association that creates a reflected admiration with the self as the object and the self-owned house as the cause, or subject. In addition to causation as a principle of association, Hume also lists resemblance and contiguity as prime principles facilitating the leap into an indirect passion. Note that Hume is going beyond the idea of appraisal in emotion to theorizing the mechanisms that link the appraisals in the case of indirect passions.

The indirect emotions only take on their full social and political significance via sympathy, Hume's key emotional disposition. He writes: "No quality of human nature is more remarkable, both in itself and in its consequences, than that propensity we have to sympathize with others, and to receive by communication their inclinations and sentiments, however different from, or even contrary to our own" (2000/[1739], 419). Hume argues that Hobbes's pessimism about human nature is simply unjustified because sympathy naturally stirs up distinctly moral sentiments beyond what can be *initiated* by education and custom. Self-interest is not the ultimate source of all our deliberations, and nor are "all moral distinctions as the effect of artifice and education, when skilful politicians endeavored to restrain the turbulent passions of men, and make them operate to the public good, by the notions of honor and shame." Hume points out that this analysis "is not consistent with experience . . . [for] had not men a natural sentiment of approbation and blame, it could never be excited by politicians" (420).

Despite this effort to establish sympathy as natural and irreducible, Hume does not want to argue that all of our moral sentiments are natural. Indeed, the distinctly political sentiments, such as a sense of justice, he explicitly deems artificial. It is important for him to establish the moral sentiments in two stages because he is trying to steer a course between Hobbesian pessimism and religious dogmatism. That is, he does not want to rely on God for the foundations of his political psychology. He sets up his politics in opposition to "two species of false religion," namely, superstition and enthusiasm. He thinks it implausible that nature has endowed us with something so specific as a natural sense for political justice (especially because most humans have not lived in large political communities until recently). But he also wants to be able to claim some basic natural moral sentiment because without it, Hobbes's undesirable political theory would follow. So Hume begins from a more modest and more plausibly natural disposition: sympathy. Humans just happen to be endowed with a propensity to vibrate in tune with the basic emotions of their fellow creatures. And from sympathy, via his theory of the indirect passions, Hume can build up more remote and complex political sentiments without recourse to anything extraordinary or mysterious: "Where, beside the general resemblance of our natures, there is any peculiar similarity in our manners, or character, or country, or language, it facilitates the sympathy. The stronger the relation is betwixt ourselves and any object, the more easily does the imagination make the transition, and convey to the related idea the vivacity of conception, with which we always form the idea of our own person. Nor is resemblance the only relation, which has this effect, but receives new force from other relations, that may accompany it. The sentiments of others have little influence, when far removed from us, and require the relation of contiguity, to make them communicate themselves entirely" (420).

The natural virtues underwrite moral behavior in relatively small social units: in the family, among friends, and perhaps at the level of the tribe. Once we move beyond small, local political communities into a necessarily abstract conception of justice, however, we find ourselves confronting the "artificial" virtues. Here our acts of political justice originally rely on enlightened self-interest—that is, the observation that small social units need each other in order to survive in a hostile world. As the principles of enlightened self-interest get set down and associated with sentiments of moral judgment, however, those sentiments become internalized in a way that begins to reflect back on our own behavior:

> We are to consider this distinction betwixt justice and injustice, as having two different foundations, viz., that of interest, when men observe, that it is impossible to live in society without restraining themselves by certain rules; and that of morality, when this interest is once observed and men receive a pleasure from the view of such actions as tend to the peace of society, and an uneasiness from such as are contrary to it. . . . After that interest is once established and acknowledged, the sense of morality in the observance of these rules follows naturally, and . . . is also augmented by a new artifice, and [it is] that the public instructions of politicians, and the private education of parents, contribute to . . . giving us a sense of honor and duty. (421)

From the point of view of contemporary political psychology, Hume's distinction between the direct and the indirect passions resonates with the distinction between the emotions generated immediately from the affect programs and those that are mediated by more complex sociocognitive mechanisms. More generally, Hume's approach points toward a focus on *developmental* and *historical* political psychologies of the emotions. Current developmental theories of moral reasoning and socialization have a very thin account of the emotions. Hume conceived of moral and political education as an education of the sentiments, and his account of our socialization into justice relies on the interaction of our emotions with our political institutions. Hume's account also suggests developmental research at the level of political societies, for example, historical accounts of political development in which the emotions are implicated or of societies making the transition out of authoritarianism (postwar Germany or the post-Communist countries).

With this more optimistic political psychology, Hume could move beyond Hobbes into a cautiously progressive liberalism based on proto-utilitarian principles. Hume saw the politics of his day as dominated by two opposing views, both rooted in false religious beliefs. The first, superstition, attracted people of a conservative temperament, and the second, enthusiasm, led liberally disposed people to ill-advised radicalism. Hume wanted to co-opt both. Thus Hume's thoroughgoing psychological naturalism, along with his attack on religious dogmatism, were in themselves part of his political theory. They undercut the rationales for superstition and enthusiasm. In their place, we are given an account of the moral sentiments that prefigures later utilitarian thinking but with an institutional twist. This proto-utilitarian element of Hume's psychology pushes him in a liberal direction by loosening distinctions based on rank and divine right and by appealing to universal moral sentiments. On the other hand, his psychological account of the origins of justice relies on our emotions' interacting with stable institutions that slowly transform prudential considerations into politico-moral sentiments. Thus, there is also a conservative check on the liberal impulses emerging from the more direct moral sentiments. So we end up with a cautiously progressive, deeply humanistic politics rooted in a deeply humanistic psychology.

CONCLUSION

Some things are ancient in the sense of being antiquated. In other cases *ancient* properly implies durability. Ptolemaic astronomy is a historical curiosity, not a living means for orienting ourselves in the universe. Aristotle's biology is also ancient in this antiquated sense, a mere historical curiosity. His psychology and his politics, however, can still startle with their vibrancy and insight. Modern political psychologists can and should dispense with what is antiquated in the historical tradition. We need no longer concern ourselves with the pineal gland or the divine right of kings. But it would be a mistake to throw away the durable with the antiquated. The impulse to theorize in systematic ways, to do psychology with political intent, serves to advance both the science of psychology and the political goals that it might serve.

CHAPTER THREE

Political Cognition as Social Cognition: Are We All Political Sophisticates?

DARREN SCHREIBER

Participation in national-level politics has been the focus of much of the political behavior literature. From seminal works such as *The People's Choice* (Lazarsfeld, Berelson, and Gaudet 1948), *The American Voter* (Campbell et al. 1960), *Public Opinion and American Democracy* (Key 1961), and *An Economic Theory of Democracy* (Downs 1957) to more contemporary work such as *The Nature and Origins of Mass Opinion* (Zaller 1992), the theoretical focus and empirical examples have drawn from national politics. Politics, however, can have a broader meaning than competition among candidates, officeholders, and parties at the national level. We can follow Aristotle's (1996) claim, originally made circa 350 B.C., that "man is by nature a political animal" and observe the evidence for his contention in family politics, office politics, church politics, neighborhood politics, and the politics existing in any assemblage of humans.

MACHIAVELLIAN INTELLIGENCE: SOCIAL COGNITION AS POLITICAL COGNITION

Some cognitive scientists, evolutionary psychologists, and primatologists have agreed with Aristotle and argued that the very nature of our intelligence is political. In a seminal paper about social cognition, Nicholas Humphrey (1976) argued that although Robinson Crusoe's task of survival on the desert island was technically challenging, the really hard problems came from the arrival of Man Friday. This line of reasoning, sometimes called the Machiavellian intelligence hypothesis (Byrne and Whiten 1988; Whiten and Byrne 1997), contends that managing the problems of the social world requires a far greater level of intellect because contexts change rapidly (see de Waal 1998). The evolution of affective states is thought to have facilitated cooperation and thus complex social structures (Lewis, Amini, and Lannon 2000), but monitoring the emotional and mental states of others requires a constant vigilance (Chance and Mead 1953). It is believed that the demands of increasingly complex social environments drove a cognitive arms race with competitive pressures leading to larger neo-cortices capable of navigating the politics of larger tribal groupings (Barton and Dunbar 1997; Dunbar 1993). One theory arising from this literature is that Robinson Crusoe's mental capacity for solving the technical problems of his mere survival evolved as an incidental benefit from the mental capacity for solving the more complex social problems that he faced (Humphrey 1976; Whiten and Byrne 1988; but see Oakley 1964).

Because there are so many different problems that result from social living, it has been argued that social intelligence is not a monolithic phenomenon but, rather, a collection of intelligences that evolved to solve particular problems in the social environment (Gigerenzer 1997; Cosmides and Tooby 2002). Andrew Whiten and Richard Byrne (1997) note that the social intelligence exhibited by primates reflects a delicate subtlety requiring at least a basic ability to manipulate the behavioral, emotional, and mental states of others and label this intelligence Machiavellian, not because it is callous but because it is subtle. Thus, for animals in a complex social environment, theorizing about the intentional states of others is one particularly important task of social cognition (Premack and Woodruff 1978; Dennett 1987).

Whereas imitation (Rizzolatti et al. 1999; Rizzolatti and Craighero 2004), symbolic thinking (Deacon 1997), language (Pinker 1994, 1999), normative judgment (Brosnan and de Waal 2003; compare Wynne 2004), and culture (Byrne et al. 2004) have all been described as kinds of social cognition emerging in primates, the argument made in the Machiavellian intelligence theories is that these capacities evolved in response to the need for a kind of political cognition. But this conceptualization of political cognition involves intimate relationships with those we encounter daily, not thinking about candidates in national elections.

The theory of this chapter is that the kinds of political cognition that political scientists usually study, namely, thoughts about values, policies, coalitions, and leaders on the state, national, or international level, have co-opted the mental apparatus evolved for solving the problems of "everyday politics" (Humphrey 1976). This conjecture follows the tradition of evolutionary arguments tracing back to Charles Darwin's (1996/[1859]) claim that "an organ originally constructed for one purpose . . . may be converted into one for a wholly different purpose."

To support this conjecture, this chapter sweeps through a diverse literature about the potential biological foundations of political attitudes and behaviors. I begin with a discussion of one proposed foundation for social cognition: mirror neurons. These neurons appear to allow us to model the actions, emotions, and thoughts of others and have been implicated in many roles that are essential for social thinking. I then discuss two important kinds of social thinking: automatic social evaluation and "theory of mind," which allows humans to understand the intentions of others. I go on to discuss how these two functional mechanisms have been connected to neuroanatomy through the default state network theory. I then describe evidence from recent functional brain imaging experiments implicating the default state network in sophisticated thinking about national politics and briefly review the major claims of the traditional political science literature about political sophistication. I argue that political scientists need to take values more seriously in their work on political sophistication and present a potential biological basis for political values and attitudes.

It is important to appreciate that not all attitudes are the consequences of deliberate or conscious choices, however, and so I distinguish between implicit and explicit attitudes. I end with a discussion of the role of coalitional cognition and social networks in political attitudes, both implicit and explicit. Evolutionary pressure generated by competition among coalitions and the individuals within those coalitions sparked more powerful cognitive capacities. The development of the mirror neuron appears to have been a critical early step in the direction of Machiavellian intelligence.

MIRROR NEURONS AS BASES FOR SOCIAL COGNITION

The recent discovery of so-called mirror neurons has presented a potential foundation for understanding the neural substrates of more complex social thinking (Gallese, Keysers, and Rizzolatti 2004). One method for studying neural function is to insert a probe directly into the neural tissue of a living animal and monitor the flow of electricity through a neuron or group of neurons. Although quite invasive, this method allows a researcher to investigate the function of particular neurons in live animals with a very high temporal resolution. In the mid-nineties, on a hot summer day in Italy, a graduate student of the neuroscientist Vitorio Gallese had inserted the probes into the premotor cortex of a macaque monkey in order to study the neural activity corresponding to manipulating objects. After preparing the monkey for the experiment, the student went out for an ice cream cone. When he returned, he noticed that each time he licked the ice cream cone, the neurons in the monkey's premotor cortex fired. This was intriguing, given that the monkey was not making any motor movements.

Further study revealed a set of 92 neurons in the premotor cortex that were active both when the monkey performed an action and when the experimenter performed the same action (Gallese et al. 1996; Rizzolatti et al. 1996). These neurons were described as mirror neurons because of their apparent ability to represent the action of another. Additional research soon identified clusters of mirror neurons in a number of different locations in the brain (Rizzolatti and Craighero 2004). Evidence that these neurons were providing mental representations of the action increased when it was discovered that neurons representing the final part of a motor sequence continued to fire when the final portion of the sequence was hidden from the monkey's view (Umilta et al. 2001).

Although macaque monkeys are capable of representing the actions of others, they are not believed to be capable of imitation. Edward L. Thorndike (1898) defined *imitation* as the capacity to learn to do an action by seeing it done and was famous for his "Thorndike boxes." Animals put into the boxes could only escape by means of a series of lever pulls. Cats and dogs could learn the sequence of events needed to escape, but he concluded that it was by trial and error, not by observation or by imitation. The consensus among ethologists is that imitation exists only in humans and probably in apes (Byrne 1995; Whiten and Ham 1992; Visalberghi and Fragaszy 2001). Thus, although the mirror neurons appear to lay a foundation for imitation, they do not guarantee it (Rizzolatti and Craighero 2004).

Mirror neurons, however, appear to do more than merely facilitate action representation. There is evidence to suggest that they play a crucial role in emotion. The expression "when you smile, the whole world smiles with you" appears to have some basis in fact. When subjects are shown subliminal images of smiling or angry faces, their facial muscles respond with smile-like or anger-like movements despite their having no conscious awareness of the stimuli (Dimberg, Thunberg, and Elmehed 2000). It is believed that the ability to represent the emotional states of others facilitates bonding and cooperation in mammals (Lewis, Amini, and Lannon 2000), and mirror neurons may play a crucial role.

Paul Ekman (1992) has identified six basic emotions that are universally recognized and have distinct facial expressions. Note that the regions of the brain that are implicated in the expression of each of these emotions have been connected to the perception of the same emotion. Feeling fear is frequently associated with activity in the amygdala, but the amygdala is also associated with the perception of fearful faces (Adolphs et al. 1994). Similarly, feeling disgusted will activate the insula, which is also activated when you observe another person experiencing disgust (Krolak-Salmon et al. 2003; Calder et al. 2000; Phillips et al. 1998; Wicker et al. 2003). Brain imaging studies of subjects looking at surprised faces activate the parahippocampal region (Schroeder et al. 2004), which also is activated when a person perceives novel information (Tulving et al. 1996). The evidence regarding sadness, happiness, and anger is less clear. Perceiving happiness in others, however, has been associated with the basal ganglia (Morris et al. 1996), a region that is also implicated in reward detection (Bartels and Zeki 2000; Knutson et al. 2001; Breiter et al. 1997). And the perception of sadness has been correlated with activation in the temporal lobe and the amygdala (Blair et al. 1999). Anger is particularly interesting because subjects have amygdala (fear?) activations when the angry gaze is directed at them (Sato et al. 2004), but experienced anger appears to most typically activate the orbital frontal cortex (Murphy, Nimmo-Smith, and Lawrence 2003).

The lesion and imaging evidence are suggestive, but more conclusive proof of the role of mirror neurons in processing of emotions has been found in direct neural recoding experiments carried out in macaque monkeys. Mirror neuron activation was observed when the monkeys both made and viewed facial expressions connected with affiliative, aversive, and fearful emotions (Ferrari et al. 2003). And imaging experiments performed with humans who were asked to express, imitate, and observe emotional displays found activations in overlapping regions (Carr et al. 2003). Note that, owing to the invasiveness of direct recording, mirror neurons have not yet been directly observed in humans (see chapter 4). The imaging evidence and the conservative nature of evolution suggest, however, that the existence of mirror neurons in humans is the most parsimonious explanation currently available.

Emotions have such strong physiological roots that the neuroscientist Antonio Damasio (1999, 2003) distinguishes emotions (described by him as changes in body and brain states triggered by the content of perception) from feelings (changes in brain states that reach sufficient intensity to be perceived by conscious awareness). The physiological roots of emotion serve regulatory purposes (for example, increasing heart rate) that support survival. But in social animals, emotions can also play an important communicative role. That the same neurons are activated when I feel fear as when I observe you feeling fear illustrates the importance of mirror neurons for social functioning.

Mirror neurons have also been linked with the facility for language. Broca's area is one of the most frequently studied regions of the brain, in part, because of its long association with language functions (Broca 1999/[1861]). Giacomo Rizzolatti (one of the discoverers of mirror neurons) and Michael Arbib (1998; see also Arbib and Bota 2003) have contended that mirror neurons found in the macaque monkey's F5 region correspond to the Broca's area in humans. Evelyne Kohler and colleagues (2002) found that neurons in F5 are activated not only when an action is seen but when it is heard, suggesting that these neurons are representing an abstraction of the action. Mirror neurons appear to have intriguing characteristics. They are activated not only during action but also during the observation of action. And they seem to facilitate the abstraction of an action into a more general representation.

Thus mirror neurons may pose a solution to the "symbol grounding" problem (Harnad 1990) identified in John Searle's (1980) famous "Chinese room" thought experiment. I discuss Searle's argument more thoroughly below, but the difficulty of learning Chinese from a Chinese-only dictionary gives one a hint of where Searle is heading. In the argument of Rizzolatti and Arbib, mirror neurons have the potential to abstract from the particulars of observation and action to a more general representation, the kind that allows for symbols and eventually language.

THEORY OF MIND

Apes may share imitation with humans, but some contend that gorillas and chimpanzees share a more impressive characteristic with us humans: theory of mind (Premack and Woodruff 1978; but see Heyes 1998). Theory of mind is the capacity to represent the intentional states of others. A wide variety of mammals appear to be capable of simultaneous emotional responses that resonate with those of their fellow mammals (Lewis, Amini, and Lannon 2000). But comprehending the intention of another is a far rarer characteristic and is not even found in all humans. For example, it is believed that some autistic people do not have theory of mind (Frith and Frith 1999).

I can fire canonical neurons in the premotor areas and achieve a particular motor sequence. Mirror neurons will fire both when I am performing the action and when I am observing you performing the action. In order to imitate, I must abstract a bit from merely observing and imagine myself in the role of the actor. But for theory of mind, I need to comprehend not only what you are doing, but why you are doing it. Believing that there is a why, in this sense, is what Daniel Dennett (1987) calls taking the "intentional stance" toward something. Dennett has argued that we can take different stances toward entities: the physical stance, wherein this entity does what it does because it obeys scientific laws; the design stance, wherein this entity does what it does because it was designed to do that; and the intentional stance, wherein this entity does what it does because it wants to. Many believe that mirror neurons are crucial for our theory of mind (Williams et al. 2001; Schulkin 2000; Gallese and Goldman 1998; Rizzolatti and Craighero 2004) and other types of social cognition (Dapretto et al. 2006). The connections among mirror neurons, the functional organization of the brain, and such high-order tasks as theory of mind, however, are still being worked out.

A classic example of theory of mind is the "Sally/Ann" task. Sally walks into a room and puts her ball into a basket. Ann walks into the room finds the ball and puts it into a box. When Sally walks back into the room, where will she look for the ball? An autistic person, lacking theory of mind, will say that Sally will look in the box. That is where the ball is and she will look there. The medial frontal cortex of the brain, located behind the center of the forehead, is activated in a variety of contexts where the subject is required to understand the intention of another actor. It has been postulated that the medial prefrontal cortex evolved from being a center representing actions (Frith and Frith 1999) to a location for representing our intentions and then to a location representing the intentions of others (Frith 2002). Problems in the medial prefrontal cortex appear to preclude autistic patients from being able to perform this task (Williams et al. 2001).

The medial frontal lobes' role in theory of mind has been supported with lesion studies (Rowe et al. 2001; but see Bird et al. 2004) and experiments using functional imaging in both healthy subjects (Fletcher et al. 1995) and patients with Asperberger's Syndome, a type of typically high-functioning autism (Happe et al. 1996). More recent imaging work has shown the medial frontal region to be active during so-called trust and reciprocity games from the economics literature (McCabe et al. 2001) and in other games of strategy such as rock, paper, scissors (Gallagher et al. 2002). It has also been implicated in non-verbal theory of mind tasks such as choosing the appropriate next panel in a comic strip without speech (Brunet et al. 2000).

THE DEFAULT STATE NETWORK

The medial frontal lobe has been also proposed as a part of the "default state network," another role that appears to be related to the theory of mind. The usual setup in a functional brain imaging experiment is that the researcher wants the subject to perform some task so that inferences can be made about the neural substrates involved in that task. Typically, this task is accompanied by a rest condition in which the subject stares at a blank screen. The resting activation is subtracted from the task activation to yield the portion of the brain that is activated during the task. In a move similar to John Cage's composition of his 1961 piece 4′33″, Marcus Raichle and his colleagues (2001) performed a meta-analysis of the rest conditions in a number of imaging studies. Their goal was to identify areas that were active during rest but diminished in activity when the subject performed any task.

The results led Raichle to postulate a default state network involving the medial prefrontal cortex and the medial posterior cortex. A diverse range of brain regions were activated during various tasks, and this default state network consistently reduced its activation when the subject switched from rest to any task. The regions that are implicated in the network have the highest resting metabolic rates in the brain and consume substantial energy resources on a continuous basis (Gusnard and Raichle 2001). Raichle theorized that this network is involved in constantly monitoring one's surroundings for phenomena that require goal-directed attention.

Raichle's theory is particularly intriguing given what is known about the areas that compose his putative default state network. As described above, the medial prefrontal cortex appears to be involved in understanding and predicting the thoughts of others (Frith and Frith 1999). And the medial posterior cortex works implicitly to evaluate the environment (Vogt, Finch, and Olson 1992) and is frequently associated with emotional stimuli (Maddock 1999). Although these regions rarely have true activations above a resting baseline in typical imaging studies, they have been activated during social cognition tasks (Greene et al. 2001; Iacoboni et al. 2004). It has also been postulated that these medial regions are involved in the representation, monitoring, evaluation, and integration of self-referential stimuli, that is, that this region is the location of the "self" (Northoff and Bermpohl 2004). Considering these theories together, we have a picture of network of brain regions that is attempting to understand our social world and relate our self to our place in that world.

The default state network theory fits nicely with the arguments by the primatologists Michael Chance and Alan Mead (1953) about the need for constant monitoring of the social environment in social animals. In his book *Chimpanzee Politics*, Frans de Waal (1998) describes the constantly shifting alliances among a group of chimpanzees. These alliances are critical to mating opportunities, food sharing, and physical safety, functions that are at the core of survival and that exert strong evolutionary pressures. Chance and Mead argue that the ability to automatically and continuously monitor alliances and potential allies in a social environment would provide an evolutionary advantage. Similarly, John Orbell and his colleagues (2004) recently demonstrated that the capacity to infer the intentional states of others and to send signals so as to manipulate the intentional states of others can facilitate the evolution of a highly cooperative disposition supporting better individual and group outcomes. Thus we can see that the capacities for theory of mind and for social evaluation enable fruitful political cognition in the context of everyday politics.

BRAIN IMAGING, POLITICAL COGNITION, AND POLITICAL SOPHISTICATION

Evidence from recent experiments with functional magnetic resonance imaging (fMRI) suggests that political cognition about national political issues utilizes the neural circuitry that apparently evolved for everyday tribal politics.[1] I and Marco Iacoboni (2004) conducted a set of experiments that examined changes in cerebral blood flow while eighteen subjects responded to questions that were either political or nonpolitical. Twelve of the subjects were college students who were members of the college Republican or Democratic club and were very politically sophisticated. Six were college students who were not politically involved and who had low levels of political knowledge.

While answering questions about national politics, the political sophisticates showed activation above a resting baseline in the medial frontal

---

1. In chapter 4 Spezio and Adolphs raise a number of concerns about fMRI and its interpretation. With fMRI, we are directly obtaining an incredibly small fluctuation in magnetic signal. From that we are making inferences about changes in the ratio of oxygenated to deoxygenated hemoglobin. And from that we are making inferences about changes in neuronal activity. With the incredibly small signal change and the tremendous variation in human neuroanatomy (consider the differing wrinkle patterns in a box of raisins), it is amazing that we get anything useful. Despite these methodological concerns, we do find statistically and substantively meaningful relationships in the data. And, as in the case of the experiments I report here, we sometimes get apparently reproducible results. The explosion in fMRI research is bringing an explosion of caveats to the method and its interpretation. But that research energy is motivated by the ability to seriously consider previously untestable hypotheses.

and the medial posterior cortices, the main areas of Raichle's default state network and areas that have been implicated in other studies of social cognition. The political novices, however, showed decreases in activity in both of these regions, suggesting that they had to increase their level of explicit cognitive effort in responding to the questions. My interpretation of these results is that political sophisticates are able to automatically use the mental tools that have developed for evaluating everyday politics and apply them to national politics. Political novices, however, do not possess sufficient experience or knowledge about how to apply the values and skills they use to navigate the politics of family and social life to the questions of national politics.

Another experiment showed significant bilateral activations in the inferior frontal lobe in a contrast of the political sophisticates and novices while they looked at political faces and nonpolitical faces. Previous research has suggested the presence of mirror neurons in these regions (Rizzolatti and Craighero 2004), and they have been activated in experiments where people both imitated and observed the faces of others (Carr et al. 2003). The preliminary interpretation of these data is that political sophisticates have a greater empathic connection to political figures than do political novices. Thus political sophistication may have an affective component (Marcus, Neuman, and MacKuen 2000) in addition to the cognitive component, which is most frequently studied by political scientists. Furthermore, the political sophisticates again had activity in the posterior cingulate while viewing political faces, consistent with the theory that they are using a capacity for implicit social evaluation to think about politics.

This kind of difference between political novices and political sophisticates was largely predicted in a paper that Matthew Lieberman and Kevin Ochsner, and I (2003) co-authored. In synthesizing the literature from social psychology, cognitive neuroscience, and political science, we expected that political sophisticates would be able to rely on implicit associations to respond to political problems and political novices would require explicit and controlled cognitive processes. We based our arguments in part on the large body of work in social psychology's "dual-processing" literature (Schneider and Shiffrin 1977; Chaiken and Trope 1999), in part on new work in cognitive neuroscience on attitudes (Lieberman et al. 2002; Lieberman et al. 2001), and in part on the decades of political scientific inquiry into the behavioral and cognitive differences between political sophisticates and political novices (Converse 1964; Zaller 1992).

As Spezio and Adolphs point out in chapter 4, there are good theoretical and empirical reasons to be skeptical of the dual-process models. If nothing else, we should be concerned that there has been such a large and continuing proliferation of dual-process frameworks, rather than a unification. On the other hand, there are areas of agreement in the nearly thirty years of work covered by this literature.

We may not have a clear sense of what exactly the top is in the top-down (as opposed to the bottom-up) versions of these theories, but many still find it useful to act as if we have some understanding of what that might mean. And even if it is possible that we will someday have adequate accounts that can nicely dispense with notions of executive, controlled, conscious, explicit, or reflective processes, it does not appear that we are quite there yet. These heuristics continue to be informative as they are tempered by the recognition that any boundaries between reflective and reflexive processes (Lieberman, Schreiber, and Ochsner 2003) are fuzzy at best. In the context of political thinking, I contend that these rough distinctions can help illuminate the differences between those who appear to be more sophisticated in their thinking about national politics and their less sophisticated counterparts.

The early work by Phillip Converse (1964) demonstrating that many people who responded to political surveys appeared to have little ideological constraint and to be temporally inconsistent in their responses was troubling to many political scientists. Converse's interpretation was that these political novices held "nonattitudes" and that "large portions of an electorate do not have meaningful beliefs, even on issues that have formed the basis for intense political controversy among elites for substantial periods of time" (245). Chris Achen (1975) claimed that "democratic theory loses its starting point" if Converse is right, and many others shared his concern.

John Zaller's (1992) research elaborated on Converse's findings and posited an information processing model to account for the results. An individual's attentiveness to political messages carried in the media would strongly predict the probability that he or she would receive a given piece of information. If a newly received piece of information was inconsistent with the other considerations already held in the mind of the recipient, then the probability that he or she would accept the new information was diminished. And when asked to respond to an opinion poll, the probability that the person would sample a given message would be influenced by the salience and accessibility of that piece of information. Zaller acknowledged that values and psychology could play a role in the processing of considerations, but his was essentially a parsimonious and powerful information-processing model.

POLITICAL VALUES AND BIOLOGY

More recent scholarship has suggested a more prominent role for values in thinking about national policy and politics. James DeNardo found that "in the face of great complexity, we are all amateur strategists" (1995, 305) and that the difference between novices and experts "is not ideological or political—it is essentially technical" knowledge (237). He found that college students often struggled in vain to apply their values to complex questions of nuclear strategy but that policy experts appeared to be applying the same kinds of value constructs to the problems with the ease afforded by extensive knowledge of how a particular missile system would impact the desired normative outcome. More recently, Mike Alvarez and John Brehm (2002) have argued that political novices are sure of what they value but, unlike experts, are unsure of how to use those values in political choices. They analyzed the structure of responses to a number of survey questions and found that uncertainty about how to apply values was far more prevalent than ambivalent conflict between two values or equivocation in values leading people to unacknowledged policy conflicts.

On the basis of the discussion above about the evolutionary importance of everyday political thinking, it would indeed be strange if most people did not have politically relevant values. We constantly need to appraise the policies we observe, obey, and implement at home, at work, and in our social structures. We frequently make choices about whom to align ourselves with in disputes among our family, friends, co-workers, and acquaintances. Although there is likely to be variation in the capacity people have for the Machiavellian intelligence exhibited in everyday politics, evolutionary pressures appear to have given most people sufficient capability to keep from getting killed or exiled as a consequence of bad choices made in their local political environment.

Thus in terms of evolution and everyday politics, at least, we are all political sophisticates, even if we all do not apply that sophistication to the realm of national politics. Many brilliant political figures have stumbled badly before an unfamiliar social group. This does not mean that they suddenly have nonattitudes but rather that they simply do not know how to apply the values and attitudes that they use regularly to this unfamiliar context.

Psychologists regularly put their lab animals into odd contexts to induce unnatural behaviors. Political scientists do the same thing with their survey respondents. An interesting question is whether humans thinking about politics (everyday or national) are more like pigeons trained to press a lever or like pigeons flying about their cage. Based on the evidence reviewed in this chapter, I contend that we are more like the pigeons flying in a cage.

Indeed, it appeared from the fMRI data we collected that political sophisticates and political novices were capable of using implicit cognitive mechanisms to respond to questions that were nonpolitical but required the application of social values. In his study of responses to a small set of questions comparing the values liberty, equality, economic security, and social order. William Jacoby (2006) found that around 80 percent of respondents in the general population possess transitive political value rankings. A portion did display some intransitivity in their preference rankings. Some of this intransitivity may be due to measurement error, but political sophistication accounts for a small part of it. The questions were phrased in terms that may not be familiar to those with very low levels of knowledge about national politics but who still might be able to operationalize these concepts in daily living.

The universality of values for which I am arguing has been suggested by a long line of research in psychology (Feldman 2003). The contention is not that everyone shares the same values. Jacoby's work demonstrates a pattern of agreement about the hierarchy of values in the aggregate view of American politics, but he also illustrates tremendous variance underlying that aggregation. The theory, however, is that nearly everyone has values and uses them constantly to approach the problems of life. The seminal work of Milton Rokeach (1973) and the more recent scholarship of Shalom Schwartz (1992, 1994) identify large sets of values from which particular cultures and individuals draw constantly. The difficulty, as far as political scientists are concerned, is in the ability to map from these values to questions of national politics.

One of the few fMRI studies of moral decision making has implicated the same neural structures that appear to underlie political cognition in political sophisticates. Joshua Greene and his colleagues (2001; Greene 2003) studied people responding to a set of moral dilemmas involving either personal or impersonal actions and found that a personal action (pushing an extremely large person off a bridge onto trolley tracks to stop a trolley from killing five people) involved activation in the areas of the default state network, whereas impersonal action (pulling a lever to reroute a train to hit one person on the tracks and thus save five others) did not. This difference helped explain the various moral choices that people indicated (they would pull the lever but not push the person), though logically the situations were equivalent (one person dies so that many may live). If mirror neurons and our capacity for theory of mind allow us to put ourselves into the shoes of others on occasion, then it is not surprising that we would more strongly identify with the person who is in close proximity (standing next to us on the bridge) than with those who are more remote (standing on the tracks).

If it truly is the intensity of simulation that differentiates the two moral dilemmas, then we have a theory that could explain moral choices in lower primates. Recently, capuchin monkeys have been shown to reject a payment that was "unfair" compared to what one of their fellow monkeys was getting for the same effort (Brosnan and De Waal 2003; but see Wynne 2004). It may be that even the simple monkeys are capable of simulating the payoff they expect for themselves and others and reacting strongly when there are inconsistencies. Jennifer Hochschild's (1981) study *What's Fair?* (which used in-depth interviews of 28 people) revealed a pattern of simulation as her subjects often imagined themselves in the position of others in society. The inconsistencies in her subjects' responses often reflected the inconsistencies in payoffs that occur in an imperfect and unfair society. It may be that our sensitivity to these inconsistencies goes back to our primate ancestors.

Other evidence for an ancient evolutionary pedigree for politically relevant values comes from work in hormones and genetics. Prairie voles are rodents well known for a strong habit of life-long monogamy, whereas the related montane vole is promiscuous throughout its life. These behavioral differences have been correlated to differences in the levels of the hormone oxytocin and differences in brain function associated with the hormone (Young, Wang, and Insel 1998; Winslow et al. 1993). Manipulated decreases in the level of oxytocin in prairie voles correlate with a reduced level of monogamy and bonding. In game theory, variation in levels of this same hormone has been found to correlate with different levels of willingness to trust a partner in a typical economic game (Zak, Kurzban, and Matzner 2004). Across related species the different levels of this hormone appear to impact socially relevant choices, and across individuals within a species, this hormone correlates with different social decisions.

Such a pattern of variation and consistency in hormone levels suggests that a genetic difference might play a role. And, in fact, genetic bases for oxytocin production and receptivity have been identified (Young et al. 1997). As a broader principle we might expect that many social and political values would have a genetic component. Social hierarchy and tribal order certainly vary among primates in a manner suggesting that an inherited characteristic is motivating the patterns.

In humans, recent analysis of genetic data in the form of twin studies has provided evidence for the partial heritability of political attitudes. Analysis of questions asked of monozygotic ("identical") and dizygotic ("fraternal") twins that were raised together or apart suggests that around 32 percent of the variance in political attitudes can be attributed to being genetically heritable (Alford, Funk, and Hibbing 2005). Although at first glance such a high level of heritability might seem surprising, in light of the preceding discussion it is easy to conceive that many politically relevant values may have a genetic component. On the basis of evolutionary principles, we can imagine that prairie voles evolved the habit of monogamous bonding as a survival strategy adaptive to their environment, just as their cousins, the montane voles, evolved a more promiscuous tendency.

We may speculate that genetic variation in oxytocin levels (and other genes and hormones) may be the reason that attitudes about living together and divorce appear to have a genetic heritability (Alford, Funk, and Hibbing 2005). It would be interesting to investigate whether humans who are more analogous to the prairie vole in oxytocin levels are more opposed to divorce and their montane analogues comfortable with living together. These attitudes might be rationalizations for genetically inherited behavioral tendencies, or they may be emotional or cognitive consequences of the inherited hormone level. But it is possible to see how evolutionary pressures could have consequences for feelings, thoughts, and behaviors that would be relevant to policy choices on a national level. Although we may not typically think about the genetic basis for political attitudes, it may well underpin some of the value structure identified by James DeNardo and William Jacoby.

Of course, I am not arguing that all political attitudes are genetic in origin. I contend that genetics is only one factor. According to the data provided by Alford et al. (2005), the environment shared by twins has an apparently small role in shaping political attitudes (about 14 percent), and the unshared environment appears to have a strong influence (about 53 percent). Thus parenting seems to have a smaller function than we might expect in the political attitudes of children, and peers seem to have a greater one (Pinker 2002). The mixture of influences in the broader environment and culture has tremendous sway.

This point is nicely illustrated in a study of fifteen tribal societies playing the economists' ultimatum game (Henrich et al. 2001). Contrary to the rational choice theory's predictions of neoclassical economics, there was substantial variation in the playing of the game across cultures. The norms utilized, however, were often quite comprehensible to anthropologists who were familiar with the contexts in which the tribes lived.

Our primate cousins also appear to have cultural variation amc (Byrne et al. 2004; Sternberg and Kaufman 2002). This manifi in customs, technologies, and behavior. But we can imagine th cultural norms would also exert a reproductive and thus genetic that could vary the distribution of genetic traits in a society.

In fact, the economist Robert Frank (1989) argued that both cheating and cheating detection should be subject to evolutionary pressures. And recently Herbert Gintis has shown that if the punishment of cheaters can evolve in a manner such that individuals receive pleasure from the act of norm enforcement, then such altruistic punishment can sustain norms of cooperation even within large societies (Gintis 2000, 2003; Boyd et al. 2003). More recently, Dominique de Quervain and colleagues (2004) identified the neural basis for altruistic punishment in the dorsal striatum, a place associated with pleasure that is active when people punish norm violators. This line of work provides an example of the way values that play a role in everyday politics can have a genetic and neural basis that is contoured by cultural and other environmental pressures.

Twentieth-century models of political decision making were heavily influenced by behaviorism and the lack of a role for philosophically meaningful choice (Watson 1913; Skinner 1938). In rational choice theory, an individual is expected to transitively rank alternatives according to preferences and to always choose the highest-ranked alternative (Downs 1957). Similarly, in the information processing model of political attitudes that Zaller (1992) presented, the individual's role is consigned to receiving, accepting, and sampling opinions in a largely mechanistic manner. These models are parsimonious, tractable, elegant, and useful, but they also leave little importance to choice as it is commonly understood.

Treating intentionality seriously does not require a resort to Cartesian dualism (Descartes, Miller, and Miller 1983; Descartes and Cress 1979). Daniel Dennett's (2003) recent book *Freedom Evolves* has woven together concepts from cognitive neuroscience and complexity theory to contend that meaningful choice is not philosophically incompatible with a strictly materialist conception. He and others (for example, Kelso 1995) contend that intentionality can be properly viewed as an emergent property (Holland 1995, 1998) of the complex system that is the human brain. Just as a swarm of ants can exhibit an aggregate behavior that is qualitatively different than the decisions of an individual ant, a human brain may be capable of choice even if we assume that the firing of each neuron is a deterministic act. Though much of the argument in this chapter may suggest a reductionist bent, I actually have the opposite agenda. I am contending that taking genetics, neuroscience, and environment seriously does not mean that we discount the notion of normatively meaningful political attitudes.

In John Searle's (1980) famous "Chinese room" argument, an argument against strong artificial intelligence, he tells a story of a monolingual English speaker in a room with two large batches of slips of paper with Chinese writing on them. The English speaker also has a set of instructions in English for matching one set of the slips of paper with another set. With much practice, the English speaker becomes so adept at the slip manipulation rules that a native Chinese speaker sliding slips of paper under the door of the room and receiving slips in response cannot tell that the English speaker does not understand a word of Chinese. Searle uses this parody of the Turing (1950) test for artificial intelligence to argue that no computer could be considered intelligent in the strong sense of the word because for the computer the symbols are processed syntactically rather than semantically, and so the symbols are meaningless and not grounded in understanding.

Although Zaller uses a broad notion of *considerations* that includes values and culture in some parts of his argument, he essentially contends that political attitudes comprise the output of an information processing system like the Chinese room—output results from systematic processing of the inputs. For a political novice who has little or no knowledge of national politics, responding to political survey questions might be like being the English speaker in the Chinese room during the first day on the job. Survey respondents who cannot identify leading political figures, the policy positions of the major parties, or use ideology as a framework for their political thinking might well be processing meaningless symbols and merely "answering questions" rather than "revealing preferences" (Zaller and Feldman 1992). I contend that for some people, however, the symbols of politics have meaning and are connected to deeply held values; these people are in the Chinese room and they speak Chinese.

Despite his rhetoric about answering questions, Zaller would be justified in noting that he anticipated a role for biological and genetic components of the political decision making process and acknowledged that those could be understood as considerations in his general framework. This, however, would be missing the heart of my critique. In Zaller's information processing framework, these biologically based considerations obtain no normatively or ontologically distinct attention. Rather, they are merely instances of the general notion of considerations. Furthermore, a review of what Zaller deduces from his founding axioms evinces no particular role for biologically rooted considerations and only a minor role for core values. In the Zaller model, one would have little reason to be concerned if a successful media campaign presented a barrage of considerations that altered a person's expressed policy preference away from some set of core values or biologically rooted attitudes. The political participant is merely answering questions in a manner akin to a machine processing information or the monolingual English speaker sliding slips of Chinese text back under the door.

It has been observed that the level of political knowledge is the most reliable means of differentiating between those who can and those who cannot consistently apply their political values and provide stable political opinions. Often, we political scientists measure political knowledge in terms of the facts that political sophisticates are able to recall (Delli Carpini and Keeter 1996; Zaller 1992). It is important, however, to recognize that facts per se do not help the citizen participate meaningfully in politics. If you know the name of the Indonesian president, whether he has the power to veto legislation, and whether his party controls the legislature, you do not have sufficient knowledge to assess whether he and his policies will conform to your values.

The knowledge of these kinds of facts is easy to measure and is believed to correlate well with the kinds of facts that do matter for assessing policies. But the facts that really help political cognition as understood in this chapter are those that allow citizens to map from the values used in everyday politics to the policy choices presented in national politics. Many people who are quite versatile in their ability to map their values onto the political problems they face in their office simply do not have the type of information that would enable them to map their values onto issues of national politics. Similarly, I would expect that the large majority of ideologically constrained political sophisticates studied by Converse (1964) and his followers would be reporting nonattitudes if asked about the politics of Indonesia or another unfamiliar country.

By necessity, we are cognitive misers and cannot have mappings in all political domains that we might encounter. The expected party differential (Downs 1957) that many people calculate for aligning with one or another faction in their work environment is orders of magnitude larger than the change in utility they would obtain from the election of a different U.S. president. With stakes that are potentially so much larger or so much more immediate, it is not surprising that citizens might choose to invest scarce resources in learning how to map their values onto the politics of their office or community rather than the politics of their nation.

My contention in this chapter, and the contention of the Machiavellian intelligence hypothesis, is that most humans (except autistics, for example) are political sophisticates with the innate capacity for highly complex political cognition. This capacity evolved because of a cognitive arms race that took place over the course of millions of years. Our incentives to obtain information about a particular value to policy mapping are what vary; our capacity for processing that mapping has a far smaller range. There are many kinds of information that help us accomplish such mapping, from logical reasoning to emotional appeals to modeling by trusted friends or experts. Some of this mapping takes place in the form of heuristics (Lupia and McCubbins 1998; Lupia 1994), and some of it takes place in terms of implicit associations.

EXPLICIT AND IMPLICIT ATTITUDES

Heuristics are cognitive shortcuts that enable people to reduce the mental effort needed to accomplish a task. One well-known example is the so-called availability heuristic. In the availability heuristic, people make judgments based on whatever information they happen to recall rather than on the complete set of information they have. This is a shortcut because they do not need to conduct an exhaustive search through all of their memories to form their response. In the dual-processing model that my colleagues and I have described previously and applied to politics (Lieberman, Schreiber, and Ochsner 2003), heuristics are represented in the *reflective* system, as part of a conscious and deliberate symbolic process.

The *reflexive* system, in contrast, plays a subconscious and implicit role in the formation of attitudes. Antereograde amnesiacs (like the main character in the movie *Memento*) are unable to form new long-term declarative memories. But it has been demonstrated that they are still able to change their attitudes (Lieberman et al. 2001). We know that this change does not come about owing to the cognitive dissonance process that Festinger (1957) described, because these people are not able to form new explicit memories. They are, however, still able to form implicit associations and relate positive or negative feedback to the stimuli. Furthermore, neural substructures that differentiate the systems that underlie implicit and explicit attitudes have been identified (Lieberman et al. 2002).

Having distinct neural substrates connected with explicit and implicit attitudes would be a mere curiosity if the attitudes did not have distinct functional properties. But whereas explicit attitudes are consciously constructed using a limited set of chunked symbolic information, implicit attitudes result from an automatic process of association among large numbers of factors that is susceptible to stereotyping bias. Furthermore, a person's implicit and explicit attitudes may be in conflict (Karpinski,

Steinman, and Hilton 2005). In many contexts, experts have been found to rely on their suboptimal intuitions of a problem or to replicate novice behavior, even when they are extremely well versed in the explicit rules or formalisms (Kozhevnikov and Hegarty 2001; McCabe and Smith 2000).

The extent to which political experts or voters who are knowledgeable about national politics rely on implicit knowledge rather than explicit knowledge is still an open question. Ideological constraint (Converse 1964), schemas (Axelrod 1973; Conover and Feldman 1984), online tallies (Lodge et al. 1975), considerations (Zaller 1992), and heuristics (Lupia and McCubbins 1998; Lupia 1994) may be relying on implicit information far more than we appreciate. Alexander Todorov and colleagues (2005) recently demonstrated that one-second exposures to the faces of candidates can yield judgments of competence that are quite predictive of electoral outcomes with no further information. Todorov demonstrates that additional information can ameliorate the impact of the instant judgment, but implicit processes and attitudes appear to have more of an effect on political judgment than traditional political science theories anticipate. Furthermore, although some have investigated the interplay between expertise and implicit judgments in other areas (see, for example, Gladwell 2005), this remains an underdeveloped area of research as regards political cognition. The differing natures of implicit and explicit processes have been particularly well studied, however, in racial attitudes (Sears et al. 1997; Dovidio et al. 1997; Phelps et al. 2000).

COALITIONAL COGNITION AND SOCIAL NETWORKS

Racial attitudes are interesting and important kinds of political attitudes, in the broad sense of *political* that I am using. In Jim Sidanius's theory of social dominance orientation (Sidanius and Pratto 1999), racial attitudes are viewed as particular cases of the more general phenomenon of ingroup-outgroup conflict. Sidanius argues that racism in America simply reflects an evolved tendency to give preferences to "us" and to discriminate against "them." His theory is consistent with the core argument of the Machiavellian intelligence hypothesis: that the continuous readjustment of alliances among complex social animals drove the cognitive competition that led to human intelligence.

Interesting evidence supporting the contention that racial attitudes are reflections of a more fundamental cognition of coalitions comes from Rob Kurzban and his colleagues (2001). In a clever experiment, Kurzban showed that although race was a prominent factor in Americans' perceptions of a story about a conflict between two teams that were divided along racial lines, it was trumped by team membership in a version of the story in which both teams were racially diverse. Kurzban argued that coalition membership was fundamental to evolution and essential to survival in early humans, whereas the recently constructed notion of racial group-ings is only able to utilize the cognitive mechanisms evolved for coalition cognition to the extent that it is consistent with the salient coalitions. He further supported the evolutionary claim in a parallel experiment demonstrating that gender, which is evolutionarily important for sexual reproduction, could not be "erased" in the easy manner that race was.

If the processing of coalitions has evolutionary roots and if politi-cal attitudes have a genetic basis, one might wonder whether political party identification has an evolutionary origin. The data from Alford et al. (2005) suggest that party identification does not have strong genetic heritability. Only 13 percent of party identification appears to be attribut-able to genetics. Around 40 percent is attributable to the "shared environ-ment" of twins and the remainder to the "unshared environment."

James Sundquist's (1983) theory of realignment can help us under-stand why party identification might not be genetically heritable. If political parties are comprised of shifting coalitions and changing social cleavages (Manza and Brooks 1999), then any politically relevant values that you inherited genetically from your parents may not map onto the same political parties. For instance, many whose grandparents were con-servative southern Democrats have found themselves in the Republi-can Party recently. Party allegiance changed as important values came to be better represented by the competing party. Frans de Waal (1998) observed that coalition alignments shifted many times during the lives of the chimpanzees he studied. Similarly, whereas one of America's main coalitional identifications is based on skin color, other societies have been divided more deeply along religious, economic, linguistic, cultural, or other lines (Sidanius and Pratto 1999).

Many children do share party identification with their parents, how-ever. This is partially reflected in the estimate that 40 percent of party identification in twins is due to shared environment. The substantial liter-ature concerning political socialization has attempted to explain why this is so and under what conditions children and parents differ (Campbell et al. 1960; Abramowitz 1983; Luskin, McIver, and Carmines 1989). One explanation is that the connection between values and political attitudes often is made at home but is made via perceptual rather than persua-sive processes (see Westholm 1999).

Although we may form many political attitudes in a personal social context (Kaz and Lazarsfeld 1955; Lazarsfeld, Berelson, and Gaudet

1948), mediated and "impersonal" (Mutz 1998) methods of political communication have a major social dimension. The evidence that political sophisticates use a portion of their brain that specializes in automatic, social processing to respond to political questions is consistent with the claim in the political science literature that politics, when meaningful, is personal. Recent work on the importance of social networks has highlighted the personal nature of political thinking. Diana Mutz (2002) has argued that people whose political discussion networks consist of others who are heterogeneous in their political views are less likely to participate in politics. She suggests that the conflicting ideas in the social network cause ambivalence in these individuals and thus reduce their likelihood of participation. Robert Huckfeldt and colleagues (2004) have used a mixture of agent-based modeling and empirical data about political discussion networks to investigate the social nature of political opinion formation. They argue for an "auto-regressive" model in which people both influence and are influenced by others with whom they discuss politics. They find that far more people participate in more heterogeneous political discussion networks than one might anticipate from a typical "contagion" model of spreading ideology. Strong partisans, however, are far more likely than typical respondents to be embedded in homogenous political networks. In Mutz's and Huckfeldt's theories, much political thinking occurs in a social context.

The social network models typically assume some kind of explicit process of attitudinal influence. Yet Curtis Hardin and his colleagues (Sinclair et al. 2005; Lowery, Hardin, and Sinclair 2001) have demonstrated that attitudes can be influenced by implicit processes as well. Using subtle signals about the beliefs of others, they demonstrate that a subject's automatic attitudes can be quickly influenced, especially when the subject likes the other people. This finding runs contrary to the supposition that automatic attitudes are the result of lifelong processes and difficult to alter (Devine 1989).

CONCLUSION

Scholars of political attitudes often conceptualize their field of inquiry as solely the study of opinions about national politics. I contend that political cognition was the driving force behind the cognitive arms race in evolving humans and that modern humans can leverage the resulting cognitive apparatus for thinking about the politics of families, communities, or nations. I believe that this new, broader view of political thinking should motivate political scientists to deepen their connections with scholars and scholarship in psychology, anthropology, genetics, neuroscience, and sociology. We should strive to align our theories with the work in these fields and develop our data collection methods in ways that facilitate assessing questions we share with these and other fields.

As we do so, I expect that political science will develop theories that are more humane and nuanced. Many current theories of political decision making are unsatisfying in their psychological realism or their normative sensitivity. I believe that the work reviewed in this chapter shows that accounting for the biological foundations of political attitudes can result in conceptualizations that are richer in their implications for moral thinking and more familiar because they comport with our everyday experience.

We humans apparently developed large neocortices so that we could navigate the politics of the complex social world in which we lived. Although we still use those tools to think about everyday politics, it appears that with particular incentives some humans choose to use these tools to apply their values to debates about problems on a national level. If this is the case, we all might be political sophisticates in our daily lives and only need a little guidance about how to be sophisticated in thinking about national politics.

CHAPTER FOUR

Emotional Processing and Political Judgment: Toward Integrating Political Psychology and Decision Neuroscience

MICHAEL L. SPEZIO AND RALPH ADOLPHS

Political psychology and decision neuroscience are interdisciplinary fields aiming at empirically informed and testable models of human judgment and decision making. Although the contexts and scopes of the fields are not identical, they overlap considerably. Moving both fields forward while maximizing their explanatory power and conceptual coherence requires energetic multilevel development (Damasio et al. 2001; Cacioppo et al. 2000). One arena for fruitful interaction, as evidenced in the literature (Lieberman, Schreiber, and Ochsner 2003; Marcus 2000; Morris et al. 2003; Winkielman and Berridge 2003; Marcus et al. 1995) and by the contributions in this volume, is the development of models that take account of the ways emotional processes work in human judgment and decision making, especially in political decisions. Attention to the role of emotional processes is also prominent in yielding progress at the interface between neuroscience and another key decision science, behavioral economics, in the field of neuroeconomics (Sanfey et al. 2003; Camerer 2003; Glimcher 2003).

We argue that the developing field of decision neuroscience, particularly where emotional processes form an intense focus of study, offers political psychology new handles on human behavior and mentation with which to investigate political judgment and decision making. Developing this interdisciplinary effort requires a clear acknowledgment of the theoretical and methodological challenges ahead, along with strategies for answering them. In addition, we articulate a theoretical framework

We express our gratitude to Ted Brader, Milton Lodge, George Marcus, Rose McDermott, Michael Neblo, Darren Schreiber, and two anonymous reviewers for very helpful comments on an earlier draft.

designed both to offer responses to the stated challenges and to inform the discussion of empirical findings that follows. Specifically, the framework allows that emotional processes contribute to human judgment and decision making in various critical ways, including ways that constitute and do not oppose adaptive outcomes. The rest of the chapter considers recent work in areas relating emotional processes to prudential decision making and reward, as well as social judgment, and closes by considering some implications of these findings for future advances in political psychology.

THEORY

Integration of political psychology and decision neuroscience for the study of political judgment has had a strong beginning owing to the use of sound theoretical frameworks of human cognition, emotion, and decision making. Yet a more comprehensive theory of the role of emotion in decision making is needed to account for the range of observations to be yielded by the interdisciplinary research program envisioned by several contributors to this volume (Schreiber, chapter 3; Cassino and Lodge, chapter 5; MacKuen et al., chapter 6; Huddy et al., chapter 9; Lupia and Menning, chapter 14). Continued success in bridging political psychology and decision neuroscience depends, then, on recognizing theoretical challenges against which progress in scientific conceptualization and communication will be measured. In this section we consider a number of challenges to developing such a comprehensive theory of the function of emotion in decision making. It is important to specify what it is that a better theory should accomplish, so that one has criteria in hand for the evaluation of new proposals. Specifically, we discuss the weight of dichotomies that inform models of human cognition, emotion, and decision making; the meaning of *cognition* and *emotion* within one of these dichotomies; and the central evolutionary and cultural context of the social environment for the normative evaluation of decisionmaking strategies. We conclude this section with a proposal for how to think about emotional processing, drawing on two highly influential and effective frameworks: appraisal theory (AT) and the somatic marker hypothesis (SMH).

The Weight of Traditional Dichotomies

Traditional models of human thought, feeling, and judgment make use of two dichotomies whose influence has weighed heavily on all subsequent scientific approaches seeking to bridge them: those between controlled and automatic processing and between cognition and emotion. To the degree to which these dichotomies are not used as heuristics but are reified in hard theoretical distinctions, they are false. Yet despite the careful, bridge-building work of many scholars, these dichotomies still wield considerable conceptual power. A brief consideration of these dichotomies and their problems is useful in recognizing their influence and perhaps avoiding them in future theory building.

The first dichotomy—indeed, dualism—we examine is that between controlled and automatic mental processing, generally instantiated in "dual process" models of human cognition (Schneider and Shiffrin 1977; Shiffrin and Schneider 1977; Simon 1979; Broadbent 1971). Dual process models hypothesize two distinct cognitive or neural systems mediating, on one hand, the top-down, goal-directed, or endogenous control of thought and activity (for example, attention), and, on the other, uncontrolled processing, labeled bottom-up, automatic, or exogenous. The former is often associated with processing that is consciously, even reflectively, directed, and a recent account has labeled it "refleCtive" processing, in contradistinction to automatic, or "refleXive," processing (Lieberman, Schreiber, and Ochsner 2003). Yet, as pointed out by Feldman Barrett et al. (2004), top-down processing need not always be under conscious control. For example, someone with a conscious goal of having a good meal at a restaurant and who makes a conscious decision to look at the menu to accomplish this goal most often will not be consciously controlling detailed visual scanning of the menu. Nonetheless, in this case the person's visual attention to the menu is under top-down control because attention was the result of a goal-directed decision, and a conscious one at that. Instead of looking out the window or at the salt shaker on the table, the person decided to look at the menu.

Although there is clear experimental evidence for some distinction between behaviors that are influenced by conscious control and those that are not, it is unclear that postulating separate, non-overlapping systems (one for controlled, the other for automatic processing) aids in understanding the mechanisms behind the data. Dual process models can cloud such understanding because they deemphasize the fact that automatic processing is always involved in human activity, even during conscious control of decision making. For example, the controlled focus of attention in recalling a specific memory involves millions of changes in the brain that are not under the conscious control of the person doing the remembering. The same is true when a person makes a political judgment, as discussed by Cassino and Lodge (chapter 5 in this volume). Further, dual process models tend to neglect the role of controlled processing in activating and modulating automatic processing, as would be the case when someone tries to remember a person she likes as opposed to a song she cannot stand or the positive and negative qualities of a candidate for whom she did not vote. Controlled processing can have clearly observable effects on the way stimuli such as words, faces, or memories are processed, though the control does not extend to the millions of brain events that take place in such processing. For example, the outcome of a visual search for a lost item in a room cluttered with objects will be influenced strongly by the image of the item that one consciously has in mind while searching for it. If one has a false image of the item in mind, finding it may take much longer, if it is found at all. So the conscious image exerts an effect on all of the processing going on during the search, without conscious control of those automatic events.

On careful consideration of the ubiquitous presence of automatic processing with controlled processing and of the demonstrable effects of controlled processing on automatic brain processes, it is clear that postulating two distinct processing systems obscures more than it reveals. Recently, some authors have acknowledged the intricate interplay of controlled and automatic processing and have called for "drastically revising the dual-process story as we now know it" (Feldman Barrett, Tugage, and Engle 2004, 567). Similarly, the account by MacKuen et al. (chapter 6 in this volume) is consistent with the idea that automatic brain processes such as those that give rise to moderate anxiety in uncertain circumstances can fruitfully influence controlled processing such as information gathering in making deliberative decisions.

Now we turn to the dichotomy between cognition and emotion. The scientific propensities in the twentieth century (compare Hilgard 1980; Scherer 1993) to devalue emotional processes in human judgment (in comparison to thought or cognition) and to divide emotional processing from "cognition" are perpetuated, perhaps unintentionally, in newer models of human judgment. Indeed, the pervasive influence of this dichotomy is responsible in part for the widespread misconception that emotion is univocally devalued within the Western philosophical tradition (Neblo, chapter 2 in this volume). Emotion has been typically characterized as automatic (as opposed to deliberative), maladaptive (as opposed to useful), innate (as opposed to learned), and so on, making it appear threatening to any systematic account of reasoned deliberative thought. Dividing emotional processing cleanly from, and devaluing it in comparison to, cognition was characteristic of dominant information processing models of human mentation through the 1980s (Simon 1979; but see Erdelyi 1974; Bruner and Postman 1947).

Although we have progressed from viewing emotions as "non-problem-solving non-behaviour" (Gunderson 1985, 72) to the point at which treating cognition as separate from and independent of emotional processing is construed by some as a "sin" against affective neuroscience (Davidson 2003), and though there is an increasing "Zeitgeist [that] seems to be dominated by efforts to integrate rather than oppose cognition and emotion" (Scherer 2003, 563), recent theoretical interpretations still draw sharp distinctions between and maintain the independence of emotional processing and cognition (Greene 2003; Marcus 2000; Goel and Dolan 2003). Further, many interactionist approaches associate emotional processing only with suboptimal or subrational outcomes in decision making (Lieberman, Schreiber, and Ochsner 2003; Lieberman, Jarcho, and Satpute 2004; Winkielman and Berridge 2003; Mellers, Schwartz, and Cooke 1998; Mellers 2000). This may be due in part to the influence of research in behavioral economics and rationality, which reports findings in terms of theoretical norms of the behaviors of interest, without consideration of potential everyday adaptive functions of the component processes under investigation (Shafir and LeBoeuf 2002; Kahneman and Tversky 1979, 1982). Several interactionist models draw on the dual process (automatic versus controlled) models of information processing discussed above and go on to restrict the domain of controlled processing to cognition absent emotional processing (Lieberman, Schreiber, and Ochsner 2003). Emotional processing often will interfere with adaptive judgment and decision making, but an unintentional or uncritical reliance on the received constructs described above will yield theoretical constructs that make no room for the possibility that emotional processes also function in ways that are necessary and adaptive.

The last word on moving beyond the dichotomy between cognition and emotion should belong to a pair of classic papers in psychology that yielded one of the laws of psychology, in this case one relating emotion and behavioral performance (Easterbrook 1959; Yerkes and Dodson 1908). The law in question is the Yerkes-Dodson Law, which simply states that performance depends on the level of emotion—often defined as arousal—such that performance is low at very low and very high levels of emotion and optimal somewhere in between. The conceptual framework of the Yerkes-Dodson Law was put forward by Easterbrook (1959) on the basis of original observations by Yerkes and Dodson (1908) in order to unify a literature showing both adaptive and maladaptive effects of emotion on various measures of performance. Interactionist models of cognition and emotion may draw on the large literature surrounding this classic work in psychology in supporting a view that accounts for adaptive functions of emotion within cognition.

The Meanings of *Cognition* and *Emotion*

After one has set aside the sharp distinction between cognition and emotion, a brief consideration of the various meanings of these terms is required before attempting to bridge the traditional distinctions between them. This is especially true for the present work toward integrating approaches from political psychology and decision neuroscience. Do political psychology and neuroscience refer to the same phenomenon when they refer to cognition? to emotion? In several important respects, the answer is no, as we will see. Discovering ways in which the two fields' uses of the terms meaningfully overlap and where they differ will aid in developing new experimental paradigms that integrate the strengths of each field for the understanding of political judgment.

Cognition

The term *cognition* is used within most philosophical treatments of judgment and decision making and mainstream views within political psychology (Marcus 2000, 247; Taber 2003; MacKuen et al., chapter 6 in this volume) as meaning "thought-knowledge" and thus referring to conscious, intentional processes (Lakoff and Johnson 1999, 11–12). Such usage is consistent with the origin of cognitive neuroscience within cognitive psychology. *Cognitive neuroscience,* which aims to "study how the brain enables the mind," emerged from a conversation in a taxicab between the cognitive psychologist George A. Miller and the neuroscientist Michael S. Gazzaniga (Gazzaniga, Ivry, and Mangun 1998, 1). The aspects of mind to be investigated were perception, attention, memory, language, learning, reasoning, judgment, and higher-order thought, all of which can come under conscious control. Given the emphasis on the role of brain processing in each of these cognitive activities and the fact that most of the brain processes would be beyond conscious control, cognitive neuroscience did not restrict cognitive to mean "conscious processing." Today, cognitive neuroscience generally follows cognitive psychology in referring to cognition as having to do with information processing, conscious or not, that contributes to any of the above-mentioned mental activities. The use of *cognition* to include nonconscious, automatic processing is a specialized usage, however, developed within cognitive psychology and neuroscience, and one that does not overlap completely with the use of *cognition* in political psychology, political science more broadly, or most other academic discourse. Thus, for the purposes of this discussion, and, we suggest, in the interest of future integrative work between political psychology and cognitive neuroscience, the term is used in its standard meaning of conscious processing for the mental activities listed above.

Nevertheless, there is still a worry that, to the extent that this approach to cognition—or conscious mental activity—relies on automatic processing, it leaves little or no room for the kind of decision making required for a deliberative democracy (Neblo, chapter 2 in this volume). Indeed, some interpretations of the influence of automatic processing leave little or no room for controlled processing at all, including that needed for setting the goals that guide decisions (Wegner 2002; Bargh and Chartrand 1999; Bargh et al. 2001). This concern is one of the motivations for dual process theories of decision making, discussed above, because this structure affords a way to retain conscious processing along with automaticity in judgment. Proponents of dual process models often associate the automatic processing system with routine discriminations, judgments or decisions that do not involve situations of novelty or deep conflict. Once such a situation arises, the controlled processing system is brought online, taking over from the automatic processing system in order to manage it. Such an approach is described for political judgment in Lieberman et al. (2003). The authors propose that political judgment relies mainly on automatic, reflexive processing (the X system) until a situation of real novelty or serious conflict arises, resulting in the activation of the conscious, reflective C system. As political sophistication increases, the X system is made increasingly coherent such that recognizing inconsistencies during political decision making becomes more automatic and more efficient, requiring less conscious control of attention and thus less need of the C system. Yet when political realities remain resistant to decisions resulting from the X system, the C system will be activated so that more nuanced political strategies may be identified.

This approach has problems because there can be no C system divorced from automatic processing. Fortunately, the dual system dichotomy is not necessary to retain a place for controlled processing in political judgment, which is necessary to deliberative democracy. There are three elements to solving the apparent problem for deliberation. The first is to recall that the learning process by which political sophistication increases, as in all cases of explicit (as opposed to implicit) learning, depends largely on controlled processing. The second is to recall the role of controlled cognitive processing in regulating processing beyond conscious control. Finally, one must recall that any experiment showing the influence of automatic processing entails evidence of controlled processing as well, without which the research participants could not have accomplished the required tasks.

This basic view is reflected in the work that Schreiber (chapter 3 in this volume) summarizes. Political sophisticates likely required deliberative control as they learned the political actors and associations inherent to political sophistication and used this knowledge early on in their development as experts. Had neuroimaging been employed during this learning process, it likely would have revealed clearly reduced activation in the "default network" associated with self-relative evaluation first described by Raichle (Raichle et al. 2001; Gusnard et al. 2001) and summarized by Schreiber, as was observed for political novices in his experiment. Similarly, that sophisticates increasingly activated this default network during political judgment, compared to a resting baseline, does not imply that they exhibited a mindless reliance on reflex. Rather, such an increase in activation indicates a more personal engagement with the task along with a style of processing that relies more on self-relative evaluations than on abstractly held associations. Indeed, recent work demonstrates that the resting default network is strongly decreased in patients with Alzheimer's, compared to healthy age-matched controls, suggesting that the network is involved in engaged, healthy cognition with respect to one's environment (Greicius et al. 2004).

Until a more complete theory of mental processing is developed, evidence of the influence of automatic processing in complex decision making and even in the setting of goals cannot be interpreted as leaving no room for controlled processing, especially during learning. Such a conclusion would be a metaphysical claim and not a scientific one.

Emotion

Gaining clarity in the meanings of key terms related to emotion is imperative in moving toward the integration of political psychology and decision neuroscience. Recent history in the field of emotion research has already yielded a case in which semantic differences concerning *emotion* were mistakenly cast as deep disagreements about functional aspects of respective models (Leventhal and Scherer 1987). To begin with, one must recognize that some operational definitions of *emotion* are restricted to a few emotional categories (fear, anger, joy) whereas others attempt to explain emotion in terms of a few theoretical dimensions such as (valence (positive-negative), arousal (low-high) and motor plan (approach-avoid-neither) that are taken to explain the categories (Heilman 1997).

Marcus et al. (2000) expressly define their affective intelligence model of political judgment in contradistinction to a valence theory of emotion (one in which emotion moves along a single dimension from negative to positive). Measurement of facial muscle tension during viewing of pleasant and unpleasant stimuli shows that the valence dimension alone cannot account for physiological responses coinciding with different emotions (Larsen, Norris, and Cacioppo 2003). Marcus et al. (2000) and MacKuen et al. (chapter 6 in this volume) prefer to model the action of emotion with a dual systems model in which the basic emotions of enthusiasm and anxiety interact to influence political judgment under different conditions. Within this model, they define *emotion* as requiring conscious awareness and *mood* as occurring at the "fringes" of conscious awareness. Things outside of conscious awareness are labeled simply "affective responses" (Marcus, Neuman, and MacKuen 2000, 40).

Other meanings of the key terms of emotional processing emotion, mood, affect, and feeling) occur within political psychology. *Emotion* and *feeling* often are used without distinction, *emotion* can be a kind of rule for categorization (Cassino and Lodge, chapter 5 in this volume), and, what is most interesting, affect can be taken as measurable via subconscious priming (ibid.) or via a verbal or written response (Huddy et al., chapter 9 in this volume).

These usages are different from those within decision neuroscience, in which affect, mood and emotion can occur independent of or concurrent with awareness. *Feeling* is generally reserved for the quale, or first-person, experience associated with emotional processing (Damasio 1994, 1996, 1999), and thus feeling requires consciousness. Perhaps most important, the demonstration of "affective response" in decision neuroscience requires a clear link to one or more accepted physiological signals and cannot be based solely on verbal responses or performance measures. Thus, *affect* retains its original connotation of developing in response to situations that palpably *affect* the body in some way. Typical measurements of affect include brain activity and psychophysiological measures such as skin conductance response (SCR), electrocardiography, muscle tension, and pupillary dilation. The difference between decision neuroscience and political psychology in construing *affect* is due to the difference in level of explanation that each ultimately seeks. The former seeks neural mechanisms for the function of emotion within decision making and therefore needs to measure emotional processing during decision processes. Political psychology aims at determining the effects of emotional categories and constructs in political judgment. Whether the emotions occur at the time of judgment or during the encoding of concepts that only later are retrieved for the purposes of judgment is less important to this latter goal than to the aims of decision neuroscience.

Still, decision neuroscience can offer political psychology tools with which to answer questions that require knowing the level of emotional processing taking place during conceptual encoding. One use of such a measure is in determining whether a verbal or written report of emotional response to a given political advertisement or news story is consistent with emotional processing at the time of viewing or requires the hypothesis of other factors, such as associative memory or the developing social context, organized (or otherwise (that is, with "spin" or not), in the wake of the publicity (Brader and Valentino, chapter 8 in this volume). Distinguishing between these possibilities could be of great interest to those involved in the design, broadcasting, and hype of political advertisements or stories. More important, such distinctions could result in better scholarly models of political judgment made in response to political broadcasts. In any case, this example shows that differences in the use of the key terms of emotional processing do not pose a barrier to integrating political psychology and decision neuroscience, provided that the differences are acknowledged and the operational definitions are appropriate for the experimental ends in view.

The Centrality of the Social

Another theoretical challenge deserves brief mention: that posed by the complexity of human social organization, in cultural and evolutionary terms, to meaningful experimental design and, in particular, to productive interpretation of results. The basic notion at play is that the "centrality of personal ties and social interactions" within human evolution and in research participants' subcultural contexts shapes the function of the component processes under investigation (Cacioppo et al. 2000, 831). Behavioral decision theorists are often eager to apply particular norms in evaluating the decisions people make under experimental conditions, and to the inferred effects of emotion on those decisions (Gigerenzer and Selten 2002; Kahneman and Tversky 1996; Gigerenzer 1994), with little attention to the role of emotion in developing and maintaining social relationships. Behavioral decision theorists sometimes argue as if it would be desirable for humans to manifest less emotional processing so that the norms of rational decision making—as set in the laboratory—could be attained. For example, Baumeister and colleagues (2005) suggest that emotional processing concurrent with decision making is so harmful that one would expect an evolutionary advantage for "people with fewer and fainter emotions" (10). Yet a person's emotional processing systems are known to be involved in effectively judging the emotions of other people (Adolphs 2001, 2002, 2003), and dysfunction in these emotional systems is likely responsible in part for such social deficits as autism (Baron-Cohen 1997; Baron-Cohen et al. 2000; Frith 2003). Social belonging is affected by deficits in social processing, and thus belonging would seem to depend on emotional processing performed concurrently with judgment and decision making in social contexts. Given Baumeister's important work on the serious detrimental effects of social exclusion on cognition (Twenge, Catanese, and Baumeister 2002; Baumeister, Twenge, and Nuss 2002), it is clear that evolutionary pressures would favor, rather than select against, emotional processing that is concurrent with judgment in social contexts. Losing sight of the centrality of the social element present in the evolutionary and cultural constraints on the range of human judgment can lead to erroneous conclusions regarding the role and necessity of emotion in decision.

In making normative evaluations about experimental results of decision making in the laboratory one must keep two things in mind. First, it is quite difficult to create naturalistic social contexts in the laboratory within which to properly evaluate the adaptive role of emotion in judgment. Second, one needs to be certain that emotional inductions or manipulations used in the laboratory result in emotional processing that is within the optimal range of emotion in a Yerkes-Dodson relation, assuming there is an optimal range for the task at hand. Consider that mood induction, such as the induction of sadness via a film clip, may result in a high level of emotion and so would predictably interfere with optimal social judgment, for example. Consider also that temporarily inactivating emotional brain centers such as the amygdala, the insula, or the orbitofrontal cortex would yield a similar performance deficit.

Recurrent Multilevel Appraisal: A Proposal for Emotional Processing in Decision Making

We now present a proposal that seeks to develop the concept of emotional processing within the context of complex decision making. We use the key term *emotional processing* instead of *emotion* to ensure that the framework allows for the categories of feeling, mood, affect, and motivation, in addition to emotion, as well as to stress the dynamic character of processing that precedes such categorization (Scherer 2000, 2003). We frame emotional processing by drawing on appraisal theory, or AT (Ellsworth and Scherer 2003; Lazarus 1991, 1991; Scherer 2003) and on the somatic marker hypothesis (Damasio 1996, 1994), resulting in a processing scheme that shares certain aspects with that described by Phillips et al. (2003).

Appraisal theory focuses centrally on the appraisal of a stimulus or situation in terms of the goals and interests of an organism. The fundamental tenet of AT "is that people evaluate events in terms of the perceived relevance for their current needs and goals, including their ability to cope with consequences and the compatibility of the underlying actions with social norms and self ideals" (Scherer 2003). Great emphasis is placed on the primary role of cognitive appraisal and the secondary role of emotional processing. The former leads to the latter, and appraisal is invoked to explain "emotion elicitation," with no role being left for emotion in the appraisal process itself. Appraisal processes can happen outside of conscious awareness and at low levels of processing, allowing for rapid, automatic appraisals. Yet in such cases emotion never contributes to but is always an outcome of appraisal. Appraisal theory is thus a "feedforward" model of emotional processing, meaning that there is no feedback of emotional processes into appraisal systems; there are only outputs of emotional processes as a result of appraisal systems.

The somatic marker hypothesis assigns to emotion precisely the opposite role. Emotional processing, according to SMH, precedes and contributes to the appraisal of events in decision making (Damasio 1994, 1996). Unlike AT, SMH assigns no explicit role to the goals—low-level or otherwise—of the person or organism in the elicitation of emotion. Rather, emotion is elicited by first categorizing an event (is it a snake in front of me or a kitten?) and then activating a link between the event category and emotional signals. The key element of the second step in this process. the link, is an association that is the result of experience. The categorization of the event and the activation of the appropriate acquired association between the event and the elicited emotion can and usually do take place outside of conscious awareness. The emotional outcome then becomes input in a decision-making process that follows the emotional appraisal. Both SMH and AT share this feed-forward structure in relating cognition and emotion.

This hypothesis developed as the result of a series of experiments conducted by Damasio, Bechara, and colleagues (1994, 1996). These involved an experimental paradigm known as the Iowa Gambling Task (IGT), in which people choose cards from four decks, turn them over one at a time, and see whether the card lists a gain or a loss to the individual who is playing. Two of the decks of cards are risky, leading to a net loss, and two are safe, leading to a net gain. It turns out that people learn the difference between the safe and the risky decks and that this learning is accompanied by developing a strong SCR prior to making a card choice from the risky decks. The hypothesis predicts that people who lack the capacity to generate SCR during the IGT should show impaired decision making because they are unable to associate a key affective response, such as SCR, with a situations involving gains and losses. In fact, patients with damage to the ventromedial prefrontal cortex show abnormalities in emotion and feeling, impaired learning on the IGT, and a failure to produce the SCR that accompanies learning.

We affirm the important contributions made by AT and SMH, and we draw on both theoretical frameworks to develop a model of emotional processing that moves beyond a feedforward structure. Moving away from feedforward schemas toward a model involving recurrent, or feedback, connections allows one to account for the complex interplay among goals, emotions, and evaluative processes within decision making. Let us begin the development of our approach by defining the instances when processing is emotional. The framework holds that an information processing function is emotional when (1) it evaluates the information present in an event in terms of an organism's own normative or autonormative outcomes (that is, goals) *and* (2) it results in affective responses in the body or in the activation of their representations in the brain. Categories of autonormative outcomes include sub- or supraliminal goals, desires, and motor plans. Norms that are external to the person, such as social norms, are included in this framework, as long as those social norms exert their action in an autonormative sense. Similarly, norms that are suggested by evolutionary history are included in our framework, as long as there is a plausible internal mechanism for their action for a given individual within a given event. One example of such internalization of evolutionary norms is the drive toward homeostasis, defined as the relatively stable internal processes responsible for the maintenance of life.

We propose a recurrent multilevel appraisal (RMA) model of emotional processing in decision making (figure 4.1). According to this model, emotional processing begins as the outcome of initial low-level evaluative processing in terms of autonormative outcomes, resulting in the activation of a set of autonomic and sensorimotor processes in the body such as heart rate, SCR, pupillary dilation, changes in skeletal muscle tone, and the representations in the brain that mediate these activations. This way of categorizing emotional processing corresponds to the "body loop" and "as if loop" categories in SMH (Damasio 1996). These are shown in table 1.1 for the RMA model. Emotional responses then go on to be used in two ways. First, they influence downstream processing in the domains

FIGURE 4.1: RECURRENT MULTILEVEL APPRAISAL MODEL OF EMOTIONAL PROCESSING

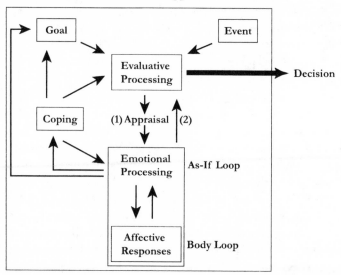

of selective attention, memory encoding and retrieval, associative learning, action planning, thought, and so on. This was already a key element of SMH. Note that some of these downstream processes could include bringing additional evaluative processing functions online, because the early function may not be sufficient to process a given situation. Second, and equally important, they are recurrent with respect to the evaluative processing functions, influencing them even as these same functions process new information coming in owing to the changes in selective attention, and so on. In other words, the evaluative processing and emotional processing functions form bidirectionally coupled, iterative loops that are extended in time. Constructs such as emotional "states" arise from integrating throughout the evaluative-emotional downstream system. Moods arise from long-lasting activation of emotional processes, and mood disorders could be due in part to the failure of proper evaluative-emotional recurrent integration.

What are some advantages of integrating AT and SMH in this way? One benefit is that the proposed feedback of emotional processing into evaluative processing functions is consistent with both affect-as-information and affect-priming models of emotional effects on judgment (Forgas 1995). Further, the current framework avoids the "amorphous affect" problem of these models, wherein both the sources and the forms of emotional inputs are only loosely defined. Drawing on SMH, we propose that activations of bodily responses or their representations are in fact the emotional responses. Also in line with SMH is the claim that these affects are required for adaptive outcomes in at least some areas of human judgment and decision making.

Our model also aids interpretation of some recent experimental results that pose some difficulty for SMH. Recall that SMH predicts that someone who is incapable of generating an affective response in the body, such as SCR, to a novel loss event should be unable to learn the difference between the risky and the safe decks in the IGT. Heims et al. (2004), however, showed that patients who were physiologically incapable of generating SCR performed no differently than did matched controls on the IGT. In contrast to SMH, which views decision making as dependent on the acquired association between an event and affective responses, RMA proposes that decision making depends on evaluative processing, which is influenced by emotional processing in the run-up to decision making. According to RMA, people lacking an SCR would continue to be able to evaluate situations, activate appropriate representations of bodily affective responses, and use this emotional processing to inform decision making. This is, in fact, what Heims et al. (2004) observed.

The final advantage is that RMA proposes a functional role for the ventromedial prefrontal cortex that is gaining support in the literature. We suggest that this cortex is required for normal evaluative processing leading to appropriate emotional processing and for the adaptive feedback of emotional processing of evaluations. This view modifies SMH, which views the ventromedial prefrontal cortex as the locus of acquired associations between events and emotional outcomes. Recurrent multilevel appraisal proposes instead that it maintains a representation of agreements between an organism's planned goals and experienced outcomes. Such a view is consistent with Raichle's work in defining a network that monitors the environment for consistency with or divergence from an organism's goals (Gusnard et al. 2001; Raichle et al. 2001, nicely reviewed in Schreiber, chapter 3 in this volume). Thus our model accounts for the deficits in judgment and decision making seen in patients with damage to the ventromedial prefrontal cortex (Anderson et al. 1999; Anderson et al. 2000; Damasio 1996). In addition, several recent studies are consistent with such a function for this cortex. In one brain activation experiment using the IGT with healthy participants, Critchley et al. (2000) showed that the start of activation in this cortex reliably preceded the peak of the SCR by 4.2 seconds. This is consistent with the possibility of an evaluative process in this brain area whose outcome participates in generating the SCR. In another experiment with healthy participants, Zysset and coworkers (2002, 2003) measured brain activation while asking subjects to agree or disagree with propositions stating either their evaluation of something or someone (for example, "Gerhard Schröder is a good chancellor") or their episodic or personal memory about something or someone (for example, "I voted for Gerhard Schröder"). There was greater activation in the ventromedial prefrontal cortex during the evaluative task than in the episodic memory task. Raichle and colleagues (2001) also reported increased activation in the ventromedial prefrontal cortex that associated with a self-referential evaluative task.

We fully expect that the RMA model of emotional processing described here will require revision on the basis of future experiments investigating the role of emotional processing in decision making, including those conducted in the domain of political judgment. One of our aims was to propose a model consistent with neuroscientific data that could be directly compared to models of emotional processing already being used by political psychologists (Cassino and Lodge, chapter 5; MacKuen et al., chapter 6; Huddy et al., chapter 9, all in this volume). We also hoped to provide an example of how key terms of emotion are used within decision neuroscience.

METHOD

There are important methodological challenges in the design and interpretation of experiments applying cutting-edge tools of decision neuroscience to the problems of interest within political psychology. We consider some challenges inherent in functional magnetic resonance imaging (fMRI) and the lesion method, both of which are important to developing theories that relate brain and behavior. Measuring the dependence of human behavior on the brain is anything but straightforward. Inferential challenges are difficult enough for methodological specialists, but for those outside a given specialty, even those within other areas of cognitive science, evaluating reports of brain-behavior associations and proceeding from them to useful inferences about brain-behavior mechanisms can be daunting. Fortunately, keeping these challenges in mind should prevent one from making key mistakes in interpreting empirical findings and in using those findings to construct new models. Because the challenges and responses to them are well described elsewhere (Adolphs 2002; Cacioppo et al. 2003; Lieberman, Schreiber, and Ochsner 2003; Raichle 2003; Logothetis 2003; Logothetis and Wandell 2004), they receive only a brief overview.

The Signal Relationship: Neural Activity and the BOLD Response

The physiological signal measured by fMRI, by far the most prominent method applied in imaging the living human brain during behavior, enjoys a complex relation to the main information processing signals in the brain. The physiological measure yielded by fMRI is the blood-oxygenation-level dependent (BOLD) signal, which varies with the amount of deoxygenated blood in the region of measurement. But information processing in the brain occurs in terms of electrical signals from neurons, not in terms of the BOLD signal. The efficiency with which the BOLD signal arises from underlying neural signals is called the hemodynamic response efficiency, and there is evidence that it differs considerably between different areas of the brain, mainly because of differences in the organization of vascular structures (Logothetis 2002; Logothetis and Wandell 2004). So brain "activation," or changes in the BOLD signal in fMRI, that occur between different regions can reflect differences in area-specific hemodynamic response efficiencies.

In addition, until very recently, neuroscience lacked a good understanding of which neural signals most closely corresponded to the BOLD signal. Most of the field assumed that the BOLD signal was directly related to and caused by electrical impulses, known as action potentials, that neurons use to communicate over longer distances. This was in part because the measurement of action potentials was long the dominant method of relating neural activity to information processing and behavior. It is still widely used and highly influential. Recently, however, the groups of Nikos Logothetis (2002, 2003, 2004) and Martin Lauritzen (Caesar, Thomsen, and Lauritzen 2003; Lauritzen 2001; Mathiesen et al. 1998) showed that the BOLD signal is not caused by action potentials of neurons at all, because eliminating all action potentials has no effect on the signal. Rather, the BOLD signal associates with smaller electrical potentials at the junctures (synapses) between neurons in the brain. This has major implications for interpretation of the BOLD signal across the entire brain, because circuits in different regions of the brain may have very different kinds of junctures between neurons even when the information output (that is, action potential) of the regions is the same. So the BOLD signal can differ depending only on differences in circuit organization for circuits in the same general area of the brain and under circumstances that yield identical numbers of action potentials.

Another aspect of brain activity measurement by fMRI is that the measured signal changes are on the order of 0.1 percent to 1 percent of the total measured signal (Raichle 2003). To understand this more fully, it helps to remember that the BOLD signal is generally a contrast in signal between two or more measurements, each conducted under some set of defined conditions. This means that reported fMRI activations, or areas where the brain seems to be lit up by bright spots, do not result from the neural circuitry in those areas going from an "off" state to an "on" state. Rather, activation is typically the result of a brain area changing from giving a signal of, say, 10 to a signal of 10.05 in a statistically significant manner. A solid grasp of the details of each contrasting condition and the differences between them is, then, crucial to drawing mechanistic inferences from evidence in the form of BOLD signal contrasts.

Individual Differences in the Brain

It is common practice in fMRI research to put all the participants' brains into one "standard" brain space using methods termed *spatial normalization*. It is widely acknowledged, however, that individual brains typically are not identical in shape, especially in the cortical regions, or, more important, in patterns of localized activations. Indeed, in normal humans there is a threefold difference in the overall size of the region of the brain that is the first step along the visual processing chain, a region called the primary visual cortex (Andrews, Halpern, and Purves 1997). Differences in functional patterns of brain activation are more striking. In a study of episodic memory, which is memory for the details of personal experiences and is a form of memory that is likely to play a significant role in political judgment and decision making (Lieberman, Schreiber, and Ochsner 2003), Gazzaniga and colleagues (2002) saw extensive individual differences in brain activation patterns that were reliable across repeated measurements. That is, different individuals performing an identical episodic memory task showed extensive and replicable individual differences in patterns of brain activity, although the individual patterns themselves did not change significantly across measurements. Grouping individual brains into a common space thus results in washing out potentially important empirically determined associations between information processing and brain activity. Increasingly, fMRI research is taking the implications of such findings into account, with recommendations that analyses using spatial normalization always be accompanied by individual analyses (Crivello et al. 2002; Miller et al. 2002; Saxe, Carey, and Kanwisher 2004). In fact, scholars are beginning to treat individual differences as important in their own right and worthy of greater empirical investigation (Kosslyn et al. 2002).

Functional MRI Activations Are Tentative Associations

Cacioppo (2003) has pointed out that whether a brain area is activated during a given information processing condition does not by itself establish that the brain area is required for the information processing function under investigation. Observed brain activation could be (1) due to a failure to control for all key contextual variables in contrasting task conditions or (2) the result of activity in another circuit in another area that actually carries out the information processing function. Conversely, failure to observe brain activation could arise in the presence of differences in neural activity if they are in different neural circuits that vary substantially in synaptic organization (Logothetis and Wandell 2004). Activation maps resulting from fMRI experiments can thus best be interpreted as hypothetical associations between information processing and brain activity. These hypotheses would require corroboration using other methods.

Note that this account of fMRI methodology in no way undermines its usefulness as an important method in understanding networks of social and political judgment. The fact is that fMRI allows what was once thought to be impossible: a noninvasive view into brain processing during complex behavior in human participants. Its limitations do not call into question the fMRI neuroimaging literature in general. Indeed, it should be obvious that any scientific methodology will have limits, and we have endeavored only to describe some of the limits of fMRI. Without such description, the exciting interdisciplinary endeavor that we foresee between political scientists and neuroscientists might not develop as rigorously as we know it can. This is especially the case because most popular accounts of fMRI research convey the false impression that the methodology directly measures brain activity, understood as neural activity or spiking. Accomplished science writers who follow neuroscience can, in their enthusiasm, convey this impression unintentionally, as was seen in a recent article on mirror neurons in the *New York Times* (Blakeslee 2006).[1]

An open acknowledgment of the limits of fMRI will, we hope, result in more sophisticated collaborations between neuroscientists and political scientists, leading to elegant experimental designs and subsequent careful interpretations of findings. The work described by Schreiber (chapter 3 in this volume) exemplifies a careful approach to collaborative

---

1. When the author of the article was contacted by one of us (MLS), she readily acknowledged that, given the basis of the fMRI signal, "mirror neurons" as defined in monkey research have not been demonstrated in the human brain.

work. Although we would characterize the existence of mirror neurons in the human brain as a hypothesis at this point, and though we would caution against too extreme a dichotomization between automatic and controlled processing, the work that Schreiber has pioneered is immensely helpful in furthering our understanding of political judgment.

The Limits of the Lesion Method

The lesion method is a classic technique usually employed to test whether a given brain area is required for an information processing function that is under investigation. A challenge to applying the lesion method is the lack of clear one-to-one correspondence between the lesioned area and the information processing function of interest. The lesion method tests patients who have sustained focal neurological damage to determine if the damaged areas associate with response abnormalities during different information processing conditions. Differences from carefully matched control subjects define any observed abnormalities. If a lesion corresponds with an information processing abnormality, it is determined that the lesioned area is required for the specified information processing function to behave normally. Yet this does not mean that the lesioned area is the locus of that function, because the damaged area could be merely a required part of a distributed circuit that enacts the function. What is more important, when experiments show normal information processing responses despite the presence of lesions, it is not possible to conclude from that result alone that a normal brain carrying out these functions would not require the areas of lesion. The absence of lesion effects could be due to brain plasticity following a lesion event, where physiological responses to a traumatic event reorganize regions outside of the original functional circuit in such a way as to restore function, as is often known to be the case (Fridman et al. 2004; Green 2003; Holloway 2003; Thulborn, Carpenter, and Just 1999; Karbe et al. 1998). Experiments with nonhuman animal models show that an overreliance on lesion data can result in the erroneous conclusion that a given brain area is not required for normal pre-lesion information processing (Moore, Rothholtz, and King 2001).

Taken together, these methodological challenges strongly suggest that construction of inferential models of information processing in the brain needs to proceed by an integrative approach, drawing on a selection of methods. Of course, the list of methods and methodological challenges presented here is not exhaustive. It could be expanded to include psychophysiology, event-related EEG potentials (that is, brainwaves), magnetoencephalography (MEG), and computational modeling. Of paramount importance prior to applying any of these approaches is to formulate and employ behavioral tasks that are sufficiently constrained and quantifiable that they can parametrically vary the processes under investigation. Assuming that one achieves this, there is a clear advantage to integrative approaches. Converging evidence obtained using a variety of methods allows scholars to weigh a model's agreement across investigative approaches to determine probabilistically the level of empirical support for each component of the model. Price and Friston (2002) recommended a variant of such an approach, and outlined it for a proposed information processing function $f(I)$, as follows: (1) identify candidate brain areas corresponding to systems performing $f(I)$ by using neuroimaging with normal subjects in two or more appropriate contrasting conditions; (2) determine whether patients with lesions specific to one or more of the candidate brain areas show deficits in behavior thought to rely on $f(I)$; (3) if no deficits are found, use neuroimaging with these lesion patients to identify "latent" candidate brain areas corresponding to systems performing $f(I)$ and proceed to step (2). Although this approach also faces the challenges outlined above, it and others like it should decrease the likelihood of inferential errors. If integrative approaches such as this are desirable for well-defined problems in the neuroscience of information processing, they are more appropriate in the study of a system as complex as human judgment and decision making in politics (Lieberman, Schreiber, and Ochsner 2003; Cacioppo et al. 2000; Adolphs 2002).

EVIDENCE

Decision and Emotion

By now there is an abundance of evidence linking lesions of the ventromedial prefrontal cortex with impaired emotional processing and with profound deficits in making adaptive decisions in ordinary life, as described in a number of recent reviews by Bechara and colleagues (Bechara 2001, 2004; Bechara, Damasio, and Damasio 2000; Bechara et al. 2001; Bechara, Tranel, and Damasio 2000). Anderson and colleagues showed that two adult subjects who sustained ventromedial prefrontal lesions prior to 16 months of age were not only more severely impaired than those with lesions sustained in adulthood when making adaptive decisions regarding their personal well-being (Anderson et al. 2000) but demonstrated something like an acquired sociopathy in their social behavior and moral decision making (Anderson et al. 1999). The precise mechanism by which circuits in the ventromedial prefrontal cortex facilitate adaptive decision making is not yet known. The somatic marker hypothesis (Damasio 1996) proposes an association between situational features and affective responses, whereas the framework of RMA emphasizes an evaluative process resulting in the activation of emotional responses. Both of these proposals may be inaccurate, however. Interdisciplinary collaborations between political psychologists and decision neuroscientists should not only result in a better understanding of how affective intelligence works, in the ventromedial prefrontal cortex and elsewhere, but also have the potential to produce mechanisms that are relevant to complex political constructs such as group identification, self-determination, and tolerance.

Social Judgment and Emotion

Judgment and decision making in the social realm shows perhaps some of the strongest association with emotional processing, where the association is measured both by examining the effects of induced moods and emotions on judgment and by associating judgments with neural systems thought to have specialized roles in emotional processing.

Social Attribution and Mood

A large and growing literature in personality and social psychology implicates the involvement of long-lasting emotional processes, or moods, when normal subjects make judgments about the emotional state, intentions, and dispositions of other people (Forgas 2000; Bower 1991; Forgas and Forster 1987). One very reliable finding is mood-congruent social attribution, wherein, for example, inducing sadness in a subject covaries with that subject's attributing sadness to another person. An important critique of this work suggests that semantic priming, rather than emotional processing, is the cause of the observed associations between mood and social judgments. *Priming* is a term meaning the activation of one concept by the presentation of another concept, a process that goes on outside of awareness. The critique proposes that mood induction techniques inadvertently use emotion-specific concepts and that conceptual priming, not mood induction, activates semantic networks, defined as structured connections between concepts related in meaning that include specific emotion concepts.

Innes-Ker and Niedenthal (2002) tested this critique by using either an emotional sentence unscrambling task or a mood induction technique prior to asking 186 subjects to attribute emotions to a person, M, based only on reading a short narrative description titled "A Morning in M's Life." Sentences fell into happy, sad, and neutral emotional categories. Mood induction used happy, sad, and neutral film clips coupled with mood maintenance for happy and sad conditions by playing music while subjects read M's story. In the sentence unscrambling task, sentence condition (happy, sad, neutral) had no effect on mood, as assessed using the Brief Mood Introspection Scale (Mayer and Gaschke 1988). In the mood induction, however, subjects in the happy condition were happier than those in the neutral condition, who in turn were happier than those in the sad condition. For sadness, the pattern was reversed. Only the mood induction technique, and not the sentence unscrambling task, resulted in mood-congruent associations between emotion condition during induction and the attribution of emotions to M in the story. That is, subjects who unscrambled sentences categorized as happy were no more likely to attribute happiness to M than they were to attribute sadness. Subjects who unscrambled sentences categorized as sad were no more likely to attribute sadness to M than they were to attribute happiness. Only when mood induction techniques were used was there a congruence effect between emotional induction condition and emotional attribution.

This important work is consistent with the position that mood-congruent effects on social attribution result primarily from mood and not of semantic priming. Further, it suggests the intriguing possibility that normal conceptual acquisition or formation in inferring the emotional states of other people requires emotional processing at some level.

Social Judgment and Neural Systems of Emotion

Is emotional processing required for making normal, adaptive judgments about the emotions, preferences, intentions, and beliefs of others? Here again, emotional processing can include but does not exclusively refer to conscious feelings, and adaptive judgments can include both those available to conscious reflection and those that are only subconscious associations that influence thought and behavior. The answer to this question appears to be yes, according to proposals that use evidence from brain areas that are implicated in normal emotional experiences and in normal social judgment and decision making to argue that emotion and social judgment use shared neural systems.

Abundant evidence has revealed that several key brain areas that either are required for normal emotional experience or are differentially activated by emotional conditions are also required for normal social judgment or are differentially activated in social judgment tasks (Adolphs 2003a, 2003b). The areas that most consistently show this association are the ventromedial prefrontal cortex, the right insula and somatosensory cortices (Adolphs et al. 2000), and the amygdala.

Bar-On et al. (2003) tested six subjects with bilateral focal lesions of the anterior and the posterior ventromedial prefrontal cortex, three subjects with unilateral lesions of the right insular and somatosensory cortices, and three subjects with unilateral lesions of the amygdala for emotional intelligence (Bar-On 1997a, 1997b) and social functioning (Tranel, Bechara, and Denburg 2002). They compared the performance of members of these groups with that of a group of control subjects who had lesions that did not involve the same brain areas. The 2003 study found no differences between any of the experimental groups and control group with regard to full IQ, executive function, perception, or memory, nor any indications of psychopathology. But each experimental group was significantly impaired with respect to emotional intelligence compared to the control group. Combining all three experimental groups yielded significant deficits in social functioning compared to controls.

Shamay-Tsoory et al. (2003) tested 12 subjects with focal lesions to the ventromedial prefrontal cortex for empathy and the recognition of social faux pas. They found that these subjects, as a group, provided significantly lower empathy scores and were significantly more impaired at recognizing social faux pas than age-matched (but not IQ-matched) controls and people with unilateral lesions to the posterior cortex of the brain.

Lesions of the bilateral amygdala impair normal attributions of trustworthiness (Adolphs, Tranel, and Damasio 1998). Stone et al. (2003) tested two subjects who sustained bilateral amygdala damage after the age of fifty in several tasks designed to assess whether these subjects could form beliefs about another person's state of mind (that is, a theory of mind). The tasks included the recognition of social faux pas and attributing feelings and thoughts to a person based only on seeing that person's eyes. Compared to age-matched (but not IQ-matched) controls lacking any lesion, the subjects with bilateral amygdala lesion performed significantly worse at detecting faux pas, and one of the lesioned subjects performed significantly worse at making social attributions based on the eyes alone.

CONCLUSIONS

The outlook for productive collaborative work between decision neuroscientists and political psychologists is promising. Methodological develop-

ments in this expanding endeavor will undoubtedly include th
participation of people with focal brain lesions in behavioral
imaging experiments. New areas of inquiry are likely to includ
the following: (1) assessing whether emotional processing is di
related to consciously held autonormative beliefs and sublimin
mative outcomes; (2) the interaction of emotional category,
intensity (valence and arousal), and stable individual dispositions in the
assessment of politically relevant propositions; (3) the role of empathy,
as distinguished from sympathy (Scheler 1954), in adaptively assessing
an opponent's political strategy; and (4) the reciprocal relation between
emotional processing and the use of metaphor in political persuasion.

PART II

Micro Models

It should not surprise one that in a collection of scholarly contributions concerning emotion, political judgment, and behavior, the largest number come from scholars studying how emotions function in and among individuals. The six chapters in this part present a rich array of approaches and topics. We begin with the contribution from Cassino and Lodge. Their work explores the central assertion of Michael L. Spezio and Ralph Adolphs and, indeed, the work of many of the other contributors, namely, that emotional processing is intimately and unavoidably involved in the evaluative and decision-making processes that follow. Cassino and Lodge present a study that argues for the pervasive impact of emotion on memory. They place their study within the motivated reasoning approach, a tradition in political psychology that Lodge (Lodge and Taber 1997) helped develop. This view holds that emotion serves mainly to aid in securing motivational goals, and this leads to the cognitive consequences that such information processing is designed to achieve. Accuracy is rarely a dominant motivational goal; rather, emotion too often sets other motivational goals, such as seeking information that bolsters preexisting values or beliefs.

The chapter by MacKuen, Marcus, Neuman and Keele offers the most recent stage of evolution of one of the earliest theories in political science (Marcus 1988). The theory of affective intelligence offers a comprehensive account of the way in which emotional preconscious processing accounts for the flux in feeling states, the consequent ways in which conscious awareness is engaged and expressed, and the judgments and behaviors that follow. A number of key foundational claims are advanced by this theory; for example, the claim that emotions are the result of preconscious appraisals, a point that is also foundational to

Cassino and Lodge. But MacKuen, Marcus, Neuman, and Keele go on to argue multiple preconscious appraisal processes are simultaneously and dynamically active and that these appraisal processes not only structure the emotions that people experience but also shape the manner and focus of conscious attention, style of judgment, and behavior. As such the theory covers structural and substantive components of theory (that is, a measurement model as well as a description of the ways in which these affective processes interact, what they respond to, and what they affect). This chapter begins with a restatement of the theory, contrasting its claims to those of the principal competitors in political science and an array of empirical findings.

Chapter 7, by Redlawsk, Civettini, and Lau, and Chapter 8, by Brader and Valentino, are direct but nonetheless friendly responses to the theory of affective intelligence. Each explores the most recent iteration of that theory by examining the distinctive effects of anxiety and aversion (Marcus 2002). Most structural theories of emotion fall into one of three camps: valence (a single dimension, approach indicating liking and avoidance, disliking), two unipolar, largely orthogonal dimensions, positive and negative (Cacioppo [1997]; Watson [1985]), and discrete, or basic, models of emotion tied to cognitive appraisal theories (for example, Roseman [1984]; Ortony [1989]; Scherer [2001]).[1] The theory of affective intelligence holds that there are two ubiquitous dimensions: anxiety (negative) and enthusiasm (positive), but that a third dimension, aversion (anger, hatred, bitterness), arises when people confront a familiar threat.

Redlawsk, Civettini, and Lau pick up where Marcus and MacKuen (1993) left off. They apply their dynamic tracing methodology to study the way emotion functions in a political campaign. They explore the way anxiety and anger function to shape attention (a recurring theme in research concerning emotion) but also the accuracy of perception (attending to one of the oldest themes in the literature about emotion, its purported capacity to blind). Brader and Valentino are interested in the issue of whether emotion serves to enhance the human capacity for judgment or to degrade it. They are concerned with the way emotion relates to contemporary assessments but are also interested in the role of preexisting beliefs and values in shaping emotional responses. Hence, stereotypes and prejudices (that is, predispositions) loom large in their analysis of how people respond to the issue of immigration. Redlawsk, Civettini, and Lau continue the tradition of work concerning emotions during political campaigns while Brader and Valentino shed considerable light on

---

1. See Marcus (2003) for a fuller exposition.

how hot button issues can be evocative and, more important, what the consequences are.

Huddy, Feldman, and Cassese demonstrate a similar interest in anger and anxiety. They rely on the literature in psychology to formulate their research. And they, as did Marcus, Neuman, and MacKuen (2000), explore the role of emotion during a time of war. Using a national panel study of Americans that covers the run-up to and the first months of the Iraq war, they map the ways in which the public experienced anxiety and anger regarding their president, the war, Saddam Hussein, terrorists, and anti-war protesters. The political consequences of emotion during times of war have long been thought to exemplify the power of emotion, but which emotion? Anxiety and anger have quite different effects, as this and the prior chapters demonstrate. These chapters warn us that the frequent temptation to declaim about "the" effect of emotion will lead us astray given that political consequences of distinct emotions are very different.

Just, Crigler, and Belt approach emotion from a different perspective than that offered by the theory of affective intelligence. This theory argues that the important effects of emotion arise in the preconscious interval between sensory signals' arriving in the brain and their subsequent expression as subjective conscious awareness. Just, Crigler, and Belt focus on the impact of conscious consideration of emotion as a vital domain in which emotion can play out its role in human affairs. This gives rise to a richer array of emotion than is offered by the theory of affective intelligence.[2] Their study reexplores the role of emotion in political campaigns by relying on the cognitive appraisal approach to emotion. They remind us that emotion may not exhaust its role in early appraisal but may have subsequent and different effects via the human capacity for reflection on expressed emotional states.

---

2. For example, the theory of affective intelligence does not measure the temporal location of an affective state. Thus, enthusiasm is in the here and now, whereas adding a temporal value enables us to distinguish between a prior experience of positive emotion (nostalgia), a present moment of positive emotion (enthusiasm), and the anticipation of a moment of positive emotion (hope).

CHAPTER FIVE

The Primacy of Affect
in Political Evaluations

DAN CASSINO AND MILTON LODGE

In large part, the cognitive revolution in psychology has been fueled by the metaphor of the mind as a computer. The human mind is seen as a remarkably sophisticated Turing machine, a device capable of perceiving and manipulating symbols in accordance with set rules. For some purposes, the metaphor is apt; for others, it can be terribly misleading.

Rather than acting as a symbol-processing device, recent arguments have held, the brain is primarily for feeling, not thinking (Le Doux 1996; Damasio 1994; 2003). To the extent that this is the case, we should question any process in which emotions are thought to be based on rational evaluation of evidence. This includes standard models of opinion formation, according to which we like or dislike something because of what we know about it: one party in an election is favored instead of another because that party's agenda will be better for the voter.

Experimental evidence, however, casts serious doubt on the viability of this reasoning. In studying the ways in which individuals evaluate issues (in this case, affirmative action and gun control), Taber and Lodge (2006) find a strong influence of prior attitudes on the evaluation of arguments. Individuals with strong prior attitudes tend to perceive affectively congruent arguments as being stronger than affectively incongruent arguments. Furthermore, when the same subjects are allowed to seek out information, they tend to search for information that would bolster their own opinions. The judgment process, in which information is integrated into an individual's existing knowledge about an object, then, seems to come after the affective process, in which the individual forms his or her likes or dislikes about an object.

In our view, this is a necessary consequence of the organization of social objects in the mind. While objects in memory can be organized by

emantic properties, such as color, size, and relation to other objects
.aving wings" is related to the object "birds"), they are hot, that is,
.tively charged. This organization—the linking of affect to concepts
long-term memory (LTM)—ensures that emotion plays a critical role
ι all of the stages of evaluation, determining what sort of processing
will be used, what information will be brought to bear, and serving as
information in the evaluation. Such processing potentially leads to serious consequences for the ways in which we think and act politically, because it means that judgments about candidates can become completely
decoupled from the information received about the candidate, leading
individuals to prefer the "wrong" side.

Affect, then, is both a characteristic associated with individual objects in memory and an organizational rule used to categorize objects in
the mind. We know that there is some dimension on which cockroaches,
disease, slavery, rainy days, and Hitler are on one end, and Abraham
Lincoln, the sun, butterflies, and lottery jackpots are on the other. When
applied to a particular object in mind, we label this dimension "affect"
and speak of an "affective tag" attached to the object, the tag representing the direction (positive or negative) and strength of the affect (Fiske
and Pavelchak 1986). Often, emotion is also the result of more diffuse
mental states, what are called moods. For our purposes, a *mood* is a diffuse state not attached to any particular object in memory. This does not
mean that mood is unrelated to affective tags: to the extent that a mood
is positively or negatively valenced, it may result in priming of objects
with similarly valenced affective tags. Affective tags and mood combine
to form the experience of emotion.

Such a definition of emotion places us near Russell's (2003) "core affect" model. This does not necessarily place us at odds with other conceptions of the role of emotions. Although we are mostly concerned
with the consequences of the positive or negative valence attached to a
mood, there is no reason why emotional states combining that valence
with arousal or aversion could not have differential effects, as Feldman,
Huddy, and Cassese (this volume) argue for anxiety and anger.

Our argument is organized thus. First, we discuss how emotion and,
in particular, affect serve to organize the mind. Second, we review existing research concerning the ways this organization leads to bias at all
stages of the evaluative process. We then use a simple experimental study
to demonstrate how the process outlined leads individuals to integrate—
or fail to integrate—information about a political candidate. Finally, we
discuss the consequences of these theories for political science and for
psychology in general.

We should note that throughout, we are discussing characteristics
the mind rather than characteristics of the brain. Although there is e
dence that different characteristics of the same mental object are sto
in different parts of the brain, we concentrate on how the mind, which
arises from the brain, is organized. As tempting as it is to associate neurons and dendrites with mental nodes and connections, at this juncture,
they are best left as metaphors.

THE AFFECTIVE ORGANIZATION OF THE MIND

There is a great deal of evidence for the use of affect as an organizational
rule in the mind. Much of it comes from work concerning the hot cognition hypothesis (Abelson 1963), which holds that information about
social objects is inevitably charged with affect (as in Bargh 1994, 1997;
Lodge and Stroh 1993) and that the object cannot be activated without
also activating this tag (see Fiske 1981; Fazio 2001; Sears 2001).

Empirical tests of the hot cognition hypothesis can be traced back
to studies making use of subliminal priming (Neely 1976). Such studies
form a straightforward application of the lexical decision task (see Collins
and Quillian 1969; Collins and Loftus 1975), in which subjects are asked
to determine whether a word flashed on a screen is an actual English
word. The subjects' only task is to press one button if the target is a legal
English word and another if it is not, as quickly as they can, without making too many errors. Unbeknownst to the subjects, they have been primed
with another word, flashed on the screen very briefly, that is either semantically related or unrelated to the target word. If the two words are
semantically related, subjects recognize the target word as being a real
word significantly faster than they do if the two words are unrelated. In a
variant, the affective decision task (Fazio et al. 1986), subjects are asked
to decide if the target word is good or bad.

In such studies, subjects are found to recognize target words faster if
they are affectively congruent to the prime word. For instance, priming
an individual with a word carrying highly negative connotations—*disease*,
for instance—allows the subjects to more quickly recognize that a word
with similar connotations, say, *cockroach*, is bad. Conversely, priming a
subject with *sunshine* makes it more difficult for the subject to recognize the negative implication of *cockroach*. This priming effect has been
shown to exist for words (Bargh et al. 1992; Hermans, De Houwer, and
Eelen 1994) and pictures (Hermans et al. 1994).

Note that this affective information is privileged: individuals are able
to recall the affective component of a social object even when they fail

to recall any of its semantic properties (Yavuz and Bousfield 1959). That is, individuals are able to offer an opinion about an object when they fail to recall any information about it. This is especially prevalent in political evaluations, where individuals may know little or nothing about the candidates in question (Lodge, McGraw, and Stroh 1989; McGraw, Lodge, and Stroh 1990). Despite what we know or fail to know about an object in memory, evaluation is inevitable: as Zajonc (1980) says, we can doubt the facts surrounding an evaluation, but we almost never call into question our evaluation.

These studies serve to demonstrate two essential points. First, the activation of an affectively charged concept in memory leads to the facilitation of other concepts with the same affective tag. This facilitation is automatic, beyond the conscious control of the individual. Second, the affective categorization of novel objects is automatic: entering an object in memory necessarily entails attaching an affective tag to the object. This is some of the strongest support for the affective organization of the objects in the mind, because individuals do not have to know anything about an object to hold it in memory but will assign it an affective tag regardless.

THE INTERPLAY OF EMOTION AND COGNITION

Emotion and cognition are exceedingly difficult to parse in nature (Lazarus 1991), and we hold that this is because they are linked in LTM and together enable the evaluation of social objects. Negativity seems to lead to deeper processing of information, whereas positivity generally leads to more heuristic processing strategies (Park and Banaji 2000; Schwarz and Bless 1991). In another line of research, Marcus and MacKuen (1993) argue that anxiety and enthusiasm play critical roles in the vote choice, with anxiety encouraging deep, effortful processing and enthusiasm stimulating interest in the campaign.

This line of research can be placed under the general rubric of motivated reasoning (see Kunda 1990). Lodge and Taber (2000) divide motivated reasoning effects into two groups, with profoundly different effects on cognition: directional motivations and nondirectional motivations.

Directional motivations involve the tendency of individuals to process information so as to reach a certain conclusion, unconsciously trading off the accuracy of that conclusion. Both the elaboration likelihood model (Petty and Cacioppo 1986) and the heuristic-systematic model (Chaiken 1987) argue that strong affect toward an object can tilt the processing of new information to ensure that the existing affect is maintained. Stronger affective evaluations are maintained, but weaker ones are subject to change owing to important stimuli. Of course, all of this is conditional on the present capacity of the individual for processing the information and the motivation to do so. When either of these is lacking, the evaluation will be the product of simplifications or heuristics, and any change in evaluation that results from such processes will likely be both short-lived and weak.

In all of these cases, an emotional response to an object being evaluated tends to alter the processing strategy of the individual to ensure a certain outcome, generally the maintenance of the current affect. This sort of directionally motivated reasoning trades accuracy in evaluations for maintenance of the current evaluation, which is considered to have an intrinsic value (Kruglanski and Webster 1996).

In contrast, nondirectional motivated reasoning pushes individuals toward a more considered evaluation, regardless of the current one. In political science, the most prominent example of this sort of motivated reasoning is Marcus and MacKuen's theory of affective intelligence (Marcus and MacKuen 1993; MacKuen, Marcus, Neuman, and Keele this volume). In affective intelligence theory, anxiety leads individuals to play closer attention to the environment and bring more information to task in processing information. In this way, a diffuse emotional response has a strong impact on the choice of information that is brought to bear on an evaluation.

Also, anxious individuals seem to give greater attention to stimuli that appear threatening (MacLeod and Mathews 1988; Fox 1993) and are more like to perceive ambiguous stimuli as threatening (Eysenck et al. 1991). Thus, emotional responses can lead individuals to make use of more information in evaluating an object.

Positive moods appear to make individuals more likely to retrieve positively valenced information, and negative moods do the same for negative information (Bower and Forgas 2001; Forgas 1995; Forgas 1994). These same effects hold when moods are long-lasting. Clinical depression, for instance, is reinforced by the inability of depressed individuals to remember information that is inconsistent with their mood (Teasdale 1983).

So emotions lead us not only to use certain processing strategies but also to make use of different information in that processing. The affective organization of objects in the mind means that affectively congruent information is most likely to brought to bear on an evaluation, potentially leading to severe biases in the outcome of the processing. In addition, moods can affect the weight given to information used to make an evaluation. Russo et al. (1996) found that individuals tended to distort information about a set of alternatives in order to support the most desirable outcome, and Olsen (1997) found that individuals believe that favorable alternatives are more likely to occur.

Finally, emotions can impact the evaluative process when they are used directly as information. That is, a negative mood can be used as a factor in deciding that an object is bad, regardless of whether the mood has anything to do with the object (see Martin et al. 1997). Schwartz and Clore (1988) argue that individuals making evaluations simply think about the object being evaluated and ask themselves how they feel: if they feel good, they evaluate the object positively. This works well, provided that their mood is not the result of some other factor (but see Martin et al. 1993). In an earlier study, Schwarz and Clore (1983) instructed subjects to recall either pleasant or unpleasant events in their past and describe the events as vividly as possible. Participants who described negative events were found to be in a more negative mood and to report a lower level of satisfaction with their lives. A participant's negative mood was used as information in answering the question regarding life satisfaction, unless the participant was manipulated so as to attribute the negative mood to qualities of the room in which the experiment was held.

In political evaluations, the online processing model (Lodge, McGraw, and Stroh 1989; McGraw, Lodge, and Stroh 1990) holds that individuals use the affective content of information they have processed about a political figure to update the affective tag attached to the candidate and then forget the information at an exponential rate. Thus, when the individuals are asked their opinion of the political figure, the most readily accessible information is their emotional response. When asked the reasons for their opinions, they simply make use of whatever affectively congruent considerations are most accessible (similar to the process suggested in Zaller and Feldman 1992).

Given the attention that the evaluative process has received in psychology and political science, a complete review of the literature would be a book in itself. The portion of it considered here is enough to demonstrate the pervasive impact of emotion on evaluation. In its diffuse and its specific forms, emotion leads individuals to make use of certain processing strategies, bring certain information to bear on evaluations, and is itself used as information for the purposes of evaluation. It is easy to see these effects as biases in cognition—emotion getting in the way of what could be a purely rational process. To the contrary, it is not clear how individuals would evaluate objects in the absence of emotion: within the framework of limited human cognition, there must be some way to determine which information is relevant at any point in time and some sort of shortcut to an evaluation when a detailed evaluation is impossible. In this way, we are in accord with affective intelligence theory, as expressed in this volume and elsewhere. Our theory of affective primacy is at odds with affective intelligence, however, in that does not hold that the shortcuts used are necessarily beneficial. We believe, rather, that in political evaluations affect often leads to serious deviations from normative decision-making theories. Of course, the perception that emotion leads to incorrect decisions is in part a result of our focus on experimental studies, in which we use participants' reliance on emotional cues to lead them astray. Although evaluations made purely on the basis of affect may not be as objectively correct as those based on a detailed review of the relevant considerations, it may be good enough for most purposes and can, in fact, sometimes prove superior to the results of conscious deliberation (as in Wilson and Schooler 1991).

Emotion certainly serves to alter the course of the evaluative process but, in doing so, may make it more, not less, efficient.

THE INTEGRATION OF INFORMATION IN CANDIDATE EVALUATION

Our model of the interplay of emotion and cognition leads us to fairly strong expectations with regard to how individuals should process new information about a political figure. When individuals are informed that they will have to make a judgment about a political figure, they should be motivated to make use of deep processing strategies to ensure that their responses will be defensible. But the primacy of affect would lead us to believe that they will be unable to do so. Furthermore, their automatic emotional response to the political figure is expected to bias their processing of other traits relating to the figure.

This experiment consists of a reaction-time study of 135 Stony Brook University undergraduates who participated in the experiment as part of the departmental subject pool. In the study, participants filled out a demographic questionnaire, including political knowledge items adapted from Delli Carpini and Keeter (1993). Then participants were asked to evaluate 40 unattributed public policy statements, including 12 that would be used later in the study. The evaluations of these statements give us a baseline for how subjects should update their affect toward the fictitious Congressman Lukas when the statements are attributed to him. If a subject has a high evaluation of the statement, it should make the affective tag attached to Lukas more positive; dislike should make the tag more negative.

In the second part of the experiment, the participants are told that they will be asked to evaluate the candidate William Lukas based on a series of statements attributed to him, and following each statement, they will be asked to decide if a word flashed on the screen is good or bad, as quickly as they can, without making too many errors. Before being shown the first statement attributed to Lukas, the participants practice the word evaluation task on the target words 30 times, without being informed that they were being primed. (In post-questioning, 11 subjects claimed to have been able to see the priming words and were excluded from the experiment.) The primes were flashed on the screen for 36 milliseconds, a short enough time to ensure that participants were unlikely to process the primes but long enough to allow for the primes to be perceived subliminally.

After the practice session, participants were presented with the first of the twelve statements attributed to Lukas. In one condition, the first three statements were pretested to be positively correlated with liking George W. Bush and negatively correlated with liking Bill Clinton. In the other condition, the first three statements were positively correlated with liking Clinton and negatively correlated with liking Bush. In both experimental conditions, the last three statements attributed to Lukas were the first three of the other experimental condition. That is, in one condition, the initial statements were pretested to appeal to liberals, and the final statements appealed to conservatives. In the other condition, the order was reversed. The six statements in the middle were selected to not significantly correlate with liking Bush or Clinton. Of course, the conceptual order of statements was set, but the statements filling out that order were shuffled. To aid in the external validity of the study, all of the statements attributed to Lukas were, in fact, statements made by Democratic presidential contender Howard Dean in 2003. The statements used are listed in the appendix.

To some extent, in studies of candidate evaluation we are forced to make a trade-off between faithfulness to the electoral environment and control over the information that participants receive about the candidates. At one extreme, we can study actual candidates and try to control for all of the information that the participants have received. On the other, we can create fictional candidates concerning whom we can control all of the information that participants receive. We opted for a controlled environment in which we could control all of the information received about Lukas, while trying to ensure that it was not a purely arti-

FIGURE 5.1: PRIMING PROCEDURE

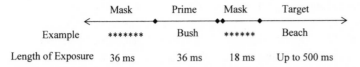

ficial environment by using statements culled from an actual presidential candidate. In some sense, our procedure is less realistic than that used by Redlawsk, Civettini and Lau (this volume), in which participants have to choose what information to receive and what information to bypass. The simpler nature of our information environment does, however, enable more direct tests of our hypotheses and also allows us to make use of a non-obtrusive measure of affect based on reaction times in the affective decision task.

After viewing each statement for a minimum of fifteen seconds, the participants began an affective evaluation task in which they were asked to decide whether the target word is good or bad by pushing labeled buttons on the keyboard (see figure 5.1). Though they generally did not realize it, the subjects were being primed with both political words (including *Clinton, Bush,* and *Lukas*) and affectively charged words (such as *lottery, beach,* and *death*) milliseconds before making the affective decision about the target words.

We were interested in the effect that the Lukas prime had on the response times to the target words. If a subject had positive affect toward Lukas, it should have taken longer for the subject to decide that a word such as *cancer* is bad, and it should have taken less time to decide that a word such as *mother* is good. If the subject disliked Lukas, the opposite should have occurred. A critical component of this analysis is that it allows us to examine the extent of the liking or disliking of Lukas without actually asking subjects how much they like or dislike Lukas. After going through all of the statements, participants completed a brief set of postexperimental questions asking them how likely they would be to vote for Lukas, where Lukas fit on an ideological spectrum, and whether they had seen the priming words.

This experimental design allows us to conduct a strong test of the primacy of affect model discussed above, with regard to the reaction of the participants to the liberal or conservative statements at the end of the sequence. Standard models of evaluation incorporating such concepts as anchoring and adjustment (as in Kahneman and Tversky 1973) that fail to incorporate the primacy of affect would hold that though these statements should not be given as much weight as the initial statements in the evaluation of Lukas, they should be evaluated in the correct direction. That is, being exposed to these affectively incongruent statements should move the affect of the participants toward Lukas in the opposite direction of the initial statements. The overall affective evaluation may still be biased in the direction of the initial statements, but the incongruent statements should have an impact in the normatively correct direction. The primacy of affect hypothesis predicts that evaluations of Lukas, when measured subliminally, should be driven most strongly by the initial evaluations of Lukas. Once the initial statements set the emotional response, the incongruent statements at the end of the sequence should do little to change it, with individuals failing to update it at all. That is, statements that should lead participants to substantially alter their evaluations of Lukas will, instead, be used to reinforce their predispositions.

The difference, in terms of normative models of evaluation, between an individual who makes minimal use of the incongruent statements and one who fails to make use of the statements at all is vital, and it is easiest to see when we put the issue in terms of the expectancy value model of attitudes (Ajzen and Fishbein 1980). In this model, an individual's attitude toward an object is the result of sum of the affective tags of all of the attached opinion objects, with each summed affect weighted by a function reflecting its immediate importance. In the expectancy value model, the weight is treated as the probability of an event occurring, but for our purposes, Anderson's (1981) conceptualization of the weight as the evaluative relevance of the implication to the current on-line tally makes more sense. In such a model, each piece of information that is relevant to a judgment is given a weight specific to that judgment, which is then multiplied by the strength of the information and summed with all of the other judgment-relevant information to arrive at a decision. This weight may be the result of agenda-setting, making a certain aspect of a candidate or issue more relevant to evaluation (McCombs and Shaw 1972; Iyengar and Kinder 1987), issue framing (Nelson and Kinder 1996), or priming (Krosnick and Kinder 1990; Krosnick and Brannon 1993).

None of the effects that may alter the weights attached to an issue necessarily cause a problem for normative models of decision making, so long as the weights attached to the issues are exogenous. A violation of this principle—a linking of the weights given to new information with existing opinion—could have serious ramifications for the correctness of one's opinions. Though it seems complex, this is far from a novel idea: all it means is that certain beliefs about an object tend to lead to similar beliefs about the relations between related objects (Judd and Krosnick 1989).

If each piece of new information about an object is weighed without regard to both the current level of affect toward the object and other information that might have been integrated previously or concurrently, then any deviation from the correct affective tag toward the object will be quickly corrected. For instance, a voter whose issue positions run contrary to that of the president might, perhaps because of an exogenous shock such as the attacks of September 2001, hold a very high opinion of the president. If all of the information about the president received is independently integrated, however, the high opinion held of President Bush in light of the attacks will fade as the voter integrates information about social and economic stances associated with the president that he does not like.

If the weighing of new information is not independent, however, as the primacy of affect model would argue, we would predict a very different result. If it were the case that the updating of information were a function of the current level of affect toward President Bush, the weights given to new information about social and economic stances would have a much smaller impact, leading the voter to return to his correct level of affect much more slowly. In the extreme case, where information deviating from the existing judgment is not at all integrated, it might never converge to the correct level. If individuals systematically give low weight to or ignore evidence contrary to their current opinions (as in Taber and Lodge 2001), they could continue to support candidates whose programs are contrary to their real interests.

Note that our hypotheses about the primacy of affect are made in regard to the affective tag attached to Lukas, not the participant's stated beliefs about Lukas. In any situation where individuals are asked to evaluate Lukas on the basis of items in their memory, they should be able to make use of the information in working memory about Lukas to arrive at a decision that comes close to being normatively correct, especially given the experimental instructions.

Overall, then, we have four hypotheses regarding participant evaluations of Lukas, two of them regarding the implicit measures of affect toward Lukas, which tap directly into the affective tags attached to Lukas, and two regarding explicit evaluations of Lukas. First, the initial statements should establish a strong affective response to Lukas in the direction of the participant's liking of the statements. Second, the final, incongruent statements should have little or no impact on participants' evaluations of Lukas. In explicit, memory-based questions, participants' responses should be results of all of the information held in working memory about Lukas. Because we expect that extra weight will be given

FIGURE 5.2: HYPOTHESIZED AFFECTIVE INTEGRATION CURVES

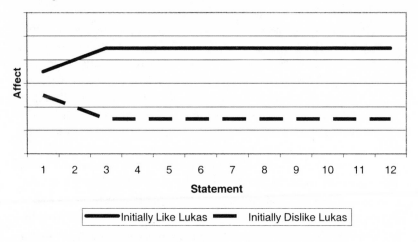

to the first and last statements, in line with primacy and recency effects, participants should place Lukas in the middle of the ideological spectrum. In explicit, affect-based questions, participants' responses should be results of the affective tag attached to Lukas. Our expectations as to the affective tag attached to Lukas can be seen in figure 5.2.

ANALYSIS

Measuring such evaluations via reaction time can be exceedingly difficult because we are dealing with differences in latency on the order of tenths of a second or less. First, we need to ensure that we are accurately recording reaction times. Common programming languages can have difficulty recording reaction times with the accuracy needed for our studies, leading us to adopt a program called Inquisit that was specifically designed for such functions. But getting a measure of the effect of the experimental manipulation on reaction times requires more than simply accurately recording them. Because practice effects can sometimes make a great deal of difference in responding to stimuli, we have to ensure that subjects have adequate practice in responding to stimuli before the recorded trial start.

Generally, analysis of reaction time measures is done with a simple analysis of variance: reaction times are decomposed into between- and within-subject elements and further decomposed to determine how much of an effect the experimental manipulation has had. In this case, however, the nature of our measurements—affect over time—lends itself to a simple time-series analysis. This has the additional advantage of providing easily interpretable coefficients, provided we create a natural scale for affect toward Lukas.

Our analysis, then, first establishes this scale with which to measure affect toward the candidate, then sets our reaction time measures to correspond to that scale. Finally, we subject these dependent variables to a series of simple regression analyses to study the differential impact of the explanatory variables on the affect toward Lukas after each statement presented in the experiment.

The nature of our dependent variable, affect toward Lukas, gives us a reasonable idea of the scale that we should use for measurement. The study includes two other political figures as primes, Clinton and Bush, and the strong negative correlation between affect toward the two figures make them natural bookends for our scale of affect toward Lukas. Although there are strong negative correlations in affect between almost any major Republican and Democratic figures (Rush Limbaugh and Edward Kennedy, for example) Clinton and Bush have the added advantage of being instantly recognizable to all subjects. None of the subjects stated that they did not have an opinion about either Bush or Clinton, a characteristic unique to this dyad.

For each subject, the average reaction time to a prime of Bush or Clinton with either a positive or a negative affective target was used to create four values: Bush-negative, Bush-positive, Clinton-negative, and Clinton-positive. Primes of Lukas with a positive affective target were put on a scale between Clinton-positive and Bush-positive, with the lower of the two values representing the high end of the scale (because faster responses represent more positive affect). The process was repeated for negative affective primes, save that the higher value represented the high end of the scale. On this scale, an affect equal to the less-liked figure (Clinton or Bush) is equal to zero; an affective response to Lukas equal to the better-liked figure is equivalent to one. The positive affect and the negative affect are then averaged together to create one measurement. For each subject, we now have twelve dependent variables, corresponding to the affect shown toward Lukas after reading each of the statements.

Such a transformation has one major advantage: our dependent variables are now on a natural scale indicating the affect toward the candidate. Unfortunately, this has failed to remove one of the other problems affecting reaction time measures: measurement error. Because the measurements that led to our dependent variables are in terms of fractions of a second, any momentary distraction or lapse of attention can lead to a values that are far different from the real reaction time. The worst instances of this are resolved by removing exceedingly high or unrealistically low reaction times: those greater than 2 seconds and those less than 250 milliseconds.

The format of our data, a series of twelve dependent variables for each subject, corresponding to one measurement of affect toward Lukas after each policy statement, lends itself easily to a time series analysis. Using Box-Jenkins ARIMA models, we can determine the effect of the statements read at the beginning and the end of the series on the affective tag attached to Lukas.

RESULTS

For the purposes of the ARIMA regression analysis, the participants were aggregated into two groups: those who, on the basis of their initial evaluations of the campaign statements, were expected to initially like Lukas, and those who were expected to dislike Lukas. In the first group were self-identified conservatives who were first exposed to conservative statements from Lukas and liberals who were first exposed to liberal statements from Lukas. The other combinations of ideology and experimental condition were expected to initially show a dislike of Lukas. For the purposes of this analysis, individuals who self-identified as moderates were excluded.

The results of the ARIMA model, without autoregressive or moving average parameters, are presented in table 5.1.

For both groups, the results strongly support our expectations. Among individuals expected to initially like Lukas, the early statements had an effect in the expected direction: an increase of one standard deviation in liking for the statement led to an expected increase in affect toward

TABLE 5.1: ARIMA regression results

	Coefficient	Standard error	P	P > z
Expected to dislike:				
Early Prior	3.53	1.08	3.26	0.00
Mid Prior	−3.93	5.67	0.69	0.49
Late Prior	0.79	2.62	0.30	0.76
Expected to like:				
Early Prior	4.66	1.75	2.67	0.01
Mid Prior	2.28	8.48	0.27	0.79
Late Prior	8.73	4.54	1.92	0.06

Note: Significant coefficients are shown in italics.

Lukas of about three and a half times the average difference between Bush and Clinton. In contrast, the late statements, which the subjects were expected to dislike, had no significant relation to affect toward Lukas.

In the series conducted with participants expected to initially dislike Lukas, the results follow a similar pattern. Early statements had a strong impact on the affective tag attached to Lukas, with an increase of one standard deviation in the evaluation of the statement increasing the expected affective tag attached to Lukas by a bit more than four and a half times the average difference between Clinton and Bush.

Note that the coefficients attached to the prior evaluations of the statements seem unreasonably large; few participants felt more strongly about Lukas than they did about Bush or Clinton. The large coefficients are mostly due to the subset of participants without a large difference in affect between Clinton and Bush: participants who dislike or like both candidates could be expected to provide unreasonably high scores on the affect scale. Previous analyses made use of a quasi-Bayesian process to correct for these problems and provided substantively similar results (Cassino 2005).

Overall, the results of this analysis strongly support our hypotheses: the initial statements have a strong impact, in the expected direction, on the affective tag attached to the congressman. In contrast, the middle and later statements have no impact on the affect tag. We should note that there are further effects evident in the data that are simply beyond the scope of the present discussion; for instance, Democrats seem to evaluate Lukas differently when they believe him to be conservative than Republicans do when they believe him to be liberal. One of the authors (Cassino) has made a further study of these effects and replicated them in national survey data; a similar asymmetry may also be present in Redlawsk, Civettini and Lau's findings in this volume.

Next, we tested our expectations regarding the post-experimental ideological placement of Lukas. In this question, participants are asked: "Based on all of the statements that you have read regarding Lukas, where would you place him on this scale of ideological positions that a person might hold?" They are then prompted to press a button corresponding to a point on a seven-point ideological scale between the positions Strongly Liberal and Strongly Conservative. Subjects were familiar with the scale because it had previously been used to evaluate the Republican Party and the Democratic Party and in a self-evaluation. Three participants who had not previously placed the Democratic Party to the left of the Republican Party were excluded from the analysis.

TABLE 5.2: Ideological placement of Lukas on a seven-point scale, by group

Group	Mean placement	Standard deviation
1	3.55	1.51
2	3.33	0.91
3	3.50	2.12
4	3.30	1.26

Note: Group 1: Conservatives, conservative statements first; group 2: Liberals, conservative statements first; group 3: Conservatives, liberal statements first; group 4: Liberals, liberal statements first.

As expected (see table 5.2), despite the differences in the affective tags attached to Lukas by the groups, all four groups placed him almost exactly in the middle of the seven-point ideological scale, with placements ranging only from 3.3 to 3.55. Moreover, the standard deviations attached to the averages make them statistically indistinguishable, and the correlation between the final measurement of the affective tag attached to Lukas and the placement is insignificant in all groups, with correlations ranging from −.04 to .15.

It seems that subjects are able to accurately respond to an explicit memory-based question. In this case, memory-based primacy and recency effects are likely to give individuals disparate views of Lukas's ideology, with the average ideology probably being close to the middle of the scale: exactly where they place him. We refer to this as a memory-based question because it requires subjects to make use of not only the affective tag attached to Lukas but also the statements that have been attributed to him.

Finally, we make use of a regression analysis to test the relation between the affective tag attached to Lukas and the explicit post-experimental evaluation question. Unlike the explicit ideological placement question, the evaluation question makes no reference to the statements that have been attributed to Lukas; instead, it simply asks subjects to place themselves on a seven-point scale of liking for Lukas, ranging from strong liking to strong disliking. Thus, we expect that participants should report, as directly as they are able, the affective tag attached to Lukas. This process should be aided by the fact that there is no perceived right or wrong answer to the question and, thus, less pressure to try to make a memory-based response. Also, their considered ideological placement of Lukas, which was not elicited until after the simple evaluation question, should have no effect.

Results of the regression bore out our expectations (see table 5.3). Of the prior evaluations of the 12 statements attributed to Lukas, only one

TABLE 5.3: Regression results

Dependent variable: explicit evaluation of Lukas

Variable	Coefficient	Standard error	t	P > t	95% Confidence interval	
Affective Tag 1	0.613	0.735	0.830	0.407	−0.855	2.081
Affective Tag 2	−0.877	0.839	−1.050	0.300	−2.551	0.798
Affective Tag 3	−0.110	0.868	−0.130	0.900	−1.842	1.622
Affective Tag 4	−0.715	0.800	−0.890	0.375	−2.312	0.882
Affective Tag 5	0.397	0.916	0.430	0.666	−1.432	2.225
Affective Tag 6	0.933	0.828	1.130	0.264	−0.721	2.586
Affective Tag 7	1.361	0.909	1.500	0.139	−0.454	3.177
Affective Tag 8	−0.164	0.849	−0.190	0.848	−1.859	1.532
Affective Tag 9	0.100	0.761	0.130	0.895	−1.419	1.619
Affective Tag 10	1.209	0.956	1.270	0.210	−0.699	3.118
Affective Tag 11	−1.199	0.870	−1.380	0.173	−2.937	0.538
Affective Tag 12	*−2.564*	*0.813*	*−3.150*	*0.002*	*−4.187*	*−0.941*
Lukas Placement	−0.059	0.324	−0.180	0.857	−0.706	0.588
Party ID	−0.115	0.310	−0.370	0.713	−0.733	0.504
Placement × Party ID	−0.017	0.086	−0.200	0.841	−0.188	0.154
Statement 1 Prior	−0.020	0.095	−0.220	0.830	−0.209	0.169
Statement 2 Prior	0.092	0.095	0.960	0.339	−0.098	0.282
Statement 3 Prior	0.055	0.110	0.500	0.619	−0.164	0.274
Statement 4 Prior	−0.089	0.114	−0.780	0.439	−0.316	0.139
Statement 5 Prior	−0.090	0.120	−0.750	0.457	−0.328	0.149
Statement 6 Prior	0.072	0.123	0.580	0.562	−0.174	0.318
Statement 7 Prior	*−0.430*	*0.121*	*−3.540*	*0.001*	*−0.672*	*−0.187*
Statement 8 Prior	−0.128	0.139	−0.920	0.362	−0.406	0.150
Statement 9 Prior	0.242	0.127	1.920	0.060	−0.010	0.495
Statement 10 Prior	−0.052	0.101	−0.510	0.611	−0.253	0.150
Statement 11 Prior	−0.031	0.104	−0.300	0.767	−0.239	0.177
Statement 12 Prior	0.029	0.084	0.350	0.727	−0.138	0.197
Constant	*5.678*	*2.143*	*2.650*	*0.010*	*1.401*	*9.956*

Note: R^2 = .368; N = 135. Italic designates key items discussed in text.

had an effect at conventional levels of significance. That coefficient, because it is attached to the seventh statement, which was pretested to be neutral, is probably the result of a Type One error. The only other significant predictor of the explicit evaluation of Lukas is the last measurement of the affective tag attached to Lukas. This variable does not account for most of the variance in the explicit evaluations of Lukas, but it does a better job than any of the other measurements of the affective tag, as would be expected. The relatively low R^2 of the entire model, .37, is most probably the result of measurement error in the dependent variable.

So when individuals are asked to place Lukas on an ideological spectrum, they make use of all the information at their disposal: the statements attributed to him. But when asked how much they like Lukas, they do not pursue such a memory-based approach. Rather, they report, as best they can, the affective tag attached to Lukas in memory. Under many circumstances, of course, this reporting could be seriously compromised, but in the absence of such intervening factors, they seem to do a fair job of it. It can also be said that this result shows the power of the affective tag. Rather than going back and reevaluating all of the information that has been presented to them, the affective tag allows individuals to know how much they like something quickly and without much cognitive effort. This summary, though convenient, is also imperfect, however, and as we have shown, is easily manipulated Whereas an effortful, memory-based approach leads individuals to one outcome—seeing Lukas as a moderate—a reliance on affect leads them to embrace the normatively incorrect bias resulting from the question ordering.

Note also that these results present something of a special case because of the order in which the statements were attributed to Lukas. If statements were presented in random order, we would expect that explicit evaluations and affective evaluations would be roughly the same because the most recent statements and the earliest statements would have similar affective content. In our experiment, however, the order of the statements ensures that the early and late statements have very different affective content, thus producing these results.

In summary, the affective tags attached to Lukas are the result of a first impression, formed by the first three statements attributed to him, with the later statements having no effect. Participants are able to access the statements attributed to Lukas in order to make memory-based judgments, but they do not do so when asked for a simple evaluation of the candidate, relying instead on their most recent affective tag. This may seem to mitigate the effects of the phenomena studied here; after all, individuals are able to overcome these biases and make normatively correct judgments. Yet there are several reasons why this is not the case. First, it is not clear how often individuals care enough about politics to make use of relatively effortful, memory-based processing strategies. Second, research into online processing has shown that individuals tend to forget the information that led them to an evaluation rather quickly, while retaining their affect toward the candidate (Lodge, Steenbergen, and Brau 1995). Thus, the capacity of the individual to overcome biases by memory-based processing should be short-lived, and judgments based on potentially flawed emotional responses should become dominant.

THE AUTOMATICITY OF EVALUATIONS

The model of emotion and cognition laid out in this chapter differs substantially from traditional models of evaluation. Rather than a cognitive calculus in which information is carefully weighed on the basis of the implications of the information for the object being evaluated, the primacy of affect hypothesis posits that evaluation is largely an emotional and automatic process. One consequence of this evaluative process is that the affect toward a social object may become decoupled from the facts about the object, potentially leading to serious errors in judgment (see Golding et al. 1990).

We wish to focus, however, on the consequences of the automaticity of evaluation. In the Lukas experiment, the moment participants learned something about the fictional candidate, they formed a positive or negative affective response to him, and this response tended to drive later evaluations. This initial emotional reaction and the biases to which it leads are entirely beyond the control of the individual. In this, though, we have not taken into consideration the experience of affective primacy. Individuals do not think of themselves as being motivated by forces beyond their control. To the contrary, even when individuals have no idea why they are evaluating an object in a certain way, they are willing to give reasons for the judgments and behavior and do not entertain the notion that their judgments are wrong. We are only aware of the outputs of our thought processes: just as we have no access to the portions of our brain that control our heartbeat, we cannot say why we form an evaluation (Gazzaniga 1985). We can offer up reasons for our evaluations, but these are not necessarily the true causes of the evaluations and may be available considerations that seem to support them (as in Zaller and Feldman 1992). The stories we tell about why we think or do things are just that: stories, based on folkloric accounts of cause and effects (Robinson and Clore 2002). We describe our own motives in much the same way as we describe the motives of others, through observations of behavior; our own stories are more convincing because of the care of our observations. For instance, voters may believe that they choose a candidate because of their own core values, but McCann (1997) finds that their values are as much a function of their candidate choice. The preference—whom do you like best?—comes first; the reasons come afterward. Hence the most basic law of electoral research: citizens vote for the candidate they like best.

Although this argument for cognition as rationalization may seem radical, it is hardly new (see Zajonc 2000; Russell 2003). Pioneering experimental work by Benjamin Libet (1985, 1993, 2004) has demonstrated the automaticity of simple behaviors such as the movement of a wrist. In a series of experiments, subjects were asked to watch a clock with a sweep second hand, and report the moment when they made the decision to flick their wrist, all while they were hooked up to EEGs and were cautioned not to think about the movement prior to the movement. Analysis of the EEGs revealed that the motor movement began approximately half a second before the conscious decision to move the wrist, but the subjects retroactively predated their conscious experience by almost exactly as much time as it took the decision (or stimulus) to reach consciousness (Libet 2004), making the illusion of conscious control over these actions compelling. If the conscious decision to do something comes well after the intention to do so has already been formed, even for a simple physical action, the notion that an individual's considered opinion precedes an automatic process is difficult to cling to.

These same processes seem to apply to judgments. Zajonc (1980, 1984) found that even when individuals are able to give a reason for their judgments, the reasons they give are not necessarily the correct ones. This can be seen in what is called the mere exposure effect, in which subjects are found to prefer Chinese ideograms to which they have been previously exposed, despite not realizing that they had seen them before. For our purposes, the most interesting element of the effect is that just as Libet's subjects misjudged when they had consciously initiated a simple physical motion so as to match up with the onset of subconscious initiation, Zajonc's subjects justified their affective responses to the ideograms. Though they had no access to the real reason they liked the ideograms, they attributed their preferences to the aesthetic value of the ideograms. Individuals seem to be excellent at explaining unconscious judgments in terms of conscious reasoning, and outside of the laboratory, there is no way to be certain that the explanations that they give are wrong. Moreover, when subjects are informed that they have been primed to affectively evaluate an object in a certain way, they are unable to overcome their automatic affective response (Winkielman, Zajonc, and Schwarz 1997). Emotional states can be misattributed, as demonstrated in the work of Schwarz and Clore (1983): in their study, participants in one condition attributed their induced negative emotional state to their satisfaction with life; in another, subjects attributed the same emotion to the room in which the experiment took place.

For political purposes, judgments based on automatic affective responses may well lead to errors, but disregarding emotions may be far more dangerous. Most voters are unable to cite more than a few reasons in open-ended questions on the NES—or able to remember the names of candidates (Neuman 1986). Reliance on the affective tag, rather than memory-based functions for making judgments about political objects, is beneficial in that it allows individuals to avoid effortful processing and, more important, provides a summary of past evaluations (Sanbonmatsu and Fazio 1990). Emotion-based evaluations may not be normatively desirable, but thinking systematically about the pros and cons of candidates and issues may be impossible for much if not all of the polity.

In this sense, our theories and results are in accord with the notion of emotion as a beneficial influence on political thinking, the basis of much of Marcus and MacKuen's work in this volume and that of many other researchers. Affect may be more efficient than other means of processing, and it may be the only avenue open for many citizens. It is also easily fooled, however, and can easily lead us to fool ourselves. Our mere likes and dislikes can tell us something about a political figure, but they become dangerous when they become reasons unto themselves. Moreover, the political appeals made to us are increasingly designed to appeal to affect, rather than reason, and, in so doing, may mislead us ever more.

Of course, it is not clear that there is anything to be done about this. As the preponderance of evidence shows, evaluation of social objects and, perhaps, of most of our mental experiences is automatic: we live a half-second behind our own actions, creating a story about why we said, thought, or did what we did. Advances in the understanding of how humans process behavior must take this into account if we are ever to explain how citizens think, reason, or act.

Appendix: Statements Attributed to Lukas

LIBERAL STATEMENTS:

- "I opposed the Congressional Resolution giving the White House open-ended authorization to attack Iraq. I continue to oppose the Bush Doctrine of preemptive war."
- "I have long advocated reversing President Bush's irresponsible tax cuts to fund more pressing needs of the country, such as universal health care."
- "I am a strong advocate of a woman's right to reproductive choice."

CONSERVATIVE STATEMENTS:

- "The Federal Government needs to resist attempts to tell states how to deal with guns beyond existing federal law."
- "Terrorists have vowed to murder Americans. We must oppose and defeat them through a relentless and hardheaded strategy that combines military force, vastly improved intelligence and law enforcement cooperation, the vigorous defense of our homeland, creative diplomacy and measures to prevent the teaching and dissemination of hate."
- "I believe the death penalty should be available to punish those who commit extreme and heinous crimes."

NEUTRAL STATEMENTS:

- "America should have been better prepared for the terrorist attacks of September 11, 2001."
- "Politicians set their clocks by election cycles. Too often their solutions to problems are two- and four-year fixes. But most of our problems require a vision that looks far into the future, fixes that must work long after that election cycle is history."
- "The federal government must recognize that an enormous number of our teachers are retiring in the coming years and provide incentives to inspire a new generation of great teachers. In addition, Washington needs to provide a cost share to help local communities fix their most rundown schools—not only improving education, but providing construction jobs as well."
- "If we are serious about improving American education, however, we must not forget that the single most important factor in how a child learns has less to do with the quality of the building, the computers or even the teachers. The most important predictor is the attitude in that

child's home toward education. We must involve parents again; we must insist that they participate in their children's education; and we must make schools and school boards responsive to parents."

- "Working with lawmakers, prosecutors, judges and law enforcement, I have cracked down on violent crime and ensured that violent felons spend time behind bars."
- "I have fought to protect family farms and cracked down on domestic violence."

CHAPTER SIX

The Third Way: The Theory of Affective Intelligence and American Democracy

MICHAEL MACKUEN, GEORGE E. MARCUS,
W. RUSSELL NEUMAN, AND LUKE KEELE

In the late 1940s and early 1950s political scientists began to make use of large national surveys to develop empirical theories of American political behavior and political judgment. From scholars at Columbia University and the University of Michigan came what has come to be called the psychological model: a now well-known and widely accepted portrait describing public ignorance of the major candidates and where they stood with respect to the predominant issues of the day. Moreover, the psychological model advanced the claim that partisan voting decisions were derived from a robust reliance on partisanship, whereas the voting decisions of independents resulted from responsiveness to "short-term" forces (hence the colloquial name "swing voters").[1] The psychological model, more commonly called the "normal vote" model, best articulated in *The American Voter* (Campbell et al. 1960), has often been taken as challenge to democracy. And although there have been many attempts to recast these findings in a more positive light (Achen 1975; Key and Cummings 1966; Mueller 1999; Page and Shapiro 1992; Stimson 2004), the challenge to the competence of the voters remains unchecked.

Another account of voting, that of rational choice, arrived shortly afterward from yet another sister social science, economics. In its initial formulation, rational choice held that voters engaged in a rational consideration of the alternatives presented to them, choosing that which best

---

1. Short-term forces are good times or bad, such as a good economy or a bad one, war or peace, scandals or their absence, a particularly good or bad candidate or campaign—and, of course, a very large part of the adult population not sufficiently interested to participate, no matter what the situation, a fact that is of considerable concern and attention (Burnham 1980; Ladd 1978; Schattschneider 1960).

served their interests (Downs 1957). Rational choice posits an attentive and thoughtful electorate that makes explicit comparisons and adjudicates among them through rational evaluation of their respective costs and benefits. A lack of empirical support for rational choice (Quattrone and Tversky 1988) led to a more qualified theory of "bounded rationality."

Each approach has attempted to deal with the problems of satisfying normative standards while dealing with seemingly intractable empirical challenges. Scholars have wrestled with the dystrophic implications of the "black and white" model advanced by Phil Converse (1964, 1966, 1970), which asserts that most people have few, if any, organized political ideas. If democracy requires an attentive and politically learned electorate and requires voters to give at least modest attention and thoughtful consideration to the policy and leadership choices before them, then neither account suffices.

We advance the claim that the theory of affective intelligence offers a comprehensive account that incorporates the insights of these two accounts of voter behavior. We argue that each of them identifies a special case of a more general range of outcomes. By this we mean that each has erroneously taken a special case of political judgment and treated it as if it were the general case.

How can it be that the normal vote and rational choice accounts are special cases, that is, theoretical specifications that apply only in some rather than in all circumstances? The two established theories presume that voters have invariant patterns of judgment and behavior. In the case of the normal vote account, voters are either partisan or not, and these immutable qualities fully control what people do, for example, whether they will pay attention (partisans do, independents do not), when they decide for whom to vote (partisans early in campaigns and nonpartisans late), and so forth. Partisans have certain qualities and they consistently display them, just as nonpartisans display their characteristic qualities (as we shall see, a similar case can be made for ideology as a stable defining quality).[2] In the case of rational choice theory (or its more recent variant, bounded rationality), voters think and act rationally all the time and in every circumstance so long as at least minimal stakes are in play. There is no logical barrier preventing the psychological and rational choice theorists from entertaining the possibility that voters shift between different decision strategies, but doing so requires formulating what the

2. John Zaller's (1992) work, justly celebrated, is the most sophisticated example of those that work from this premise. His Receive-Accept-Sample (RAS) explains how people attend and respond to information.

alternative strategies might be and what would initiate shifting from one to another. The theory of affective intelligence offers an alternative account that specifies the alternative strategies, the factor that shifts voters from one strategy to another, and the consequences.[3]

Perhaps the most often noted feature of the theory of affective intelligence is that it makes the counterconventional claim that emotion's impact is largely functional and rational. Equally important, it explains how emotion controls the way in which voters make political judgments. We argue that the effect of anxiety is largely conditional. This conditionality generates a model that is far more dynamic than a conventional model. Conditionality enables an important "if then" component that allows the theory of affective intelligence to model two courses of action for each individual. It is this conditionality, operationalized as statistical interactions, that enables the theory of affective intelligence to subsume what are most often seen as contending and antagonistic theories, the psychological, or normal vote, and rational choice approaches.

THE POLITICAL GEOGRAPHY OF AFFECTIVE INTELLIGENCE

The theory of affective intelligence holds that people have two basic decision strategies available and that they easily move from one to the other and back again. Why do people need more than one strategy? If people have the capacity to be rational why do they not rely on that capacity in all situations given that rationality promises much and its opposite, irrationality, promises so little? The standard answer is that rationality, as a cognitive process, is very demanding (even for those who might be gifted in its practice) and so its demanding character prevents its universal display.

The theory holds that rationality is appropriate only in some situations. More fundamentally, the theory holds that people have alternative decision strategies because different environments require them. The theory identifies two geographies, each of which demands a different strategy. In the first, the geography of familiar situations, it is efficient to swiftly and automatically (Bargh and Chartrand 1999) rely on previously learned routines. People in familiar and recurring choice situations can rely on the same decision-making strategies as they have in the past, for often,

3. We do not mean to imply that these are two discrete and thereby mutually exclusive strategies. Indeed, they may form ends of a continuum with a mixture of both available when both are engaged.

past success predicts future success. Moreover, the swift and deft management of social and behavioral interaction depends on unself-conscious modes of articulating speech and action. It is costly and unnecessary to use the time and effort required to arrive at a decision via explicitly rational calculation when the same decision has to be made again and again in the same environment. If all Democratic and all Republican candidates advance the same consistent policy stances, then why invest the time to learn about the newest candidate? If today's economic situation seems similar to yesterdays, why watch the business report? In such situations, what worked before, what becomes embedded in the heuristics of choice, operates to swiftly avail us of prior choices that will likely be as effective in the present as they were in the past.[4] In such circumstances, voters display habitual choice as their decision strategy.

But we do not always find ourselves in the domain of the familiar. Sometimes, we find ourselves in unexpected and novel situations. When we find ourselves in the political geography of uncertainty, we cannot safely or prudently rely on past lessons, especially lessons that are embedded in automatic judgments (Bargh et al. 1992). Practiced routines become unreliable guides and are likely to be ill suited to novel terrain. The theory of affective intelligence holds that in such circumstances we turn to the less often used mode of explicit consideration. Rationality, as a decision-making process, if not well suited to the familiar realm of habit—being too time-consuming and too costly—is critical to managing uncertain conditions (see table 6.1).

Increased anxiety tells us when we are entering the geography of uncertainty.[5] Absence of anxiety tells us we are in the realm of the safe and familiar and that we can rely on past actions that will, as they have before, successfully manage our lives. And in such circumstances people display habituated choice as their decision strategy. But there is more at stake than merely asserting that the central role of anxiety has been ignored.

---

4. *Heuristic*, as we use the term, is synonymous with the following equivalent terms: *preference, predisposition, conviction, standing decision, affective disposition, value, opinion,* and *attitude*. Some of these, e.g., *value, opinion,* and *attitude*, are thought to be primarily semantic and consciously available, whereas others, e.g., *preference* and *predisposition*, may be less accessible (Wilson 2002; Wilson, Kraft, and Dunn 1989; Wilson and Schooler 1991). Notwithstanding that distinction, people often make current choices by relying on some previously learned standards, and we take all of the above terms to depict embedded choices, however they have been acquired or however they maybe expressed.

5. We do not claim infallibility for emotional preconscious appraisals. As with conscious perception, preconscious appraisals may well be erroneous and, further, share with conscious assessments the prospect of elite manipulation.

TABLE 6.1: Responses to political geography

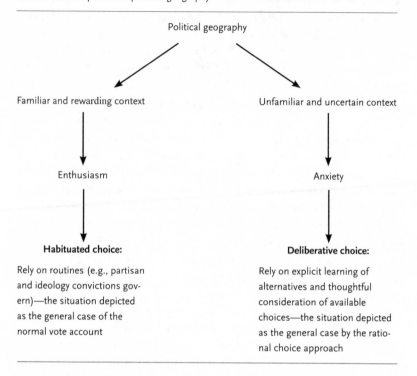

Political geography

Familiar and rewarding context

Unfamiliar and uncertain context

Enthusiasm

Anxiety

Habituated choice:

Rely on routines (e.g., partisan
and ideology convictions govern)—the situation depicted
as the general case of the
normal vote account

Deliberative choice:

Rely on explicit learning of
alternatives and thoughtful
consideration of available
choices—the situation depicted
as the general case by the rational choice approach

We argue that the theory of affective intelligence significantly revises conventional thinking about electoral behavior in America.

Spezio and Adolphs (chapter 4 in this volume) argue that affective processes and cognitive processes are simultaneously and continuously active, raising a question as to whether their careful critique of dual models of emotion and cognition applies to our work. Their view is one we concur with, though that might sound surprising given our adoption of a dual model of affect and cognition (with habit and hence the affective processes that sustain execution of habits being more dominant at some times and less so at others). As Spezio and Adolphs clearly state, neuroscience generally defines *cognition* as information processing, whether conscious or not. With such a definition affective processes become one variant of cognition (since affective processes are primarily but not exclusively information processing). We use the older, traditional meaning of *cognition*, "to cogitate," that is, to *expressly* think and reflect before acting (and here also affective processes are active, though not the same as sustained execution of habits). And though the revelation of nonconscious roles for cognition is important (and likely to become more so as neuroscience progresses), the role of expressed consideration has importance not only to our lives as humans but in particular for the special role it plays in liberal political democracy. Only by public sharing of our intentions, goals, and values can we resolve our differences and reach common purpose via democratic political mechanisms.

THE THIRD WAY: RECONSIDERING AMERICAN POLITICS

The standard view of the American electorate, derived largely from the psychological school developed over the course of the past fifty years, articulates a set of expectations that have become conventional wisdom. We demonstrate how the theory of affective intelligence recasts many of these conventional assertions.

CONVENTIONAL WISDOM 1: PARTISAN VOTERS DECIDE BY MEANS OF INTRANSIGENT RELIANCE ON DEEPLY HELD CONVICTIONS

Normal vote assertion: Dispositions anchor partisans and ideologues. A representative and current example of this view is given by Stimson (2004, 183): "The committed partisans make their decisions long in advance, many before the campaign begins, before the candidates are known."

Affective intelligence elaboration: Dispositions are used when appropriate and abandoned when inappropriate. Hence we expect that partisans will assert loyalty, but when they are anxious, we should observe a propensity for rejecting reliance on established partisan convictions.

The theory of affective intelligence argues that voter competence is dynamically responsive to the strategic character of the political geography. For this purpose, being rational is using different strategies of choice depending on the political context. First, it makes rational sense that voters rely on heuristics in familiar, recurring situations because they yield a high probability of success. Second, it makes rational sense to abandon heuristics when situations are novel and or uncertain and instead rely on considered judgments based on contemporary information. Hence voters are sophisticated to the extent that they shift from reliance on heuristics to considered judgments when conditions change from certain and familiar to uncertain. And it is rational for voters to return to reliance on heuristics when conditions return to normal. It, therefore, follows that voter sophistication comprises the ability to rely on predispositions under the appropriate circumstances as well as the ability to abandon them in other appropriate circumstances.

CONVENTIONAL WISDOM 2: SWING VOTERS DETERMINE ELECTION OUTCOMES

Normal vote assertion: Election outcomes depend on the dynamic of the swing vote and mobilization (turning out the partisan base). Partisans are intransigently loyal, but they may turn out at higher or lower levels in any particular election as a result of particular mobilization (and demobilization) efforts. But it is, as Stimson (2004, 182) describes, the independent voter who is decisive in an election: "That leaves the horse race to be decided by those of middling interest and knowledge, but no commitment to one side, our score keepers. Attentive to outcomes, not party or ideology, they are not involved enough to care much about the early, primary, stage of the campaign. They sit on the sideline as judges, watching to see what the parties will do. They are detached, usually having no party and not wishing to involve themselves in producing a candidate."[6]

Affective intelligence elaboration: Partisan defection is a more frequent and consequential part of every election than one might expect from the normal vote model. Election outcomes are largely the result of a party's securing a net advantage in partisan defection, not the movement of swing voters.

The claim of partisan intransigence is central to the standard view although election narratives have long noted that partisans may support the candidates of the other party (for example, "Reagan Democrats" or "Clinton Republicans"). Hence our understanding of campaigns and how they are run largely misses an important feature of American elections: effective political campaigns often turn on their ability to recruit support from the hostile opposition.

6. Many Americans who could participate if they were sufficiently motivated ignore elections. Again, Stimson (2004, 181) offers a representative account: "The inattentive never tune in. They answer questions when pressed, but their answers signal neither conviction nor intent. Mostly they will not vote, constituting the great bulk of the eligible electorate which sits out even presidential elections."

CONVENTIONAL WISDOM 3: AMERICAN ELECTIONS ARE NATURALLY PERIODIC

Normal vote assertion: Scholars have noted a cyclical pattern in American politics whereby periods of liberalism are followed by periods of conservatism and so on (Stimson 1991). The standard view has little to say about why such sinuous shifts take place.

Affective intelligence elaboration: The public pays more attention than the conventional wisdom holds but not as a constant feature of all voters or of most elections. Attention levels rise and fall according to emotional signals about the strategic character of the political geography. Moreover, attentiveness does not automatically lead to partisan cheerleading (loyalty). Major events (for example, shifts in economic conditions) impact the electorate through the mechanisms of emotional appraisal. In addition, as administrations gain greater success they cause anxiety among their partisan base and generate the conditions of defection. Moreover, cyclical patterns (from conservative to liberal to conservative) may have their foundations in the emotional responses to governance. Hence the theory of affective intelligence has macro as well as micro implications.

The theory of affective intelligences advances a counterintuitive explanation: the more successful governments are at enacting their policy proposals, the more likely they are to generate anxiety among their supporters. That is, support for a government will begin to crumble as the party leaders have success in enacting their programs. We expect that as governments achieve more of their political goals, thereby changing familiar terrain into the unfamiliar, their partisan supporters will become increasingly anxious, creating the conditions that make them open to withdrawing their support. This latter pattern may provide a critical element in accounting for the cyclical pattern of American politics.

In sum, we expect that partisans play an active role in determining election outcomes by shifting from reliance on their established convictions to deliberation about the best options when unfamiliar conditions generate anxiety about their "normal" choice. We also expect that, as a result, the net defection among partisan camps advantaging one party or another will have a considerable impact on election outcomes.

We now turn to the empirical evidence for the hypotheses we have advanced. At the center of these claims is that anxiety is a pivotal assessment of the nature of the immediate circumstances. The level of anxiety should modify the mode of rationality to ensure that the appropriate form of rationality is articulated: reliance on tested convictions in familiar and settled circumstances, on one hand, and attentive and deliberate consideration of the available choices in novel and unsettled circumstances, on the other.

In this discussion we use the American National Election Studies (ANES) for the five presidential elections from 1980 to 1996. This group of data sets contains the measures that we have previously used (Marcus, Neuman, and MacKuen 2000) and hence allows for comparable analyses.[7]

IDEOLOGY AS A POLITICAL DISPOSITION

For much of the twentieth century Americans used the liberal-conservative ideological continuum to talk about the character of politics and policy. Despite the prevalence of ideological terminology in politics, however, it is clear that the terms have no precise meaning for many citizens and that specific understandings of ideology vary widely. Nevertheless, the general meaning of the terms *liberal* and *conservative* is largely consensual at any given time, particularly among politicians and elite commentators who have no trouble sorting out the "liberal" and "conservative" actors and policy options. The extent to which the electorate, on the other hand, uses ideology to structure political thinking has long been a matter of scientific interest. Clearly, there is a real difference between the intellectual frameworks of political elites and ordinary people, with the latter using ideological terms idiosyncratically and indifferently (Converse 1964, 1975).

During the past quarter-century, more and more Americans have started to use ideology to organize their political world. As a quick measure of ideological literacy consider the ability of citizens to (1) choose to identify themselves as liberal or conservative, (2) understand that political parties and candidates can be associated with one side or the other, and (3) correctly describe the Democratic Party or the Democratic candidate as more liberal than the Republican counterpart. This is a relatively easy task (Jacoby 1995) because it implies nothing about the citizens' conceptualization of liberalism and conservatism or their willingness to translate their own identification into a judgment about the parties or candidates. Nevertheless, it is a reasonable standard of a functional "ideological literacy" in that it reveals citizens' ability to get the terms straight. This is a major concern of ours because our view of predispositions is

7. In the 2000 ANES the emotion measures were slightly modified (a change we approve of). In order to ensure that the data analyses are not contingent on using different measures, we restrict our analyses to the data from 1980 through 1996.

FIGURE 6.1: THE GROWTH OF IDEOLOGICAL LITERACY OVER TIME

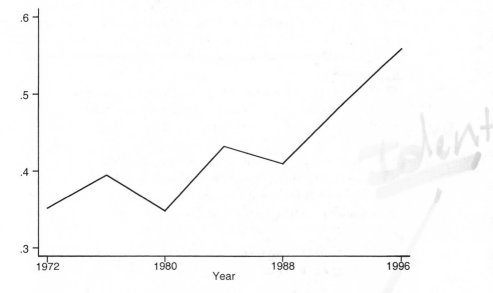

that they are functional, that is to say, that they exist to provide a reliable guide to action. Hence, that people may label themselves "liberal" or "conservative" does not establish that they can and do competently use these terms of reference in making political choices.

Figure 6.1 shows that ideological literacy has grown steadily. It plots the percentage of literates as identified by the ANES from 1972 through 1996—the portion of the public that chooses an ideological identification (including "moderate") and can correctly identify the Democrats as more liberal than the Republicans.[8] Only 35 percent of the public could do so in 1972, an election year in which Richard Nixon painted George McGovern as a liberal, But by the 1980s this portion increased to more than 40 percent, and by the end of the century, it reached 57 percent. By this measure, the public is catching up with the terms of elite political discussion. This is important because the ideologically literate public does use its ideological disposition as a guide for voting. During this period,

8. For this measure we use the standard seven-point scale prompts where the respondent is asked to choose a position from "Extremely Conservative" to "Moderate" to "Extremely Liberal" and then asked the positions of the two parties and their presidential candidates. Someone is ranked as literate if he or she chooses some position and gets the parties and presidential candidates straight. Below, when we use the full range of the ANES data (including the off-year election studies), we score as literate those who merely get the parties correct (in the off-year studies there are no presidential candidates).

ideological identification worked nearly as well as party identification as a predictor for how citizens will vote for candidates for the presidency and for the Senate (MacKuen, Erikson, and Stimson 1988)—a relation that appears to be relatively constant. The rise in literacy supports the conclusion that the electorate as a whole has voted increasingly along ideological lines.

Given the importance of ideology as a political disposition, we want to understand how the systems of affective intelligence modulate ideology's operation. In the past forty years, the party system has evolved to produce ideologically consistent partisan alternatives across the country so that, much of the time, the Democratic candidate will consistently offer a more liberal alternative than the Republican. Understanding the similarities and differences between the two dispositions (party and ideology) and their reliance on affective intelligence will push our understanding further.

AFFECTIVE INTELLIGENCE AND THE MODULATION OF POLITICAL DISPOSITIONS: IDEOLOGY

The ability of anxiety to modulate partisan dispositions has already been shown to be substantial and consistent with the predictions of the theory of affective intelligence (Marcus, Neuman, and MacKuen 2000). We examine the theory's effect on ideological dispositions as opposed to partisan dispositions. In the analyses that follow, we use the same analytic approach that we previously used to assess reliance on partisan identification as the habituated basis for political choices, but we add reliance on ideological convictions as another habituated predisposition to see whether it functions in much the same fashion.[9] So in table 6.2

---

9. The candidate likes and dislikes are the volunteered comments about the candidates, summed up for directional content. For the candidate policy proximity we use the seven-point issue scales set out by the ANES staff in each election from 1972 to 1996, relying on the investigators' judgment to get the right items. For each issue we calculate the simple distance from the individual's preferred policy choice and the individual's *subjective* perception of the candidate's position on the scale. Then we subtract the candidates' position from the respondent's placement and sum up straightforwardly across the different issues of the day. All variables are rescaled to a unit interval—bounded by the range of the variable's possible responses—to make the coefficients roughly comparable. We use linear regressions to make substantive interpretations relatively easy. Of course, the dichotomous nature of the dependent variable makes this a tradeoff between statistical probity and substantive feel. Anxiety is measured by the repeated ANES questions about whether the candidate had done anything to make the respondent feel angry or afraid. Although these items were not explicitly designed for the current theoretical test, they do well enough.

TABLE 6.2: Affective intelligence modulation of disposition's impact on vote choice, 1980–96, ideologically literate voters

	Partisanship		Ideology	
	Complacent about your party's candidate	Anxious about your party's candidate	Complacent about candidate with same ideology	Anxious about candidate with same ideology
Partisanship	.62	.39	—	—
	(.02)	(.03)		
Ideology	—	—	.80	.35
			(.04)	(.05)
Policy comparison	.19	.35	.21	.42
	(.03)	(.04)	(.03)	(.05)
Candidate qualities	.31	.46	.31	.47
	(.02)	(.03)	(.02)	(.03)
Constant	.18	.28	.10	.33
	(.01)	(.02)	(.02)	(.03)
N=	1995	1013	1610	808
Adjusted R^2	.80	.64	.79	.64
RMSE	.22	.30	.22	.30

we include results for partisanship for comparative purposes. We might normally expect self-identified liberals to vote for the Democratic candidate and conservatives to vote for the Republican. And, given the ideological literacy of our target group, we can be sure that they understand the relative attractiveness of the two parties' candidates. So there is no surprise when the third column of table 6.2 shows that ideology dominates the choice of complacent voters—voters who feel no uneasiness about "their" candidate. On the other hand, when engaged by their emotional alert mechanisms, people do change their behavior. As was the case with partisanship, we see that the reliance on disposition diminishes: compare

---

The scores are the averages of the two items normed to the unit interval. The astute reader will note that Feldman, Huddy, and Cassese (Chapter 9 this volume) show, as have others (Ax 1953; Lerner and Keltner 2001), that anger and fear are quite different (both as to underlying neurological foundations and as to impacts on cognition and behavior). The distinction between anger and fear is also a vital component of the theory of affective intelligence (Marcus 2002). Yet the measures of anger in the NES series function as measures of anxiety because for the most part presidential candidates do not stimulate anger. For a fuller discussion of this point, see Marcus et al. (forthcoming).

FIGURE 6.2: AFFECTIVE INTELLIGENCE MODULATION OF VOTING MODEL: ANXIETY ABOUT
IDEOLOGICALLY COMPATIBLE CANDIDATE

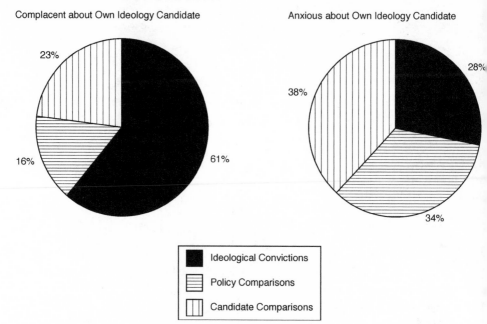

Complacent about Own Ideology Candidate   Anxious about Own Ideology Candidate

Ideological Convictions

Policy Comparisons

Candidate Comparisons

Source: American National Election Surveys, 1980–96.

0.80 with 0.35. And, similarly, when reliance on disposition declines the
importance of contemporary factors such as candidate quality and policy
positions increases in about the same sort of way.[10]

We can see this graphically in figure 6.2. Complacent voters, defined
as those who have no anxiety about the candidate leading their party, rely
on their dispositions, be they partisan or ideological. But when emotionally stimulated to reasoned consideration, that is to say, highly anxious
about their party's candidate, citizens reduce their reliance on disposition
and increase their weighing of contemporary information.[11]

10. Table 6.2 presents two models. One focuses on partisanship, replicating the analyses
we have previously presented (Marcus, Neuman, and MacKuen 2000). The second focuses
on ideology as the conviction of interest. Because these two convictions are highly interrelated, we present them separately. In these models, the voters' assessments of the candidates'
quality and policy positions reflect idiosyncratic interpretations due to the voter and the
candidates and not to a standardized partisan or ideological perception. The multivariate
analyses control for the biasing effects of the dispositions on the candidate assessments.

11. To be a bit more precise, we use the same estimation method as we used previously
(Marcus 2000). A common regression model is defined that includes interaction terms

The affective intelligence story applies to ideology just as it does to partisan convictions. Without disturbance, people rely on their heuristics and efficiently deal with the information that lies out in the political world, largely by casually seeing that which confirms their established views. When things seem awry, however, people's emotions signal a need for reconsideration of the choices before them, and they begin to rely more heavily on specific and contemporary information.

THE ROLE OF PARTISAN DEFECTION
IN PRESIDENTIAL ELECTIONS

If partisans shift from robust reliance on their partisan and ideological convictions to an attentive and rational reconsideration of the proposals and candidates offered by the major parties, then it is likely that the steadfastness of partisans may be overrated. One way we might capture the behavioral consequences of the loosening of partisan and ideological predispositions by anxiety is by examining the number of people who vote for a candidate of opposite partisan and ideological ties. This "defection" is, in fact, the ultimate sign of the abandonment of partisan and ideological instincts. Normally, we expect party and ideology to act as powerful cues in the voting booth, for even citizens identifying themselves as partisan "leaners" tend to rely heavily on partisan cues when they vote (Keith et al. 1997). We examine how anxiety contributes to these partisan defections during elections.

First, we review the level of defection by party and by year. We use the ANES data for these analyses as well. As a result, our data actually measure inclination to defect, because we use the vote intention variable to classify people as party loyalists voting for their own candidate or not (defecting). Because the actual vote is not available, we may overestimate the actual level of defection because late movement may return one to the party with which one is identified. We are not concerned with the accuracy of the sample statistic as an estimate of the population parameter but with the dynamics involved. This provides preliminary evidence of the variability of the phenomenon under consideration.

Figure 6.3 displays the percentage of partisans, Democratic and Republican, who are inclined to defect for each of the presidential campaigns

---

(e.g., anxiety × partisanship). We can then estimate what would happen if people are very anxious by setting the value for anxiety at 1 (we norm all variables to a common 0–1 range). And, as in this case, we see that the result is to sharply reduce the impact of partisanship (from .62 to .39). For the complacent, we set anxiety to 0.

FIGURE 6.3: DEFECTIONS BY PARTISANSHIP AND BY YEAR, 1980-96

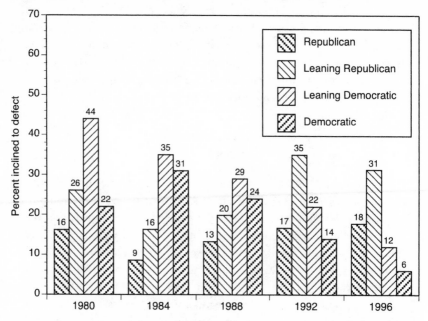

Source: American National Election Surveys, 1980–96.

from 1980 through 1996. The proportion of defectors is hardly minuscule. The overall pattern of probably disloyal voting among partisans does not support the popular view that presidential elections are primarily determined by swing voters.

Certain well-known verities are displayed in these data. Weak partisans are inclined to defect more than committed partisans, though it is interesting to note that this difference is often not very great (see, for example, 1980, 1984, and 1988 for Republicans and all but 1980 for Democrats). And Democrats, in general, are less loyal than are Republicans (as seen in 1980, 1984, 1988, but not in 1992 and 1996). Still there is considerable variability among Republicans. Second, partisan defection seems remarkably volatile. In these five elections, among Republicans, excluding the leaners, the figures range from 18 percent to 9 percent, a ratio of 2:1. Among Democrats, again excluding leaners, the ratio of defection ranges from a high of 31 percent to a low of 6 percent, a ratio of 5:1. It is apparent that partisans have a choice beyond whether to show up or stay home. Many partisans vote for the candidate of the other party. Sometimes, on balance, defection advantages the Republican. In 1984, 31 percent of Democrats were inclined to defect whereas only 9 percent of Republicans were similarly inclined, a net advantage of 22 percent for the Republican Party. Sometimes the net advantage goes to the Democrat. In 1996, 18 percent of Republicans were inclined to defect whereas only 6 percent of Democrats were similarly inclined, a net advantage of 12 percent for the Democratic Party. Given that partisans, including the leaners, constitute about 89 percent of the electorate (only about 11 percent are true independents), these defection rates are of considerable importance in determining which party captures the White House. Consider that in the closest of these elections, 1992, when defections were most evenly matched, Bill Clinton's campaign had a net advantage of approximately 3 percent, and though Clinton drew almost twice as much support from the true independent vote than did George H. W. Bush, the larger partisan vote meant that Republicans contributed more support to Clinton than did the swing voters.[12] So it is clear that defection occurs in all elections, though the level of defection varies from election to election.

The results of the 2004 presidential elections also support that conclusion. According to exit polls, Democrat John Kerry won the independent vote 49 percent to 48 percent, but he suffered greater defections (11 percent of Democrats reported voting for George W. Bush) than did Bush (6 percent of Republicans reported voting for Kerry).[13] Had Kerry held the defection rate of Democrats to a level equal to that of the Republicans, he would have won the race. Defection also accounts for the results in the important battleground states. Ohio and Florida also showed greater defection among Democrats than among Republicans (and again, if they have been equal, Kerry would have won both states). New Hampshire, the one state that Kerry captured that in 2000 had voted, narrowly, for Bush, the defection advantage went to Kerry (95 percent loyal, 5 percent defection, and for Bush, 91 percent loyal, 9 percent defection). The overall pattern of disloyal voting among partisans does not support the popular view that presidential elections are primarily determined by independent, swing, voters.

We have shown that when citizens become anxious they are more likely to abandon partisanship and ideology as ironclad guides to political

---

12. In this exercise we are assuming equal propensity to vote, a presumption that undoubtedly overestimates the impact of the independent vote. On the other hand, we have excluded the undecided from these calculations, which is likely to understate the role of independents since they have a higher proportion of undecided among them than does the partisan group. Still, all in all, it remains that partisan defection contributes the larger proportion of the winning margin.

13. http://www.cnn.com/ELECTION/2004/pages/results/states/US/P/00/epolls.0.html.

behavior. This implies a fairly simple mechanism by which affective assessments are structured as simple valence judgments. That is, anxiety has a simple effect on defection whereby as anxiety increases, so does the probability of defection. Such a view of emotional mechanisms is both popular (Osgood, Suci, and Tannenbaum 1957; Schwarz and Clore 2003) and temptingly parsimonious. Emotional cues enable us to quickly determine whether we like (and hence should approach) or dislike (and avoid) something. In politics, it is equally common sense to expect that people vote for those they like and against those they dislike (Kelley 1983).

But reality is probably more complicated. According to the theory of affective intelligence, as in many structural theories of emotion (Cacioppo and Berntson 1994; Cacioppo, Gardner, and Berntson 1997; Plutchik and Conte 1997; Tellegen, Watson, and Clark 1999a; Tellegen, Watson, and Clark 1999b), "positive" and "negative" affect are neither anchors of a single bipolar dimension nor uniformly devoted to approach and avoidance. We deal with this complication in two ways. First, in order to ensure that we can discriminate between the older assertion that a simple liking or disliking of candidates is sufficient to explain partisans inclination to defect, we can control for both enthusiasm for one's own partisan candidate and enthusiasm for the candidate of the other party in a model of electoral defection. Second, we might also expect anxiety to act on nonpartisan criteria for defection. That is, we might expect voters to defect should they observe that their own candidate has poor qualities or that the opposition is closer in term of issue distance. But these effects should be more potent in the presence of anxiety, because the engagement of anxiety makes these nonpartisan cues more salient.

Since our previous work has shown that incumbents are the primary emotional focus of the electorate, we concentrate on partisans who have an incumbent in the race (Marcus, Neuman, and MacKuen 2000).[14] The standard account holds that partisan affiliation anchors voters because their emotional attachment to party also provides the foundation for their voting choices (Miller and Shanks 1996). Incumbency adds a further challenge to the affective intelligence theory's alternative account. Voters, partisans no less than the general electorate, have a vested reliance on established political leadership that serves to provide the certainty and regularity that cannot be obtained by self-reliance. Thus, Republicans in 1984, 1988, and 1992 and Democrats in 1980 and 1996 should have been

14. Challengers have, in general, had limited success in an generating emotional response to their candidacy, whether enthusiasm or anxiety, certainly far less than incumbents (Marcus, Neuman, and MacKuen 2000).

doubly resistant to any provocation to defect because they were bolstered by partisanship and the power of incumbency. Moreover, the conventional account holds that partisanship and incumbency are each anchored in symbolic and hence emotional attachments and needs (Edelman 1964; Elder and Cobb 1983; Sears 2000). The theory of affective intelligence holds that anxiety shears these attachments and generates the conditions for rational reconsideration of the vote choice that in turn opens up the prospect of partisan defection.

We test this model of defection below. In brief, we make defection (with whether the voter is loyal, intends to vote for own party's candidate, or intends not to as the dependent variable) a function of anxiety about one's party's candidate, issues comparison (high coded as closer to the other party's position than to that of the subject's party's candidate), candidate qualities (coded as are issues), and interaction terms for anxiety with issues and with candidate qualities, as well as enthusiasm for each of the two candidates.[15]

In table 6.3, column 1 presents the results for Republican partisans when they held the White House and had an incumbent seeking reelection. The results are consistent with general conventional expectations: enthusiasm for Republican candidates, partisan intensity, education, and campaign involvement each bolstered loyalty. On the other hand, issue positions, enthusiasm for the Democratic candidate, and a comparison of candidate qualities favorable to the Republican led to defection. Anxiety about the Republican candidate did not have much of an impact on defection, and to the extent it did, the more anxious were *less* inclined to defect.[16] The interaction of anxiety with issue positions was highly significant, however, and shows, as we have previously argued, that anxiety changes the mode by which voters determine whom to support. In this case (as was also the general case with Democratic partisans), anxiety by itself did not so much motivate defection as it opened up a critical examination of the particulars of that specific election with a focus on a rational comparison of the issues, with the results of that assessment then yielding a deliberate choice. And when that comparison favored the other party, partisans defected.

We show the interaction between comparative issue distances and anxiety by plotting the probability of defection against issue distances

15. We also add education, partisan intensity, political involvement, and dummies for election year (expecting, as results confirm, that more devoted partisans and the politically involved are less likely to vote across party lines).

16. The coefficient is marginally significant (p=.06).

TABLE 6.3: Defection when incumbent is of same party, 1980–96

	Defection by partisan Republicans in 1984, 1988, 1992 (n = 1899)	Defection by partisan Democrats in 1980 (n = 679)	Defection by partisan Democrats in 1996 (n = 725)
Constant	−4.89	2.44[ns]	−1.37[ns]
	(2.58)	(1.97)	(2.77)
Enthusiasm for one's own	−1.93	−2.94	−2.44
party's candidate	(.21)	(.33)	(.58)
Enthusiasm for other party's	2.07	1.89	2.58
candidate	(.23)	(.36)	(.60)
Anxiety about one's own	−4.49*	.88[ns]	22.34
party's candidate	(2.58)	(3.29)	(7.05)
Issue distances	4.47	4.79[ns]	−1.61[ns]
	(2.04)	(3.81)	(5.52)
Candidate qualities	5.80	1.35[ns]	6.68[ns]
	(1.67)	(2.71)	(2.71)
Anxiety by issues interaction	12.87	−2.71[ns]	41.15
	(5.22)	(6.50)	(13.87)
Anxiety by candidate	−0.63[ns]	16.56*	1.18[ns]
qualities interaction	(3.49)	(5.75)	(7.29)
Partisan intensity	−1.33	−1.79	−0.95[ns]
	(.46)	(.40)	(.57)
Education	−0.63	1.30	−1.34[ns]
	(.26)	(.42)	(.72)
Campaign involvement	−0.64	−.71[ns]	−1.13[ns]
	(.29)	(.45)	(.72)
Pseudo R^2	.34	.47	.46
% correctly classified	89%	87.7%	94.9%
Log likelihood	−522.04	−208.94	−99.58
χ^2 likelihood ratio	526.80	365.44	169.92

Source: American National Election Surveys, 1980–96.

[ns] Not statistically discernible from zero. * p = .06. All others statistically significant.

FIGURE 6.4: PROBABILITY OF DEFECTION AMONG REPUBLICAN PARTISANS
AS A FUNCTION OF THE INTERACTION BETWEEN ANXIETY AND REPUBLICAN
ISSUE POSITIONS

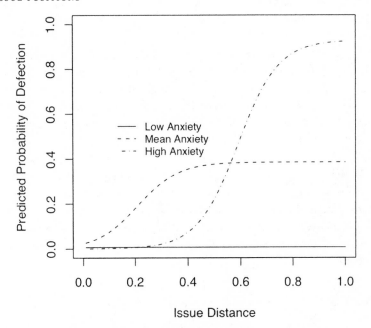

Issue Distance

Source: American National Election Surveys, 1984, 1988, 1992.

across three levels of anxiety, holding the other variables constant at their means. Figure 6.4 shows how the probability of defection among Republican partisans as anxiety moves from its lowest levels, when Republican partisans are feeling complacent, to its highest, when they are most anxious. As figure 6.3 shows, when an issue comparison favors the Democrats there is little prospect of defection if anxiety is at a minimum, but as anxiety increases in the same circumstances, the probability of defection moves to well over 90 percent. Partisans are not nearly the intractably loyal group that conventional wisdom portrays them to be.

Column 2 in table 6.3 shows that a focus on issues is not always the primary desiderata of rational, that is, anxious, voters. In 1980, when President Jimmy Carter was seeking reelection in the midst of the Iran hostage crisis, double-digit inflation, and unemployment, the key interaction term is not about the issue differences between Carter and his opponent, Ronald Reagan. Rather, the interaction of anxiety and candidate qualities is instead the key force behind defections. This suggests that Reagan attracted Democratic partisans, the so-called Reagan Democrats, not by appealing to a more conservative array of issues but rather by suggesting he had more of the "right stuff" to be president. Anxiety was harnessed to Jimmy Carter's suitability for a second term, which led to a comparison of Carter's qualities to those of Reagan, and Democrats who found Carter wanting defected.[17]

Column 3 of table 6.3 shows the results for 1996, when President Bill Clinton was challenged by Republican Robert Dole. The results in this case are quite similar to those for Republican partisans. Anxiety initiates an explicit rational comparison of the parties' issue positions, with loyalty and defection the possible outcomes (and in 1980 and 1996 low levels of anxiety were sufficient, because of their interactive effects with candidate qualities and comparisons of the issues, respectively, to guarantee defection). So again we witness how the surveillance system of affect detaches partisans from efficient and automatic reliance on the dispositions system of affect (in this case, the expression of standard partisan and ideological positions). And when the surveillance system is active, what follows is a close reappraisal that has clear behavioral consequences in the voting booth.

THE MACRO CONSEQUENCES OF ANXIETY

The shifting of the American electorate from more liberal to more conservative predilections and back again is well known (Burnham 1970; Stimson 1991). The role of economics, in the form of business cycles, helps account for such sinuosity (Alesina, Londregan, and Rosenthal 1983). In addition, political movements, whether liberal or conservative, seem to have a natural life span, finding enthusiasm when young and exhaustion when older. If they are long enough, such cycles might reflect the passage of age cohorts whose political convictions are defined by the characteristics of their times (the Great Depression, World War II, Vietnam, or, most recently, 9/11).

The theory of affective intelligence substantially revises the conventional wisdom about the periodicity of elections. That a downturn in the economy would cause anxiety and hence diminish support for an administration at election time is hardly a novel prediction, nor a prediction that could discriminate between this and any other theory. Administrations do more than simply manage the economy (with the limited tools available). Administrations also have policy goals that they seek to advance by way of creating laws. But as they do so, they change the envi-

---

17. As before with Republican partisans, anxiety had no direct impact on the odds of defection. Anxiety functioned indirectly, through its interaction with candidate qualities.

ronment. New laws compel new behavior (either by applying sanctions to discourage current behaviors or by offering inducements to engage in new behaviors).

The theory of affective intelligence advances a counterintuitive claim: that a regime's supporters should become increasingly anxious as the administration becomes increasingly successful and that this dynamic should be more robust than the comparable increase in anxiety among the administration's detractors. We derive this prediction by noting that supporters of an administration are wedded to a world they already find familiar and congenial by virtue of the many predilections that offer reassuring guides to their everyday life. Having an administration in power that shares their commitments defends those predilections. Having an administration dynamically and effectively change the world will, we predict, make the regime's supporters increasingly nervous as the administration achieves its policy goals.

In order to test the claim of affective intelligence theory, we need to develop a model that includes the features that would account for the observed periodicity in American politics. Primary among the characteristics of governments is their management of public affairs—and it is surely in the political interests of presidents to be seen as competent rather than incompetent managers. In the contemporary United States, the most common standard of government competence (whether it makes sense or not) is management of the economy. Presidents who preside over economic booms are presumed to have done well, and those who encounter harsh times on their watch will find themselves having to defend their record. As an indicator of a sitting president's economic fortunes, we use the University of Michigan's Index of Consumer Sentiment, a set of ongoing surveys that assess the public's views of the contemporary economy.[18] Unremarkably, the theory of affective intelligence predicts that anxiety should rise and that the surveillance system should become active when the economy plummets. And, unremarkably, this prediction is sustained. When we model individual-level anxiety as a function of national economic conditions, we see a strong negative relation: the better the

18. The Index of Consumer Sentiment combines measures tapping retrospective and prospective assessments of family finances and "business conditions." These stem from national surveys, now conducted on a monthly basis, taken from 1952 through the present. We use the year's average sentiment (that is, for January to December of the election year) as a proxy for contemporary economic conditions. In this sense we use information about both the recent past and the immediate future that might go into popular perceptions of the incumbent's economic management. We have rescaled the measure to the unit interval to make it roughly comparable to our other measures.

economy, the lower the anxiety, and the worse the economy, the greater the anxiety. The numbers are large and statistically solid. Performance matters for affective intelligence.

Another feature is policy. We know that many citizens are only dimly aware of national policymaking and would be surprised to see that they react to legislative victories and defeats. To be sure, few citizens can enunciate anything specific about what the Congress and the president have done during the past year. And yet, from a normative point of view, we should at least hope that they are able to react to surges of liberal or conservative changes in national policy. It is surely the case that citizens do react in terms of their preferences for policy change. Evidence from the past half-century shows that when the national government passes liberal legislation, the public's demand for liberal policies drops discernibly, and when the government passes conservative policies the public begins to demand more activism (Erikson, MacKuen, and Stimson 2002). It this periodicity that we seek to illuminate.

The question is whether people's affective intelligence operates to capture changes in national policymaking. By all accounts, we should expect that the passage of liberal legislation will lead to an increase in anxiety about liberal presidents and that the passage of a conservative program will lead to worries about conservative presidents. Success by presidents in pushing their policy agendas will typically exhaust their symbolic reservoir because that very success will impel changes that, even if welcome, generate a counterreaction based on the public feeling that things have gone far enough. We test this proposition by modeling incumbent anxiety as a function of the number of major (liberal-conservative) laws that were passed by Congress and signed into law by the president during the year preceding the election campaign.[19] We expect a negative relation, and this expectation, too, is sustained.

Putting the pieces together in the first column of table 6.4, we observe an elementary model of incumbent anxiety written as a function of our two macro-level political conditions: economic performance and partisan policymaking. Taken together, each is statistically and powerfully

19. We use a version of David Mayhew's (1991) major laws. These include pieces of legislation thought at the time to be significant (and described as so in the year-end reviews of the *New York Times* and the *Washington Post*). The series has been updated by Jay Greene using the same methodology. We have coded the particular laws as liberal or conservative, double-counting landmark legislation such as the 1996 welfare bill (Erikson, MacKuen, and Stimson 2002).

TABLE 6.4: Incumbent- and challenger-elicited anxiety as a function of macro-level politics and individual-level political dispositions and evaluations, 1980–96, ideologically literate voters

Issues	All voters		Incumbent's supporters		Challenger's supporters	
	Incumbent-elicited anxiety	Challenger-elicited anxiety	Incumbent-elicited anxiety	Challenger-elicited anxiety	Incumbent-elicited anxiety	Challenger-elicited anxiety
Index of consumer	−.22	−.05[ns]	−.32	−.16[ns]	−.12[ns]	−.02[ns]
sentiment	(.05)	(.05)	(.07)	(.08)	(.08)	(.06)
Major laws passed	.33	.03[ns]	.38	.02[ns]	.24	.01[ns]
(prior year)	(.04)	(.04)	(.05)	(.06)	(.06)	(.05)
Partisanship	−.31	.22	−.24	.14	−.12	.10
	(.02)	(.02)	(.05)	(.06)	(.06)	(.05)
Ideology	−.21	.27	−.12	.36	−.31	.14
	(.03)	(.03)	(.04)	(.05)	(.04)	(.04)
Policy comparison	−.29	.20	−.12	.26	−.46	.15
	(.03)	(.03)	(.04)	(.05)	(.05)	(.04)
Constant	.94	.13	.89	.23	.83	.15
	(.04)	(.04)	(.07)	(.05)	(.07)	(.05)
N	4548	4546	2235	2234	2052	2050
Adjusted R^2	.27	.18	.09	.06	.12	.02
RMSE	.34	.35	.32	.39	.36	.29

[ns] Not statistically discernible from zero.

related to people's feeling complacent or uneasy about the incumbent. We can use these results to model the substantive consequences of the public's assessment of the economy and of an administration's translating its agenda into law. The difference between the best and worst years in consumer sentiment in our sample is enough to move anxiety downward by a little more than a quarter of its effective range. More striking, the difference in the most and least successful presidential policy years yields movement of about one-half of the range. Good times lead to a reduction in anxiety; success in a legislative agenda leads to an increase in anxiety. The picture is different for challengers. The second column of the table shows an identical model, positing feelings about the challenger to be a function of the political environment. It is fairly clear they are not. The coefficients for both of the macro political measures are decidedly small, and the performance measure is statistically insignificant. The surveillance mechanism's emotional cues about incumbents do reflect genuine shifts in the political world, but the cues given about the challengers do not. And, of course, this is exactly what we would expect from affective intelligence: the surveillance emotions should reflect some reasonable approximation of reality and not represent a mere extrapolation from standing dispositions.[20]

Of greater interest is that, by dividing voters into supporters and opponents of the candidates, we can test whether the theory of affective intelligence works as a signaling device for supporters to alert them to the potent consequences of the success of the administration. It is conventional to presume that these factors work not for supporters but only for those in opposition, inasmuch as supporters should encourage the success of an administration in enshrining agreed-on policies in law. In this case, however, dividing voters into supporters of the incumbent administration and those opposed to it shows that anxiety is increased more among the former than among the latter. The signal that something is changing works for opponents and for supporters. This is absolutely critical because it is the supporters, after all, who will use the affective surveillance system to interrupt their routine reliance on partisan and ideological dispositions. And, as we have seen, when these dispositions are interrupted, defections may follow.

CONCLUSION

It is quite common to describe people as manifesting uniform characteristics: people are liberal or conservative, engaged partisans or inattentive independents. The established theories that we have discussed, the rational choice and the psychological, are exemplars of this approach.[21] A core assertion of the theory of affective intelligence is the fundamental imperative of knowing at the earliest moment the character of the political geography in which one finds oneself. Preconscious appraisals identify our location as either in the realm of the familiar, where reliance on existing habits is efficient and productive, or the realm of the unexpected

20. For the macro political causal forces, it is anxiety about only the incumbent that carries a political signal.

21. Hence, when repeated studies show that people depart from rationality, rational choice theorists retreat to some lesser version, such as "bounded rationality," rather than consider the alternative that we advance: sometimes and in some circumstances people are quite rational whereas in perhaps most other circumstances they are not, and for good reason (Marcus 2002).

and unfamiliar, where a different mode of decision making if required. Our uniform capabilities include both the capacity to rely on heuristics and the capacity to engage in explicit deliberation. The theory of affective intelligence provides an account of why we have both capabilities and when each is likely to be manifested.

The theory offers important insight into the dynamic character of political dispositions. It holds that people use heuristics such as partisan and ideological convictions when they are most likely to achieve conservation of limited cognitive resources. Reliance on heuristics enables one to secure rational, that is, near optimal results.[22] Thus we expect that partisan loyalists and the ideologically driven are likely to most often rely on their dispositions to formulate their political judgments. But they are also likely to set aside those firmly held convictions and apply those limited cognitive resources in the service of deliberate judgment when appropriate to do so. As a result, the micro picture of intransigence in the face of contentious information is not a universal truth.

Furthermore, the macro expectation that elections turn on how the least informed of likely voters decide how to vote is also a portrait that misses a crucial dynamic, namely, that the defection of partisans has far greater weight in determining who wins and who loses in American elections. The record of presidential elections in the past quarter-century amply shows that defection is the principal explanation for electoral outcomes and that defection arises from two sequential steps. First, the campaign that can induce anxiety in its opponent's partisan and ideological base creates an opening that can be used to encourage defection. But in order for defection to occur, that campaign must have an issue or a candidate that will attract voters who make a thoughtful comparison because of their anxiety.

An older tradition, the cognitive appraisal theory of emotion, holds that feelings are informed by self-conscious considerations (Ortony, Clore, and Collins 1988; Roseman, Antoniou, and Jose 1996). As discussed by Crigler, Just and Belt (chapter 10 in this volume), the way in which people understand their feelings may have impacts above and beyond those that are impelled by the multiple preconscious systems that are the focus

---

22. By *optimal* we do not mean that some newly implemented analysis would not yield some marginal improvement over that resulting from reliance on a pertinent heuristic. Rather, we mean that reliance on the heuristic provides a highly certain and, if conditions are as they have been, favorable result. Furthermore, embedded with the heuristic is the learned capacity for implementing said decision (something not generally available to support a newly derived solution).

of the theory of affective intelligence.[23] But to properly explore the role of preconscious affective appraisals and post-awareness affective intro-spection requires a research design that can identify and specify each distinct array of influences. Perhaps it is time to abandon the largely spatial metaphor that shapes our understanding of reason and passion, cognition and affect, a metaphor that construes these two states as concurrent but distinct and often antagonistic (their "separateness" often articulated in such familiar tropes as heart and mind). The spatial metaphor misleads by distracting us from the temporal sequencing tasks that are the core responsibilities of preconscious appraisal systems, responsibilities that control and are followed by conscious awareness and thereafter by intro-spection and refection (Libet 2004; Marcus 2002). By abandoning this metaphor we would gain a fuller and more incisive understanding of the dynamic capabilities that people have to adapt to the different demands and challenges that democratic politics presents.

Cassino and Lodge (Chapter 5 this volume) illustrate another point of contention. It has long been held that emotions provide an assessment that resolves the critical evaluative issue of approach to situations, objects, or people that we like or desire as against avoidance of situations, objects, or people that we dislike and avoid (Tooby and Cosmides 1990). This notion of emotion as valence has the advantage of parsimony. It makes the further presumption that emotion "tags" items in declarative memory (Fiske 1981; Fiske and Pavelchak 1986). We hold that this view, and the research it has spawned, miss essential and powerful roles for emotion. The first is that emotion is rarely experienced as a simple valence, like-dislike (Marcus 2000). The second is that, though the role of emotion is associative memory is ignored by this conception, what we do, as contrasted with what we think, is largely driven by associative memory, not declarative (or semantic) memory (especially when people choose automatic reliance on extant heuristics). Third, as a consequence, by ignoring the role of anxiety, the dynamic shifting from one decision strategy to the other (and back) is largely missed by the theory of emotion as valence?[24] Fourth, Brader and Valentino (chapter 8 in

---

23. And in this as well, neuroscience can be useful in applying its methodological apparatus to understanding the discrete emotions that result from conscious consideration (Takahashi et al. 2004).

24. Furthermore, though Cassino and Lodge couch their findings as contradicting the normative implications of the theory of affective intelligence, their findings are quite consistent with the theory of affective intelligence. One of the major tasks of affective appraisals is to give the earliest assessment of the immediate context, classifying the environment as familiar and rewarding, familiar and punishing, or unfamiliar and uncertain. That an

this volume) find that anger is driven by prejudice, a relationship that is fully consistent with the theory of affective intelligence (Marcus 2002). Anger, as we have labeled this class of emotion aversion, is driven by confrontation with familiar punishing stimuli and by the commitment of psychic and physical resources to learned defensive and aggressive behavioral routines.

Finally, though not likely to be the sole explanation, the theory of affective intelligence provides another counterintuitive insight. The cyclical character of American elections may have its roots not only in the way the "moderate middle" moves but also in the way that partisan supporters of a successful administration respond to its success. That partisan opponents become more determined to oppose successful administrations is hardly novel (on that score the theory of affective intelligence has no dispute with conventional wisdom). But that partisan supporters become more anxious than the administration's opponents, with attendant political consequences, is hardly conventional wisdom. As such the theory of affective intelligence provides a framework that has macro applications (see chapters 12 and 13 in this volume). Although the theory provides a reason to expect robust and comprehensive roles for preconscious affective appraisal systems, other paths are also worth exploring.

By incorporating elements of the rational choice and the psychological theories and by and specifying the conditions when each is likely to be applicable, we resolve the long-lived conflict between an attractive normative macro theory—rational choice—and a seemingly more accurate but normatively disappointing micro theory: psychological (or normal vote) theory. The theory of affective intelligence offers empirical promise for new lines of inquiry that can reveal hitherto unknown dynamics of political behavior and judgment. It also provides a micro-account of a political psychology that sustains a normative portrait of democracy that is more encouraging than has previously been thought plausible.

---

initial emotional appraisal, having identified which of these contexts we are in, would thereafter impact subsequent information is precisely what the theory of affective intelligence says ought to happen.

CHAPTER SEVEN

Affective Intelligence and Voting: Information Processing and Learning in a Campaign

DAVID P. REDLAWSK, ANDREW J. W. CIVETTINI, AND RICHARD R. LAU

After devoting many years to voting behavior studies focused on cognition, recent research has turned toward the important role that emotions play in political decision making. No longer can we subscribe to the idea that passion is antithetical to reason; important research in neuroscience has suggested that there can be no reason (or effective decision making, at least) without emotion (Damasio 1994, 1999; Spezio and Adolphs, chapter 4 in this volume). In this chapter we seek to demonstrate how initial feeling toward a political candidate influences the evaluation of new information and how emotional reactions to that new information influence learning. Building on Marcus, Neuman, and MacKuen's (2000) affective intelligence thesis, we use dynamic process tracing (Lau and Redlawsk 1992, 1997, 2001a, 2001b, 2006; Redlawsk 2001, 2002, 2004) to present voters with a campaign in which evaluative expectations are often violated and emotional responses to candidates are heightened. An initially preferred candidate becomes suddenly and unexpectedly less attractive, while an initially rejected candidate begins taking positions that are very close to the voter's own. The result should be conflict between the initial evaluation and new information, allowing us to test the

The study reported in this chapter was supported by funding from the Department of Political Science at the University of Iowa and the Center for the Study of Group Processes, Department of Sociology, University of Iowa. Thanks to Lisa Troyer for helping secure funding and providing lab space and thanks to the bevy of research assistants who worked on this project: Jason Humphrey, Kimberly Brisky, Karen Emmerson, Michelle Bagi, Matt Opad, Stephanie Hood, Trisha Soljacich, Francisco Olalde, Laura Patters, Megan Adams, Conor Moran, Garrett Hanken, and Mike Biderman. An earlier version of this chapter was presented at the Annual Meeting of the Midwest Political Science Association, Chicago, IL, April 15–18, 2004.

expectations of affective intelligence at the most basic level of candidate information: an individual piece of information.

Contrary to classical notions of cool, emotionless decision making, affect is the force that organizes and drives how we make sense of new information. But in order to understand this process we must be able to track what happens as voters actually encounter information about candidates, something not possible in existing studies of emotion, which rely primarily on survey research (Marcus and MacKuen 1993; MacKuen and Marcus 1994; Marcus, Neuman, and MacKuen 2000) or experiments that do not include a comprehensive political campaign environment (Wolak et al. 2003). Although Cassino and Lodge (chapter 5 in this volume) come closest to what we have in mind, campaigns are dynamic events, and the emotional reactions they generate occur as the campaign happens. Thus we turn to a methodology that allows us to track the specific items that voters learn about candidates and their emotional responses to those items.

THEORETICAL PERSPECTIVE: AFFECTIVE INTELLIGENCE

Marcus and colleagues focus squarely on emotions rather than cognition in identifying the way in which response to a candidate generates specific behaviors. Following Cacioppo and Gardner (1999), they separate affect into two subsystems: a disposition system and a surveillance system. These two systems are responsible both for how we react to novel situations *and* how we use habitual behaviors. The dispositional system monitors habit, or scripts, and allows us to perform tasks without consciously considering them. When expectations are not challenged by new information, we can safely rely on habitual responses to incoming stimuli. The central emotion of the dispositional system is enthusiasm; when these habitual responses suffice, enthusiasm is generated. From the perspective of affective intelligence, then, even the simplest of habits relies on affective processing. Moreover, the dispositional system operates before conscious awareness (Damasio 1994). "Affective primacy" is central to the theory of affective intelligence.

The surveillance system is activated when something unexpected is encountered, producing anxiety in such novel situations.[1] Anxiety drives conscious attention to a problem, which in turn promotes learning. Thus, when new information is incongruent with habitual response or habitual response produces outcomes that are inconsistent with expectations,

---

1. Marcus and colleagues seem to equate novel situations with being threatened; the new or unexpected appears to be always threatening, at least initially.

conscious awareness occurs. As a result, it should take longer to process information that is incongruent with habitual predispositions. Conscious awareness is reserved, in a sense, for times when expectations are violated; the surveillance system acts as a sort of cipher that prevents the needless waste of mental resources. Therefore, when we are conscious of our emotions they are more likely to be negative (Derryberry 1991; Pratto and John 1991). Because novel information generates conscious awareness, activation of the surveillance system—and thus negative emotion—promotes learning. The key affective component of the surveillance system, anxiety, can, then, be considered a correlate of active learning. This is perhaps the most important substantive claim of affective intelligence. The surveillance system has value from an evolutionary perspective, since heightened anxiety implies a more careful consideration of what to do next. Of course, the context of a presidential election is substantially different from survival, the primary motivation of evolution: threats in the political environment are quite different from those that might put one's life on the line. Even so, Marcus and colleagues show evidence that emotional responses to presidential candidates produce results that look quite similar to those produced by presumably more dangerous stimuli.

The theory of affective intelligence is primarily a theory about the place of emotions in a decision-making process. Yet little time has been spent dealing with what happens once conscious awareness is activated. It may be that individual decision-making processes respond in ways that are disproportionate to the emotional response generated prior to consciousness. Steenburgen's (2001) work on a conservatism bias in Bayesian updating suggests that if the surveillance system generates conscious awareness, information that is incongruent with expectations is likely to carry less weight than do the expectations themselves. This implies that once an evaluation of a candidate has become habitualized, moderate amounts of information contradicting that evaluation may not be enough to alter it. The learning effects that Marcus et al. report may not be the same across all levels of incongruent information. Sometimes voters may learn—if we consider learning to be making "rational" and "accurate" adjustments to existing evaluations—and sometimes they may not.

It may take a large amount of incongruent information to alter evaluations. Given the association of anxiety with threat, considering this process in terms of the level of threat in the environment is useful. In a low-threat environment, where relatively little incongruent information is encountered, the conservatism bias (Steenbergen 2001) might well mediate the effects of anxiety. But in a high-threat environment, where a great deal of new information may be incongruent with prior expectations, the conservatism bias might be overridden as more active consideration of the new information takes hold. It could be that while the surveillance system alerts us to the fact that our expectations and the new information may be in conflict, we still rely on habitual predispositions unless the threat level is sufficiently high. Since learning only occurs in this state of conscious arousal, this also implies that learning may not always lead to different decisions, even when the new information contradicts expectations.[2] And of course, in a very high-threat environment it may be that anxiety becomes debilitating rather than facilitating. After all, the idea of "test anxiety" in popular parlance seems to suggest that too much anxiety lowers performance.

The importance of this point about threat levels should be clear. Although affective intelligence is about emotional responses to individual pieces of information, the broader environment in which that information is situated is critically important (Pantoja and Segura 2003). Yet to date little has been done to assess the effects of different levels of environmental threat.

Marcus and colleagues employ survey data from the American National Election Studies (ANES) to demonstrate the effect of emotional processing on candidate evaluations. Their central finding is that whereas anxiety promotes learning about the candidates, enthusiasm, the key emotion of the dispositional system, does not do the same. Though somewhat persuasive, this finding is based solely on global affective evaluations and overall summaries of learning, whereas affective intelligence theory is about how specific stimuli generate emotional responses and how emotional processes monitor our actions. In order to test the theory more directly in a candidate environment we must know how voters react to individual items of information and which emotional responses they associate with them. This necessitates a methodology more comprehensive than survey research; it requires knowing precisely what information has been encountered and what affective response occurred for each piece of information. In this chapter we employ dynamic process tracing, an experimental methodology that permits us to know exactly what information voters encounter, in what order, for how long, and their emotional reactions to each piece of information. We use dynamic process tracing to create a presidential primary election environment

---

2. Motivated reasoning research (Kunda 1990; Lodge and Taber 2000; Redlawsk 2002) provides some evidence of exactly such a process. These studies routinely show that evaluations are not updated in a straightforward Bayesian manner. Cassino and Lodge (Chapter 5 in this volume) further develop this point.

where voters (subjects) learn about candidates, and as they do we track their information search and affective responses.

This chapter proceeds in four sections. We begin by considering a series of hypotheses generated by affective intelligence theory. In addition to hypotheses to confirm the basic findings of Marcus and colleagues, we consider the degree to which voter-candidate issue distance generates emotional responses and the role played by the overall threat level in the political information environment. We also consider whether the valence of prior expectations—that is, whether a candidate is a preferred or rejected candidate—matters in generating affective responses. Next we describe the dynamic process tracing methodology and the experiment used to collect the data. Third, we detail the findings from our experiment and consider how well they meet our expectations. Finally, we discuss the implications of our findings and directions for future research.

HYPOTHESES

Affective intelligence is best understood as a response to individual informational stimuli based on existing evaluative affect. If a voter likes a candidate and learns new information that is congruent with that expectation, presumably little will happen because the disposition system is not disrupted. Conversely, new information that is incongruent with existing beliefs activates the surveillance system and its associated processes. This activation may lead to a number of consequences for voters and their perceptions of candidates.

Before we can examine this process, we must first identify how affective responses are generated by the relative congruence of existing expectations and new information (Steenbergen, Kilburn, and Wolak 2001). Consider first a preferred candidate, one receiving a high initial evaluation. Voters should be *enthusiastic* about such a candidate and when encountering information conforming to expectations should have that enthusiasm reinforced. But once emotionally invested in this candidate, an encounter with new information that violates expectations should result in a negative response. This negative reaction might be *anxiety* (a sense of concern that the candidate is not quite what was expected) or *anger* and a feeling of betrayal by the preferred candidate. Whether such responses should also be expected for a rejected candidate is less clear. Once they have determined that they dislike a candidate, voters might simply avoid processing any new information about that candidate. Without any (positive) emotional investment in the candidate, new negative information (which confirms expectations) would simply be par for the course. Encountering information that is contrary to expectations (finding a position to be "good") might generate interest. Even so, this kind of incongruence (a rejected candidate taking a liked position) might not have the same emotional impact as a liked candidate taking a disliked position.

The underlying proposition is that affective responses can be generated by the interaction of the global affective evaluation of the candidate and the processing of new information about that candidate at the level of the individual item. This leads to Hypothesis 1:

H1: When voter-candidate agreement is high on a particular issue, voters will express enthusiasm about the candidate. When voter-candidate agreement is extremely low—the candidate is very distant from the voter—voters will express anger. When information is not distant enough to generate anger, but not close enough for comfort, voters will express anxiety toward the candidate. Although these affective responses will occur in the same direction for both preferred and rejected candidates, they will be attenuated for rejected candidates.

If encountering new information can generate affective responses, what does the affect do? Affective intelligence suggests that threatening stimuli activate the surveillance system, enhancing processing and leading to learning. Ultimately, anxious voters may be informed voters. But how would this be exhibited at the level of individual stimuli? One possibility is to examine processing time. Redlawsk (2002) shows that incongruent information generally takes longer to process, though he uses only a simple binary measure of voter-candidate issue distance. A more nuanced view suggests that the disposition and surveillance systems may generate very different levels of processing. An enthusiastic response to new information for a preferred candidate should not require extra processing because it is in line with expectations. But when an affective response is a result of information that threatens prior expectations, processing time should increase. It is not clear a priori, however, whether to expect increased processing time with both anxiety and anger. Anxiety, which presumably heightens attention, should increase processing time. Anger, though, is an aversive response and can be clearly differentiated from anxiety (Huddy, Feldman, and Cassese, chapter 9 in this volume.) Even so, it seems that in order to become aware that one is angry, something more than routine processing is required. This yields Hypothesis 2:

H2: All else being equal, enthusiasm generated by new information will not increase processing time over affectively neutral information.

New information that activates the surveillance system and generates anxiety will take longer to process than other information. Information that generates anger will also require additional processing time.

Thus far we have focused directly on the interaction of existing global affect and new information. But the environment itself may have differential levels of threat with concomitant implications for how new information is perceived. In a low-threat environment, where most of what is learned is congruent with expectations, new incongruent information may be quite conspicuous and thus seem particularly threatening. But it is also possible that this information, atypical and uncommon, may be heavily discounted after only a cursory look because most of the rest of the information in the environment simply confirms expectations. So it may take a particularly strong affective reaction to influence processing in a low-threat environment. Alternatively, in an environment where initial evaluations are regularly challenged by new incongruent information, that which generates enthusiasm will probably not result in increased processing because there are plenty of threatening things to watch out for. Although we make no formal hypotheses about the effects of the overall level of threat in the environment, we intend to explore these differences.

Finally, because processing is made more careful by a certain amount of anxiety, affective intelligence suggests that the result is learning. Responses such as anger may, however, lead to aversion—a move away from the object. If anxiety generates learning, we should see greater information search as anxiety increases.[3] Learning cannot be unbounded, however: a real election campaign has an ending at a specific time. Accordingly, so does our simulated campaign. At some point a decision must be made, which will attenuate how much additional learning anxiety can actually generate. On the other hand, aversion effects should be more apparent because an angry voter can choose to ignore the offending candidate given that alternatives exist.

In addition to greater information search, learning can be evidenced by more accurate placement of candidates with respect to issues. Anxious voters may be better able to place candidates with regard to issues, but what

---

3. At the same time, as noted above, extreme levels of anxiety may not enhance processing. That having been said, in a political environment we might expect that high enough levels of anxiety would simply lead to rejection of a candidate and consideration of a different one. Thus we might not expect to find debilitating anxiety levels, unless a voter simply grew anxious about all the options available in the election, in which case she might simply abstain. Unfortunately, we are not in a position to directly test this proposition.

about angry voters? Presumably an aversive effect would mean less learning, resulting in less accurate recognition of the candidate's positions. The possibility also exists that enthusiastic voters would fail to be as accurate as anxious voters, for two reasons. First, they are presumably not motivated to greater information search. Second, enthusiasm toward a candidate might blind a voter to that candidate's weaknesses and leave the voter unswayed by any evidence that might contradict prior beliefs (Lodge and Taber 2000; Redlawsk 2002). Two related hypotheses are thus suggested:

H3a: Activation of the surveillance system as evidenced by greater anxiety will result in more information search focused on the candidate who generates anxiety. Anger, however, will result in aversion, evidenced by less information search. No effects for enthusiasm on information search are expected.

H3b: Greater overall anxiety toward a candidate will result in a more accurate placement of that candidate with respect to issues. Both greater enthusiasm and greater anger will result in less accurate placement. As with Hypothesis 2, the overall threat level of the environment may attenuate or accentuate effects expected for learning, and thus we will investigate the effects of the threat environment on learning.

DATA AND METHODS

Most affective intelligence studies rely on survey research, which generally measures affect at one point in time, often after the campaign is over and without any knowledge of the detailed information that contributed to the voter's affective responses.[4] But surveys cannot tell us about the role of affect in candidate evaluation *during* a campaign. Process tracing, an approach borrowed from the psychology and marketing research literature, controls the information environment while continually monitoring the decision-making process as it happens (Ford et al. 1989; Jacoby et al. 1987).

Dynamic Process Tracing

Process tracing techniques using static information boards have been used to look at voting behavior (Herstein 1981), political decision making

---

4. Cassino and Lodge (Chapter 5 in this volume) do examine individual pieces of information and their impact on the evaluation of political figures, but in doing this they provide one of the few exceptions that prove the rule.

(Riggle, Johnson, and Hickey 1996; Avery and Riggle 2000), and political information search (Huang 2000; Huang and Price 1998). Unfortunately, this traditional approach suffers from a significant flaw limiting its applicability to voter decision making. The information board presents items in a matrix of alternatives by attributes, with all candidates and issues readily and equally accessible. The campaign environment, however, is not so neatly organized. Politics is messy; information comes and goes somewhat chaotically. Alternative policy options and candidates do not sit neatly on a shelf waiting to be examined and compared. Moreover, citizens certainly do not have unlimited time to devote to candidate comparison-shopping. Thus, we need a technique to mimic the flow of a political campaign while retaining the ability to trace information search and decision making as they happen.

We devised dynamic process tracing (Lau and Redlawsk 1992, 1997, 2001a, 2001b, 2006; Redlawsk 2001, 2002, 2004) to accomplish this. Whereas static information boards allow easy access to all available information, the dynamic board emulates the ebb and flow of a political campaign over time. Early election information is predominately about candidate attributes, including polls and personal characteristics. As the election continues, information flows change, resulting in the availability of more issue positions, alongside endorsements of the candidates by interest groups. New statements appear at the top of a computer screen in one of six colored boxes, proceed down the screen, disappear, and are replaced by other items. Subjects access detailed information such as "Rodgers' Position on Iraq" and read a "card" on the screen listing the details; thus they have the opportunity to learn a wide range of information about the candidates. Meanwhile the system unobtrusively collects data detailing what information subjects access, how long they spend processing each discrete piece of information, their likes and dislikes about each candidate and issue, and more. This dynamic design combines the advantages of the traditional static information board approach to process tracing—knowing exactly what information contributes to a decision—with the chaotic and somewhat overwhelming information environment that defines modern political campaigns.

Experimental Design

Data were collected using a dynamic process tracing experiment simulating a presidential primary election campaign. Subjects first completed a relatively standard political attitudes questionnaire. They then participated in a twenty-minute primary election with four candidates from their chosen party seeking the presidential nomination. In all cases the campaign involved either four Democrats or four Republicans only, with no out-party candidates. Information about the candidates, from personal qualities to issue positions to polls and endorsements, became available in a controlled fashion designed to mimic information flow during a typical campaign.[5] Subjects initially knew nothing about the candidates because all were fictitious. Subjects were told that their ultimate goal was to learn whatever they thought they needed to know to decide which candidate to support in the primary.

Following the campaign, subjects voted and evaluated all four candidates on a standard feeling thermometer. They then were asked to record everything they could recall about each candidate. For half of the subjects this test was unexpected; the other half had been warned they would be tested in the pre-campaign instructions.[6] Then, for each recorded memory, the experimenter asked whether that memory made the subject feel any combination of anxiety, enthusiasm, or anger. Next subjects recorded everything that could be remembered that they liked and disliked about the candidate for whom they had voted and provided the experimenter with the underlying reasoning for the choice.

Subsequently, subjects were shown the title (not the content) of each individual item of information they examined and asked a series of questions. The first was whether the subject recalled examining the item. If not, no other questions were asked and the experimenter moved to the next item. If the item was recalled, the subject was asked whether it had been clicked on by mistake and then asked to recall the affect associated with the item. Did the item make the subject feel anxious, enthusiastic, or angry?[7] A total of 117 subjects (primarily undergraduate students) participated in the experiment during the fall of 2001 and the spring of 2002, and each was paid $10. Table 7.1 summarizes the procedure.

5. The timing and type of information available was based on a study by Lau (1995) that examined the kind and frequency of information about candidates presented in newspapers during the 1988 presidential campaign.

6. This manipulation examines whether on-line processors (Lodge, McGraw, and Stroh 1989) looked different from memory processors (Redlawsk 2001) in the way they responded to affectively incongruent information. No differences of consequence were found for the affective intelligence thesis, and as such it will not be mentioned further in this chapter.

7. Across 117 subjects an average of 8 percent of items were reported as chosen "by mistake." Usually this happened when the subject immediately reaccessed an item after having just looked at the same item. Some subjects had a little more difficulty than others with the mouse, clicking on items when they did not intend to do so.

TABLE 7.1: Experimental procedures

Procedure	Time allotted
Online questionnaire	30–40 minutes
Vote preference, political knowledge, interest, activity, issue positions and attitudes, and group and political person feeling thermometer evaluations	
On practice session	5–10 minutes
Designed to familiarize subjects with the working of the dynamic information board	
Campaign simulation	20 minutes
Participate in a primary election for chosen party, learn about candidates, vote, evaluate all candidates	
Memory test	10–15 minutes
List everything remembered about each of the four candidates and indicate affective reactions to these memories to the experimenter	
Decision process and likes/dislikes	10 minutes
Describe how the decision to support one candidate was made, list likes and dislikes for the chosen candidate	
Information review	20–30 minutes
With experimenter, review the title of each piece of information examined for each subject, indicating whether the item can be recalled and if so whether it was accessed by mistake, and the affective reaction to the information	
Debrief and dismissal	5 minutes

Experimental Manipulation

The dynamic environment allows us to focus on how voters respond to information that is affectively congruent or incongruent with expectations. Information was manipulated so that candidates did not take the same positions for all subjects; instead, positions regarding issues were systematically varied relative to subjects' own positions regarding the same issues. Subjects began the experiment by examining whatever they wished about the candidates (from what was available). After five minutes the experiment was interrupted by a "Gallup Poll" asking, "If the election were held today, which candidate would you vote for?" Subjects chose from among the four candidates in their primary and then rated all four candidates on a feeling thermometer, after which they returned to the task of learning about candidates.

TABLE 7.2: Information congruency manipulation

Manipulation	Preferred candidate	Rejected candidate
All congruent information	100% of issues are as close as possible to subject's position	100% of issues are as far as possible from subject's position
75% congruent information	75% of issues are as close as possible to subject's position, 25% as far away as possible	75% of issues are as far as possible from subject's position, 25% as close as possible
50% congruent information	50% of issues are as close as possible to subject's position, 50% as far away as possible	50% of issues are as far as possible from subject's position, 50% as close as possible
25% congruent information	25% of issues are as close as possible to subject's position, 75% as far away as possible	25% of issues are as far as possible from subject's position, 75% as close as possible

Note: All manipulations begin after the initial interruption for a Gallup Poll question.

Following the poll question, the issue positions taken by the preferred candidate (the one a subject would vote for) and the rejected one (the one with the lowest evaluation) were randomly manipulated in one of four conditions. For one-quarter of subjects, all subsequent issue positions taken by these two candidates conformed to the subject's expectations. That is, for the preferred candidate, all issues matched as closely as possible the subject's preferences, whereas the rejected candidate's positions were as far away as possible from the subject's preferences. This maintained congruency between positions taken by those candidates and the expectations the subject had developed about them. The remaining three experimental conditions varied the percentage of congruent information at 75 percent, 50 percent, or 25 percent, with the preferred and rejected candidates manipulated simultaneously.[8] Table 7.2 summarizes the manipulation.

8. Although the campaign environment contains a wide range of information in addition to issues, including group endorsements, candidate personality traits, polls, and candidate background characteristics, as a practical matter it was only possible to manipulate the issue positions. Subjects were asked their opinion about 27 issues in the pre-experiment questionnaire using a standard seven-point scale. Candidate positions regarding these issues were determined before the study by expert ratings of a range of positions on each of the issues. Eight possible positions ranging from extremely liberal to extremely conservative were available for each of the issues. When a subject chose to examine a particular issue the system determined (1) which experimental manipulation was in force, (2) which candidate was being selected, (3) the subject's own position

Operationalization of Key Concepts

The congruency manipulation was designed to confront most voters with information that would generate anxiety and perhaps anger, providing a clear test of the affective intelligence theory's assertion that voters will not pay particular attention (beyond routine processing) to information unless it represents an unexpected threat. As noted above, the overall threat level in the environment may be an important factor. Manipulating the amount of incongruent information that is encountered enables us to examine voters in high- and low-threat environments. Subjects in the all-congruent and 75 percent congruent conditions faced a relatively low-threat environment, and those in the 50 percent and 25 percent congruent conditions faced a high level of threat to their initial expectations.

Two measures are used to operationalize learning. One simple measure is the amount of information about a candidate that was examined after the Gallup poll interruption. Presumably, the more one examines, the more one learns. But this is complicated by the time limitations of the campaign; of necessity, spending more time on one candidate means spending less on others. Thus when we examine learning about a candidate we control for the total amount of information examined for all candidates. The second—and more direct—measure of learning comes from asking subjects to identify the positions of the preferred and rejected candidates regarding specific issues. Because the actual positions of the candidates are known, the difference between subject placement and a candidate's position is readily calculated, providing a measure of how accurately subjects know the candidates. This requires recording the subject's perception of the candidate's position and the fact that the issue was accessed during the campaign. Of the four issues queried in the post-experiment questionnaire—environment, taxes, affirmative action,

---

regarding the issue; then it matched an available issue position to the candidate based on the congruency/incongruency manipulation in effect. The issues actually manipulated varied by subject because the manipulation was dependent on which issues subjects chose to examine. Because the number of issues examined for any given candidate also varied by subject—and was generally higher for the preferred candidate than for the rejected candidate—the actual percentage of congruent/incongruent information never exactly met the specific percentage targets. The two candidates who were neither preferred nor rejected in the poll were not manipulated and thus took positions that may or may not have fit the subjects' own preferences in any given case. These two candidates are ignored in the analyses that follow.

and defense spending—only affirmative action has enough nonmissing values for both of these requirements.

Global candidate evaluation is measured by a feeling thermometer labeled at 100 degrees with the phrase "Extremely Favorable," at 0 degrees with the phrase "Extremely Unfavorable," and at 50 degrees with the phrase "Neither Favorable nor Unfavorable." Subjects evaluated all candidates using the thermometer following the initial poll and after casting their vote.

Affect at the individual item level was measured during the information review, when subjects were given the opportunity to express their affective reactions to the information they examined. As the title of each item was displayed the experimenter asked a series of questions, beginning with whether the subject recalled looking at the information. If the answer was yes, the subject was asked to recall whether the item represented by the title made him or her feel anxious, enthusiastic, or angry about the candidate. This was done for all information examined by the subject for all candidates.

FINDINGS

We should first establish that the manipulation of threat in the environment operated as expected. Subjects who learned only affectively congruent information about the preferred and the rejected candidates should have found the task of deciding between the candidates to be relatively easy. Conversely, those who were faced with unexpectedly incongruent information should have found the decision more difficult. Following the experiment, subjects were asked to rate how confident they were that the decision they made was the correct one. Figure 7.1 shows these ratings by the relative amount of incongruent information encountered (in quartiles). As expected, the more they encountered incongruent information, the less confident subjects were that they had made the right choice.

Affective Reactions to Issue Congruency

Hypothesis 1 suggests that specific issue positions taken by preferred and rejected candidates can generate affective responses in voters. Studies often simply assume that the greater the distance between the voter's preferences and candidate's positions, the greater the likelihood of a negative affective reaction (for example, Wolak et al. 2003.) Although Steenbergen, Kilburn, and Wolak (2001) have found some support for

FIGURE 7.1: CONFIDENCE IN VOTE CHOICE BY INCONGRUENCY QUARTILE

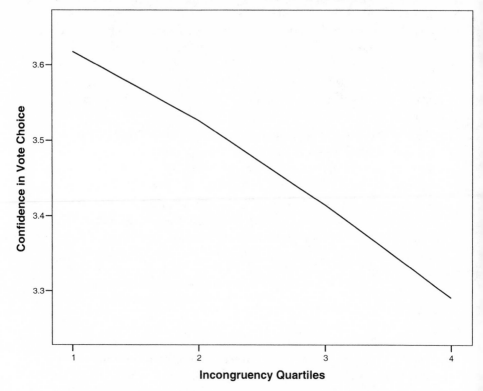

this, it is unclear whether we can make such an assumption (Redlawsk 2002). Fortunately, making an assumption is unnecessary because congruency is known for many of the issues presented to voters in the simulation, the initial candidate preference is measured, and affective reactions are reported by subjects. In addition to supporting our expectations that affect can be activated by issue congruency, a strong relationship would provide additional evidence that the congruency manipulation works as expected and that recall of affect is reasonably accurate for the issues we used. In general, a greater distance between the positions of the subject and the candidate ("issue distance") should dampen enthusiasm, increase anxiety, and perhaps generate anger. Though we expect similar patterns for preferred and rejected candidates, the relationship should be stronger for a preferred candidate.

Multiple analytical approaches strongly support Hypothesis 1. Subject-candidate issue distance is clearly correlated with affective reactions. Table 7.3 summarizes the zero-order bivariate correlations at the individual

TABLE 7.3: Bivariate correlations and subject-candidate issue distance, by affective response, analyzed by individual issue

	Enthusiastic	*Anxious*	*Angry*
Preferred candidate, n = 661	−.264***	.173***	.258***
Rejected candidate, n = 400	−.277***	.187***	.229***

Note: Cell entries are the zero-order correlations between subject-candidate issue distance and the recall of affective response to the issue.
*** p < .001.

issue level of analysis.[9] The greater the voter-candidate issue distance, the less the reported enthusiasm for the candidate with respect to that issue. Conversely, the greater the distance, the more likely it was that the issue made the subject anxious or angry, with anger showing a stronger correlation than anxiety but not as strong as enthusiasm. The pattern holds for preferred and rejected candidates and is shown graphically in figure 7.2, which plots the likelihood that any given issue will generate an affective reaction by the distance in quartiles between the subject and the candidate regarding that issue.[10]

These data support our contention (also supported by Thomas and Diender 1990) that subjects can accurately recall their affect toward information when prompted to do so. Another way to examine this question is to consider the overall mean voter-candidate issue distance for

9. Each case involves a subject accessing a candidate's issue stance. Thus, each subject is responsible for multiple cases in this analysis.

10. Figure 7.2 shows an interesting pattern that might be called "stickiness" in the affective responses, especially for the preferred candidate. As would be expected, issue distance in the first quartile is very likely to generate enthusiasm and much less likely to generate anxiety or anger. This does not change for items in the second quartile. For the preferred candidate, it is only when a candidate position becomes especially distant from the subject's position (in the third and fourth quartiles) that enthusiasm finally wanes and anger and anxiety increase. This may be indicative of motivated reasoning—the tendency to discount or avoid negative information about a liked alternative (Redlawsk 2002; Lodge and Taber 2000) and confirmatory decision making (Lau and Redlawsk 2006).

But the same is not true of the candidate rejected in the early poll. Reading backwards—because the fourth quartile represents the information that is most congruent with expectations for the disliked candidate—the same level of "stickiness" is not present. Moving from more distant positions to closer ones results in a fairly consistent change in enthusiasm, anxiety, and anger. Thus the motivated reasoning effects that may occur for a liked candidate do not appear to operate to the same extent for a disliked candidate.

FIGURE 7.2: VOTER-CANDIDATE ISSUE DIFFERENCE AND AFFECTIVE
RESPONSES TO ISSUE ITEMS

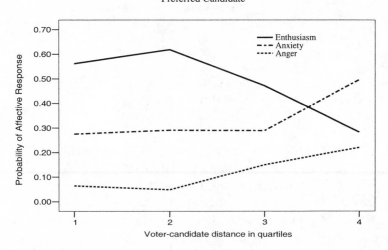

Preferred Candidate

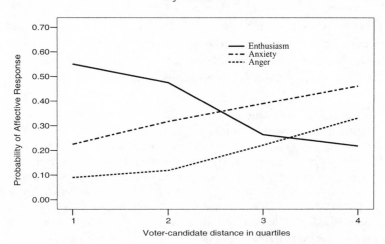

Rejected candidate

each of the three specific affective reactions. In general, we expect that
issues that generate enthusiasm will exhibit minimal distance between
the candidate and the voter. Conversely, issues that make voters angry
should show a large distance between the candidate and the voter. Anxiety is likely to be somewhere in between—not close enough for enthusiasm but not far enough away to generate anger. Figure 7.3 displays the
relationships we find in our study.

Preferred candidate

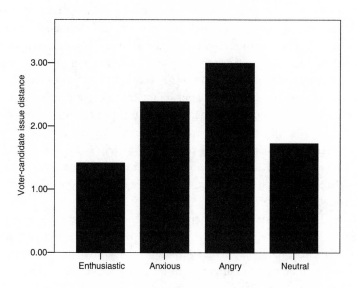

Rejected candidate

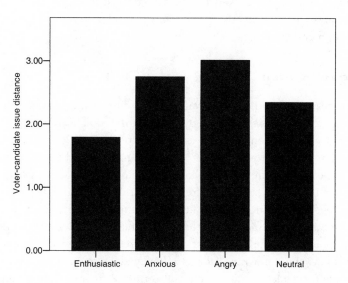

Affective responses to the preferred candidate again appear as expected. Items that generate enthusiasm are on average no more than 1.3 points distant from the subject's position (using a standard 7-point scale.) But items with an average distance of 3 points generate anger. Why 3 points? Maybe it is because that distance places the candidate and the voter on opposite sides of the political spectrum or, for those holding the most extreme positions (1, 7), it places the other right in the center (4). A smaller distance simply makes the voter anxious (mean about 2.4) but not angry. A similar pattern appears for the rejected candidate, with a caveat. Voters become enthusiastic about a rejected candidate's position at a further distance than for a preferred candidate. The mean distance that generates enthusiasm for a rejected candidate is 1.8, compared to 1.3 for the preferred candidate. Apparently, finding a previously rejected candidate who is within shouting distance of one's own position generates some enthusiasm.

Overall we find strong support for Hypothesis 1. As the distance between a voter's issue preference and a candidate's issue position gets larger, anxiety or anger is in fact generated. This provides a foundation for the direct analyses of affective intelligence suggested by Hypotheses 2 and 3. Because affective responses to issue positions are both reasonable and predictable, we suggest, subjects' responses for other types of information are also likely to be reasonable. Accordingly, the following analyses use all the information subjects encountered and reported on, not merely issues.

Affect and Processing

Hypothesis 2 tests whether activation of the surveillance system results in more careful processing. The dynamic information board records the amount of time spent reading each piece of information. Processing time is measured from the time the item appears on the screen until the subject clicks on a "done" button to indicate that she is finished, to a hundredth of a second. Unfortunately, this is not directly useful as captured. People differ in their levels of manual dexterity. Because the time measurement includes both reading and the physical act of clicking a mouse, we adjust the raw time by regressing it on the number of words in each item, within subjects (Redlawsk 2002). For each subject the result includes a unique constant term that represents the mouse click. All reading times are then adjusted within subject by subtracting the constant from each item's raw time. The resulting adjusted reading time is used as the processing measure.

Of course, processing is dependent on many things that are innate to the information itself and to the person doing the processing. The most obvious is that if there are more words in an item it will take longer to read. This is mediated, however, by each subject's reading ability, so we control for this using a measure of reading speed (in seconds) calculated from the time it took subjects to read the instructions at the beginning of the study. Other controls include subject education, age, and political expertise, along with the experimental manipulations. In addition, because subjects routinely spend much more effort learning about preferred candidates, a simple binary measure of whether each item is about a preferred candidate is included.

Examining processing time creates an interesting challenge for analysis. Essentially, the times needed to process information are nested within subjects, so that for each subject there are multiple measures of processing time, one for each item that the subject examined. The data set therefore contains as many entries per subject as there were items examined by the subject. Consequently, a simple OLS analysis is not appropriate (Steenbergen and Jones 2002). Instead, we specified a mixed linear model, allowing for effects within subjects and between subjects.[11] We present the marginal effects for each affective response in figure 7.4.[12] For each affective response we show three panels. The first is the marginal effect for affect, with lines representing preferred and rejected candidates. The second and third panels present high and low threat levels for preferred and rejected candidates, respectively.

Turning first to enthusiasm, we see no effects for processing time, regardless of the model specification: whether for a preferred or a rejected candidate, whether in a high or low threat environment, enthusiasm, as expected, has no statistically significant effect on processing.[13] Thus we find support for the assumption that the disposition system represents essentially status quo processing. The results for anxiety and anger are more complex. Both appear to increase processing time, as expected, but not consistently. As the first panel in the anxiety series shows, anxiety

11. For this analysis and the analysis reported in table 7.2, complete multivariate models were developed, controlling for subject age, expertise, education, reading ability, and vote choice. In the interest of clarity, only relevant results are reported here. Full models are available from the first author.

12. These effects are estimated at the mean for each covariate in the data.

13. The line for high threat shows some change in processing time for rejected candidates (as seen in the third panel), but this difference is not statistically significant and should not be considered a substantive difference, either.

FIGURE 7.4: AFFECTIVE RESPONSE AND PROCESSING TIME

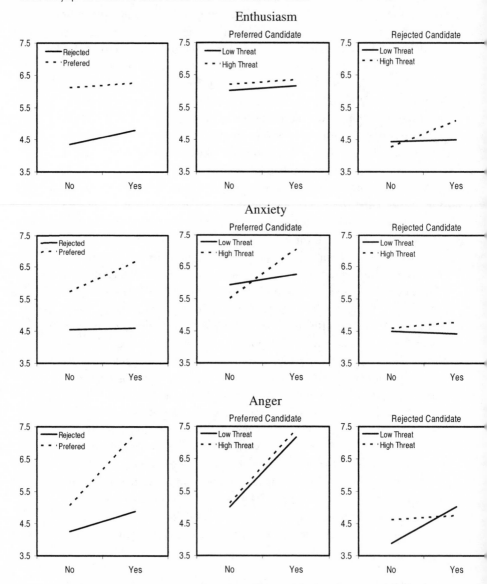

operates only for preferred candidates; encountering information that generates an anxious response significantly increases processing time (F = 7.447, p < .01). But further investigation shows that the effect is limited to the high-threat environment, where a great deal of unexpected information is encountered. Only in that specific environment do subjects take significantly longer to process anxiety-provoking information

(F = 3.306, p < .1). Perhaps this occurs because for a preferred candidate, such information is less expected than it is for a rejected candidate, and thus more jarring. But small amounts of such information (low levels of threat) do not invoke much additional processing effort. Anxiety only enhances processing when the environment becomes significantly threatening to prior expectations.

Anger, which, we suggested, might create an aversive reaction, appears not to do so, at least in terms of processing time. From the initial panel in the anger series in figure 7.4 we see that only a preferred candidate generates effects for anger, a reasonable result given that negative information about a rejected candidate would actually be expected. But the effect is to increase the amount of time spent processing anger-inducing items, not to reduce it (F = 11.156, p < .01). Examination of the second and third panels indicates that for the preferred candidate the threat environment does not matter. Whether embedded in an environment with little unexpected information or a lot of it, items for which subjects expressed anger generated longer processing times, all other things being equal—there is no interaction effect with threat. The overall pattern of figure 7.4 and the models that underlie it suggest general support for affective intelligence as expressed in Hypothesis 2, but only under certain conditions. Initial evaluation matters, but the surveillance system generally is activated only when negative stimuli are encountered about a preferred candidate. And, as anticipated, enthusiastic responses to information do not result in increased processing time for either a preferred or a rejected candidate.

Affect and Learning

Are anxious voters better voters? New, threatening information activates the surveillance system, increasing both anxiety and anger and generating more careful processing. Hypotheses 3a and 3b suggest that heightened anxiety leads to learning. Two measures of learning are available: the amount of information examined for a given candidate and the accuracy of the placement of candidates with respect to issues. For preferred and rejected candidates, we know how much information each subject encountered and how accurately subjects placed those candidates regarding the issue of affirmative action. Marcus and colleagues examined affirmative action (Marcus, Neuman, and MacKuen 2000; MacKuen et al. 2001; Wolak et al. 2003), and so we have a direct comparison to their work. Accurate placement is measured as the absolute distance between the subject's placement of the candidate on a liberal-conservative scale and the known position that the candidate took on the same scale.[14]

Table 7.4 reports OLS regression models assessing the effects of anger, anxiety, and enthusiasm on the amount of information examined for preferred and rejected candidates. Affective reactions are measured as the percentage of all items examined that generated each affective response. Although only the affect variables are shown in table 7.4, the full models control for subject age, expertise, education, reading ability, information search, and vote choice. Because our previous analyses show that preferred and rejected candidates should be examined independently, we do so in this case as well. Model 1 in the table examines the data controlling simply for the threat environment; Model 2 disaggregates the data by preferred and rejected candidates and threat levels.

A clear aversion effect for anger toward the preferred candidate is seen in Model 1. As subjects report encountering more items that generate anger, they are significantly less likely to continue searching for information about that candidate. Subjects learn that there is something wrong, and they respond by trying some other candidate. This effect is absent for the rejected candidate, regarding whom anger seems to have little influence. Conversely, items that generate either anxiety or enthusiasm increase the amount of information seeking, but only about two-thirds as much as anger decreases it. Although no processing effects were found for enthusiasm, when new information generates enthusiasm—whether about the preferred or the rejected candidate—subjects focus more on that candidate, relative to others. Once again, anxiety only operates on the preferred candidate. In fact, anxiety appears to suppress searching for the rejected candidate, though the coefficient does not reach significance.

Turning to Model 2 in table 7.4, we see varying effects depending on the level of threat in the environment. When threat is high, anxiety results in greater information search, as we had anticipated, but only for the preferred candidate. In a low-threat environment, the search effects of anxiety are attenuated and do not reach significance. Whereas the earlier analysis showed that anger increases processing time for preferred candidates for both threat levels, here anger does not direct information search in a high-threat environment. In a low-threat environment where

14. Candidate issue positions are known with certainty because we assigned the issue positions to each of our candidates. Each issue statement was rated by experts (a group of faculty members and graduate students) on a scale from 1 (very liberal) to 7 (very conservative). The mean of these ratings was assigned as the known candidate issue position.

		Model 1		Model 2			
				High threat		Low threat	
		Preferred	Rejected	Preferred	Rejected	Preferred	Rejected
Amount of information examined:[a]							
Anger		−6.968*	−1.649	−4.179	−4.784	−21.262*	.830
		(3.980)	(1.989)	(4.568)	(3.095)	(10.709)	(2.774)
Anxiety		4.622*	-1.823	7.081*	−.279	2.802	−3.208
		(2.472)	(1.448)	(3.743)	(2.264)	(4.070)	(2.115)
Enthusiasm		4.185*	5.646**	1.522	6.495*	8.647*	4.888*
		(2.327)	(1.643)	(3.799)	(2.558)	(3.252)	(2.453)
Adjusted R^2		.479	.640	.341	.593	.514	.660
		112	110	55	56	57	54
Mean accuracy of placement on affirmative action:[b]							
Anger	Yes	1.31 (9)	1.29 (9)	.72 (5)	1.40 (3)	2.05 (4)	1.23 (6)
	No	1.32 (53)	2.00 (24)	2.07 (21)	2.19 (14)	.84 (32)	1.74 (10)
	t	.029	1.957*	3.431**	1.410	−1.40	1.058
Anxiety	Yes	1.36 (20)	1.78 (8)	1.06 (10)	2.05 (4)	1.66 (10)	1.50 (4)
	No	1.34 (42)	1.82 (25)	2.28 (16)	2.05 (13)	.71 (26)	1.57 (12)
	t	−.164	.074	2.651*	−.004	−2.223*	.120
Enthusiasm	Yes	1.03 (26)	1.80 (9)	2.26 (7)	1.63 (6)	.58 (19)	2.13 (3)
	No	1.53 (36)	1.81 (24)	1.64 (19)	2.27 (11)	1.41 (17)	1.41 (13)
	t	1.605	.016	−.909	.763	2.850**	−2.214*

[a] Entries are OLS regression coefficients, standard errors in parentheses. Combined affect measures compare to items generating a neutral affective reaction. Full model includes controls for subject age, expertise, education, reading ability, total information search, and vote choice.
[b] Entries are mean distances between subject perception of a candidate and the candidate's actual position, number of cases in parentheses. Smaller values represent more accurate placement.
* $p < .1$; ** $p < .01$; *** $p < .001$.

the few anger-generating items stand out, however, there is a significant *aversive* effect for the preferred candidate but not for the rejected one. It is interesting that enthusiasm exhibits strong positive effects for all conditions except the preferred candidate in the high-threat environment, counter to the expectation of Hypothesis 3a. On the other hand, the findings for anger and anxiety support the hypothesis, at least for preferred candidates.

The bottom half of table 7.4 reports mean differences in the placement of candidates' positions regarding affirmative action, with smaller values representing more accurate placement. For this purpose, affect is a binary indicator of whether the candidate's position regarding affirmative action generated the particular affective reaction.[15] Thus we directly examine the voter's response to the candidate's position and the accuracy of the voter's placement of the candidate. Though some evidence that affect relates to learning is visible, the results are only suggestive at best, given the low value for n in some cells. Model 1, which examines preferred and rejected candidates, actually shows little evidence of learning about candidate's positions regarding affirmative action. The only significant result is that for anger toward the rejected candidate. Subjects for whom the candidate's affirmative action stance generated anger were significantly more accurate in placing the candidate. Anger appears memorable, if nothing else.

Model 2 shows a number of learning effects for the preferred candidate in both environments. In a high-threat environment, anger and anxiety both show learning effects, and subjects are much better able to place their preferred candidate. In the low-threat environment, however, both affective responses lead to *less accurate* placement. This makes sense for anger, given that anger ought to generate aversion. The reason why this should be so for anxiety towards the preferred candidate is less apparent. For the rejected candidate, neither anger nor anxiety shows any effects in either threat condition. When a candidate's affirmative action stance generates enthusiasm, placement effects are again mixed. In the high-threat condition, there appears to be a tendency to do worse in placing the preferred candidate when enthusiastic about that candidate, while

---

15. With limited numbers of cases available, attempts to build full OLS models predicting placement failed, except for the preferred candidate in the high-threat situation. The results reported are t-tests of the mean placement distance by affective reaction. A correlational analysis controlling for subject expertise and the amount of information acquired about the candidates results in similar patterns, as does a full model for the preferred candidate in a high-threat situation.

enthusiasm tends to lead to more accurate placement for the rejected candidate. Neither effect reaches statistical significance. The direction is reversed low levels of threat, where enthusiasm toward the preferred candidate results in greater accuracy, but an enthusiastic response to the rejected candidate results in lower accuracy. These latter results provide tentative support for Hypothesis 3b, though the results again suggest that the affective intelligence thesis does not apply in every circumstance.

DISCUSSION

Existing studies of affective response have been hampered by reliance on aggregate-level data with no knowledge of the details that go into reported global evaluations. The data collected for the present study represent a significant improvement. We employ a dynamic process tracing environment that captures details about what goes on in a campaign that simply have not been available in the past. We capture information about every piece of information examined by a subject, building a data set that includes not only the typical global measures (candidate evaluation, affective response, and the like) but also information about what went into those global variables. Because the theory of affective intelligence is constructed around affective reactions to individual-level stimuli, this project represents a significant improvement over previous studies.

The weight of the evidence supports aspects of the affective intelligence thesis, albeit with important caveats. Anxiety, which is presumed to cause heightened attention and processing, only operates for preferred candidates and in an environment where there is substantial information that defies expectations. In a high-threat environment anxiety leads to more careful processing, more effort to learn about the candidate who generates the anxiety, and better assessment of that candidate's position on the issue of affirmative action. But in a low-threat environment, anxiety appears to do very little to increase either processing efforts or learning. Furthermore, regardless of threat environment, anxiety does not have any effects on processing information about rejected candidates. Thus it seems there may be a threshold: if there is too little anxiety in the environment learning is not activated, and though we could not test the idea, it seems likely that too much anxiety would also impede learning.

Anger, which ought to generate aversion, exhibits the expected effect, at least in low-threat environments. In such environments greater attention is paid to information that invokes anger, but when that anger is aimed at an initially liked candidate, aversion occurs as voters turn toward other candidates. The result is a tendency to incorrectly recall where such a candidate stands with regard to issues. As with Huddy, Feldman, and Cassese (chapter 9 in this volume), we find that anxiety and anger are clearly distinct, with differing effects on information search and learning.

Finally, according to affective intelligence, the role of enthusiasm should be relatively neutral; that is, enthusiasm toward a preferred candidate should be the norm. Whereas enthusiasm has no effect on processing time, we find that greater enthusiasm results in more information search, although that search does not always produce more accurate issue placement. This finding is particularly interesting given that the prior affective intelligence studies suggest a small role for enthusiasm (the disposition system) in driving information search.

The original affective intelligence studies were dependent on survey research, but the theory is one of individual information effects. Thus dynamic process tracing, a methodology designed to track the way in which voters acquire and respond to campaign information piece by piece, gives us a more direct way to understand how information affects voter decision making. That our findings support much of the basic thesis of affective intelligence—though only for preferred candidates—is promising. But the anomalies that we have found require additional study. A future direction may include consideration of the way motivated reasoning effects—the tendency of people to maintain existing evaluations in the face of countervailing information (Kunda 1990; Lodge and Taber 2000)—interact with different kinds of affect to explain both heightened processing and the observed limits to accurate perception of new information.

The current study has limitations. Subjects were primarily undergraduates and thus may have had less stable political attitudes and responses (Sears 1986). Information flow, though it mimics real presidential campaigns, is primarily dependent on text-based material. Furthermore, the only information manipulated in this study was that regarding candidates' issue positions and endorsements. All other candidate information—personality, background, polls—was unaltered and reasonably positive across all candidates. Thus subjects might well have been cross-pressured by candidates who became increasingly unlike initial expectations, maintaining very positive personalities. Although this could be realistic, for analytical purposes a certain amount of control was probably lost. A more complete study would fully manipulate all types of candidate information.

The results may be a function of limitations in the data collected for this study. Or they might suggest that within the context of an election campaign, the effects of global candidate affect, new information, and the interplay of multiple candidates are more complicated than they first appear. Regardless, the best way to study a process that occurs over time such as affective reaction to candidates during an election campaign is to study it as it happens, not long afterward. Data collected via dynamic process tracing studies have the potential to provide insights that are unattainable by survey research or experiments that fail to account for the dynamic nature of election campaigns.

CHAPTER EIGHT

Identities, Interests, and Emotions: Symbolic versus Material Wellsprings of Fear, Anger, and Enthusiasm

TED BRADER AND NICHOLAS A. VALENTINO

Much of the literature concerning affect and politics emphasizes the impact of emotions on political behavior and judgment, although recent studies also shed light on the ability of political events and communication to trigger emotions. For the most part, researchers have been concerned with the causes and effects for citizens in general and have paid little attention to individual differences in emotional reactions to politics. There is good reason, however, to expect that different people will react differently to the same events, issues, and candidates. For example, the intensity of enthusiasm responses to a given stimulus differs along personality dimensions such as extroversion-introversion (Watson 1988). Similarly, research concerning fear appeals, as well as appraisal theories of emotion, have long suggested that efficacy (locus of control) can condition the experience of anger or anxiety in response to a given stimulus (Lazarus 1991; Witte and Allen 2000). Thus different people, or the same people at different times, may have dramatically different emotional experiences in response to the same political event, issue, or candidate.

In this chapter we explore the antecedents of emotional reactions to an important contemporary political issue: immigration. We examine the extent to which citizens' emotional reactions to increasing immigration can be explained by differences in their personal attributes and circumstances. In doing so, we focus on the long-standing distinction between deeply ingrained symbolic identities, or predispositions, on one hand, and material circumstances, or self-interest, on the other, as factors in political explanations. Affective intelligence theory suggests that emotional states condition the power of each of these factors in explaining political attitudes and behavior (Marcus, Neuman, and MacKuen 2000). This claim is supported by evidence that citizens base their decisions more ✓ heavily on evaluations of current circumstances under conditions of fear and more heavily on predispositions under conditions of enthusiasm (Brader 2005; Marcus, Neuman, and MacKuen 2000). In other words, affective intelligence raises the exciting possibility that the long-running and sometimes contentious debate about the roles of reason and emotion in political decision making can be reconciled.

Unfortunately, to date, the theory has not been subjected to extensive empirical scrutiny. Though survey-based tests of the implications of affective intelligence have been supportive, only a few controlled experiments have shed light on the particular ways fear and enthusiasm condition the impact of predispositions on political attitudes (Brader 2005; Brader and Valentino 2005). Several chapters in this volume test various implications of this theory. The present chapter attempts to take the logic of the theory back one step in the causal chain: What are the individual differences that contribute to the experience of the emotional states? In particular, who is likely to react with fear, anger, or enthusiasm to a given attitude object?

Affective intelligence theory, it seems to us, might lead one to expect significant differences across models used to predict the incidence of these emotional states. For reasons we explain below, variation in symbolic dispositions (for example, prejudice and group identities) should be strongly linked to emotions such as enthusiasm, whereas variation in current circumstances (for example, material or economic interests) should be most strongly linked to fear and anger. The literature concerning symbolic politics, and in particular racial resentment theory, would make a different prediction: prejudice should be tied strongly to all three emotions, but perhaps most strongly to anger.

IDENTITIES, INTERESTS, AND EMOTIONS

We can simplify the myriad motivations underlying public opinion to three primary ingredients—material interests, group dispositions, and values (Kinder 1998). Although quantitative research concerning values, or political principles, has been limited until recently, research concerning interest-based and group-based explanations has been prolific for decades. For example, political scientists have long regarded economic considerations as key determinants of political attitudes and voting behavior (Fiorina 1981; MacKuen, Erikson, and Stimson 1992; Zaller 2001). An equally impressive collection of studies shows the central place of group orientations in American public opinion (Brady and Sniderman 1985; Campbell et al. 1960; Nelson and Kinder 1996), or what some have called "symbolic politics" (Sears 1993). Many studies explicitly pit the explanatory power of self-interest against that of symbolic predisposi-tions, and the evidence suggests that under most circumstances policy opinions derive far more from symbolic factors (Citrin and Green 1990; Kinder 1998; Sears and Funk 1991). ✓

Research about attitudes toward immigration resembles the larger public opinion literature in its focus on these ingredients. Several stud-ies have shown that a mix of prejudice, economic concerns, and values explains support for restricting immigration to the United States (Burns and Gimpel 2000; Citrin et al. 1997; Fetzer 1994; Kinder 2003). Studies of anti-immigration attitudes in Europe have reached similar conclusions, finding opposition rooted in perceived threat to the dominant group, eth-nocentrism, and economic insecurity (Quillian 1995; Sniderman et al. 2000). Scheve and Slaughter (2001) find that less-skilled workers (that is, those facing the most competitive pressure from immigrants) are more likely to oppose immigration but also find that opposition is no greater among workers in "gateway communities" where immigrants are con-centrated. Finally, researchers have found that negative reactions to im-migration are tied to national pride or nativist conceptions of national identity (Citrin et al. 1994; Jackson et al. 2001). Overall, the evidence suggests that both material and symbolic factors play a role but that the latter are generally dominant.

There is mounting evidence that the relevance of these sorts of fac-tors in political and social judgment may depend on a person's emotional state. Affective intelligence theory posits that political judgment and be-havior are guided by two basic emotional systems in the brain (Marcus, Neuman, and MacKuen 2000). The disposition system, which generates enthusiasm, facilitates the development and execution of learned routines by monitoring the environment for signs that one's goals are being met. The surveillance system, which generates anxiety or fear, facilitates the redirection of attention and higher reasoning functions when a potential threat to one's well-being is detected.[1] Therefore, reliance on behavioral

1. The terms *anxiety* and *fear* hold various meanings in both academic and everyday par-lance. We use these terms interchangeably in this chapter to refer to the primary affective response to threat, which emerges from what Marcus and colleagues (2000) call the sur-veillance system (and which they call anxiety). In the English language, people use a large number of synonyms to describe feelings within the anxiety-fear emotion family (Lazarus 1991). They may report feeling frightened, uneasy, alarmed, terrified, worried, apprehen-sive, stressed, or scared, to name a few examples. In some cases, the terms merely convey differing degrees of intensity. The terms can also imply qualitatively different reactions, however. For example, a person might reserve the term *fear* to describe the state of extreme

predispositions should increase with enthusiasm, and thoughtful consideration of current circumstances should increase with anxiety. Consistent with these predictions, survey and experimental evidence shows that enthusiastic citizens base their political evaluations more heavily on party identification or preexisting preferences, and anxious citizens base their evaluations more on new information or comparisons of candidates' issue positions and qualities (Brader 2005; Kinder and D'Ambrosio 2000; Marcus, Neuman, and MacKuen 2000; Way and Masters 1996).[2] These emotional systems enable individuals to switch adaptively from one mode of judgment to the other as the situation demands. As a result, MacKuen and colleagues (this volume) argue, affective intelligence helps to reconcile the vision of symbolic, habitual voters that is rooted in social psychology and the vision of rational decision-makers that is rooted in economic theory.

Enthusiasm and fear (with their low-arousal counterparts, depression and calm) are the major emotions of affective intelligence theory. Although scholars have recognized that anger can be important in politics (Conover and Feldman 1986; Kinder 1994), its place in affective intelligence theory and other structural approaches to the study of emotion remains unclear. Although it is possible to identify situational antecedents that ought to distinguish anger and fear (Lazarus 1991), both emotions can emerge in response to threats and, indeed, in response to the same threat (for example, the terrorist attacks of September 11, 2001). In fact, in the initial formulation of affective intelligence theory, the authors treat self-reports of fear, anger, and disgust all as measures of anxiety (Marcus, Neuman, and MacKuen 2000). As Huddy and colleagues (this volume) show, however, the effects of anger are often distinct from those of fear

---

fright produced by imminent threats to life and limb, which some scholars attribute to a separate "fight or flight" system. Clinical psychologists also distinguish anxiety disorders characterized by hypersensitivity in the perception of and reaction to threats from phobias characterized by an extreme and seemingly unwarranted fear of particular situations or objects. We do not consider such distinctions here. We believe that in politics, references to fear ads, economic anxieties, "Medi-Scare" tactics, and partisans who are uneasy about the performance of their candidate all imply the same emotion, and that is the emotion which affective intelligence theory assigns to the surveillance system. Moreover, the verbal self-reports used by political scientists and social psychologists to measure emotional reactions assume that anxiety, fear, and other synonyms belong on a common scale, and respondents typically validate that assumption by answering the questions similarly.

2. This pattern of findings is largely consistent with work in social psychology that finds that positive moods affect information processing by increasing reliance on stereotypes and existing belief structures and negative moods promote greater consideration of new information or circumstances (Bless 2001; Isbell and Ottati 2002).

(see also Lerner and Keltner 2000, 2001). More recently, Marcus (2003) has tried to reconcile the place of anger in affective intelligence theory by arguing that it is often indistinguishable from anxiety but, under certain conditions, can emerge as the separate dimension of aversion. According to this view, anger or aversion is a product of the disposition system and manifests itself as a sort of negative enthusiasm whenever a person encounters a familiar source of opposition. Therefore, this distinction between the political role of anger and that of fear cries out for further attention. We hope to add a small piece of the puzzle by exploring the distinctiveness of the antecedents of these two emotions relative to enthusiasm and to one another.

Researchers have only begun to investigate the *sources* of political emotions. Studies that draw on the affective priming paradigm in social psychology have shown that nonpolitical, incidental cues, such as pleasant smells and subliminal images, can elicit emotions with consequences for political evaluation (Isbell and Ottati 2002; Way and Masters 1996). Of more direct consequence for politics, researchers have found that peripheral cues such as facial expressions or advertising imagery that are embedded in political communication can arouse emotions and thereby affect political judgment and behavior (Brader 2005; Huddy and Gunnthorsdottir 2000; Sullivan and Masters 1988). Finally, new work demonstrates that media portrayals of political candidates, issues, and events can trigger emotional reactions that mediate the impact of news on attitudes and behavior (Brader, Valentino, and Suhay 2004; Hutchings et al. 2006; Lerner et al. 2003; see also Graber, chapter 11 in this volume).

Although much work remains to be done on effects and external causes, few studies have examined individual differences in order to shed light on the internal sources of political emotion. In this chapter, we investigate the individual precursors of enthusiasm, fear, and anger about immigration among U.S. citizens. We are especially interested in the extent to which material circumstances and social or political identities shape these emotions. Are symbolic predispositions, interests, or both behind emotional responses to immigration, and does the answer depend on the emotion? By asking the questions in this way, we depart from the studies cited above, which emphasize the external or perceptual causes of emotions (that is, situational appraisals and the events or environmental cues that trigger them). We do not deny the relevance of such antecedents. To the contrary, we take for granted that both conscious and nonconscious perceptions of one's situation can directly precipitate emotional responses, as suggested by appraisal theories of emotion (Lazarus 1991; see also Just, Crigler, and Belt, chapter 10 in this volume). We simply wish to step back and examine which sorts of individual differences trigger specific emotions, presumably by making the appropriate appraisal more or less likely.[3] In particular, we ask whether symbolic predispositions or material circumstances better enable us to predict who will feel enthusiastic, anxious, or angry about the test issue of immigration Appraisal theories offer few clues as to whether or how these broad categories of individual factors differentially predict specific emotions, but affective intelligence theory hints at a connection.

One might wonder whether our expectations imply a mechanism that is starkly different from a basic tenet of existing theories of emotion. Namely, if emotions trigger the use of predispositions instead of contemporary information in current evaluations, as theories like affective intelligence suggest, then how can predispositions and contemporary circumstances also moderate the experience of these emotions in the first place? Our argument is that such feedback loops are quite possible and even probable; the brain is replete with processes of this sort. Prior work on affective intelligence theory has not focused closely on the precursors of emotional reactions. Like most theories of emotion, however, it acknowledges that predispositions, personality traits, or personal circumstances can alter the probability that an event or issue will trigger a particular emotional reaction. Marcus and colleagues (1995), for example, make just such an argument for personality characteristics in the domain of civil liberties judgments. The emotion, once triggered, would then alter strategies for evaluating the present circumstance, reinforcing the use of predispositions or boosting reliance on information. Thus our investigation does more to complement existing theories of emotion than it does to revise or contradict them.

HYPOTHESES

Our expectations are rooted in the claims of affective intelligence theory and the literature about symbolic politics. Affective intelligence theory posits that political enthusiasm is closely tied to such "habituated, long-term forces" as partisanship, ideology, and group identity (Marcus, Neuman, and MacKuen 2000, 52). The disposition system, from which

3. Unfortunately, we do not presently have the data to test the link between these attributes and situational appraisals. Therefore, it is possible that the findings in this chapter speak reliably about individual differences only for the issue of immigration (and among native residents in the United States). A more complete investigation that includes perceptual-level precursors would consider the appraisal or appraisals most likely to be elicited by a given political person, issue, or event among individuals who are similarly situated in terms of attributes, dispositions, or material conditions.

enthusiasm springs, enables citizens to act efficiently by deploying these habits of the mind, monitoring the success of those actions, and modifying habits in light of experience. The theory also posits that political anxiety is closely tied to rational calculation of costs and benefits based on available information (61). The surveillance system, from which anxiety springs, enables citizens to break free of reliance on habits and devote greater attention to their immediate environment when the circumstances warrant. Marcus and colleagues propose these relationships to highlight they ways in which emotions affect reliance on political predispositions and contemporary considerations.

We ask whether the relationships stretch farther such that habit and circumstances also differentially contribute to the generation of emotions. This is not logically necessary, nor is it a necessary implication of affective intelligence theory. The contention that enthusiasm modulates the relevance and application of predispositions and that anxiety triggers greater consideration of immediate circumstances does not require that predispositions and circumstances are better predictors of enthusiastic and anxious reactions, respectively. Nonetheless, affective intelligence theory's contention that distinct brain systems tie habits to enthusiasm and reasoned calculation of contemporary information to anxiety leads us to speculate that the associations could go both ways. If they do, then, when comparing the precursors of enthusiasm and fear, we would expect long-term predispositions to have greater influence over levels of enthusiasm and evaluations of current circumstances to exert greater influence on levels of anxiety. Given the concern of Marcus and colleagues (2000) with vote choice and emotional reactions to candidates, the central predisposition in their analyses is party identification, and contemporary information consists of issue proximity and evaluations of candidates' traits. Given our focus on emotional reactions to the issue of immigration, we follow the public opinion literature (Kinder 1998) in examining the role of group predispositions such as prejudice, patriotism, and partisanship, as well as the role of material interest as embodied in financial and economic assessments, occupational vulnerability to competition from immigrants, and the level of immigrants in the local population. Material interest is a major component of contemporary circumstances and one that is especially relevant to debates about the causes of opinion about immigration (Kinder 2003; Scheve and Slaughter 2001; Sniderman et al. 2000).[4] We thus arrive at the following two hypotheses:

4. We regard material interest as a substantial constituent of current circumstances. This is consistent with the way in which Marcus and colleagues (MacKuen et al. Chapter 6

H1: Symbolic predispositions, such as those rooted in social identities, will have a greater impact on levels of enthusiasm than on levels of fear.

H2: Material interests, such as those based on personal finances or employment, have a greater impact on levels of fear than on levels of enthusiasm.

The symbolic politics literature (Sears 1993), and in particular racial resentment theory (Kinder and Sanders 1996), would, ostensibly, make a competing prediction. Racial resentment is rooted in the combination of whites' negative reactions to the perceived violation of basic American values such as individualism by blacks and a generalized negative affect toward that same group. If we extend this theory of white resentment toward blacks to that of white resentment toward Hispanics, it is reasonable to expect a strong association between prejudice and all emotional reactions to immigration. In other words, because the theory suggests that attitudes about groups are rooted in emotion, positive and negative emotional reactions should be strongly associated with prejudice (albeit in different directions) toward an outgroup. If we were to make a specific prediction, however, it would be that prejudice is most closely tied to *anger* because of its obvious conceptual similarity to the notion of *resentment*.

In keeping with other recent studies (for example, Huddy, Feldman, and Cassese, chapter 9 in this volume), we examine whether the individual precursors of anger can be distinguished from those of fear and enthusiasm. If anger is indeed part of the disposition system, predictions should be similar to Hypothesis 1: symbolic predispositions play a greater role in explaining anger. Anger and fear often share certain antecedent conditions, however, especially the presence of a threat, suggesting that we should expect similar individual precursors for those negative emotions. Researchers have also typically found a strong correlation between

---

in this volume; Marcus, Neuman, and MacKuen 2000) distinguish reliance on symbolic predispositions from rational calculation in light of contemporary information. The specific factors we analyze below—views of economic conditions, personal financial concerns, present vulnerability of one's employment to labor market competition, and the number of immigrants moving to the area—are all elements of a citizen's contemporary circumstances that could affect how she responds to immigration (and, indeed, these have been central to political economic cost-benefit approaches to explaining opinion about immigration [Scheve and Slaughter 2001]).

self-reports of anger and fear. In sum, prevailing evidence leads us to predict similarity between anger and fear with regard to their causes.

H3: The individual precursors of anger should closely parallel those of fear. Thus, material interests have greater impact on levels of anger than on levels of enthusiasm.

Our interpretation of symbolic politics theory suggest that a slightly different pattern of results might emerge, with anti-Hispanic prejudice playing a consistently strong role across these emotions but perhaps maximized in the case of anger.

H4: Prejudice has a strong impact on all emotional responses to immigration, decreasing enthusiasm and increasing fear and anger. The strongest linkage should be with anger.

METHODS AND MEASUREMENT

To test for the effects of identities and interests on emotional reactions, we focus on the issue of immigration. Public opinion about immigration, as we noted above, has roots in both symbolic predispositions and material interests. Thus it is a promising issue for examining whether these factors shape responses to immigration through distinct emotional channels.

We tested the hypotheses with data from a nationally representative survey of 354 adult Americans. The survey was conducted by Knowledge Networks, a Web survey company that maintains a large respondent pool by offering free Internet access in exchange for occasional participation in surveys. The company randomly draws samples from a large pool, but it can also stratify samples based on known demographic characteristics of participants in the panel.[5] Given limited resources and ethnic and racial group differences in attitudes about immigration, our sample is stratified to include only non-Hispanic white citizens. Subjects from 46 states completed the survey between October 21 and November 5, 2003. The median interview length was 16 minutes. The median respondent was 46 years old with some college education and a $45,000 annual income. Fifty-two percent of respondents were women. Thirty-one percent identi-

---

5. Knowledge Networks recruits families into its pool by contacting a random sample of U.S. households. According to the company, the recruitment ("response") rate for joining the panel is 56 percent, and the completion rate for the survey reported in this chapter was 77 percent.

fied themselves as Republicans, and 28 percent identified themselves as Democrats.[6]

The survey also included an experiment designed to examine how people respond to certain types of information about immigration. Given our interest in the individual-level predictors of emotional reactions, we focus on the survey as a whole rather than the experiment in this chapter. The experiment employed a 2 × 2 design, in which we manipulated the emphasis in a news story on consequences of immigration and the presence of ethnic identity cues. Subjects in a control group read about government efforts to track the relationship between cell phone use and car crashes. In order to check whether ignoring the experiment affects our tests of the hypotheses, we performed the analyses on the control group alone. The results confirm that we would indeed reach the same conclusions. The full survey simply provides a more powerful test.

In the initial portion of the survey, respondents answered questions regarding their political predispositions and feelings about the economy. After reading a news story, respondents answered questions about the article and their feelings and opinions about immigrants and immigration. Knowledge Networks had previously collected information from all respondents regarding their background and household characteristics.

In order to measure emotional reactions to immigration, several items were asked shortly after exposure to the news story. Following a distractor question about the informativeness of the news story, the following preface appeared on screen: "Now, moving on, we would like to know how you feel about increased immigration. The following questions will ask you how you feel when you think about the high levels of immigration to this country." Participants were then asked, "How anxious (that is, uneasy) does it make you feel? (Very anxious, somewhat anxious, a little anxious, or not anxious at all?)" In randomized order, the emotional response items were *anxious, proud, worried, hopeful,* and *angry.* We combined *anxious* and *worried* into a single measure of fear and *proud* and *hopeful* into a measure of enthusiasm. We used the *angry* item alone to measure anger. These scales were all coded to run from 0 to 1, as were all of the independent variables described below.

So that we could explore the antecedents of emotional reactions to immigration, we included questions tapping several dimensions of social

6. We were able to conduct the survey with the support of Time-Sharing Experiments for the Social Sciences (TESS), an infrastructure project funded by the National Science Foundation that facilitates data collection for projects approved through a double-blind peer review process.

and political identity, including prejudice, nationalism, party identification, and ideology. We constructed a measure of prejudice toward Hispanics by summing responses to three questions. Two were modified versions of the standard racial resentment scale (see Kinder and Sanders 1996) and asked respondents the extent to which they agreed or disagreed with the following statements:

1. "Irish, Italian, Jewish and many other minorities overcame prejudice and worked their way up. Hispanics should do the same without any special favors."
2. "Over the past few years, Hispanics have gotten less than they deserve."

The third prejudice item asked about admiration for Hispanics: "We would like to ask whether you have ever felt admiration for Hispanics. Please tell us whether you have felt admiration for Hispanics very often, fairly often, not too often, or never." Our measure of nationalism is based on two items. Each of these questions asked the respondents how strongly they agreed with the following statements:

1. "There are some things about America today that make me feel ashamed of America."
2. "The world would be a better place if people from other countries were more like Americans."

We measured party identification with the standard branching question format and seven-point scale used by the American National Election Study. We used a respondent's rating of "conservatives" on a feeling thermometer as a proxy for conservative political orientation.[7]

In addition to these symbolic predispositions, we measured several dimensions of economic or material interest. In order to measure economic insecurity, we asked respondents about their personal financial concerns: "We are interested in how people are getting along financially these days. So far as you and your family are concerned, how worried would you say that you are about your present financial situation? (very worried, somewhat worried, a little worried, not worried at all?)" In order to measure perceptions of the national economy, we asked, "Now thinking about the economy in the country as a whole, would you say that OVER THE PAST YEAR the nation's economy has gotten better, stayed

7. All of the agree-disagree items appeared together with similar items in randomized order.

about the same, or gotten worse?" We also included two measures of objective circumstances that might influence respondents' estimation of how immigration affects their lives. The first is the percentage of residents in the respondent's state who are foreign-born, according to the 2000 U.S. Census. The second is a dichotomous measure of whether the respondent is employed in an occupation involving relatively low-skilled and manual labor.[8] Finally, our analysis includes standard measures of age, gender, and educational attainment as control variables.

THE STRUCTURE OF SELF-REPORTED FEELINGS ABOUT IMMIGRATION

Before exploring the precursors of emotional reactions, we examine the structure of self-reported feelings about immigration. Psychologists have demonstrated that variation in emotional self-reports can typically be simplified as falling along two dimensions, though they have disagreed about whether to characterize those dimensions in terms of valence and arousal or negative affect and positive affect.[9] In addition, scholars have identified the occasional emergence of a third dimension, when anger becomes distinguishable from fear (Marcus et al. 2006). In constructing and analyzing measures of emotion, therefore, Marcus and colleagues advise political psychologists to be alert to the underlying dimensions that structure any particular set of self-reports and about the number and type of questions appropriate for capturing these dimensions.

In this regard, our measures of emotion have advantages and disadvantages. One advantage is that we asked how the respondent currently feels about a very specific policy issue. Another is that we offered respondents a range of options to express the intensity of their feelings. We also deliberately included *angry* among the emotion terms so that we would be able to detect aversion if it emerged as distinct from anxiety (Marcus et al. 2006). Unfortunately, limitations on resources prevented us from using a longer list of emotion terms to strengthen the scales. In particular, we were limited by having only a single item to capture anger or aversion.

In order to examine the structure of emotions about immigration, we factor analyzed responses to the five items mentioned above: anxiety, worry, anger, pride, and hope. In table 8.1 we present the simple unconstrained and unrotated solution. Two factors emerged with eigenvalues

8. We coded respondents as having a "labor" occupation if they said they worked as a mechanic, repairer, tradesperson, laborer, or material mover.

9. For a review of research concerning the structure of emotion, see Marcus (2003).

TABLE 8.1: Factor analysis of emotional reactions to immigration: unrotated solution

Emotional reactions	Factor 1: Valence	Factor 2: Arousal
Anxious	.82	.38
Worried	.81	.38
Angry	.81	.24
Proud	−.69	.58
Hopeful	−.67	.61
Eigenvalues	2.91	1.05
Variance explained	58.21	21.00

Note: Entries are drawn from the component matrix (utilizing principal components extraction).

greater than 1. The first is obviously a valence dimension, with negative and positive emotions loading highly but with opposite signs. The second factor, contributing much less explained variance than the first, appears to be some form of arousal, with all five variables loading on the factor in the same direction. These results are consistent with Russell's (1980) valence-arousal conceptualization of the structure of emotion. We found further evidence for this interpretation when we examined the correlation between the scores for each factor and responses to an item asking how excited they were about immigration. The term *excited* seems to capture general feelings of arousal, though it can be associated with positive affect. The correlation between the valence factor and excitement is −.25, and the correlation with the arousal factor is .41. For this reason, we left responses to excited out of our measure of enthusiasm.

When we rotate the solution, as shown in table 8.2, we also get the familiar result that Watson (1988) demonstrated: the two dimensions now are best labeled "positive" emotions (hope and pride) and "negative" emotions (anxiety, worry, and anger). Although either set of dimensions is sufficient to describe the emotional reactions, affective intelligence provides a theoretical rationale for thinking about the emotions in terms of positive and negative dimensions—that is, disposition and surveillance (see Marcus 2003). Note that we do not see the emergence of a third factor in the rotated solution that might indicate a separate dimension for aversion to immigration. This already suggests that, consistent with our hypothesis, the precursors of anger will mirror those of fear. Nonetheless, in order to complete our theoretical tests, we keep the two measures separate for the analyses to follow. We will be able to see if the sources of fear and anger are identical without foreclosing the possibility that some differences will be visible.

TABLE 8.2: Factor analysis of emotional reactions to immigration: Varimax rotated solution

Emotional reactions	Factor 1: Negative	Factor 2: Positive
Anxious	.88	−.17
Worried	.88	−.17
Angry	.80	−.28
Proud	−.22	.87
Hopeful	−.19	.89

Note: Entries are drawn from the structure matrix (utilizing principal components extraction).

SYMBOLIC AND MATERIAL SOURCES OF EMOTION

We now turn to the question of how these different emotional reactions to immigration are linked to different identities and interests. Our goal is to test whether the relationship suggested by affective intelligence theory, that between distinct emotional states and either predispositions or reasoned consideration of circumstances, extends to the origins as well as the effects of emotions. Our concern is with the individual dispositions or circumstances that may serve as antecedents to emotions regarding immigration. Affective intelligence theory leads us to expect that symbolic predispositions are most closely aligned with the experience of enthusiasm, whereas material interests are most closely aligned with the experience of anxiety. The relationship between these factors and the experience of anger is more difficult to predict because anger has similarities to both enthusiasm *and* fear. We expect, however, that material interests will be most closely aligned with anger because the stimuli or situations that elicit anger and fear are often similar, whereas anger and enthusiasm are more similar in the kinds of effects they have on behavior.

Table 8.3 shows the results for regression analyses for fear about increased immigration. In the table, three models are tested (one in each column). In the first column, we examine the impact of identity variables on fear reactions. Only prejudice directed toward Hispanics is significantly related to anxiety, and the effect is substantively enormous. Since each variable is recoded to run from 0 to 1, the coefficient for anti-Hispanic prejudice indicates that moving from the lowest to the highest value for prejudice causes a shift of more than three-quarters of the entire range of the dependent variable. None of the other symbolic predispositions, including nationalism, party identification, and conservatism,

TABLE 8.3: The determinants of fear reactions to immigration

	Model 1	Model 2	Model 3
Identity variables:			
Anti-Hispanic prejudice	.77***		.62***
Nationalism	.02		−.04
Party identification	−.02		.00
Conservatism	.05		.13
Interest variables:			
Personal financial concern		.18**	.21***
Negative view of national economy		.06	.03
Foreign-born persons in the state		.05	.07
Occupation as a laborer		.17***	.18***
Demographic controls:			
Age			.24**
Gender			.09**
Education			−.18*
Constant	−.14	.28***	−.30*
Adjusted R²	.13	.06	.23
N	335	347	333

* p<.05; ** p<.01; *** p<.001.

are significantly associated with anxiety about immigration. In the second model, we see that two of the four interest variables are significantly associated with fear reactions. Personal financial concern and being a laborer both led to significantly higher levels of fear. National economic concerns and the percentage of foreign-born residents in the state are unrelated to fear reactions. Looking at the adjusted R^2 of each model, we see that the identity variables, principally prejudice, explain roughly twice as much variance (13 percent) as the interest variables do (6 percent). Finally, in the full model, which includes identity and interest factors as well as demographic control variables, we find the effects unchanged. In other words, prejudice and material interests independently predict fear reactions to immigration.

Next we turn to the precursors of enthusiasm about immigration. Table 8.4 presents the results. In the first model we find evidence confirming that symbolic predispositions are linked quite powerfully to the expression of enthusiasm. Anti-Hispanic prejudice is strongly and negatively associated with enthusiasm about increased immigration, whereas

TABLE 8.4: The determinants of enthusiasm reactions to immigration

	Model 1	Model 2	Model 3
Identity variables:			
Anti-Hispanic prejudice	−.90***		−.80***
Nationalism	.18*		.22**
Party identification	−.12*		−.15*
Conservatism	.07		.04
Interest variables:			
Personal financial concern		−.02	−.02
Negative view of national economy		−.08	−.09
Foreign-born persons in the state		−.05	−.06
Occupation as a laborer		−.09*	−.02
Demographic controls:			
Age			−.02
Gender			.01
Education			.14*
Constant	.87***	.36***	.82***
Adjusted R^2	.23	.01	.24
N	335	347	333

* p<.05; ** p<.01; *** p<.001.

Republican party identification predicts a more modest but still rather sizeable decline in enthusiasm. We find that nationalism is positively associated with enthusiasm, such that the more respondents believed that the world would be a better place if people from other countries were more like Americans, the more enthusiastic they were about immigration.[10] Affect toward conservatives was not significantly associated with enthusiasm in this model. These variables explain nearly one-quarter of

10. If scholars examined only the bivariate relationships or failed to include a full range of predispositions in the model, then they would miss this positive impact of nationalism. The simple correlation between nationalism and enthusiasm about immigration is practically zero (.01), whereas the correlation with negative emotions is positive (fear = .10, anger = .18). In the bivariate case, however, the covariation of nationalism and anti-Hispanic prejudice hides the fact that nationalism is tied to positive feelings about immigration, while giving rise to the spurious impression that nationalism is tied to negative feelings about immigration.

TABLE 8.5: The determinants of anger reactions to immigration

	Model 1	Model 2	Model 3
Identity variables:			
Anti-Hispanic prejudice	1.10***		.93***
Nationalism	.16		.10
Party identification	−.06		−.04
Conservatism	.00		.10
Interest variables:			
Personal financial concern		.27***	.25***
Negative view of national economy		.09	.08
Foreign-born persons in the state		.12^	.18**
Occupation as a laborer		.18**	.11*
Demographic controls:			
Age			−.02
Gender			.04
Education			−.25**
Constant	−.49***	.10	−.53**
Adjusted R²	.22	.08	.30
N	336	348	334

^ p < .10; * p < .05; ** p < .01; *** p < .001.

the variance (23 percent) in enthusiasm. Among the interest variables, only holding a labor occupation has a significant (negative) impact on enthusiasm for immigration, and it accounts for almost none of its variance. More important, this small association disappears in the omnibus model (Model 3) because it is an artifact of failing to control for education. In general, the evidence is consistent with theoretical predictions that enthusiasm is more strongly linked to predispositions than to material interest.

The third emotion we explored was anger. Our expectations were less clear than in the other cases because the prior work suggests that anger might be associated with aspects of the disposition and the surveillance systems. The results, displayed in table 8.5, suggest that, in fact, anger has some antecedents in common with both fear and enthusiasm. Once again anti-Hispanic prejudice is strongly associated with the emotional reaction, but this is the only identity variable that significantly predicts anger about increased immigration. The effect of prejudice on anger exceeds its impact on fear by nearly 50 percent, suggesting closer kinship with enthusiasm.[11] As with fear, however, material interest also plays a strong role in generating anger. Personal financial concern, the share of foreign-born residents in the respondent's state, and holding a job as a laborer are all related significantly to the expression of anger about immigration. These effects are unchanged when included in an omnibus model, suggesting again that interests and identities contribute independently to anger.

Looking at the omnibus models in tables 8.3 through 8.5, we find that the set of precursors for each emotion differs in significant ways that are largely consistent with predictions. In comparing the contribution of each factor across emotions, we are less interested in the direction of the impact, which should switch predictably between positive and negative emotions, than in the magnitude of the impact. Consistent with the first hypothesis (H1), symbolic predispositions such as partisanship and nationalism have a greater effect on levels of enthusiasm than on levels of fear (p < .05 and p < .10, respectively). The coefficient for prejudice is also stronger in the case of enthusiasm, but the difference in the size of these coefficients is not statistically significant. There is also support for the second hypothesis (H2): Material interests such as personal financial concerns and working as a laborer have a greater effect on levels of fear than on levels of enthusiasm (p < .01 in each case). The third hypothesis (H3) is borne out in the similarity of the models for fear and anger. In fact, the interest variable represented by higher levels of foreign-born residents is significant only in the anger model, where its impact is statistically distinct from that for enthusiasm (p < .05) but not that for fear (p < .15). As noted, however, the absolute impact of prejudice is greater for anger than for fear (p < .05), making it closer to and in fact larger than the impact of enthusiasm, though this difference is not significant. This is consistent with the fourth hypothesis (H4), drawn from symbolic politics theory, which sees prejudice as closely tied to resentment. Similarly, the fourth hypothesis is supported by and serves to qualify the first hypothesis in that prejudice is not only significant but also is the most potent explanatory factor for all three emotions.

Figure 8.1 provides a visual overview of the extent to which each emotion draws on symbolic and material wellsprings by displaying the *relative* rather than the absolute impact of each set of factors based on the omnibus models in tables 8.3 to 8.5 (using the same method as Brader

---

11. The difference in the magnitude of the coefficients is statistically significant (p < .05).

FIGURE 8.1: RELATIVE CONTRIBUTIONS OF IDENTITY AND INTEREST
FACTORS TO PREDICTING EMOTIONAL REACTIONS TO INCREASING
IMMIGRATION

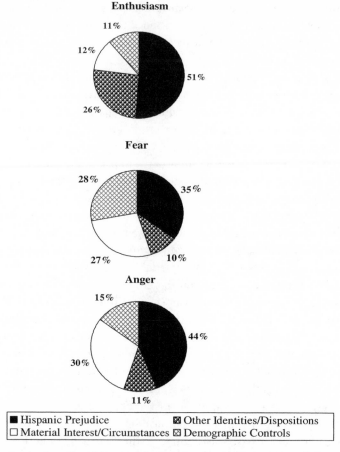

Note: Graphs show the relative contribution of each set of factors to predicting enthusiasm, fear, and anger in reaction to increasing immigration. Values are calculated by dividing the sum of effects in each category by the sum of all estimated effects from the full models in tables 8.3–8.5 (cf. Brader 2005; Marcus, Neuman, and MacKuen 2000).

2006, 131–133, and Marcus, Neuman, and MacKuen 2000, 115–120). The distinct pattern across emotions, especially when comparing enthusiasm to either of the negative emotions, parallels in many respects the pattern for the effects of emotion on the relevance of predispositions and contemporary circumstances (see MacKuen et al., chapter 6 in this volume, figure 6.3; Brader 2006, 133).

SUMMARY AND CONCLUSIONS

Our goal in this chapter has been to explore the impact of individual differences in identities and interests on emotional reactions to immigration. Although existing theoretical approaches make no explicit predictions about which individual difference factors would be most strongly tied to particular emotional reactions, we used affective intelligence and symbolic politics theories as our guides. We would have liked to reach strong conclusions about which of these two approaches fares best, but we are, to put it bluntly, unable to do so. Our results provide at least partial support for both.

In support of affective intelligence theory (Marcus, Neuman, and MacKuen 2000), we found that individual differences in material interests and current circumstances are powerful predictors of self-reported anxiety (but not enthusiasm) about immigration. Predispositions such as nationalism and party identification, on the other hand, powerfully predict levels of enthusiasm about immigration, but not levels of anxiety. In light of the similar causal roots (as opposed to effects) of anger and fear, we expected the antecedents of anger to closely resemble those of anxiety, and that prediction was borne out by our results: material circumstances such as financial concerns, working in a labor occupation, and a high percentage of foreign-born persons in the state all predict anger about increasing immigration, but nationalism and party identification do not influence levels of anger.

One set of findings is not explicable in terms of affective intelligence but does seem consistent with symbolic politics theory (Kinder and Sanders 1996; Sears 1993). The relationship between prejudice toward Hispanics and all three emotions is consistently strong. In fact, prejudice is the most potent predictor by far in every case. Americans' implicit linkage between Hispanics as a group and the issue of immigration is clearly powerful. Moreover, consistent with the conception of prejudice as rooted significantly in resentment toward the outgroup, prejudice toward Hispanics is most closely tied to anger. We hesitate to make too much of a single comparison in judging the explanatory power of an entire theory, but it is interesting that anger, rather than enthusiasm, is tied most closely to prejudice, yet anger and fear are otherwise so parallel in terms of individual-level precursors. Scholars of emotion and politics continue to wrestle with the proper place of anger alongside the better-studied emotions of enthusiasm and fear. Our results suggest that more work needs to be in done conceptualizing the precise sources and role of anger in theories of emotion and politics.

Why does prejudice predict levels of anger, fear, and enthusiasm so strongly and consistently, when one might infer from affective intelligence theory that, as a predisposition, it should be much more closely tied to the experience of enthusiasm than of fear? One possibility is that group-related predispositions such as anti-Hispanic prejudice play a special role when it comes to emotional reactions to issues or other political objects with clear relevance to the group, such as immigration. If prejudice itself is built in part on a long-running affective reaction to a group, as theories of symbolic racism (Sears and Henry 2003) and racial resentment (Kinder and Sanders 1996) claim, then we might in fact expect those with greater levels of prejudice to be more highly emotionally reactive to issues that invoke thoughts about disliked groups.[12] This view also seems consistent with recent psychological work concerning the power of group-based emotions, such as intergroup emotions theory (Dumont et al. 2003; Mackie and Smith 2002) and a sociofunctional threat-based model of prejudice (Cottrell and Neuberg 2005). None of this, of course, directly contradicts affective intelligence theory, which explicitly predicts a close link between enthusiasm and predispositions, on one hand, and anxiety and contemporary circumstances, on the other, *only in regard to the effects of those emotions.*

Still, our findings beg the question of how the loop is closed: if prejudiced people feel anxious when confronted with issues that invoke the disliked group, then how and why does that predisposition get reinforced? Because new information is supposed to be weighted heavily in conditions of anxiety, one might imagine that the predisposition itself would be undermined, at least some of the time. One possible path toward reconciling these findings with the predictions of affective intelligence would be to explore the encoding and recall of information that is collected during the experience of anxiety. Huddy, Feldman, and Cassese (chapter 9) suggest that although anxiety might stimulate attention to new information, as the original theory predicts, it might also interfere with the processing (encoding and recall) of that information. Such selectivity effects would then prevent a predisposition such as prejudice from being revised during or after the experience of anxiety in the political realm.

Marcus and colleagues (2000) argue that affective intelligence theory can reconcile the previously antagonistic views of public opinion as rooted in either symbolic predispositions or material interest and

---

12. Thus, from this, we might similarly expect party identification to play an especially strong role in predicting emotional reactions to candidates in partisan elections, whether the emotion is enthusiasm, fear, or anger.

rational choice. We, indeed, find evidence of the emotion-specific relevance of symbolic and material factors. But the persistent and powerful role of prejudice as a precursor of all emotions suggests that affective intelligence theory (currently) offers partial but not complete purchase on reconciling the symbolic and the material domains.

CHAPTER NINE

On the Distinct Political Effects
of Anxiety and Anger

LEONIE HUDDY, STANLEY FELDMAN, AND ERIN CASSESE

Research concerning emotions has had growing influence on the study of political behavior, producing valuable insights into the emotional underpinnings of political beliefs. George Marcus, Michael MacKuen, and colleagues (1993, 2000) have argued for the centrality of emotion in political decision making. Their theory of affective intelligence focuses on two weakly related dimensions of affect, anxiety and enthusiasm, that have distinct effects on political judgments. In their research, anxiety enhances interest in political matters and inhibits citizen reliance on longstanding political beliefs in arriving at political decisions, whereas enthusiasm influences candidate choice and encourages active interest and involvement in a political campaign. In addition to demonstrating the intricate interconnectedness of affect and cognition, these findings hold important implications for everyday politics. Marcus and colleagues conclude that candidates who engender anxiety cause voters to seek out more information about a campaign, whereas candidates who elicit enthusiasm are more likely to foster active campaign involvement. Their research concerning affective intelligence thus goes beyond a simple demonstration of the political relevance of emotion to underscore the differentiated political effects of specific emotions elicited by political events and candidates.

Evidence of two distinct dimensions of political affect has emerged in other studies of political reasoning (Abelson et al. 1982; Marcus 1988;

We thank David Redlawsk, Andrew Civettini, and Ann Crigler for helpful comments on an earlier draft of this manuscript. This research was supported by Grants SES-0201650, SES-9975063, and SES-0241282 from the National Science Foundation. We gratefully acknowledge the assistance of George E. Marcus, Michael MacKuen, and Charles Taber in data collection.

Brader 2006) and is consistent with a large body of research in psychology concerning the structure of emotions more generally. Two distinct dimensions of self-reported positive and negative affect commonly emerge in social psychological research, and the dimensions are usually only weakly negatively related (Marcus 2003; Cacioppo et al. 1999; Watson et al. 1999; Tellegen et al. 1999; see Marcus 2003 for a summary). From a political vantage point, this means that someone can feel both positive and negative emotions toward a political candidate, producing a complex set of reactions to the candidacy. Emotion researchers in psychology use slightly different names for their models and underlying dimensions, but there is broad consensus that the two dimensions are tied to a basic approach-avoidance behavioral system. Negative emotions are linked to the avoidance of aversive stimuli, whereas positive emotions encourage approach toward rewarding stimuli.

This neat picture of distinct, weakly related negative and positive emotional reactions has met with a growing challenge, however, from a number of social science subfields including behavioral decision theory (Lowenstein 2001; Lerner and Keltner 2000, 2001), social psychology (Berkowitz 2003; Bodenhausen et al. 1994; Mackie et al. 2000; Skitka et al. 2004). and political science (Conover and Feldman 1986; Marcus 2003). The major objection to the prevailing two-dimensional valence model is its inability to explain consequential differences among specific types of positive and negative emotions. In particular, researchers question whether negative emotions such as sadness, anger, and anxiety produce the same cognitive consequences and behavioral outcomes. Anxiety, for example, is typically equated with risk avoidance, whereas anger is tied to risky action (Lerner and Keltner 2000, 2001).

Recent research confirms that it is possible to distinguish among different negative political emotions. Marcus and colleagues (2000) observed three distinct emotional reactions to Bill Clinton: the two familiar dimensions of enthusiasm and anxiety and a third aversion factor conveyed by disgust and anger. Differing negative reactions also have divergent political consequences. Conover and Feldman (1986) found, for example, that anger but not anxiety about the national economy fueled disapproval of President Ronald Reagan. Experimentally manipulated anxiety but not anger heightened the perceived likelihood of future terrorism (Lerner, Gonzalez, Small, and Fischhoff 2003). And Skitka and colleagues (2004) observed higher levels of political tolerance among anxious individuals in the aftermath of 9/11 but lower levels of tolerance among those who were angry.

These findings lead to two important conclusions about the treatment of emotion within political research. First, it is important to distinguish among different negative emotions in order to understand their distinct effects. Second, the effects of different negative emotions need to be contrasted simultaneously because responses such as anxiety and anger are related but distinct, making it difficult to isolate their specific political effects. In this study we differentiate between anger and anxiety as distinct negative reactions to the Iraq war and examine their unique political effects.

TWO-DIMENSIONAL VALENCE MODELS

Careful analysis of the structure of self-reported emotions confirms the existence of distinct positive and negative dimensions (Cacioppo et al. 1999; Marcus 2003; Watson et al. 1999; Watson and Tellegen 1985; Watson and Clark 1992). In the most sophisticated version of this model, Watson and colleagues (Tellegen et al. 1999; Watson et al. 1999; Watson and Clark 1992) posit and test the existence of three hierarchical levels of emotion: a single, higher-level bipolar dimension (pleasant-unpleasant), an intermediate level of dissociated positive and negative affect referred to as positive and negative activation, and a lower level of more discrete emotions such as anger and anxiety. The two dimensions of positive and negative affect or activation are central to this model. In general, we refer to this as the two-dimension valence model.

The central focus on two valence dimensions fits with assorted evidence that they are basic to the way in which emotion is experienced. Positive and negative affect are tied to core aspects of personality: positive affect is linked to extraversion and negative affect is tied to neuroticism (Watson et al. 1999). The two valence dimensions (along with more specific emotions) are consistent across situations and types of measurement, suggesting a close match between affective experience and long-standing predispositions (Watson and Clark 1992). Moreover, the two-dimensional valence model has been neatly equated with two basic motivational systems that developed as part of human evolution: approach and avoidance. The approach system is linked to motivated goal-seeking behavior that produces positive emotions by directing an individual toward experiences and situations that produce pleasure and reward. In contrast, negative affect is linked to avoidance designed to protect against harm and the occurrence of negative outcomes (Cacioppo et al. 1999; Cacioppo, Gardner, and Bernston 1997; Watson et al. 1999). The existence of distinct behavioral approach and avoidance systems is further supported by the involvement in their activation of differing regions of the brain and different neurochemical pathways (Davidson 1995).

This functional approach to emotions, based on the notion that emotions serve decidedly utilitarian and basic evolutionary functions linked to approach and avoidance motivations, helps explain the weak link between positive and negative affect. Negative emotions are likely to surge under conditions of threat but may be muted at other times. In contrast, positive emotions are more common and ongoing. It is thus possible to experience a range of positive emotions without any noticeable shift in negative feelings, although positive affect is likely to decline under conditions of extreme negativity. As a result, positive and negative dimensions of affect are modestly correlated (at around −.45; Watson et al. 1999). This correlation increases significantly under various conditions: high levels of negative emotion, after having made a decision, and as one gets closer to action (Cacioppo et al. 1999; Watson et al. 1999).

BEYOND VALENCE: THE DISTINCT EFFECTS OF ANXIETY AND ANGER

The two-dimensional valence model of positive and negative emotion is thus conceptually clean, mapping onto approach and avoidance motives. But it does not account for the distinction raised earlier among different types of negative emotions, such as anger and anxiety. According to the valence model, all negative emotions should be associated with heightened vigilance and with the avoidance of danger consistent with their link to an avoidance motivation more generally. Anxiety conforms to this pattern, but anger does not. Indeed, anger has commonly been equated with behavioral approach, not avoidance, raising further doubts about any simple correspondence between valence and functional approaches to affect (Carver 2004; Berkowitz and Harmon-Jones 2004; Harmon-Jones and Allen 1998; Harmon-Jones and Sigelman 2001; Lerner and Keltner 2000; Mackie et al. 2000; Marcus 2003).

It is perhaps useful at this point to examine anger and anxiety in greater detail to better understand their distinctive political effects. Consider their origins first. Clinical and cognitive psychologists regard anxiety as a response to an external threat, especially a personal threat, over which the threatened person has little control (Bower 1988; Eysenck 1992). In contrast, anger arises in response to a negative event that frustrates a personally relevant or desired goal (Carver 2004; Lazarus 1991; Stein, Trabasso, and Liwag 2000) and is intensified when the event is caused by a specific agent and viewed as unjust or illegitimate (Clore and Centerbar 2004; Ortony et al. 1988; Smith and Ellsworth 1985; Shaver,

Schwartz, Kirson, and O'Connor 1987; Weiss, Suckow, and Cropanzano 1999).[1]

Anxiety and anger also have different consequences. Anger is linked not only to action but also to a series of cognitive outcomes that propel someone toward actions such as less careful and systematic processing of events, the diminishment of perceived risks, and greater tolerance for risky action. In contrast, anxiety's link to avoidance produces a heightened sensitivity and attention to threat, an overestimation of risks, and more careful information processing. The distinct effects of anger and anxiety make clear the need to better understand their political consequences. We consider each of these distinct consequences in turn to explore their possible political implications.

Risk Assessment and Action

Anxiety commonly produces an overestimation of risk, leads to risk-averse behavior (Eysenck 1992; Lerner and Keltner 2000, 2001; Lerner et al. 2003; Raghunathan and Pham 1999), and is especially likely to increase the perceived risks associated with personally relevant negative events (Butler and Mathews 1987). In contrast, anger tends to decrease perceived threat and leads to heightened risk-taking behavior. Supportive evidence comes from behavioral decision research. Lerner and Keltner (2000) found that anxiety increased the perceived risk of dying from various common causes, whereas anger decreased risk estimates. This is consistent with evidence summarized by Lerner and Keltner (486) that angry people lead more risk-prone lives and tend toward greater optimism. They are, in fact, just as optimistic as happy people when contemplating the future (Lerner and Tiedens in press). In addition, striking differences in the behavioral consequences of anxiety and anger suggest that the widely reported link between general negative feelings and increased pessimism is caused by anxiety, not anger (see Lerner and Keltner 2000 for a summary).

The differing behavioral effects of anxiety and anger lead to specific predictions about their impact on support for government policy. Consider support for overseas military action designed to punish terrorists or curtail terrorism. Anxious individuals should oppose any military action that is seen as dangerous and risky, especially to oneself. In contrast,

---

1. See Berkowitz and Harmon-Jones 2004 for an exception. They believe that all of these factors intensify anger but that it is precipitated very generally by any kind of negative event.

angry individuals, especially those who are angry at terrorists, should be less inclined to see military action as risky and more supportive of it as a consequence. These expectations concerning the political impact of anxiety are supported in our research concerning reactions to 9/11 in which anxious individuals were less supportive than were nonanxious Americans of military intervention in Afghanistan (Huddy, Feldman, Taber, and Lahav 2005). Anger should operate very differently, reducing perceived risks associated with action and leading to support for aggressive military intervention. We did not examine anger in our original research on 9/11, however, and were therefore unable to test this additional prediction. The current study is designed to extend research into the political effects of emotions by examining the simultaneous effect of anxiety and anger on support for the Iraq war.

Political Motivation

Ample research in cognitive psychology and neuroscience demonstrates that anxiety leads to heightened interest in and focus on threatening stimuli (Eysenck 1992; Le Doux 1996; MacLeod and Mathews 1988; Mathews and MacLeod 1986; Mogg et al. 1990; Öhman 2000; Yiend and Mathews 2001; Williams et al. 1997). This effect occurs in experimental lab settings but has also been demonstrated by Marcus and colleagues for political phenomena outside the lab. In their research, individuals who feel anxious about presidential candidates exhibit slightly greater interest in campaigns, care more who wins, and follow campaigns more closely in newspapers and magazines even after controlling for their level of general political interest (Marcus and MacKuen 1993; Marcus et al. 2000).

Two-dimensional valence models predict that any form of negative affect, including anger, will heighten attention to negative stimuli because it produces a heightened sensitivity to threat. From that perspective, anger, anxiety, and a whole host of other negative emotions should elicit increased attention to threatening environmental stimuli (Gray 1987; Watson et al. 1999). Pratto and John (1991) provide supportive evidence that negative emotions produce greater vigilance and attention to negative stimuli. This is also consistent with pervasive evidence that negative affect motivates more effortful and systematic processing and directs attention to new, external information (Bless 2001; Bless et al. 1992; Clore et al. 2001; Schwarz 1990).

It is unclear, however, whether anger also heightens vigilance toward threatening stimuli. Berenbaum and colleagues (1995) provide tentative evidence that anger does not do so, at least in terms of the amount of thought given to threatening events. They presented students with various negative scenarios, asked them to write down everything they would expect to think and feel, and then indicate how strongly they would experience each feeling. When these responses were analyzed, feelings of anxiety produced greater thought but not much action, as expected. In contrast, anger initiated action but little thought. This provides tentative evidence that anger does not increase attention to negative events, as indicated by the amount of thought given to them. This is consistent with the notion that angry individuals are more inclined toward action than toward vigilance, a proposition that we test by examining the effects of anger and anxiety on news consumption and various other indicators of attention to the Iraq war.

Depth of Cognitive Processing

Negative moods tend to deepen levels of cognitive processing (Bless et al. 1992). Marcus and colleagues confirm that anxiety has this effect on political information processing (Marcus and MacKuen 1993; Marcus et al. 2000). They found that Americans who feel anxious about one of the presidential candidates show greater interest and learn more than do less anxious individuals about the candidate's issue positions (although the deeper level of thought given to political problems by anxious individuals does not always facilitate learning; Feldman and Huddy 2005). As noted above, Berenbaum and colleagues (1995) also found that anxiety is associated with increased thoughtfulness. The link between anxiety and deeper levels of cognitive processing is consistent with the notion that anxiety heightens vigilance and leads to a careful analysis of the threat inherent within a given situation in order to avoid harm.

The link between negative emotion and deeper levels of thought does not appear to extend to anger, however. In fact, anger is often associated with lower levels of cognitive effort and less thorough cognitive processing than is anxiety (Bodenhausen et al. 1994; Lerner, Goldberg, and Tetlock 1998; Lerner and Tiedens in press; Tiedens 2001; Tiedens and Linton 2001). Tiedens (2001) found, for example, that people who were induced to feel angry made inferences about others based on chronically accessible scripts, indicative of superficial processing, whereas those who were sad considered a greater number of alternatives. In research by Bodenhausen et al. (1994), angry people engaged in more stereotyping than those who were sad and were more convinced by superficial aspects of a persuasive speech. Lerner and Tiedens (in press) conclude that "angry people engage in relatively automatic, superficial, and heuristic processes." In general, the evidence suggests that angry people, consistent with their orientation toward action, may be faster to arrive at a decision and take shortcuts to do so. We examine the links between political knowledge, anxiety, anger, and support for the Iraq war to further explore these relationships.

In summary, past research provides convincing evidence that anger and anxiety have distinct effects. Anxiety is best characterized by heightened vigilance, increased sensitivity to threat, and behavioral avoidance. In contrast, anger is associated with superficial and possibly rapid decision making, a lowered sensitivity to risk, and an orientation toward action. In contrast to a simple two-dimensional valence model, these two negative emotions can generate diametrically opposed predictions about the implications of negative emotion for political beliefs and action.

THEORETICAL APPROACHES AND SPECIFIC NEGATIVE EMOTIONS

If the two-dimensional valence model cannot account for the obvious distinction between anxiety and anger, what other approach can? We tentatively consider two main classes of explanations: appraisal theories and a broad class of approaches that we refer to collectively as a functional neuroscience perspective. Within appraisal theories, differing negative emotions are caused by the perceived features of a situation. From this perspective, anxiety, anger, shame, sadness, and a range of other negative emotions arise from factors such as one's perceived control over a given situation and certainty about the course of events. In other words, the way someone perceives, understands, and analyzes the development of a specific situation determines his or her emotional reaction to it. In this approach, cognition typically precedes affect (but see Berkowitz and Harmon-Jones 2004 for an exception) and produces fine-grained negative and positive emotions in response to specific events. In contrast, the functional neuroscience perspective blends evidence about the physical location of different emotions in the brain with a functional approach-avoidance framework in which emotions are tied to behavioral tendencies (Carver 2004; Davidson, Jackson, and Kalin 2000; Gray 1994). This approach is similar to the functional approach applied to standard two-dimensional valence models discussed above but, rather than simply equating all negative emotions with an avoidance motive, this perspective accounts for a more clearly differentiated set of emotional and behavioral responses.

Appraisal Theory

According to appraisal theories, people assess a given situation along several distinct dimensions, and the ensuing appraisal determines their emotional reactions to the event (Lazarus 2001; Smith and Ellsworth 1985). Four appraisal dimensions are most pertinent to the distinction between anger and anxiety: responsibility for the event, control of the event, whether the situation is pleasant, and certainty about what has happened and will happen next (Smith and Ellsworth 1985). Both anger and anxiety are characterized by an understanding that an event is unpleasant and typically caused by external factors. Anger and anxiety differ, however, in the degree of perceived certainty and control inherent in the precipitating event (Tiedens and Linton 2001). From an appraisal perspective, anger arises when negative events are clear and certain and action against the responsible agent is seen as likely to succeed (Lazarus 1991; Weiss et al. 1999). In contrast, anxiety is characterized by reduced feelings of certainty and a lack of perceived control over events. This explains why anger produces action whereas anxiety leads to avoidance and heightened perceived risk (Lerner and Keltner 2001). Appraisal theory thus has the virtue of being able to clearly differentiate among numerous negative and positive emotions.

But appraisal theory also has a number of drawbacks. First, it does not address the effects of emotions on cognition. As noted above, anxiety is expected to enhance attention and thoughtful cognitive processing, whereas anger is not. This is difficult to reconcile with appraisal approaches in which cognition drives emotion, not vice versa (but see Roseman and Smith 2001 for a contrary view). Second, the notion of a cognitive appraisal is difficult to operationalize. Consider Lazarus's (1991) reference to "two kinds of appraisal processes—one that operates automatically without awareness or volitional control, and another that is conscious, deliberate and volitional" (169). If appraisal occurs outside conscious awareness, how can it be measured and differentiated from emotional reactions that also occur outside conscious awareness? And how can an unconscious appraisal be differentiated theoretically and empirically from an automatic affective response to a conditioned stimulus? This question regarding the level of consciousness at which cognitive appraisals take place has yet to be successfully resolved by appraisal theorists (see, for example, Ellsworth and Scherer 2003). Third, it is possible that cognitions and emotions operate in a recursive loop in which cognitions influence emotions, which influence cognitions, in turn—making it difficult to know whether cognitive appraisals are causes or consequences of differing emotional states. We should add that not all appraisal theorists view appraisals as the sole source of emotion (see Just, Crigler and Belt, chapter 10 in this volume).

As a consequence, we leave open the possibility that cognitive appraisals drive emotional reactions but also turn to functional neuroscience approaches as a second possible basis for distinguishing among different positive and negative emotions, especially anger and anxiety.

The Functional Neuroscience Approach

The functional neuroscience approach differs from cognitive appraisal theories in several respects. First, functional neuroscience models allow emotions to influence cognitive activities outside of conscious awareness well before conscious appraisals have been formed about a given situation as a conditioned response (CR), secondary conditioned response (SCR), or unconditioned response (UCR) to a specific stimulus. This clearly differs from cognitive appraisal theories in which appraisals of a situation (at either the conscious or the unconscious level) drive emotional reactions. Spezio and Adolphs discuss this process in greater detail (Chapter 4 in this volume) in their description of Damasio's (1994) somatic marker hypothesis. From this perspective, a specific stimulus elicits a particular emotional response through their pairing over time, not through the contemporary appraisal of a given situation. This link is essentially the arrow from affective response (part of the "body loop") to conscious emotional processing (the "as-if loop") in Spezio and Adolphs' depiction of the recurrent multilevel appraisal model. In that sense, emotions are seen as formative and not merely derivative of cognitive activity within a functional neuroscience approach (Marcus 2003).

Second, the functional neuroscience approach is grounded in the neuroscience literature, which locates emotional reactions in parts of the brain that are differentially associated with approach or avoidance motives (Davidson et al. 2000). This perspective accounts for differences between discrete emotions such as anxiety and anger by demonstrating their location in differing parts of the brain that are, in turn, associated to varying degrees with approach and avoidance behavior. Contemporary approaches to appraisal theory can also be considered functional in this sense because they pair emotions with broad action tendencies (for example, the appraisal-tendency framework discussed in Lerner and Tiedens 2004). The key difference is that functional neuroscience approaches focus on two broad behavioral systems—approach and avoidance—with obvious roots in evolutionary theory and specific locations in the brain. In contrast, appraisal theories account for a broader and more differentiated range of actions.

Carver (2004) provides one variant of a functional neuroscience model. Building on the work of Jeffrey Gray, he argues that anger is part of the approach system (the behavioral activation system in Gray's terminology), whereas anxiety is tied to avoidance, or the behavioral inhibition system (see also Marcus 2003). There are slight differences between Gray's and Carver's approaches, but basically negative emotions arise in Carver's system when either approach or avoidance is blocked; positive emotions emerge when avoidance or approach is successful. Thus, according to Carver, anger is associated with moderate levels of frustration (when the goal is not yet lost) and is accompanied by increased effort, whereas anxiety more typically produces avoidance. Carver finds that a dispositional sensitivity to reward is tied to angry responses in an experimental situation, whereas a long-standing sensitivity to threat is linked to greater anxiety. This confirms the link between anger and approach, on one hand, and anxiety and avoidance, on the other, although others note that anger and anxiety do not always produce different action tendencies (Wacker et al. 2003).

There is also neurological evidence linking anger and approach behavior (Davidson et al. 2000). Gray's behavioral activation and inhibition systems (BAS and BIS) have been localized in different parts of the prefrontal cortex. Recent research confirms the link between anger and action by locating anger in regions of the brain such as the action-positive region of the frontal cortex that are associated with the behavioral activation system (Harmon-Jones and Sigelman 2001; Harmon-Jones and Allen 1998).

The association between anxiety and risk aversion and anger and risk-taking is consistent with Carver's functional approach to emotions. Greater sensitivity to threat helps explain why anxiety leads to avoidant behavior: anxiety increases perceived risks, and the need to avoid threat takes on greater urgency as a consequence. This process can be clearly adaptive in a threatening environment. Anger, on the other hand, deemphasizes any perceived risks and precipitates action. The link between anger and action, and anxiety and inaction is supported in findings reported by Berenbaum and colleagues (1995). Mackie and colleagues (2000) also find that anger at an outgroup strongly predicts a desire to argue with, oppose, and attack outgroup members.

Carver's model is thus plausible but by no means universally accepted. Cognitive appraisal models retain a loyal following (see Just,

Crigler, and Belt in this volume; Ellsworth and Scherer 2003). And evidence from neuroscience that anger, anxiety, and other distinct emotional reactions originate in distinct functional regions of the brain remains tentative. At best, we can suggest that the functional neuroscience approach remains an intriguing alternative to cognitive appraisal theories as an explanation for the distinct effects of anger and anxiety. There have been several recent attempts to reconcile the differences between appraisal theories and functional neuroscience approaches, but these models, though appealing in broad outline, lack sufficient specificity. Consider Spezio and Adolphs' recurrent multilevel appraisal model, a blend of Damasio's somatic marker hypothesis, in which affect flavors cognition, and appraisal theory, in which cognition drives affect (see figure 1.1, this volume). The devil lurks in the details of their model, raising a number of unanswered pivotal questions. What happens when a cognitive appraisal is at odds with an automatic affective response? Are there circumstances under which a conditioned affective response overwhelms a cognitive appraisal or when a cognitive appraisal trumps an automatic affective response? These questions are central to political decision making in which immediate emotional arousal (for example, in response to the burning World Trade Center towers) may be at odds with considered intellectual reasoning (for example, the low odds of being victimized by a terrorist attack). A model that blends the two approaches is appealing, but more work is needed to do this successfully.

DATA AND KEY MEASURES

Sample

The data for this chapter are drawn from the Threat and National Security Survey (TNSS), a three-wave national panel study. The analyses are based largely on the second and third waves of the study, which focus on political reactions to the Iraq war. The first wave of the survey was conducted via telephone with a national sample of 1,549 adults over the age of 18 between early October 2001 and early March 2002, focusing on psychological reactions to 9/11 and support for government antiterrorism policy. The initial sample was drawn as a weekly rolling cross-section with roughly 100 individuals interviewed each week throughout this period. The first month's data were collected by Schulman, Ronca, and Bucuvalas, Inc.; the remainder of the data (including waves 2 and 3) was collected by the Stony Brook University

Center for Survey Research. The cooperation rate (AAPOR COOP3) for the survey was 52 percent.[2]

The second wave of data collection occurred in October 2002, after congressional debate about the war had ended. Of the original interviewees, 858 were re-interviewed between 7 and 12 months later for a re-interview rate of 55 percent. An additional 221 respondents were added to the panel from a fresh RDD sample drawn to the same specifications as the original. This new component was designed to serve as a check on panel effects, attrition, and composition. The cooperation rate for this new component was 56 percent. A more complex third wave of data collection occurred in 2003. Half the sample was recontacted during the Iraq war starting on the day after the war's onset (March 20, 2003) and continuing until April 10, 2003, roughly at the official end of the war as announced by George W. Bush. The other half was interviewed some time after the war had ended, from May 20 until June 18. In wave 3 we were able to re-interview 612 individuals from the original panel and 117 of those introduced in wave 2 for a re-interview rate of 68 percent of those interviewed for wave 2. All three waves of the survey were roughly 20 minutes in length. The second and third waves focused on reactions to terrorism and support for the Iraq war.

Questions about Emotions

The second and third waves of the study included batteries of questions focused on emotional responses to a number of targets: anti-American terrorists, Saddam Hussein, a war with Iraq, and anti-war protesters (in wave 3 only). Respondents were presented with three items designed to measure anxiety—*nervous, scared,* and *afraid*—and three to measure anger—*angry, hostile,* and *disgusted*—in response to each target. For the Iraq war and anti-war protesters respondents were also asked to report three positive emotion items: *enthusiastic, proud,* and *hopeful.* Respondents were asked to report how much (very, somewhat, not very, and not at all) a given target had made them feel each emotion. The items for anger, anxiety, and positive emotions were intermixed for each target. Overall, respondents reported a total of nine (anxiety, anger, and positive) emotions toward the Iraq war and anti-war protesters, and six

2. There was no difference in response rate between the two survey organizations, and response rates were similar to those obtained in recent RDD surveys using a different sampling frame but similar methodology (Steeh, Kirgis, Cannon, and DeWitt 2001; Losch et al. 2002).

emotions (anxiety, anger) toward Saddam Hussein and terrorists. Our use of the term *affect* is consistent with much social science research but differs from standard neuroscience usage (as noted by Spezio and Adolphs, this volume), in which an affective response entails physiological signals.

Nine emotions toward President Bush were also assessed in the survey. We do not report them in detail because they comprised an unusually tight single negative-positive factor, making it impossible to separate anger from anxiety or negative from positive emotions. This raises an important question about how reliably different emotions can be distinguished. As noted above, there are situations in which distinct positive and negative dimensions collapse into one, as happened for Bush (cohering into Watson, Tellegen, and colleagues' first-level bipolar dimension; Tellegen et al. 1999). Of the three conditions noted above under which this collapse can occur, a combination of high levels of negative emotion and post-decisional consistency could help explain strong bipolar reactions to President Bush. Many Americans had made a decision about Bush in the 2000 presidential election. More important, Bush was widely disliked at the time by Democrats, and strong negativity toward him on the part of Democrats may have fueled equally strong defensive support for him among Republicans, resulting in the single bipolar positive-negative reaction observed in our data. There has been too little research to enable us fully to understand the conditions under which anger and anxiety are separable (as opposed to forming a single negative dimension). It is clear from our data that complex negative objects such as war and terrorism elicit diverse negative reactions.

THE STRUCTURE OF EMOTIONAL RESPONSES

One of the crucial debates underlying recent research concerning emotions is the extent to which specific negative emotions such as anger and anxiety go together or can be clearly differentiated. We tackle this issue first, by focusing on the structure of negative emotions toward the different targets: the war, terrorists, Saddam, and anti-war protesters. We begin with a confirmatory factor model in which each constellation of negative and positive emotions (anger, anxiety, and enthusiasm) is treated as a latent emotion factor and the correlations among the latent factors are estimated to better determine their dimensional structure. Estimated correlations among distinct emotions can be biased by systematic measurement error because of respondents' tendency to report feeling all or no emotion, potentially attenuating the negative link between positive and negative feelings (Green, Goldman, and Salovey 1993). To get around this, we included a response set factor in each model.

Estimation of the response factor was not completely straightforward. In general, identification of models with a common response set factor is difficult when items have the same response format. A standard approach is to force each item to load equally on the response set factor, leaving only the factor variance to be estimated. In these data, even the variance could not be estimated simultaneously with the other parameters. To deal with this, we estimated a series of factor models with different fixed values for the response set factor variance. This procedure was designed to determine the response set variance that best minimized the fit functions. For waves 2 and 3, the best fit in factor models suggested a response set variance that was about one-eighth the size of the variance of the emotion factors. Values for the response set variance well above and below this value had little substantive effect on the results. None of the conclusions we draw are changed significantly by fixing the variance of the response set factor somewhat higher or lower.

We used the Mplus program to estimate all confirmatory factor models (Muthen and Muthen 2004). The Mplus program models the relationships between the latent variables and discrete indicators as ordered probit functions to avoid the questionable assumption that the (four) response categories for the emotion items are continuous. Treating discrete response categories as continuous can produce misleading fit statistics and, with skewed response distributions, inconsistent parameter estimates.

Specificity of Negative Emotions

To get at the underlying structure of emotions concerning the war and terrorism, we estimated two separate models (one in each wave), testing the existence of distinct emotion factors (positive, anxiety, anger) for each target. The correlations among the latent emotion factors *within* each target for waves 2 and 3 are shown in table 9.1. The correlations among latent emotion factors *across* targets for waves 2 and 3 are shown in table 9.2. The correlations from the wave 2 model are thus split across tables 9.1 and 9.2. The same holds for correlations from the wave 3 model. In both waves, all individual items load highly on their respective target-emotion factor (for example, anger, hostility, and disgust toward Saddam Hussein). These specific item loadings have been omitted

TABLE 9.1: Correlations among latent emotion factors *within* distinct targets

	October 2002	
Factor	Anger	Anxiety
Iraq war:		
Positive emotions	−.53	−.41
Anxiety	.64	
Terrorists:		
Anxiety	.43	
Saddam:		
Anxiety	.56	
	March–June 2003	
	Anger	Anxiety
Iraq war:		
Positive emotions	−.43	−.31
Anxiety	.58	
Protesters:		
Positive emotions	−.89	−.03
Anxiety	.39	
Terrorists:		
Anxiety	.44	
Saddam:		
Anxiety	.54	

Note: Entries are maximum likelihood estimates of the correlations among the emotion factors. Entries in the top panel are from a single model estimating all target-emotion factors in wave 2. This same model was used to generate estimates in the top panel of table 9.2. Entries in the bottom panel are from a single model estimating all target-emotion factors in wave 3. This same model was used to generate estimates in the bottom panel of table 9.2. Both models include a response set factor.

in order to conserve space. The overall fit statistics for the two models are very good.

Several findings emerge from these two tables. First, the models shown in table 9.1 confirm the modest negative relation between positive and negative emotions observed in typical two-dimensional valence models after correction for measurement error (about −.45). This link is essentially confirmed in the current study, with very similar estimated correlations among the emotion factors in the two waves. The correlations between

TABLE 9.2: Correlations among latent emotion factors *across* distinct targets

Factor	October 2002			
	Protesters	Terrorists	Saddam	General
Anxiety:				
Iraq war		.68	.73	.87
Terrorists			.76	.84
Saddam				.91
Anger:				
Iraq war		.07	.15	
Terrorists			.66	

	March–June 2003			
	Protesters	Terrorists	Saddam	General
Anxiety:				
Iraq war	.38	.69	.68	.82
Protesters		.43	.48	.52
Terrorists			.74	.84
Saddam				.86
Anger:				
Iraq war	−.09	.19	.26	
Protesters		.46	.45	
Terrorists			.63	
Positive emotions:				
Iraq war	−.71			

Note: Entries in the first three columns are maximum likelihood estimates of the correlations among the emotion factors. Entries in the first three columns of the top panel are from a single model estimating all target-emotion factors in wave 2. This same model was used to generate estimates in the top panel of table 9.1. Entries in the first three columns of the bottom panel are from a single model estimating all target-emotion factors in wave 3. This same model was used to generate estimates in the bottom panel of table 9.1. Entries in the last column are from two separate models (one for wave 2 and another for wave 3) in which anxiety is a function of a single second-order anxiety factor (replacing the correlations among the anxiety factors). All models include a response set factor.

positive emotions and the two negative emotions range from a weaker value of −.31 (anxiety and enthusiasm for the war in wave 3) to a stronger negative link of −.53 (anger and enthusiasm for the war in wave 2). In general, the modest negative link between positive and negative emotions indicates that Americans felt a mix of both about the Iraq war.

The correlations for anti-war protesters in wave 3 are a little less straightforward, as seen in table 9.1. The estimated correlation of positive emotions with anxiety is not significantly different from zero (−.03), whereas the correlation between positive emotions and anger is −.89. Thus positive emotions and anger toward anti-war protesters are virtually bipolar, whereas anxiety is a relatively distinct response, pointing to an important distinction between anger and anxiety.

Second, there is a clear distinction in reported feelings of anxiety and anger across the different targets, ranging from a high of .64 for the Iraq war in wave 2 to a low of .39 for anti-war protesters in wave 3 (as seen in table 9.2). These correlations indicate that anger and anxiety are positively related, but far from synonymous, as expected. To confirm that anger and anxiety are indeed distinct negative emotions, we also estimated two models (one for wave 2 and one for wave 3) in which a single negative-emotions factor was specified for the three anxiety items and the three anger items for each target and compared the results to models with a distinct latent factor for anxiety and anger. In waves 2 and 3 the separate anger and anxiety model was a much better fit to the data than a single negative-emotions model. This demonstrates that Americans had related but distinct feelings of anger and anxiety toward the war, terrorists, Saddam Hussein, and anti-war protesters.

Generality of Anxiety across Targets

Data presented in table 9.2 yield one more intriguing finding. Anxiety tends to generalize across the different targets to a greater extent than does anger, consistent with related evidence that anxiety may be a basic response that colors reactions to events very generally (Huddy et al. 2002; Berenbaum et al. 1995). In both waves, anxiety toward terrorists, Saddam, and the Iraq war are strongly correlated. The mean correlations are .72 in wave 2 and .70 in wave 3. In wave 3, there is also evidence that anxiety toward anti-war protesters correlates with anxiety toward the other three targets, albeit at somewhat lower levels. As a further test of the generality of anxiety, we estimated a second confirmatory factor model for each wave that replaced the correlations among the anxiety factors with a second-order, generalized anxiety factor. In both waves, anxiety toward terrorists, Saddam, and the war loaded in excess of .8 on the generalized anxiety factor. In wave 3, anxiety toward anti-war protesters had a loading of .52 on generalized anxiety.

Sizeable positive correlations among the anxiety factors are even more impressive when the cognitive links between these targets are scrutinized more closely. It is reasonable to expect that people who feel negatively toward Saddam and terrorists will have relatively few negative feelings toward the Iraq war, resulting in a negative correlation among anxiety items.[3] But *anxiety* about the war bears a strong *positive* relation to anxiety toward terrorists and Saddam, indicating that individuals tend to feel anxious about all three. Similarly, individuals who feel negatively about anti-war protesters should feel much less negative about the war, and this is indeed observed among positive emotions. Those who felt positive about the war felt very few positive emotions about anti-war protesters, as shown in table 9.2. But once again, the correlation between anxiety toward these same two targets is positive (.38), indicating that respondents who felt anxious about the war also felt anxious about war protesters.

In contrast to the substantial correlations among the anxiety factors, anger is a more fine-grained and target-specific emotion. As seen in table 9.2, anger toward the war is virtually uncorrelated with anger toward terrorists and Saddam (and anti-war protesters in wave 3). Reactions to the other targets—Saddam, terrorists, and anti-war protesters—are more likely to elicit negative feelings among those who support the war and indeed go together more tightly. This is seen in the modest positive correlations among measures of anger toward all three targets in table 9.2. These patterns more neatly fit logical expectations that negative feelings toward Saddam, terrorists, and protesters go together. But there is no evidence of a general anger factor comparable to the general anxiety factor that cuts across diverse objects.

Analysis of the dimensions underlying feelings toward the Iraq war and related objects indicate that anger and anxiety are distinct emotional responses. The two negative feelings are moderately correlated, suggesting the possibility of a general negative emotion dimension. However, anger and anxiety cannot be reduced to a single dimension of negative emotion for any of the examined targets. There is also some hint in these analyses that anxiety and anger comprise qualitatively different emotional responses, with anxiety but not anger generalizing across intellectually diverse targets.

POLITICAL CONSEQUENCES OF ANXIETY AND ANGER

We now turn to a direct comparison of the effects of anxiety and anger, drawing exclusively on data from wave 2 that were collected in October

---

3. The correlations between anger toward terrorists and Saddam and *positive* emotions toward the war are approximately +.3 in both waves.

2002, some months before the war began. We avoid use of data from wave 3 for these purposes because we are interested in the link among emotions, the perceived risks of war, and support for it. Once the war had begun in March (corresponding to wave 3 of our data) its associated risks became more readily apparent. Thus, we do not present the findings from wave 3, although they are very similar to those presented for wave 2.

We examine the impact of anxiety and anger on the three distinct political factors discussed above: interest and motivation, perceived risks associated with the war and support for it, and the depth of cognitive processing underlying attitudes toward the war. In each analysis, anxiety is measured as the combination of anxiety toward Saddam Hussein and anxiety toward terrorists, and anger is measured as anger toward the same two targets. Anxiety and anger toward the war were excluded from both measures because it seemed circular to include them as predictors of war support. Moreover, anger toward the war was only weakly related to anger toward Saddam and terrorists, as shown in table 9.2. Both scales are constructed to vary between 0 and 1.[4]

Political Motivation and Media Involvement

In examining the effects of anxiety and anger on attention to the Iraq war and media news consumption, we consider three dependent variables. The self-reported amount of thought about the war was assessed with a scale formed from six questions. The first asked, "Over the last week or two, how much thought have you given to a possible war with Iraq?" The other five questions asked how much thought they had given to the effects of U.S. military action in Iraq on the U.S. economy, the threat of terrorism to the United States, the situation in the Middle East, the help we would get from U.S. allies in the war on terrorism, and Saddam Hussein's willingness to use weapons of mass destruction against U.S. troops. The estimated reliability of this scale is .82, and it is constructed to range from 0 to 1. The second variable is a single question that asked respondents how often they had talked to friends, family, co-workers, or neighbors about a possible war with Iraq (very often, somewhat often, not very often, or not at all). Responses were recoded to range from 0 (not at all) to 1 (very

---

4. The anxiety and the anger scales have large estimated reliabilities. The reliability (coefficient alpha) of the anxiety scale is .91; it is .85 for anger. The correlation between anxiety toward terrorists and Saddam in the confirmatory factor analysis is .76, and the comparable correlation for anger is .66.

TABLE 9.3: Effects of anxiety and anger on motivation and media attention, wave 2
(October 2002)

Variable	Thinking about the war	Talking about the war	Observing media coverage
Anxiety	.21 (.03)	.16 (.04)	.07 (.04)
Anger	.12 (.03)	.06 (.05)	.11 (.04)
Age	.025 (.004)	.012 (.007)	.081 (.006)
Education	.005 (.003)	−.001 (.004)	.015 (.004)
Female	−.08 (.01)	−.08 (.02)	−.14 (.02)
Race or ethnicity			
Black	.02 (.03)	.10 (.04)	.07 (.04)
Hispanic	.06 (.03)	.08 (.05)	.02 (.04)
Other	−.04 (.03)	−.06 (.05)	.01 (.05)
Party ID (Republican)	.03 (.02)	.02 (.03)	.03 (.03)
Ideology (conservative)	−.02 (.02)	−.04 (.04)	.01 (.03)
Authoritarian	−.05 (.02)	−.09 (.03)	−.10 (.03)
Constant	.34 (.05)	.45 (.08)	−.05 (.07)

Note: All entries are unstandardized regression coefficients with standard errors in parentheses. Coefficients in italics are at least twice the size of their standard error.

often). The final variable is a scale formed from two questions: the number of days in the past week respondents reported watching national television news, and the number of days on which they read about national
events in a newspaper. This measure was rescaled to range from 0 to 1. In
addition to the effects of anxiety and anger, regressions also examine the
impact of age, education, gender, race or ethnicity, party identification,
ideological identification, and authoritarianism on attention and media
exposure.[5] These results are shown in table 9.3. All multivariate analyses
rely on regression analysis.

In past research, anxiety has typically predicted political interest and
attention. This relationship is replicated in these data. Individuals who felt
anxious about Saddam and terrorists thought and talked more than others did about the war. They were not, however, significantly more likely

5. Age is an ordinal variable coded in ten-year intervals, education is coded in years,
gender is coded 0 if male and 1 if female, race/ethnicity is composed of three dummy
variables for black, Hispanic, and other (with white as the excluded category), party identification and ideology are standard seven-category measures recoded to range from 0 to
1 with 1 indicating Republican and conservative identifications, and authoritarianism is a
three-item scale ranging from 0 to 1 (see Feldman and Stenner 1997).

than nonanxious individuals to watch television or read a daily newspaper, although findings are in the right direction and almost reach statistical significance.

We had been uncertain as to whether anger would stimulate political attention over and above the effects of anxiety. Some studies have found that general negative affect causes heightened vigilance toward threatening stimuli. There is some support for this prediction in table 9.3. Angry individuals were more likely to think about the war and consume news media than were nonangry individuals, although they were no more likely to talk about the war. Thus, increasing levels of anxiety and anger are both consistently related to higher levels of involvement and attention. With regard to thinking and talking about the war, the coefficient for anxiety is substantially larger than that for anger; with regard to self-reported media attention, the coefficients for anger and anxiety are roughly comparable. Anxiety may be a greater stimulus to political attention than anger, but both variables remain significant predictors for two of the three indicators of motivation and attention.[6]

Several other variables consistently influence political involvement. Older people were substantially more engaged with the war than were younger people; they thought significantly more about it and more frequently watched or read the news. Women were significantly less likely than men to have consumed news media, thought, or talked abut the war; authoritarians also paid less attention to the war than did nonauthoritarians. In addition, increased education enhanced media attention, Hispanics were more likely than Anglos to think about the war, and blacks talked about it more often than did others.

Overall, our results are consistent with theoretical models of the effects of negative affect on attention. Both of the negative emotions considered, anxiety and anger, have broadly similar effects on attention to politics. As both emotions increase, respondents are more likely to report thinking about the Iraq war, talking about it, and, to a more limited extent, attending to national television news and newspapers.

Perceived Risks and Support for the Iraq War

Our second test of the differing effects of anger and anxiety focused directly on the Iraq war; in this instance, our predictions were more

---

6. The coefficients indicate the estimated change in the dependent variable as each emotion varies from its lowest possible score (no reported anxiety or anger) to its highest possible score.

clear-cut. Anger and anxiety were expected to have opposite effects: anxiety was expected to elevate the perceived risks of the war and promote opposition to it, whereas anger was thought to minimize perceived risk and promote support for the war. To assess the war's perceived risks, respondents were asked about their concerns that a war in Iraq would hurt the U.S. economy, increase the threat of terrorism against the United States, make the situation in the Middle East less stable, and decrease help from U.S. allies in the war on terrorism. These four questions were combined into a measure of risk assessment that ranges from 0 to 1 to gauge the total number of potential risks perceived by respondents.[7] The risk Saddam Hussein posed to the United States and its allies was included as the second measure of perceived risk. The threat posed by Saddam was assessed by combining the perceived risk that he would attack the United States with weapons of mass destruction (WMD) and use WMD against neighbors in the Middle-East and the likelihood that he actively supported terrorist groups targeting the United States. The three items form a reliable scale (α = .71).

We also constructed a measure of support for the war from four questions: "How strongly do you favor or oppose U.S. military action against Iraq?"; "How strongly do you favor or oppose U.S. military action against Iraq even if it means the U.S. armed forces might suffer a substantial number of causalities?"; "How strongly do you favor or oppose U.S. military action against Iraq without the support of the United Nations?"; and "How strongly do you favor or oppose sending large numbers of U.S. ground troops into Iraq?" Responses to these four questions have a mean inter-item correlation of .76 (α = .92). The results of the three regression equations are shown in table 9.4.

Consider perceived risk first. Increased anxiety about Saddam and terrorists is associated with a heightened perception that the war in Iraq involved substantial risks, consistent with our initial prediction. The coefficient for anxiety is significant and large. In contrast, anger has the opposite effect. In line with much past research, anger lowers the perceived risk of deploying troops to Iraq. Its effects are also sizeable. Anxious people not only view the war as risky, but they are also more likely to view Saddam as a threat. In the case of Saddam, angry people have the same view. Anger increases the perception that Saddam posed a risk, perhaps because this perception boosted support for the war and military action.

7. We do not report a reliability coefficient for this scale because it is designed not to tap a single latent construct but rather to simply count up the number of distinct perceived risks, which do not necessarily scale together.

TABLE 9.4: Effects of anxiety and anger on perceived risks and war support, wave 2 (October 2002)

Variable	Risk	Threat from Saddam	Support for war
Anxiety	.17 (.04)	.07 (.03)	−.17 (.04)
Anger	−.25 (.04)	.26 (.03)	.41 (.04)
Age	.008 (.006)	−.009 (.004)	−.029 (.006)
Education	.009 (.004)	−.004 (.003)	−.007 (.004)
Female	.01 (.02)	.04 (.01)	−.06 (.02)
Race or ethnicity			
Black	.03 (.03)	−.10 (.03)	−.19 (.03)
Hispanic	.03 (.04)	−.08 (.03)	−.15 (.04)
Other	.05 (.04)	−.10 (.03)	−.14 (.04)
Party ID (Republican)	−.14 (.03)	.06 (.02)	.21 (.03)
Ideology (conservative)	−.06 (.03)	.10 (.02)	.16 (.03)
Authoritarian	−.06 (.03)	.06 (.02)	.11 (.03)
Constant	.45 (.07)	.49 (.05)	.32 (.07)

Note: All entries are unstandardized regression coefficients with standard errors in parentheses. Coefficients in italics are at least twice the size of their standard error.

Thus, the effects of anxiety and anger go together, but in different ways. Anxiety promoted the perception that the war was risky *and* that Saddam posed a threat to the U.S. and his neighbors, consistent with the general effects of anxiety on heightened risk perceptions. In contrast, anger diminished the perceived risk inherent in a war with Iraq but boosted the threat posed by Saddam; both perceptions are consistent with support for military action against Iraq.

The link between anger and action is further borne out by the opposing effects of anxiety and anger on support for the war. Anxious people were more likely to oppose the war than were angry people. Overall, the pattern of findings presented in table 9.4 is consistent with earlier predictions that anxiety increases perceptions of risk and promotes risk aversion and anger reduces sensitivity to risk and motivates support for action against a threatening source.

As expected, Republicans, conservatives, and authoritarians were substantially less likely than Democrats, liberals, or nonauthoritarians to see risks in a war with Iraq, more likely to view Saddam as a threat, and more likely to support military intervention. Older people, women, and minorities were less supportive of the war than were younger people, men and whites; conservatives and the highly authoritarian were more supportive of the war than were liberals and those who are low in authoritarianism.

Thoughtful Cognitive Processing

Anger and anxiety were predicted to have opposite effects on the depth of respondents' thought about the Iraq war. Anger was expected to produce less thoughtful information processing, whereas anxiety was expected to increase the amount of effort put into thinking about the war. Findings presented in table 9.3 provide partial support for this hypothesis: anxiety substantially increased thought about the war. But anger also significantly increased the amount of thought given to the war, which complicates the notion that angry people process information less carefully. Before rejecting the notion that anger promotes superficial cognitive processing, it is important to examine it more closely because self-reported thought about the war tells us little or nothing about the depth or quality of that thought.

To further test the impact of anxiety and anger on thoughtfulness, we examined the degree to which respondents based their opinions about the Iraq war on factual information about Iraq. In essence, we view a strong connection between information about Iraq and estimates of the risks of and support for the war as indicative of thoughtful processing. In contrast, opinions derived in the absence of information are viewed as based on less thoughtful processing. To test that relationship, two interaction terms—anxiety and information, and anger and information—were added to the regression equations presented in table 9.4. Information was assessed as the number of correct responses given to five objective questions about Iraq: the name of one country that shares a border with Iraq, the name of the capital city of Iraq, the name of the Middle Eastern television network that broadcast statements by Osama bin Laden and al Qaeda, the name of the ruling political party in Iraq, and the name of the major ethnic group that lives in the north of Iraq. Responses to these five questions go together very strongly, with a mean tetrachoric correlation of .78. The information scale varies from 0 to 5 with a mean of 1.8 and a mode of 1 correct answer. For this analysis, information was recoded to range from 0 to 1 (5 correct answers).

Findings from these enhanced regression analyses, presented in table 9.5, lend support to our original hypothesis that angry individuals hold less thoughtful opinions about the war than do others. As seen in the table, there is a large interaction between anger and information for all three war-linked attitudes. Among the least angry, those who knew more about Iraq saw greater risks associated with military action before the onset of the war, viewed Saddam as less of a threat than did the less knowledgeable, and were more likely to oppose the war than those who were

TABLE 9.5: Effects of anxiety and anger on perceived risks and war support: added effects of political information, wave 2 (October 2002)

Variable	Risk	Threat from Saddam	Support for war
Anxiety	.12 (.06)	.11 (.04)	−.10 (.06)
Anger	−.07 (.06)	.13 (.05)	.25 (.06)
Information	.35 (.10)	−.31 (.07)	−.06 (.02)
Anxiety * Information	.11 (.12)	−.12 (.09)	−.04 (.02)
Anger * Information	−.47 (.13)	.36 (.10)	.09 (.03)
Age	.006 (.006)	−.007 (.004)	−.027 (.006)
Education	.006 (.004)	−.000 (.003)	.004 (.004)
Female	.03 (.02)	.02 (.01)	−.08 (.02)
Race or ethnicity			
Black	.04 (.03)	−.11 (.03)	−.21 (.03)
Hispanic	.03 (.04)	−.08 (.03)	−.15 (.04)
Other	.06 (.04)	−.11 (.03)	−.15 (.04)
Party ID (Republican)	−.14 (.03)	.07 (.02)	.22 (.03)
Ideology (conservative)	−.04 (.03)	.09 (.02)	.15 (.03)
Authoritarian	−.05 (.03)	.05 (.02)	.10 (.03)
Constant	.35 (.07)	.57 (.05)	.41 (.07)

Note: All entries are unstandardized regression coefficients with standard errors in parentheses. Coefficients in italics are at least twice the size of their standard error.

less well-informed. Among angry individuals, however, these effects disappeared almost completely (as seen by numerically combining the coefficient for information with that for the interaction between information and anger). The effects of information among angry individuals are close to 0 for all three dependent variables in table 9.5. This implies that the opinions of angry individuals were simply unrelated to their knowledge of Iraq. Information acquired about Iraq by nonangry individuals in the build-up to the war influenced their view of Saddam and the war's risks but had absolutely no impact on the opinions of those who were angry with Saddam and terrorists.

We also had expected anxious individuals to hold more thoughtful positions regarding the war. There is slight support for this idea, although the findings do not reach statistical significance. The effects of information increased modestly as anxiety increased. For example, the coefficient for information in the equation predicting the perceived risks of the war increases from .35 among the least anxious to .46 among the most anxious. The interaction between anxiety and information almost reaches statistical significance for attitudes toward the war in a two-tailed test and would be significant in a one-way test. Thus there is weak but tentative support for the hypothesis that anxiety increases thoughtfulness. Taken together, our findings suggest that anger increases self-reported thought but decreases thoughtfulness. In contrast, anxiety increases thought and may marginally increase thoughtfulness.[8]

DISCUSSION

Overall, the findings from this study strongly vindicate the differentiation of negative affect into distinct emotions such as anger and anxiety and pose a clear challenge to the two-dimension valence model, in which all negative emotions are viewed as a single entity. Anger and anxiety are related. But they are also distinct and have strikingly different political consequences. Consider perceptions of risk of and support for the Iraq war. Anger leads to a reduced perception of the war's risks and promotes support for military intervention. In contrast, anxiety heightens perceived risk and reduces support for the war. As a consequence, a combined measure of negative affect lends no insight whatsoever into public opinion about the war (in analyses not shown here), leading to the erroneous impression that negative emotions did not matter one way or the other in shaping support for the war. The reality could not be more different. It is not unduly dramatic to view the balance between Americans' feelings of anger and anxiety as the key to understanding the future trajectory of public support for the war in Iraq.

The differing political effects of anxiety and anger go hand in hand with other responses that bolster the hypothesized link between anger and a propensity toward action, on one hand, and anxiety and a proclivity for greater caution on the other. As noted, angry people tend to minimize the risk of action, whereas anxious people elevate it. Lower levels of perceived risk among angry people are likely to facilitate steps toward potentially risky action, as noted by Lerner and Keltner (2001). Elevated perceptions of risk, however, tend to heighten a sense of caution and raise the threshold for taking risky actions.

8. Our results may seem at odds with Brader and Valentino's findings (Chapter 8 in this volume) that anti-Hispanic prejudice equally influenced angry and anxious responses to immigration. It is difficult to compare the two sets of findings, however, because Brader and Valentino do not test the greater hypothesized influence of prejudice on attitudes toward immigration among angry respondents than anxious ones. A stronger connection between prejudice and views of immigration among angry respondents than among anxious ones would be consistent with the link observed in our data between anger and less effortful political reasoning.

Anger also minimized the connection between knowledge about Iraq and opinions about the war, suggesting that anger may facilitate the adoption of opinions designed to propel action by ignoring contrary information about possible risks. Angry people were not less well informed about Iraq; they scored roughly the same as nonangry individuals on the five-item knowledge quiz in October 2002. But the effects of information on support for the war were quite different among angry and nonangry Americans. Knowledge had very specific effects among nonangry individuals: it diminished their sense that Saddam posed an imminent threat and heightened the perceived riskiness of the war. In contrast, angry individuals held the same amount of information about Iraq, but it did not undermine their support for the war or increase the war's perceived risks as it did for others. We view this as evidence that angry individuals put less effort into thinking about the war, which is consistent with past research on the effects of anger (Lerner, Goldberg, and Tetlock 1998; Lerner and Tiedens in press; Tiedens 2001; Bodenhausen et al. 1994; Tiedens and Linton 2001), but it could also indicate more effortful counterarguing on their part. We are unable to test these alternatives in this study.

Evidence that anger counteracted the negative impact of factual knowledge on support for the war is somewhat at odds with Schreiber's contention (chapter 3 in this volume) that sophisticates employ different neural mechanisms than others do to think about politics. Schreiber argues that sophisticates rely on the "default state network" used to think about social life more generally to process political information, rendering their political judgments less effortful. Our empirical evidence that anger reduces the intellectual effort put into thinking about politics by sophisticates and nonsophisticates alike challenges Schreiber's conclusion by raising questions about the pervasiveness of differences according to sophistication. Nonangry sophisticates do draw different conclusions than nonsophisticates about the necessity of a war with Iraq. But this difference is not necessarily consistent with Schreiber's position because it could arise from effortful processing among sophisticates who connect general information about the Middle East with arguments against going to war with Iraq.

We had also expected anxiety to increase thoughtfulness about the war because of the well-known link between anxiety, heightened threat sensitivity, and risk avoidance. There is clear evidence that anxious individuals saw the war as more risky and were more reluctant to support military action. But evidence that anxious people engaged in more thoughtful information processing was mixed at best. On one hand, anxiety increased self-reported thought about the war and heightened conversations with others about it. This suggests greater attention to the war. There was only weak evidence, however, that anxious people relied more heavily than others on factual knowledge to decide their position regarding a war with Iraq. Information reduced support for the war among anxious individuals (a finding that almost reached statistical significance), which is consistent with the predictions of affective intelligence theory (Marcus, Neuman, and MacKuen 2000). But this effect was confined to support for the war overall. Well-informed, nonanxious individuals were just as likely as the anxious to see the war as risky and view Saddam as a threat.

In conclusion, our findings raise serious concerns about the prevailing two-dimensional valence model of emotion. According to this model, all negative emotions should work in similar fashion, although various researchers concede that specific emotions can have somewhat divergent effects in particular instances (Cacioppo et al. 1999; Watson et al. 1999). But none of the two-dimensional models come close to explaining why two specific negative emotions such as anxiety and anger have competing and diametrically opposed effects on political attitudes. A functional neuroscience approach in which anger is associated with approach and anxiety with avoidance—or cognitive appraisal theories that posit a link between anger and greater action and anxiety and caution—would fit our findings and those of others much better (Carver 2004; Lerner and Tiedens in press). Ultimately, more research is needed to flesh out the various effects of distinct negative emotions and explain why anger and anxiety are so closely associated in self-report data yet have such distinct consequences.

CHAPTER TEN

Don't Give Up Hope: Emotions, Candidate Appraisals, and Votes

MARION R. JUST, ANN N. CRIGLER, AND TODD L. BELT

We know that this election presents America with a real stark choice: A choice between hope and fear; between unity and division.

BILL CLINTON, *A Man from Hope*

Campaigns are built on emotions. These emotions range from the raw passions of a cheering crowd to individual feelings about candidates, parties, issues, and elections. The purpose of this chapter is to examine how citizens' emotions about candidates influence two aspects of the campaign: vote choices and expectations about the results. Whereas the literature about emotions in campaigns emphasizes the critical role of fear, our study addresses the importance of hope in connecting individuals to political objects. As the campaign unfolds, citizens experience the emotion of hope for their preferred candidates with the expectation that these candidates will bring favorable political leadership or enact favorable policies. Because hope is oriented to an unknowable future, it is often accompanied by fear of a different outcome. During an election campaign a compensatory relation develops between hope and fear about opposing candidates. We rely on appraisal theory to explain how emotions are related to assessment of candidate traits or issue positions. Our data suggest that hope is a powerful coping mechanism that can mold perceptions about candidates and bias information search. By the end of the campaign, supporters attach hope to the preferred candidate's chances of winning the election. The result may be false hope for a favored outcome even when there is ample evidence that a preferred candidate is going down to defeat. Whether hope is true or false, we show that hope is the key emotion in voting decisions and is essential for the democratic process.

EMOTIONAL APPRAISAL AND AFFECTIVE INTELLIGENCE

Note that our study of emotions is not about states of being but is, rather, about emotions attached to objects, specifically, emotions about candidates in elections. Because we are convinced that the experience of emotions about a candidate is intertwined with assessments, our analysis draws on appraisal theory. According to many psychologists who have developed appraisal theories of emotion and cognition, emotion is best understood in relation to perception, cognition, and motivation (see, for example, Arnold 1960; Brothers 1999; Cassino and Lodge, chapter 5 in this volume; Crigler, Just, and Belt 2006; Ekman and Davidson 1994; Ekman and Scherer 1984; Lazarus 1991; Martin and Tesser 1996; Oatley 2000; Plutchik 1980; Redlawsk, Civettini, and Lau, chapter 7 in this volume; Roseman and Smith 2001; Schorr 2001; Smith and Kirby 2001). Although there are many variations, what appraisal theories have in common is the claim that specific emotions are elicited through a process of evaluation or appraisal (conscious or unconscious) of people, communications, events, or life situations (Roseman and Smith 2001).[1] Appraisal theory argues that all emotions have a cognitive component that is either preconscious or conscious and may be generated "in response to perceived, remembered, or imagined events, and by automatic or controlled processing" (Roseman and Smith 2001, 7; see also Arnold 1960; Izard and Buechler 1980; Lazarus 1991; Smith and Kirby 2001). We share the view of Spezio and Adolphs (chapter 4 in this volume) that a dualistic view of cognition and affect is misleading and that the relation between emotion and cognition is interactive.

The role of evaluation is critical for understanding why different people may respond to the same situation with different emotions and to explain why the same individual may respond differently to the same situation at different times or why individuals in different circumstances may experience the same emotion (Harré and Gillett 1994). In each case, the evaluation of the situation, along with its relevance to and congruence or incongruence with a person's goals or motives, is critical to the emotion an individual experiences (Breznitz 1986; Lazarus 1991; Roseman

1. Although we embrace appraisal theory in the campaign context, we do not believe that appraisal is the only source of emotion. We agree with Izard (1999) and others that there are multiple and mixed causes of emotions, such as neural, sensorimotor, motivational, and cognitive processes. We also agree with many appraisal theorists who recognize that appraisals not only cause emotions but are also components and consequences of emotional responses (Roseman and Smith 2001, 14–15).

1991; Smith and Lazarus 1990). Almost all emotions share the appraisal of importance; that is, individuals must appraise something as important in order to feel most emotions about the object. Happiness, joy, and hope as well as some of the more negative emotions such as fear, sadness, and anger require some familiarity with the object being appraised.

Typologies of emotions have generated a great deal of scholarly debate. Some researchers view emotions as falling simply along positive and negative dimensions, but others differentiate, for example, between primary and secondary emotions, between named and felt emotions, and between cognitively processed and noncognitively processed emotions. Still others, including the authors, distinguish among a range of discrete emotions (see, for example, Abelson et al. 1982; Belt, Just, and Crigler 2005; Calhoun and Solomon 1984; Fredrickson 2003; Lazarus et al. 1980; Smith and Ellsworth 1985; Wierzbicka 1999). The self-reported semantic representations of emotions, such as those derived from survey research, lend themselves to the description of discrete emotions.

Appraisal theory is consistent with the identification of discrete emotions attached to particular objects. Linguists and psychologists are debating the question of the universality of emotions, but at least some emotions appear to be robust across cultures (Ekman and Davidson 1994; Ekman and Rosenberg 2005; Wierzbicka 1999). Some have argued that analyses using discrete emotional categories are less accurate than those employing valence or multiple dimensions (in application, only two or three dimensions); the more parsimonious analyses lose both accepted validity and explanatory power. This is a general analytic problem. There is a well-recognized trade-off between reliability and validity. The fewer the categories, the greater the reliability and replicability across units and across researchers. The greater the number of categories, the greater the accepted validity and usefulness. For example, scales with five, seven, or ten points are more difficult to replicate than dummy variables, but dummy variables provide less explanatory power.

We rely in this research on appraisal theory rather than affective intelligence theory in part because of the nature of our question. Affective intelligence theory argues that emotions exist in a circumplex, one axis of which is positive and the other negative.[2] Appraisal theory

2. Researchers disagree as to the proper names of these axes. Cassino and Lodge (chapter 5 in this volume) refer to them as positive and negative moods. The labels "mastery" and "threat" (see Marcus 1988) and the labels "enthusiasm" and "anxiety" (see Marcus and MacKuen 1993; Marcus, Neuman, and MacKuen 2000) have also been used.

permits us to measure the dynamics of emotions over time (see Huddy, Feldman, and Cassese, chapter 9 in this volume). For example, during election campaigns citizens appraise and reappraise candidates and other objects. The campaign dynamically generates emotions that lie along the same dimension and on an orthogonal dimension. To emphasize discrete emotions is not to say that these emotions may not be linked or arranged across one or more dimensions. We agree with Brader and Valentino (chapter 8 in this volume) and Huddy et al. (chapter 9), who argue that failing to distinguish among discrete emotions may yield misleading interpretations.

THE IMPORTANCE OF HOPE

Appraisal theory is appropriate for complex and temporally sensitive emotions such as anxiety, fear, and hope because it is precisely the evaluation of the situation in particular external and internal contexts that elicits anxiety, fear, and hope. Some of these evaluations happen without any conscious effort, as in an individual's fear response to a roaring, charging lion. Other evaluations, however, may require more cognitive work. This is especially likely for the emotions that are future-oriented, such as hope (Averill, Catlin, and Chon 1990; Groopman 2004; Lazarus 1991; Roseman and Smith 2001; Snyder 1994; Snyder, Cheavens, and Michael 1999).

Given that some emotions are more highly integrated with cognitions than others, hope is clearly one of the most cognitively integrated emotions. According to Snyder, "How we *think about and interpret* our external environment is the key to understanding hope" (1994, 12, emphasis in original).[3] Hope is intimately associated with appraisal of the environment and the estimated possibility of a preferred outcome (Averill et al. 1990; Kierkegaard quoted in Ben Ze'ev 2000, 474; Nussbaum 2001, 28). In their work, Fridja, Kuipers, and ter Schure (1989) find that unlike other joylike emotions, hope is not characterized by a sense of self-agency or controllability. Instead, hope's appraisal is associated with uncertainty.[4] Hope is the named emotion that is best predicted on the "basis of appraisal and action readiness cues," and appraisal is the more important of the two factors (Frijda, Kuipers, and ter Schure 1989,

---

3. People who feel hopeless have ill-defined goals, see limited, if any, paths to their goals, or have "no willpower to set out to accomplishing their goals" (Snyder 1994, 12).

4. Other emotion terms associated with unexpectedness are *anxiety, fear*, and *surprise*.

216).[5] The evidence of the close tie between hope and estimates of future outcomes is that people who believe an outcome is impossible will not continue to hope.[6]

Hope and fear share an assessment of the probability of a certain outcome that accompanies the behavioral intention of attraction to or repulsion from an object (Ben Ze'ev 2000, 475).[7] The emotion of fear has long been regarded as essential for self-preservation—in terms of the animal response of "fight or flight"—and is therefore regarded as a genetically programmed evolutionary human adaptation (Ben Ze'ev 2000). Like fear, hope can be regarded as essential for survival (Groopman 2004). Hope permits individuals to face the future with equanimity, but like fear, hope depends on feedback from the environment. In a recent interview with the medical researcher Jerome Groopman, the psychologist Richard Davidson argues that hope is an emotion that is integrated with cognition. Davidson explains: "I understand hope as an emotion made up of two parts: a cognitive part and an affective part. When we hope for something, we employ, to some degree, our cognition, marshaling information and data relevant to a desired future event. . . . But hope also involves what I would call affective forecasting—that is, the comforting, energizing, elevating feeling that you experience when you project in your mind a positive future" (Groopman 2004, 193).

Because of their orientation toward the future and the anxiety of uncertainty attached to hope and fear,[8] it is likely that both encourage individuals to seek greater information, at least about possible outcomes. Hope becomes particularly necessary when full information is impossible, as it inevitably is in regard to the future actions of a candidate. Even if a voter had complete information about the characteristics of

5. Some researchers argue that positive emotions in general are useful "antidotes" to negative emotions and their associated narrow behavioral repertoires (Fredrickson and Branigan 2001).

6. We distinguish hope from optimism. Optimism is a general positive attitude (Ben Ze'ev 2000, 477). Hope is different from a general optimistic outlook or personality trait. Hope is attached to a particular object. Hope is specific and relates the individual to important objects.

7. The possibility that the outcome may not be favorable means that hope is almost always accompanied by anxiety. For that reason Lazarus argues that hope is a "mixed" emotional state (2001, 65).

8. Some researchers would argue that the cognitive processing involved in future-oriented emotions such as hope means that hope is not a true emotion (Lazarus et al. 1980; Lazarus 1991; Clore and Ortony 2000; Cicero 2002). Others take the view that cognition is integrated with emotions (Damasio 1994).

a candidate—the personality, experience, political record, and so on—a voter would still have to have faith about what the candidate would do in a set of unknowable future circumstances (Fromm 1968).

Feelings of hope are necessary to decision making, because people need an emotional "upheaval" if they are to take action (Isen 2000; Nussbaum 2001). Scholars agree that hope is an important element in decision making and the sociopolitical function of voting (Averill et al. 1990, 89; Isen 2000). Positive affect (the "mastery" or "enthusiasm" dimension) for a candidate is an important, if not essential, ingredient in the vote decision (Belt, Just, and Crigler 2005; Just, Crigler, and Belt 2006; Marcus 1988, 745; Marcus and MacKuen 1993; Marcus, Neuman, and MacKuen 2000). Hope and enthusiasm are not identical, however. Hope, because of its orientation toward the future, involves a level of uncertainty about the candidate and how he or she will perform in the future. Moreover, hope offers the possibility of transformation from the current state of affairs (whether perceived as positive or negative) to a better situation in the future. Enthusiasm reflects only a positive emotional appraisal of the candidate. It does not convey uncertainty. It is present-oriented rather than future-oriented. And enthusiasm does not offer the promise of transformation. Hope, therefore, is distinct from enthusiasm and integral to the process of representation. Individuals hope that their representatives will act for them in the future in a way that is compatible with their values and goals. Hope is a particularly powerful political emotion because it links the individual's goals for the future with the democratic process (Barber 1972; Kinder 1994). During the campaign, hope becomes critically attached (or not) to candidates. Our first hypothesis is, therefore, one about the political importance of hope.

H1. Importance of hope. Hope is the most important emotion in the campaign, becoming crucial at the end of the campaign when citizens vote for a candidate.

Compensatory Emotion Appraisal

In emphasizing the importance of hope, we fully recognize that citizens feel a range of different emotions about the competing candidates.[9] Dur-

---

9. For example, at the outset of the 1996 presidential campaign, Republicans felt a great deal of anger toward Bill Clinton, the incumbent president, whereas Democrats felt a great deal of hope about the incumbent.

ing the campaign, people's emotions about candidates are dynamic and develop in a compensatory process (Lodge 1995, 136). For example, a person who feels angry at one candidate may need to develop hope for an opposing candidate in order to forge a positive voting decision. A person who feels hopeful for one candidate may become angry at the opponent as a result of the battles waged during the campaign. Campaign messages are tailored to the emotional state of the potential electorate, building on various positive and negative emotions. In an experimental study, Ira Roseman and colleagues found that students responded most favorably to emotional appeals that matched the way they had been feeling before the exposure, except for those who felt afraid. Subjects who reported feeling fearful responded more favorably to hopeful rather than to fearful messages (Roseman, Abelson, and Ewing 1986). The relation between hope and fear leads to our second hypothesis.

H2. Compensatory emotion appraisal. Hope for one candidate is closely related to fear of the opposing candidate.

Consistent Emotion Appraisal

Because the appraisal process entails evaluation, it is reasonable to ask what is being considered in the evaluation process. People use a variety of considerations to evaluate the candidates, such as candidate personality traits (which may be summative judgments in the on-line processing of the campaign), memories of events, issue positions, and the relative placement of candidates with regard to issues (spatial modeling), as well as economic retrospection and prospection (Abelson et al. 1982; Fiorina 1981; Just et al. 1996; Kinder 1994; Lodge 1995; Marcus 1988; Popkin 1991; RePass 1971; Zaller 1992). Whether conscious or unconscious, emotional appraisal links the individual with the political world.

Appraisals of candidates' traits and issue positions are processed in relation to one's own goals. Depending on the nature of the campaign, individuals more or less attribute to candidates their own goals, sense of agency, and pathways for achieving goals. Will a particular candidate help or hinder the achievement of one's goals? Are there substantial differences between the candidates? Is the opposing candidate threatening the achievement of the individual's potential goals? Does the closeness of the race activate the individual's sense of agency in terms of voting (that is, does the individual feel that her vote will matter)?

The process of emotional appraisal of candidates during the campaign aligns individual emotions about candidates with evaluation of the candidates' issue positions and personal traits. For example, the belief that a candidate is not trustworthy may erode the feeling of hope and build the feeling of fear; but feeling hopeful about a candidate may actually contribute to the belief that a candidate is trustworthy and cares about people like oneself. As hope for a candidate increases over time, individuals become more consistent and appraise all of a candidate's traits and issue positions in positive ways and appraise the opponent's in negative ways.

The reason why hope and fear are so important in elections is that they are future-oriented emotions that implicitly compare citizens' judgments about the past with their desires for the future. After all, the point of a campaign is to decide the future direction of the polity. Appraisal of candidates is an important component of hope and fear. These appraisals involve not only the candidates' partisan identifications but also assessments of the candidates' policy positions vis-à-vis one's economic circumstances and appraisal of the candidates' personal traits, especially in terms of governance. We therefore offer a consistency hypothesis. It is similar to Iyengar and Kinder's theory of "projection" (1987), which involves making evaluations of the president consistent with the overall evaluation, even in the face of contrary news.

H3. Consistent emotion appraisal. Evaluations of candidate traits are and become increasingly consistent with the compensatory emotions of hope and fear.

Biased Information Search Strategies

During presidential campaigns, the electorate is bombarded with information. Emotional appraisals of candidates become easily remembered heuristics for decision making (Oatley 1999). Herbert Simon, in comparing humans to computers (1967), argued that emotions are useful because of the limitations of human cognition. Because there is never enough time to process all of the information that is necessary for decision making, emotions are a planning and management device that human beings use to override the serial processing of information; in other words, emotions truncate cognitive processing. According to Simon, emotion as "an interruption mechanism . . . allows the processor to respond to urgent needs in real time" (1967, 39). Emotions are, therefore, adaptive in that they make decisions possible in time-bound situations. For example, the pull of emotions may enforce individual consistency with strategies of attention to campaign messages and events.

Given the information overload of a presidential campaign, emotions act as a heuristic to tame the information tide (Graber 1984). Although there are conscious and unconscious processes of emotion in the appraisal of candidates, "in order to increase the chances that hoping, rather than worrying, will take place, there is need to *bias the information processing itself* in favor of positive thoughts and images" (Breznitz 1986, 300, emphasis in original). Individuals who feel hopeful about a candidate are inclined to view the events and to interpret the messages of the campaign in a manner that is consistent with their preferences. That is, individuals not only come to hold consistent emotional appraisals of the candidates but also modify their information search strategy to support their appraisals.

H4. Hope biases information search. Individuals who feel hope regarding a candidate will attend to news about the campaign and watch that candidate's party's convention on television.

False Hope

Over the course of the campaign, increasing emotional attachments to the candidates are associated with greater certainty about voting decisions and greater emotional investment in the outcome, both of which motivate participation.[10] The connection with hope for the candidate and hope for the outcome of the election also explains the anxiety that individuals feel in anticipation of Election Day. The more one feels hope for the supported candidate, the more one fears that the desired election outcome is at risk—that one's hope may be dashed. Hope appears to function as a coping mechanism for many voters, screening out disconfirming information and, for some voters, leading to false hope. Breznitz distinguishes "mature hoping" from "hoping with denial," which, he argues, is delusional (1986, 302). Individuals who are hopeful about a candidate may *hope against hope* that their candidate will be elected in the face of evidence to the contrary. Therefore, we posit a false hope hypothesis.

H5. False hope. Biased information acquisition and perception may lead to false hope regarding election outcomes.

10. The emotional attachment to candidates and outcomes by the end of the campaign (as well as the social desirability of voting) helps explain why the overwhelming majority of survey respondents report a great likelihood of voting. Given that our study employs a panel design, our respondents are more likely than those in a cross-sectional survey to report a high certainty of voting.

METHODS AND DATA

The current research, part of a project called Campaign Discourse and Civic Engagement,[11] relies on a panel survey conducted in five waves during the 1996 American presidential campaign. The panel survey design is suited to examining the interactions of campaign messages and citizens' emotional evaluations of the candidates over time. (Appendix A presents a summary of the panel design.)

The sample was made up of a 1,002-person national RDD (random digit-dialed) sample of United States citizens who were at least eighteen years of age plus an additional sample of New Hampshire residents.[12] The first wave of the panel survey went into the field at the conclusion of the primary elections in mid-June 1996, with the majority of collection occurring in July. A total of 1,457 respondents completed the telephone questionnaire in an average time of 37.2 minutes per respondent. Subsequent waves of the panel were conducted in late July (wave 2), in early September after the national party conventions (wave 3), in the last three weeks of October (wave 4), and after Election Day (wave 5).[13] We focus on waves 1 and 4 of the panel (the telephone surveys, which we refer to as July and October).

The survey instruments included closed and open-ended questions to assess citizens' involvement in politics, evaluations of the presidential candidates, exposure to and attention to media reports about the campaign, and levels of political knowledge, as well as a series of demographic characteristics. The candidate evaluation questions covered emotional, evaluative (for example, feeling thermometer), and issue topics. Respondents' emotions were attached to the two major candidates specifically. Two questions were used: Has Clinton/Dole ever made you feel (adjective)? How often would you say you have felt (adjective)? The adjectives included *angry, hopeful, afraid, worried, respectful,* and *enthusiastic*.[14]

11. Funding for this project was provided by the Pew Charitable Trusts, the Ford Foundation, and the National Science Foundation Grant #SBR9601418.

12. The New Hampshire sample was not significantly different from the national sample in terms of the variables examined here, and therefore the two samples were combined for this analysis.

13. In order to maximize response rates, we used a variety of cash and gift incentives, introductory or reminder letters, and multiple telephone recontact attempts (response rates are provided in appendix A).

14. Candidate feeling thermometer and trait items (i.e., really cares about people like you, provides strong leadership, is knowledgeable, is trustworthy, and gets things done) from the NES were employed. In addition, respondents were asked to compare the can-

Exposure to and attention to news about the campaign were measured in detail for many possible media sources. Frequency of use and the amount of attention paid to the news were assessed for network evening news programs and local newspapers. The panel survey specifically addressed the interaction of campaign communications, the role of positive and negative emotions, involvement in the campaign, and enthusiasm about one's vote choice (see appendix B for the wording of all survey items used in the following analyses).

The 1996 Presidential Campaign

In 1996 the incumbent president, Bill Clinton, defended his record of peace and prosperity. The strong economy helped the president establish a commanding lead over his Republican challenger, the former Senate Majority Leader, Robert Dole. The challenger countered Clinton's advantage regarding economic issues with a proposal to make a substantial cut in income taxes. He also launched a series of advertisements attacking the record and values of the incumbent. The ads served mainly to convince the electorate that Dole was a negative campaigner and did little to diminish Clinton's standing in the polls. Meanwhile, Dole was forced to respond to media assessments that he was falling behind in the race. In the end, Clinton won a second term by a substantial margin.

RESULTS

Our study of the 1996 election campaign generally confirmed the hypotheses described above. In particular, they showed the importance of hope, its compensatory relation to fear, and the consistency of hope and fear with appraisal of candidates. We also suggest how this process operates by showing how hope biases the citizen's search strategy in the campaign, which affects perceptions of information and expectations about the outcome of the election.

H1. Importance of hope. Hope is the most important emotion in the campaign, becoming crucial at the end of the campaign when citizens vote for a candidate.

We hypothesized that a winning campaign must generate or maintain hope in order for a candidate to be assured of victory. Looking at the level

---

didates' positions regarding such issues as crime, taxes, Medicare, abortion, and reducing the deficit.

FIGURE 10.1: PERCENTAGE OF RESPONDENTS INDICATING EMOTIONAL
RESPONSE TO CANDIDATES

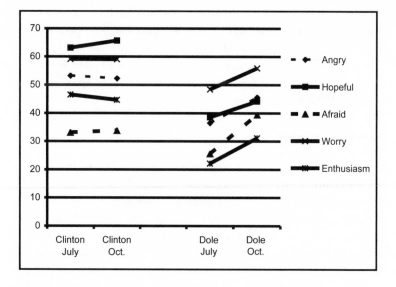

and trajectory of emotions over the course of the 1996 campaign, we see
that our respondents reported hope for the winner, President Clinton,
far more than any other emotion for either candidate. At the outset of the
campaign, hope for Clinton was much greater than hope for Dole (see
figure 10.1). As we would expect from Kinder's research (1994), in July
all emotions were more widely felt for the incumbent than they were for
the challenger, who had yet to be formally nominated. Emotions about
Clinton, the known quantity, did not vary a great deal from July to October. In contrast, all of the emotions for Dole increased sharply during
the campaign. Although hope regarding Dole increased from July to October, the increase was smaller than for any other emotion about Dole.
The result was that by the end of the campaign, the percentage of respondents expressing hope about Clinton far exceeded the percentage reporting hope about Dole (Clinton = 65.7 percent; Dole = 44.2 percent).

Figure 10.1 also shows that, as we expected, hope and enthusiasm are
distinct emotions. Far more respondents reported that they felt hope
than enthusiasm for either candidate. Changes in hope and enthusiasm
during the campaign are not correlated. Whereas hope and enthusiasm
for Dole increased during the campaign, only hope increased for Clinton. These differences may reflect the starting positions for these emotions. Enthusiasm for Clinton was felt by almost half of the respondents
in July, compared to less than a quarter for Dole. One could argue that

Dole voters had more emotional ground to make up than did Clinton voters.

There was virtually no increase in the percentage reporting fear regarding Clinton from July to October, but the percentage of respondents reporting fear with respect to Dole increased during the campaign. As with Clinton, more respondents reported hope than fear with respect to Dole. The percentage of respondents reporting fear with respect to Clinton was less than those reporting it for Dole (Clinton = 33.8 percent; Dole = 39.5 percent). The effects of emotions are reported in the results of two regression models estimating these effects, one for the beginning (July) and the other for the end of the campaign (October; see table 10.1). At the outset of the campaign, hope for the candidates and party identification were significant factors in voters' preference, along with other emotions. Looking at the Beta coefficients in a regression on the differential feeling thermometer of Clinton and Dole (which is correlated at 97.16 percent with the vote),[15] hope for Clinton and Dole in July contributed strongly and at about the same level as party identification to the voters' preference. By the end of the campaign, however, hope regarding Clinton was the strongest contributor to candidate preference. It is interesting that by the end of the campaign, economic retrospection and prospection fell in line with candidate preference, suggesting that the campaign not only aroused hope regarding both Clinton and Dole but also stimulated economic rationalization of the voting preference.

Table 10.1 shows that hope was the most important candidate emotion, but it also indicates that fear was also present in the early and late stages of the campaign, although it was greater at the end of the campaign. We hypothesized that the logic of compensatory processing, as suggested by Lodge, would increase the relation between hope and fear over the course of the campaign.

H2. Compensatory emotion appraisal. Hope for one candidate is closely related to fear of the opposing candidate.

The correlation of hope regarding Clinton and fear regarding Dole jumped from .243 to .376 from July to October. The correlation of hope regarding Dole and fear of Clinton received a similar boost, jumping from .329 to .386 in October. Table 10.2 shows the results of a factor analysis of all positive and negative emotions about Clinton and Dole. Three factors

15. Similar results have been found by Granberg and Brown (1989, 174).

TABLE 10.1: Predicting differential feeling thermometer (Clinton-Dole)

	July			October		
	B	SE	Beta	B	SE	Beta
Emotions about Clinton:						
Hope	16.059***	1.619	.191	21.020***	1.844	.234
Enthusiasm	10.390***	1.538	.128	6.246***	1.680	.073
Worry	−7.480***	1.571	−.091	−5.750**	1.749	−.066
Fear	−7.731***	1.581	−.090	−5.547**	1.720	−.061
Anger	−9.802***	1.521	−.120	−9.704***	1.640	−.113
Emotions about Dole:						
Hope	−17.837***	1.646	−.214	−15.084***	1.877	−.175
Enthusiasm	−11.467***	1.772	−.117	−13.439***	1.859	−.146
Worry	7.110***	1.480	.087	6.226***	1.757	.072
Fear	8.710***	1.677	.094	10.776***	1.782	.123
Anger	5.635***	1.466	.067	6.701***	1.616	.078
Party identification	−4.426***	.391	−.219	−3.876***	.434	−.183
Economic prospection	3.462	3.078	.018	7.695*	3.495	.036
Economic retrospection	2.691	2.412	.017	6.835*	2.749	.040
Issue knowledge	−10.139***	2.658	−.060	−8.945**	2.921	−.049
Gender (male)	−1.618	1.246	−.020	−4.571***	1.362	−.053
Race (white)	−.597	1.872	−.005	−1.593	2.031	−.012
Income	−2.006	2.770	−.012	−1.128	2.972	−.007
Education	1.945	2.587	.013	−.272	2.763	−.002
Age	−.080*	.039	−.032	−.041	.042	−.016
R^2	.722			.736		
N	1,296			1,153		

Note: Multiple regression analyses. Variables measured at corresponding times.

* $p < .05$; ** $p < .01$; *** $p < .001$.

were extracted in the rotated component matrix. In July, factor 1 showed extremely high loadings for fear, anger, and worry about Clinton *as well as* hope and enthusiasm for Dole. Negative feelings about Dole and positive feelings about Clinton, however, constituted two other separate factors. The results suggest that from the outset, support for the challenger derived substantially from negative feelings about the incumbent. This is not unexpected, because the incumbent is better known and people have a much longer period of time to establish their feelings about the incumbent than they do about the challenger. The reverse, however, was not the case.

TABLE 10.2: Rotated component matrix of emotions

	July components			October components		
	1	2	3	1	2	3
Emotions about Clinton:						
Hope	−.224	.240	.773	.670	−.442	.104
Enthusiasm	−.082	.286	.783	.686	−.372	.226
Worry	.703	.117	−.264	.012	.741	.231
Fear	.722	.172	−.223	−.020	.788	.205
Anger	.680	.134	−.306	−.037	.746	.164
Emotions about Dole:						
Hope	.717	−.403	.107	−.223	.370	.755
Enthusiasm	.683	−.322	.280	−.100	.259	.831
Worry	−.007	.752	.159	.777	.047	−.197
Fear	.007	.768	.153	.777	.082	−.203
Anger	.022	.700	.143	.725	.094	−.191

Note: Extraction method: principal component analysis. Rotation method: varimax with Kaiser normalization.

Negative feelings about Dole (factor 2) and positive feelings about Clinton (factor 3) were separable at the beginning of the campaign. We undertook additional factor analyses of the emotions that formed these unique inverse relationships (Clinton positive/Dole negative and Dole positive/Clinton negative).[16] In these analyses, positive emotions about Clinton and negative emotions about Dole were separable: they formed distinct factors. In the case of positive emotions about Dole and negative ones about Clinton, however, only one combined factor could be extracted, indicating that these emotions were closely related at the beginning of the campaign.

By the end of the campaign, however, the pattern of emotions among Clinton supporters looked just like the pattern for Dole supporters. The first factor extracted is a combination of hope and enthusiasm for Clinton and fear, anger, and worry about Dole. It appears that the campaign brought a convergence of compensatory emotions among Clinton supporters similar to that experienced by Dole supporters from the beginning of the campaign. Further factor analyses of corresponding compensatory emotions (Clinton positive/Dole negative and Dole positive/Clinton negative) shows

16. Not reported in table 10.2.

that in *both* cases only one component can be extracted.[17] The results confirm a strong campaign effect on the emotional responses to candidates. By the end of the campaign, positive feelings about one's preferred candidate become enmeshed with negative feelings about the opponent, even if those sets of feelings were separable at the outset of the campaign. Very likely, candidate attacks during the campaign have the unintended effect of invigorating the compensatory emotions of the opposition's supporters. Negative compensatory emotions may account for the "boomerang" effect of negative ads first described by Gina Garramone (1984).

H3. Consistent emotion appraisal. Evaluations of candidate traits are and become increasingly consistent with the compensatory emotions of hope and fear.

We explored the relation between emotions about and traits of Clinton and Dole over the course of the campaign in another set of factor analyses (see table 10.3). Early in the campaign in July, the first two factors were symmetrical; they were positive emotions and trait appraisals of Clinton and positive emotions and trait appraisals of Dole. The third factor represents negative emotions about Dole. By the end of the campaign in October, compensatory emotions emerged as expected. The first factor is made up of positive feelings and trait appraisals of Clinton along with negative feelings about Dole. The third factor consists of positive feelings and positive trait appraisals of Dole, but with no negative feelings about Clinton. The second factor shows a strengthening correlation among emotions and trait assessments. It represents primarily negative feelings about Clinton, but it also includes negative appraisal of his traits. The results again show that by the end of the campaign, negative feelings about at least one of the candidates translated into negative trait assessments for that candidate. The findings of the factor analyses support the notion that during the campaign, compensatory emotions led to negative appraisal of the opposing candidate. We can assume that the ongoing relation between emotions regarding candidates and trait appraisal is fed by political advertising and coverage of the candidates in the media. The ongoing appraisal is consistent with the arguments of Spezio and Adolphs (chapter 4 in this volume).

H4. Hope biases information search. Individuals who feel hope regarding a candidate will attend to news about the campaign and watch that candidate's party's convention on television.

17. Not reported in table 10.2.

TABLE 10.3: Factor analyses: Emotions and trait appraisals

	July components			October components		
	1	*2*	*3*	*1*	*2*	*3*
Emotions about Clinton:						
Hope	.672	−.041	.338	.684	−.388	−.072
Enthusiasm	.597	.041	.436	.694	−.278	.013
Worry	−.502	.399	.381	.030	.736	.216
Fear	−.527	.351	.323	.063	.697	.192
Anger	−.594	.307	.311	−.006	.702	.199
Emotions about Dole:						
Hope	−.288	.715	−.027	−.098	.418	.655
Enthusiasm	−.161	.663	.088	.013	.360	.637
Worry	.109	−.218	.698	.702	.113	−.278
Fear	.158	−.202	.681	.707	.080	−.302
Anger	.082	−.209	.650	.651	.131	−.287
Clinton traits:						
Cares about people	.816	−.108	.153	.614	−.609	−.084
Strong leader	.812	−.175	.166	.557	−.628	−.143
Trustworthy	.809	−.207	.096	.510	−.641	−.189
Gets things done	.766	−.134	.086	.516	−.609	−.088
Dole traits:						
Cares about people	−.164	.729	−.324	−.303	.168	.728
Strong leader	−.101	.738	−.204	−.174	.102	.746
Trustworthy	−.097	.722	−.341	−.265	.094	.731
Gets things done	−.052	.716	−.205	−.119	.113	.750

Note: Rotated component matrix. Extraction method: principal component analysis. Rotation method: varimax with Kaiser normalization.

Our fourth hypothesis deals with the expected interrelation between emotions and media consumption. Based on the research of Marcus, Neuman, and MacKuen (2000), we expected that fear would be the primary emotional stimulus to campaign attention. Our results show, however, that hope regarding both candidates was a significant factor in stimulating attention to the respective party conventions and to television network news. The results of probit analyses regarding party conventions followed from the logic of support for a party's candidate. Hopefulness about a candidate in the early phase of the campaign led to watching televised coverage of that candidate's party convention later in the campaign (see table 10.4). The influence of hope on television news viewing was candidate-specific, however. In models predicting television news viewership, we found, contrary to Marcus (1985), that early feelings of hope about Clinton, rather than fear of either candidate, stimulated television news usage later in the campaign. The reverse was not true. Neither hope about Dole nor fear of Clinton stimulated television news usage. These results confirm the hypothesis that hope biases information search strategies. It would have been difficult for a hopeful Dole supporter to find reinforcing information on network television news, which was preoccupied with the horserace that Dole was losing (Just, Crigler, and Buhr 1999). Dole supporters appear to have sought confirming information (the Republican Party convention) and avoided challenging information (the campaign horserace) on television news. Once again, our results support the recurrent multilevel appraisal model of Spezio and Adolphs (chapter 4 in this volume).

Table 10.4 does not offer support for the proposition that only fear stimulates attention to information sources. Hope is by far the most important influence in reinforcing messages, but it is also more significant than fear in encouraging later engagement with campaign information.

If positive and negative emotions arouse attention to the media, does attention to campaign media stimulate positive and negative emotions? We examined the question of how emotion-based appraisals of the candidates may be affected during the campaign by respondents' media usage (controlling for partisanship, issue knowledge, and demographic identities). We found that viewing the national parties' conventions had a significant influence on the emotional appraisals of both the incumbent and the challenger (see table 10.5). Respondents who watched the Democratic convention became more hopeful about Clinton and more afraid of Dole. As expected, the converse was true for those who watched the Republican convention. People who watched the Republican convention became less hopeful about Clinton and both more hopeful about and less afraid of Dole. For the challenger, the national convention presents a crucial stage for forming an emotional relationship with voters. These results suggest that the compensatory relation between hope and fear is heightened during the conventions, when candidates articulate their messages and draw distinctions between themselves and their opponents.

H5. False hope. Biased information acquisition and perception may lead to false hope regarding election outcomes.

TABLE 10.4: Predicting media usage

	Watched Democratic convention	Watched TV news (Oct.)		Watched Republican convention	Watched TV news (Oct.)
Emotions about Clinton:			Emotions about Dole:		
Hope	.227*	.530***	Hope	.227*	.147
	(.108)	(.146)		(.113)	(.145)
Enthusiasm	.063	−.003	Enthusiasm	.233	.207
	(.105)	(.144)		(.130)	(.169)
Emotions about Dole:			Emotions about Clinton:		
Worry	.032	.140	Worry	.092	.038
	(.099)	(.133)		(.105)	(.141)
Fear	.120	−.114	Fear	.085	−.122
	(.116)	(.152)		(.109)	(.137)
Anger	.004	.025	Anger	.026	−.132
	(.097)	(.129)		(.102)	(.133)
Party identification	−.069**	.048	Party identification	−.006	−.025
	(.025)	(.034)		(.025)	(.032)
Economic prospection	.390	.399	Economic prospection	.222	.311
	(.215)	(.272)		(.214)	(.267)
Economic retrospection	−.080	.257	Economic retrospection	−.092	.246
	(.165)	(.211)		(.166)	(.207)
Issue knowledge	.231	.178	Issue knowledge	.143	.246
	(.178)	(.231)		(.182)	(.229)
Gender (male)	.027	−.028	Gender (male)	−.049	−.058
	(.085)	(.112)		(.086)	(.111)
Race (white)	−.453***	.055	Race (white)	−.177	.027
	(.151)	(.173)		(.138)	(.173)
Income	−.003	.577*	Income	.067	.628*
	(.190)	(.247)		(.191)	(.244)
Education	.196	−.234	Education	.333	−.144
	(.175)	(.232)		(.176)	(.231)
Age	.007**	.010**	Age	.007**	.010**
	(.003)	(.004)		(.003)	(.004)
Pseudo R^2	.050	.058	Pseudo R^2	.032	.037
N	1,048	1,048	N	1,043	1,043

Note: Probit analyses. Standard error in parentheses. Independent variables measured in July.

* $p < .05$; ** $p < .01$; *** $p < .001$.

TABLE 10.5: Predicting October emotions

	Emotions about Clinton			Emotions about Dole	
Clinton models	Hope	Fear	Dole models	Hope	Fear
Emotions about Clinton:			Emotions about Clinton:		
Hope	1.472***		Hope	1.136***	
	(.103)			(.097)	
Fear		1.247***	Fear		1.188***
		(.092)			(.101)
Media usage:			Media usage:		
Watch TV news (Oct.)	.060	−.011	Watch TV news (Oct.)	.050	.073*
	(.040)	(.036)		(.036)	(.035)
Watch Dem. convention	.943***	−.006	Watch Dem. convention	−.289	.565**
	(.263)	(.217)		(.227)	(.214)
Watch Rep. convention	−.827**	.244	Watch Rep. convention	.921***	−.486*
	(.264)	(.219)		(.231)	(.219)
Party identification	−.217***	.109***	Party identification	.189***	−.162***
	(.029)	(.025)		(.026)	(.024)
Issue knowledge	−.071	.448*	Issue knowledge	.089	.367
	(.205)	(.188)		(.193)	(.188)
Gender (male)	−.070	−.230*	Gender (male)	−.041	−.219*
	(.101)	(.091)		(.092)	(.088)
Race (white)	.060	.014	Race (white)	.268	.095
	(.172)	(.148)		(.150)	(.137)
Income	−.339	−.156	Income	.249	−.063
	(.228)	(.203)		(.206)	(.195)
Education	.032	.260	Education	−.164	.255
	(.210)	(.185)		(.188)	(.182)
Age	−.012***	−.004	Age	−.002	−.008**
	(.003)	(.003)		(.003)	(.003)
Pseudo R^2	.396	.219	Pseudo R^2	.291	.213
N	1,085	1,085	N	1,070	1,077

Note: Probit analyses. Standard error in parentheses. Independent variables measured in July except as noted.

* $p < .05$; ** $p < .01$; *** $p < .001$.

Our fifth hypothesis stated that the more hope an individual has about a candidate, the more likely the individual will believe that the outcome of the election will be favorable for that candidate but that exposure to media coverage of the horserace will decrease false hope. Specifically, the more hope respondents had regarding Dole, the more they would be likely to think the election would be close. Since Dole was widely predicted to lose, we can infer that hope biases judgment in favor of the preferred outcome. Voters could find lots of evidence supporting the probability that Clinton, who was regarded as the front-runner, would win. Therefore, the more hope respondents felt regarding Clinton, the more they felt the election would *not* be close, although the effect was not as great as the bias for the preferred outcome for Dole.

Respondents who viewed network news were less likely to expect the election to be close. Content analysis of network news from the 1996 campaign shows that the emphasis was on the aspect of the campaign as a horserace (Hess Report 2000; Just, Crigler, and Buhr 1999). It would have been hard for television news viewers to avoid knowing that the race between Clinton and Dole was not expected to be close. But regardless of these factors, the strongest influence was hope about Dole—those who felt hopeful about Dole experienced false hope, in expecting that the election outcome would be close.[18]

CONCLUSION

Results of our analysis show that the feeling of hope with respect to a candidate is a crucial factor in voting preference but that the future-oriented emotions of hope and fear are closely related. Our data show that in some instances, hope regarding the preferred candidate and compensatory fear

---

18. We estimated two probit models predicting the expected closeness of the election (close = 1, expect Clinton wins = 0). In our first model we included emotions about Clinton, in the format coefficients (standard error, significance): Clinton/hopeful = $-.269(.101, p < .01)$; Clinton/afraid = $.221$ $(.091, p < .05)$; network news usage = $-.272$ $(.132, p < .05)$; gender = $-.214(.083, p < .01)$; income = $-.482$ $(.185, p < .001)$. For the Dole emotions model: Dole/hopeful = $.438$ $(.095, p < .001)$; Dole/afraid = $-.269$ $(.091, p < .01)$; network news usage = $-.295$ $(.133, p < .05)$; gender = $-.251$ $(.084, p < .01)$; income = $-.536$ $(.186, p < .01)$. Both models control for the effects of caring who wins, watching both party conventions, party identification, economic prospection and retrospection, issue knowledge, race, education, and age (the influence of all controls is not statistically significant). For the Clinton model, pseudo R^2 = $.055$, n = 1030. For the Dole model, pseudo R^2 = $.071$, n = 1028. Note that along with Dole supporters, lower-income and female respondents also expected the election to be close.

of the opposing candidates are present from the outset of the campaign. When hope regarding the preferred candidate is not accompanied by fear of the opponent, the messages of the campaign can stimulate compensatory emotions of hope and fear concerning the opposing candidate.

Appraisal of candidate traits is intimately related to emotions even at the outset of the campaign. Nonetheless, appraisals of the traits of competing candidates at the outset of the campaign—unlike emotional appraisals—appear to be independent of each other. Increasing compensatory negative emotions about an opposing candidate, however, leads to negative appraisal of that candidate's traits by the end of the campaign.

Whereas previous research has shown that fear stimulates information-seeking behavior, we find that hope in fact spurs use of important campaign communication including political conventions and television network news. It is reasonable to think that because hope, like fear, is a transformative emotion, people seek support for their future expectations. In the search for information, however, hope may bias the process of information-seeking. The intimate association of hope and fear is further illustrated by the fact that both can stimulate an individual to seek out information during the campaign. The classical philosophers who inveighed against hope for clouding judgment were correct. There is a caveat, however. People who are exposed to information are less likely to hold false beliefs about future outcomes. Respondents who paid attention to the media (notably television news that was preoccupied with the horserace) were not likely to hold false hope for the losing candidate.

The evidence about the role of emotions and appraisal in campaigns also shows that campaigns serve important informational functions. Campaigns contribute to the ongoing reappraisal of the candidates. These continuing appraisals involve candidate traits, economic assessments, and group identifications. Hope about a candidate is a coping mechanism for many voters, motivating them to search for reinforcing information and to screen out disconfirming information.

Much has been made about messages of fear in campaigns, particularly concerning the impact of negative political ads, but messages of hope are also pervasive. Hopeful messages are epitomized by speeches given at party conventions. Hope is the emotion embedded in campaign promises, which are the staple of candidate interactions with voters. It makes sense to think of hope as the quintessential democratic emotion. Hope forges the political connection between the candidates' promises and the citizens' votes.

Hope and enthusiasm are not distinguishable at the end of the campaign because by that time the future is now. That concurrence explains why hope and enthusiasm may not be easily distinguished in cross-sectional survey analysis. Our findings about the dynamic and reciprocal emotions of hope and fear, the ongoing relation between appraisal and emotion, and the development of compensatory feelings about candidates do not reveal whether there is a contradiction between the neuroscience underlying affective intelligence theory and the emphasis of appraisal theory on cognitive and discrete emotion. We can attempt to resolve these questions via future experimental research. Further study could show how these important reciprocal processes operate and how emotions are related to preconscious and conscious appraisals. This kind of research calls for greater collaboration between the study of politics and the neuroscientific study of emotion.

Appendix A: Study Summary

In the first wave of the panel study, a total of 1,457 respondents completed the telephone questionnaire (CATI) in an average time of 37.2 minutes per respondent. Subsequent waves of the panel were conducted in late July (Wave 2), in early September after the national party conventions (Wave 3), in the last three weeks of October (Wave 4), and the final round after Election Day (Wave 5). In order to maximize response rates, we used a variety of cash and gift incentives, introductory or reminder letters, and multiple telephone recontact attempts.

The panel is summarized in table 10A.1.

TABLE A.1

		Dates in field			
	Wave 1, June 18– Aug. 15	Wave 2, July 22– Aug. 16	Wave 3, Sept. 9– Nov. 5	Wave 4, Oct. 10– Nov. 5	Wave 5, Nov. 21, 1996
Methods	CATI	Video Questionnaire	Mail	CATI	Mail
No. of variables	360	45	37	277	37
Total N	1,457	787	1,119	1,265	1,066
Overall response rate	73%	56%	79%	87%	75%
RDD N	1,002	507	755	835	693
RDD response rate	68%	51%	78%	83%	71%
NH N	455	280	364	430	373
NH response rate	87%	62%	80%	95%	82%

The response rate was calculated as follows:

$$\frac{\text{total sample} - \text{ineligible cases} - \text{nonsample cases}}{\text{total sample}}$$

Ineligible cases included persons who were sick, non-English speakers, or otherwise unavailable during the survey period. Nonsample cases included telephone numbers not associated with a household or households with no U.S. citizen or adults.

Appendix B: Survey Question Wording and Variable Codes (ordered as they appear in the figure and tables)

CANDIDATE EMOTIONS

"We would like to know something about the feelings you have toward the candidates for president. I am going to name a candidate and I want you to tell me whether something about that candidate or the candidate's positions on the issues has made you have certain feelings like anger or hope. The first (or next) candidate I am going to ask you about is [candidate] (Bill Clinton or Bob Dole). Has [candidate] ever made you feel [adjective] (afraid, angry, enthusiastic, hopeful, or worried)?"

    0. = No
    1. = Yes

CANDIDATE FEELING THERMOMETERS

"I'd like to get your feelings toward some of our political leaders and other people who have been in the news these days. I'll read the name of a person, and I'd like you to rate that person using something we call the feeling thermometer. You can choose any number between 0 and 100. The higher the number, the warmer or more favorable you feel toward that person; the lower the number, the colder or less favorable. You would rate the person at the 50 degree mark if you felt neither warm nor cold toward [that person]. If we come to a person whose name you don't recognize, you don't need to rate that person. Just tell me and we'll move on to the next one. The first person is [candidate] (Bill Clinton or Bob Dole). How would you rate him using the thermometer?"

    Actual score, 0 through 100.
    Differential Feeling Thermometer = Clinton Score – Dole Score

PARTY IDENTIFICATION

"Generally speaking, do you usually think of yourself as a Republican, a Democrat, an Independent, or what? [if Democrat or Republican] Would you call yourself a strong (Democrat or Republican) or not a very strong (Democrat or Republican)? [if Independent or other party] Do you think of yourself as closer to the Democratic Party or the Republican Party?"

    1. = Strong Democrat
    2. = Weak Democrat
    3. = Leaning Democrat
    4. = Pure Independent
    5. = Leaning Republican

6. = Weak Republican

7. = Strong Republican

ECONOMIC RETROSPECTION

"We are interested in how people are getting along financially these days. Would you say that you (and your family living there) are better off or worse off financially than you were a year ago? Is that [much better or somewhat better/much worse or somewhat worse] off?"

0.000 = Much worse

0.250 = Somewhat worse

0.500 = Same

0.750 = Somewhat better

1.000 = Much better

ECONOMIC PROSPECTION

"Now looking ahead—do you think that a year from now you (and your family living there) will be better off financially or worse off or just about the same as now? Is that [much better or somewhat better/much worse or somewhat worse] off?"

0.000 = Much worse

0.250 = Somewhat worse

0.500 = Same

0.750 = Somewhat better

1.000 = Much better

ISSUE KNOWLEDGE: SUMMARY INDEX OF FOUR QUESTIONS

Question 1. "As President, do you think Bill Clinton or Bob Dole would be tougher on crime, or do you think there wouldn't be any difference between them?" (Dole correct=1)

Question 2. "As President, do you think Bill Clinton or Bob Dole would be more likely to lower taxes or do you think there wouldn't be any difference between them?" (Dole correct=1)

Question 3. "As President, do you think Bill Clinton or Bob Dole would be more likely to protect Medicare benefits or do you think there wouldn't be any difference between them?" (Clinton correct=1)

Question 4. "As President, do you think Bill Clinton or Bob Dole will make it more difficult for women to obtain abortions in this country, or do you think there wouldn't be any difference between them?" (Dole correct=1)

The number of correct answers was added together to create the following index:

0.000 = 0 correct answers
0.250 = 1 correct answer
0.500 = 2 correct answers
0.750 = 3 correct answers
1.000 = 4 correct answers

GENDER (DETERMINED IN SAMPLING)
0. Female
1. Male

RACE
"Would you mind telling me your race or ethnic origin? Are you white, black or African American, Hispanic, American Indian or Alaskan Native, Asian, Pacific Islander, or some other race?"
0. = Nonwhite
1. = White

INCOME
"To get a picture of people's financial situation, we need to know the general range of incomes of all people we interview. Now, thinking about (your/your family's) total income from all sources (including your job), did (you/your family) receive $5,000 or more in 1995? [if yes] Was it $15,000 or more? [if yes] Was it $25,000 or more? [if yes] Was it $35,000 or more? [if yes] Was it $50,000 or more? [if yes] Was it $75,000 or more? [if yes] Was it $100,000 or more?"
0.000 = Under $5000
0.143 = $5000–$14,999
0.286 = $15,000–$24,999
0.429 = $25,000–$34,999
0.571 = $35,000–$49,999
0.714 = $50,000–$74,999
0.857 = $75,000–$99,999
1.000 = $100,000+

EDUCATION
"What is the highest grade of school or year of college you have completed? [if 0–11 years] Did you get a high school diploma or pass a high school equivalency test? [if 13+ years] What is the highest degree you have earned?"

0.000 = No HS degree
0.250 = HS graduate
0.500 = Some college
0.750 = College graduate
1.000 = Postgraduate

AGE
"What is the month, day and year or your birth?"
Actual age in years computed and recorded.

VIEWERSHIP OF PARTY CONVENTIONS
"In talking to people about the political party conventions last summer, we found that many people watched the coverage of the conventions on television and some did not. How much of the (Democratic or Republican) party convention did you watch?"
0.000 = None
0.333 = A little of the coverage
0.667 = Some of the coverage
1.000 = All of the coverage

VIEWERSHIP OF TV NEWS
"On which of the television network news programs do you watch campaign news most often (*World News Tonight* on ABC, *The NBC Nightly News*, *The CBS Evening News*, or some other network news program)? (= Network). How many days in a typical week do you watch campaign news on [network]?"
0.000 = None
0.250 = Once or twice a week
0.500 = Three or four times a week
0.750 = Five or six times a week
1.000 = Every day

EXPECTED CLOSENESS OF THE RACE
"Regardless of whom you are supporting, who do you think will be elected President in November, Bill Clinton, Bob Dole, or some other candidate? Do you think the presidential race will be close, or will [candidate] win by quite a bit?" Answers were combined such that:
0.0 = Not close, Clinton will win
0.1 = Close ("false hope" condition)

CARING ABOUT WHO WINS

"Generally speaking, would you say that you personally care a good deal who wins the presidential election this fall, or that you don't care very much who wins?"

0.0 = Don't care very much
0.1 = Care a good deal

PART III

Macro Models

Part III extends affective politics from neurological and psychological theories of the brain and of the individual to broad-gauged theories about how politics works at the societal level. Clearly, matters of consequence for individuals as emotional beings will have an impact on how they interact with each other and produce political outcomes. What is important, and largely unknown, is precisely how much of the theory of political affect gets translated into our theories of politics. Each of the chapters in this part takes a cut at that translation, showing how emotion may well move beyond the individual and into the polity.

Chapter 11, by Doris Graber, pushes emotion-driven attention out of the laboratory and into the buzzing confusion of everyday life. She uses Pew's monthly surveys for the period 1986–2003 to identify news stories that captured the attention of a majority of the public and then examines the ways in which the most engaging stories differ from comparable news stories that missed the mark. Employing a careful and thorough empirical assessment of the news stories and their associated media coverage, in each case examining the actual news footage with an eye for nuance, she is able to assess the character of coverage in great detail. Factors such as the dramatic presentations or the nature of the characters or the story framing all are linked to attention. But the single dominant theme is that events that generate substantial losses of life or physical damage are more likely to capture the public's attention than are similar sorts of events that were substantially less harmful. The data thus accord well with the psychological expectation that people will pay closest attention to matters that generate fear or anxiety. This expectation is confirmed in the real world, outside the contrived setting of the laboratory, and is confirmed directly rather than indirectly in terms of measured attention.

This is all true in general tendency but not true in every instance. As ever, additional factors arise that confound the inference, including the amount of media coverage accorded to different stories and the nature of the news environment that competed for the audience's attention. And the exact comparability of news events is a matter of substantive judgment rather than experimental manipulation. These are, of course, the sorts of factors—extraneous, endogenous, and sometimes unmeasured—that complicate the transfer of neurological or psychological theory to the real world. But it is accomplishing that transfer that will make understanding the neurological and the psychological useful for understanding the political.

In chapter 12, David C. Leege and Kenneth D. Wald argue for emotion's central role in their view of cultural politics. Informed by considerable empirical work (Leege et al. 2002), they suggest that the last half-century of American electoral politics has been driven by the association of the parties and candidates with different subsets of American cultural identification. They argue that the art of using images and symbols lies in political strategists' properly selecting emotional appeals that elicit cultural responses. Their reading of the history, then, suggests that emotion, and especially the emotions of fear and loathing, lies at the heart of this enterprise. Political professionals, employing tactics consistent with the ideas explored in this volume, have portrayed their political opponents as threats to the core self-definitions of various subgroups in order to alter the fundamental coalitional structure of the parties. In this chapter especially, the authors show that white evangelical Protestants (on one hand) and white business and professional women (on the other) have reversed the link between their cultural identification and their political affiliation. Although the analyses cannot reliably link the contemporary science of emotion to particular emotional appeals, much less specific theories about emotional appeals to concrete tests of success and failure, it is clear that the language of self-identification, cultural symbols, and threat is a language that resonates with the enterprise. By focusing on the cultures and subcultures that define meaning in American politics, Leege and Wald show the way for political emotion to move our understanding far beyond the more elementary neurological and psychological claims of affect and effect.

In chapter 13, Peter F. Nardulli and James H. Kuklinski examine the electoral politics of the past thirty years to see how political dynamics have been moved by threats to economic prosperity, individual safety, and collective physical security. Their analysis is set at the county or city level and thus considers how communities and localities (rather than individuals) change their macro political behavior when their well-being is under attack. The authors emphasize two points: (1) their analyses are consistent with the emotional theories laid out in this volume, but (2) those same analyses do not decisively inform the theoretical debate about political emotion. For example, they establish that threatening conditions (unemployment, crime, warfare), especially in conjunction with one another, lead communities to punish incumbents. And further, these threats differentially affect the parties depending on party reputation and issue ownership. Such patterns are surely consistent with much of the theoretical work developed in this volume—and many authors would be happy to conclude with a satisfied confirmation. But Nardulli and Kuklinski go beyond the simple inference. They are especially keen to point out that macro-level analyses simply cannot tell us which emotions are brought into play or much about the conditionality of emotional engagement at the community level as opposed to the individual level. The theoretical links between the mechanisms of emotion and the mechanisms of community-level politics are not sufficiently crisp.

This general problem will be evident as the discipline begins to translate emotional theory, which is naturally rooted in the brain and the individual, to the broader canvas of the polity. Matters that seem straightforward to either the neuroscience of stimulus and psychophysical response or the psychology of individual experience will quickly become problematic when they are translated to the macro environment. It is clear that the processes that translate the activity of neurons into personal experience will not be the processes that translate individual action into political outcomes. The micro theories and macro theories are not mere extrapolations or interpolations of one level into the other.

And yet our discipline will be much richer when we can incorporate the science of political emotion into theories of politics. Political actors of all stripes know that emotions underlie much of our political life. Politicians, political strategists, news producers, and political commentators use emotional language every day: it is easy enough to use common sense to sketch out casual knowledge. The science of politics will start to make more serious advances, however, when we begin to introduce more rigorous theoretical structure to our intuitive grasp of emotion and then work out how that structure shapes the goals, strategies, and institutions of political life. This will prove an enormously challenging and rewarding task. The next three contributions make an excellent start at this endeavor: they show the way forward.

CHAPTER ELEVEN

The Road to Public Surveillance: Breeching Attention Thresholds

DORIS A. GRABER

THE PROBLEM

Social scientists have identified numerous elements that make news stories arousing. But they have failed to explain why some news stories arouse nearly universal attention while others attract only small audiences. For example, when the Pew Research Center for the People and the Press conducted nationwide surveys from 1986 through 2003 to assess the extent of attention to widely reported television news stories, it found that only a tiny portion of the stories—73 in 1,016, or 7 percent—had attracted "a great deal" of attention from 50 to 80 percent of the audience.[1] These stories all had characteristics identified by social scientists as highly arousing, shocking audiences into some kind of action such as closer surveillance of the situation. It is puzzling that other stories featuring very similar topics and characteristics attracted maximum attention from far fewer viewers. Less than half of the audience, often much less, claimed to have paid a lot of attention to them. It is also puzzling that so few stories overall contain factors that are emotionally compelling enough to induce viewers to pay close attention to them and that so many stories about events with vast political consequences were so widely ignored.

What accounts for the difference between stories that engage the body's surveillance system—the warning mechanism in the brain that stimulates enhanced vigilance—and news stories that leave the audience placid?

Shikha Jain's assistance was crucial in conducting the massive content analysis performed in this chapter. I am grateful for her help.

1. Based on calculations from data available at http://www.people-press.org/database.html. This site is also the source for the data in this chapter's tables.

What makes a story a bombshell? Is there a threshold that attention triggers must cross to turn noteworthy stories into monumental news?

Why the Answers Are Politically Important

Answers to these questions are important because most people obviously overlook many highly significant stories or fail to commit them to memory. That impairs their ability to perform effectively as citizens who monitor their government to the extent required in well-functioning democracies. If social scientists can determine what propels some important stories into the limelight while others languish in the shadows, they may provide purveyors of political messages with better tools to capture attention for information that citizens should know. The news media may then be able to fulfill the functions that the sociologist Michael Schudson laid out for them in his analysis of the requirements of citizenship in the twenty-first century.

Schudson (1998) contends that, even when most citizens fail to stay on top of all important political information, the needs of democratic civic life can be met if citizens merely monitor the news for signals about major political threats to themselves or their communities. The media or other opinion leaders must provide such signals, which are akin to a fire alarm that arouses citizens' attention and propels them to investigate the situation and take appropriate action. The interplay between news media and monitorial citizens produces the connection between citizens and their government that is vital in democracies.

Answers to questions about attention arousal are also important because they shed further light on many social scientific theories related to triggering attention to news stories and to storing them in long-term memory. We need to know what kinds of stimuli set the attention-arousal process in motion and how they propel large numbers of heterogeneous citizens to pay close attention to vital information in the news.

The Potency of Threats

Multiple surveys of citizens who have been exposed to television news show that stories reporting direct threats to their safety or suggesting that social norms have been violated stimulate them to pay attention to the information that signals the danger (Marcus et al. 1995). In fact, as the Pew polls have shown, the stories that attract the largest audiences almost always involve fear-arousing situations. In the Pew surveys, respondents were asked whether they were following selected important news

TABLE 11.1: Story topics receiving very close attention from 50 percent or more of respondents in 1986–2003 Pew surveys

Focus of high-attention stories	Share of high-attention story pool
Violence-prone foreign involvements	34.2%
U.S. terrorism and hostage crises	20.5
Sharp increases in gasoline prices	13.6
Natural disasters (e.g., floods)	9.5
Man-made disasters (e.g., explosions)	6.8
Heinous crimes	6.8
Human interest (e.g., toddler in well)	4.1
Patriotism (e.g., flag-burning)	2.7
Presidential election	1.3

N = 73 peak attention stories.

stories that had received ample television news coverage within a few weeks prior to the survey date very closely, fairly closely, not too closely, or not at all closely. Other questions within the survey were unlikely to influence the responses because the news interest questions were usually asked as lead-offs within a larger survey. Each survey included four to ten questions about attention to news stories, depending on the flow of important events. The average for the period 1986–2003 is roughly five stories per month. Table 11.1 shows the distribution of story topics in the maximum arousal categories—stories noted by 50 percent or more of the survey respondents.

It is easy to understand why the two top categories shown in table 11.1 are anxiety-producing. Americans fear foreign involvements that might lead to massive American casualties including deaths, and they are well aware of the harm done by terrorist acts on U.S. soil or the dangers facing the country when Americans are held hostage and risky rescue operations are possible. Such events could impact people's own lives at any time, even when they are not directly involved. Events covered in the next two categories pose major dangers to people's economic security, as well as threatening life and limb. Rising gas prices can ruin personal transportation and heating budgets and raise the costs of commodities that most people use in everyday life. They can also arouse anger when these stories explicitly state—as they did—that businesspeople are gouging consumers and reaping huge profits. Reports about floods, earthquakes, hurricanes, and weather extremes stir people emotionally because they put large numbers of people at risk of death or injury and economic calamity and there is no way to predict where they will strike. In the remaining five categories listed in table 11.1, the only surprise is the fact that presidential elections reached the top attention level only once between 1986 and 2003 and that Supreme Court cases involving patriotism issues such as flag burning and the recitation and wording of the Pledge of Allegiance are on the top-level attention arousal list.

Emotional Arousal Theories

The fact that nearly all of the high-attention stories involved threatening, dramatic situations suggests that emotional arousal theories provide an explanation. As great story tellers throughout history have known, stories about emotion-laden events that people regard as potentially threatening for themselves are exceptionally appealing to audiences. They pay attention to such stories, they commit them to memory, and they may be stimulated to actions related to the information conveyed by the story.

Neuroscientific studies shed light on the physiological reactions that explain the arousal phenomenon. They show that storing and retaining such stories in memory is facilitated because emotional arousal releases stimulants into the bloodstream that sensitize perceptions and heighten their impact (Gazzaniga 1992, 1998; Damasio 1994, 1999, 2003; Goleman 1995). As Antonio Damasio (2003) has noted, this is nature's way of forcing people to pay attention to potential threats to their survival. Responses to potent emotional stimuli are largely automatic. Human beings detect them ultrafast because the responses, like gut reactions, occur below conscious levels of information selection.

The physiological consequences of the emotional arousal rapidly mobilize people's cognitive resources so that they can deal intelligently with the challenges they face. That does not necessarily mean that they make the most appropriate choices. It does mean that they pay attention and deliberate about coping behavior. Research also shows that the information about the danger need not come from direct experience such as encountering a dangerous animal or a violent storm. Experiencing such things vicariously, via news stories, is sufficient (Bradley 2004; Bradley et al. 2001; MacKuen et al. 2001). In fact, news stories may be exceptionally stirring because they report about actual happenings (Sundar 2003).

Marcus, Neuman, and MacKuen (2000) put the arousal phenomenon into a broader context. According to their theory of affective intelligence, if individuals sense a serious threat arising from politics or other situations, their surveillance system becomes instantaneously mobilized so that they pay close attention and follow through with action, if indicated. Core emotions such as hatred, anxiety, fear, and high elation are especially potent motivators that are likely to stimulate people to pay close attention to information about the threat and to retain it in long-term memory.

Under most circumstances, when the information suggests that no unusual reaction is required, the matter is handled by the disposition system, which activates routinized responses to the stimulus (Dillard and Peck 2000). Weak arousal stimuli are often ignored or the response may be haphazard, such as cursory attention to news. Most people, most of the time, handle political stimuli that require little fresh thinking with routine reactions that belong to their disposition system. But when the emotional mechanisms in their surveillance systems signal serious danger, higher-level decision-making capacities are activated, leading to heightened attention to information and more active information searches (MacKuen et al. 2001; Bradley 2000; Marcus, Neuman, and MacKuen 2000).

The Arousal Potential of Mediated Political Messages

Political communication scholars have studied the consequences of emotional arousal primarily by focusing on arousal tactics in propaganda messages and in political speeches and advertisements aired during election campaigns. For example, John Nelson and Bob Boynton, in *Video Rhetorics* (1997), analyzed the themes that politicians commonly use in televised political advertisements, such as the "daisy" ad in 1964, the "bear" commercial in 1984, and the Willie Horton ad in 1988, to tug at the heartstrings of audiences. In their advertisements politicians typically argue that the nation faces imminent serious disasters, such as nuclear explosions, war, or murderers prowling city streets, that have been ignored or mishandled by their opponents. The candidate promoted by the advertisement is the only one who can cope with the crisis, thereby saving the viewers from mortal danger. There is ample evidence that such evocations of serious threats and promises of relief conveyed through news media capture audiences' attention (Edelman 1964; Brader 2006).

Several major theories about arousal of attention in response to news media stimuli are also compatible with the idea that emotional arousal heightens people's desire to pay attention to information. For example, uses and gratification theories postulate that needs for information determine news choices. According to these theories, people selectively pay attention to news stories that promise to satisfy various needs (Rosengren et al. 1985; Winkielman and Berridge 2003). The need to survey the environment and discover potential threats requiring protective action qualifies as a powerful motivator. Incentive theories of motivation suggest that the motif of self-protection may be so strong that a weak stimulus such as an unattractive news story may motivate protective behavior. Socials scientists also contend that "people's liking for stimuli may be influenced by rudimentary affective and perceptual mechanisms. These rudimentary mechanisms can generate 'sub-rational' preferences that may be decoupled from higher cognitive processes underlying rational beliefs about the stimulus" (Winkielman and Berridge 2003, 665).

Agenda-setting theories are also relevant. Research into the potency of news stories to attract attention and influence the audience's thinking has demonstrated that audiences recognize the signals that journalists embed into news stories to cue the audience that the story requires their attention (MacKuen 1984; Iyengar and Kinder l987; Iyengar 1991). For example, television news, which is the public's main source of political information, signals importance of stories to viewers by reporting them repeatedly, by placing them in the first part of the broadcast, by devoting an above-average amount of time to reporting the stories, by verbally labeling them as important, by choosing graphic words and pictures, and by announcing within the broadcast that the stories are forthcoming. Attention to various aspects of the story is also guided by the overall framing and delivery of the narrative and by the choice of particular sounds, colors, and vistas to make major points.

Discovering Attention Thresholds—The Hypotheses

Based on the reasoning presented thus far, the key to resolving the attention-arousal puzzle seems to lie in producing fear- or anxiety-arousing content and alerting the audience to the impending dangers. Accordingly, we designed our research to test hypotheses concerning the combination of factors that stimulate fear and anxiety and lead to widespread, careful attention to news stories. To explore the distinctions between news reports with high and low arousal potential, we concentrated on highly arousing stories that were matched by news reports involving very similar situations that turned out to be far less captivating. The Pew surveys provided us with an ideal data set because they involved large national samples of randomly chosen respondents interviewed periodically over a period of seventeen years.

Because of the large sample size, the ever-present idiosyncratic factors in information selection and processing need not concern us in this project. The same holds for social desirability biases, given the diversity of story topics and rates of attentiveness to similar topics. The study focuses solely on the characteristics of news stories and the prevailing political and social environment likely to influence average people's news choices and news consumption habits because we lack information about audience responses beyond the claims they made about attention to the story. Considering polling logistics and ethics, it would, of course, be impossible for us to re-interview these respondents in person to investigate the personal reasons that prompted their news choices and their subsequent reactions and actions. We hope to explore some aspects of the impact of idiosyncratic factors in follow-up experiments, however.

The five hypotheses tested in our study are as follows.

1. Stories that move a high proportion of audience members from disposition to surveillance systems, as shown by high attention to news, have many more fear-arousing elements than do their less potent counterparts.
2. Stories that move a high proportion of audience members from disposition to surveillance systems, as shown by high attention to news, have many more stimuli that suggest that grave harm is imminent for the self or significant others than do their less potent counterparts.
3. Stories that move a high proportion of audience members from disposition to surveillance systems, as shown by high attention to news, have many more signals of journalistic importance than do their less potent counterparts.
4. Stories that move a high proportion of audience members from disposition to surveillance systems, as shown by high attention to news, are embedded in a far more supportive context of political and social events including news than is the case for their less potent counterparts.
5. Arousing fear reactions in large heterogeneous audiences requires combinations of interacting fear-producing stimuli occurring at the individual and the societal levels.

The first four hypotheses follow clearly from our prior discussion. The fifth one, the importance of interaction effects, requires a bit more explanation. Sociopsychological events that are likely to arouse fear reactions involve various physiological, psychological, and contextual levels. To understand their impact fully requires a multilevel integrative analysis, as Cacioppo and Visser (2003, 650–51) note: "The principle of multiple determinism specifies that a target event at one level of organization . . . can have multiple antecedents within or across levels of organization." It is therefore essential to be alert to interaction effects and to explore a variety of factors that, in combination, may produce results that differ from those witnessed when fewer factors and levels are examined. The analysis of various combinations of attention triggers should shed light on the conditions under which the composite becomes potent enough to arouse the surveillance system and induce large numbers of viewers to pay attention in situations when single factors or other composites fail to elicit that level of arousal.

THE RESEARCH DESIGN

What kinds of potential emotion triggers did we examine? As indicated, the project began with identifying news stories that people claimed to have followed very closely in response to questions asked in nationwide surveys representative of the entire U.S. population. We selected stories that one-half or more of the respondents to Pew surveys had followed very closely for which we could find mates with scores below 50 percent and more than twenty points lower than the top-rated story. We were able to identify thirteen story groups composed of a total of thirty-seven news stories, covering different types of topics. Attention score gaps ranged from 29 to an extreme of 61 points between the most compelling and the least compelling story in each grouping. The mean gap score was 31 percent if one excludes the outlier figure. The diversity of topics covered by these story groups and the diversity of the situations surrounding them allowed us to test whether the elements that make stories exceptionally attractive are specific to particular story types and situations or apply generally to all widely noted news stories.

For each case, we secured videotapes of all relevant stories aired on ABC, CBS, NBC, and CNN in the month prior to the survey. We excluded snippets of twenty seconds or less because they rarely have much impact on viewers given their limited verbal and visual content. Our reported findings about each story group are based on stories from all the networks combined, because we did not know which stories individual viewers had watched. We realize, of course, that it is unlikely, though not impossible, that individual respondents watched all the pre-survey broadcasts covering each story in our sample.

We then verified that news stories that we had initially selected were truly comparable in content. Many were not, forcing us to eliminate six story groups. For example, in a group of stories covering students who shot and killed classmates in school settings, it seemed pointless to include a story of much lesser gravity in which a single student was attacked and sustained only minor injuries. Story groupings that turned out to have features that made comparisons questionable were cases involving Terry Nichols's role in the 1995 Oklahoma City bombing, comparisons between the racial aspects of the O. J. Simpson murder trial and the Rodney King case, comparisons of reports of multiple U.S. Supreme Court cases involving flag-burning, the Pledge of Allegiance and abortion, comparisons of coverage of major hurricanes in 1992, 1999, and 2003, and comparisons of high-casualty airline crashes in 1989, 1996, and 2001. We dropped a group of nine comparable stories about gasoline prices because the single group that scored at low arousal levels focused on price reductions, whereas all of the others focused on price increases.

The next step in research design was the development of a coding scheme that would cover all the factors that singly or in combination may account for the attractiveness of a story. What are these factors? It is a very long list, indeed, which grew as the research progressed because we added factors that became apparent only with the analysis of newly examined cases.

We began with an obvious factor: story content. Did the contents of highly arousing stories involve shocking events that potentially affected the survival of audience members or people close to them? What were these events, where, when and how and why did they happen, and who (or what) were the actual or presumed perpetrators and victims? Would it be easy for audience members to imagine themselves facing a similar situation? Were the stories cast into frames that facilitated identifying with the persons involved in the story?

Story framing is important because it has a strong impact on whether and how news stories are processed and recalled by audiences (Entman 1993; Nelson and Boynton 1997; Graber 2001). For coding story framing, we borrowed categories from Neuman, Just, and Crigler's book *Common Knowledge* (1992) because that study also involved analyses of the impact of frightening situations. In *Common Knowledge* the authors discuss economic frames, which stress profits and losses, human impact frames, which tug on heartstrings, conflict frames, which picture politics as perennial contests, powerlessness frames, which emphasize individuals' impotence in controlling events, and morality frames, which stress the moral values inherent in stories.

Details of presentation also affect the potency of stories and need to be examined (Nimmo and Combs 1985; Zillmann and Brosius 2000). We coded details such as the length of the broadcast, the number of live or taped scenes, the repetition of scenes and themes in subsequent broadcasts, the nature of visuals and audio features, and camera angles and distances. All these factors can influence attention to stories. For instance, close-ups are more involving than distance shots because they show faces in the intimate way people see them when they are face-to-face with each other. Familiar human faces create greater arousal than do those of unknown individuals because they are apt to stir previously stored positive and negative feelings about the person in viewers' memories.

Children and attractive old people are more likely to be noted and arouse sympathy because they activate inherent instincts to protect the next generation and parent-like figures (Winkielman and Berridge 2003). Bright red blood oozing from wounds, ashen faces, or fly-covered babies may stir feelings of fear, anxiety, disgust, and even horror. Whether that leads to greater attention to news or to news avoidance remains an open question, judging from studies of vividness effects (Taylor and Thompson 1982; Gibson and Zillmann 1993; Sundar 2003). Compared to reporting events after they have occurred, live broadcasts tend to attract more attention because threatening breaking news generates a greater sense of reality and urgency (Miller 2004). Breaking news alerts viewers to the fact that ongoing happenings have to be watched to allow for protective behaviors.

Sounds can have a strong impact on attention arousal and memory. They can stir emotions by themselves or they can amplify the emotional impact created by pictures. They can make messages persuasive that might otherwise be bland (Nelson and Boynton 1997; Brader 2006). Tone, pitch, and tempo can produce a broad range of feelings such as attraction, revulsion, sympathy, and fear. Since the qualities of delivery are crucial, it is important to record not only the tone and texture of voices but also the nature of background sounds including music and environmental noises such as sirens, aircraft noise, and barking dogs.

Research has demonstrated that people's ability to remember stories suffers when verbal and visual messages are poorly coordinated, forcing the viewer to simultaneously absorb different ideas about the story and then attempt to coordinate them. Aside from politically sophisticated individuals, viewers often are unwilling to undertake this difficult intellectual maneuver (Rahn et al. 1994; Rahn and Cramer 1996). For purposes of the current study, we rated disparities between words and pictures as weakening the likely impact of the message on the audience. By contrast, we considered it a boost for the impact of messages if they contained explicit signals that this was important news. Examples of such signals are reporters or anchors announcing the forthcoming story earlier in the broadcast, placing the story in the opening portions of the newscast, and devoting an above-average amount of time to them. Longer stories allow reporters to supply more contextual information that makes stories more dramatic and more meaningful.

As part of recording the emotional climate portrayed by the story's visuals and sounds, we paid close attention to the facial expressions, body language, and verbal language of the main characters, as well as those of reporters and anchors shown or described on screen. Recorded reactions include emotions such as anger, hostility, fear, sorrow, joy, and excitement as well as evidence of low-key reactions such as calmness, detachment, or boredom. Similarly, we coded the tone, word choices, and other delivery characteristics of spoken messages.

Coding facial expressions is especially important and, fortunately, has become well systematized (Ekman 1983; Masters and Sullivan 1993). Recent research suggests, however, that coding of visible expressions may miss subliminal expressions of anger, fear, disgust, or happiness that are presented and observed below the level of awareness (Winkielman and Berridge 2003). Traditional research thus far has largely been able to record only observable phenomena, leaving the subliminal and the subconscious beyond researchers' grasp.

Scholars of facial expressions have amply documented the ways in which core feelings are reflected in a person's face. They have also shown that observers are adept at recognizing these facial cues to feelings. In our coding, we recorded how long the facial signals persisted for a screened subject because a fleeting expression might be missed whereas a persistent one would most likely be noticed. In addition to facial expressions, we rated the physical attractiveness of the main characters in the story in light of prevailing standards and the social acceptability of their displayed or reported behaviors.

Several coding categories were designed to assess which collective memories were likely to have a bearing on survey respondents' interactions with the story. Knowledge about shared memories can provide clues to how new information is likely to be categorized and evaluated. For example, we coded whether stories referred to similar events in the past, priming the audience to recall these events and the associated feelings and reactions. We also coded the presence or absence of messages that indicated that evaluations of the situation were controversial. We thought that controversies raise the specter of cross-pressures that sap opinion strength, as public opinion research indicates.

Finally, we examined other events reported at the same time as our key story, searching for miscellaneous message enhancers and detractors—features that might increase or diminish the story's impact. For instance, news that one hundred people died in a forest fire will pale in significance when paired with a story reporting the death of almost two hundred thousand people in a tsunami. Identifying information that might modify message potency is also important because people often are strongly attracted by stories that shed further light on events that have already caught their attention. Alternatively, audiences may be distracted from stories that deviate from their current news focus. Widespread feelings of anxiety about world conditions might also affect how people respond to new anxiety-producing events.

Our analysis of the influence of contextual factors extended to other news in the same broadcasts that preceded or followed the story in question. For example, surrounding stories might have contained messages that suggested that the event in question was likely to recur, possibly in the respondent's own community. Fear about recurrence of an event or joyful anticipation of a recurrence might result in greater arousal, which, in turn, might produce above-average attention and better recall. Conversely, on slow news days, even a story with comparatively low appeal is likely to shine. A brief description of all case groupings follows; the high-attention cases are listed first in each group.

BROADCAST DATES AND ATTENTION SCORES FOR CASE GROUPINGS

1. The *Challenger* and *Columbia* space shuttle explosions
   Cape Canaveral, Florida, July 2–31, 1986; audience high attention score = 80%
   Erosion of O-rings allowed the shuttle to explode within seconds of ignition at an altitude of 46,000 feet. The entire seven-person crew was killed. This widely watched event occurred January 28, 1986. Interview questions were asked five months later.
   Other news at the time: The hostage crisis in Lebanon; Israeli raids in Lebanon; arms negotiations with Soviets

   Kennedy Space Center, Feb. 1–28, 2003; audience high attention score = 46%
   Damage to the shuttle's heat shield sustained during launching caused it to break up and crash 16 minutes before its anticipated landing on February 1, 2003. The entire seven-person crew was killed.
   Other news at the time: U.S. tensions with Iraq and with Korea

2. The racial violence cases involving the Rodney King beating: the incident and its aftermath
   Simi Valley, California, May 1–8, 1992; audience high attention score = 70%
   An investigation of the Rodney King beating led to acquittal of the four policemen accused of assault. Anger about the verdict then led to racial riots throughout Los Angeles.
   Other news at the time: The Persian Gulf War

Los Angeles, March 5–21, 1991; audience high attention score = 46%

Rodney King, a black motorist, had led police on a high-speed chase through the northern suburbs of Los Angeles on March 3, 1991. After he was captured, three white Los Angeles police officers kicked, stomped on, and beat King with a metal baton as their supervisors watched.

Other news at the time: Gorbachev visited the United States

3. The school shooting cases

Littleton, Colorado, April 20–28, 1999; audience high attention score = 68%

Two high school seniors, ages 17 and 18, who felt that they were treated as outcasts by other students entered their school and discharged multiple weapons. When the rampage was over, they had killed thirteen people and themselves.

Other news at the time: The NATO campaign in Yugoslavia; the bombing of Serbia

Jonesboro, Arkansas, March 24–31, 1998; audience high attention score = 49%

Two students, ages 11 and 13, armed with rifles and handguns, opened fire on fellow students and teachers, killing four students and one teacher. The older student was allegedly angry about being jilted by a girlfriend.

Other news at the time: President Clinton's visit to Africa to discuss genocide in Rwanda, AIDS, and the African economy; meetings with South Africa's Nelson Mandela

Springfield, Oregon, June 13, 1998; audience high attention score = 46%

One student, age 15, opened fire on fellow students, killing 2 and wounding 24. He had killed his parents on the previous day because he was angry about his father's chastising him for an illegal gun purchase. The event took place 23 days prior to the June newscast.

Other news at the time: The funeral in Texas of James Byrd, an African American murdered in a race crime; ethnic cleansing and fighting in Kosovo

Santee, California, March 5–23, 2001; audience high attention score = 39%

One student, age 15, opened fire on fellow students, killing 2 and wounding 13. Presumably, he had endured frequent bullying and was seeking revenge.

Other news at the time: An unprecedented plunge of the Dow Jones index; NASDAQ hit its lowest level in 28 months. Vice President Dick Cheney was hospitalized

4. Reacting to invasions abroad: The Kuwait and Yugoslavia cases
Kuwait City, Kuwait. August 1–8, 1990; audience high attention score = 66%

An army of 100,000 Iraqi troops invaded Kuwait and seized the country in five hours. The dispute involved claims over two strategic islands and oil resources. News of sanctions by the United States, Britain, and the USSR followed this segment of the broadcast.
Other news at the time: U.S. hostages were released from Monrovia, Liberia

Karlovac, Yugoslavia, December 23–29, 1991; audience high attention score = 5%.

Croations and Serbians fought each other over control of territories claimed by both in the former Yugoslavia. The central government declared proclamations of independence by Slovenia, Macedonia, and Croatia illegal.
Other news at the time: Georgia and Russia fought over Georgia's refusal to join the new Commonwealth of Independent States; Christmas stories from around the world

5. The multilateral military intervention cases: Bosnia and Iraq
U.N. headquarters, February 1–8, 2003; audience high attention score = 62%

The U.N. discussed plans for a multilateral intervention in Iraq to forestall military ventures by the regime of Saddam Hussein. The main event was an address by U.S. Secretary of State Colin Powell on February 5 explaining the need for preemptive war.
Other news at the time: The *Columbia* space shuttle explosion; Americans abroad targeted by terrorism; Bush funded HIV/AIDS fight in Africa and Caribbean

United States and Bosnia, May 1–22, 1993; audience high attention score = 24%

The U.N. and and United States discussed sending troops into Bosnia, which was engaged in civil war. The purpose of the intervention was protection of ethnic minorities from extermination by Bosnian Serbs. Air strikes were contemplated.

Other news at the time: U.S. intervention in Haiti; Nelson Mandela elected president of South Africa; former president Nixon's death; U.S. intervention in Haiti

6. Hunting foreign dictators: The Panama and Haiti cases
Panama City, Panama. January 1–11, 1990; audience high attention score = 60%
On December 20, 1989, the U.S. invaded Panama to capture and prosecute President Manuel Noriega for drug trafficking. Noriega surrendered on January 3, 1990. The U.S. invasion force of more than 25,000 soldiers was sent after a U.S. marine was shot. The mission was controversial because it produced a high toll of Panamanian casualties and property damage.
Other news at the time: Trouble between the USSR and Iran along the Azerbaijani border; a suspect in a sensational Boston murder case committed suicide

Port-au-Prince, Haiti, September 6–18, 1994; audience high attention score = 23%
Starting on September 19, 1994, 20,000 U.S. troops occupied Haiti to oust the military regime, restore democracy, and return exiled president Jean-Bertrand Aristide to power
Other news at the time: Fighting in Sarajevo led to cancellation of papal visit; the crash of a USAir flight killed 132; the start of the O. J. Simpson murder trial

7. The Somalia humanitarian intervention cases
Mogadishu, Somalia, January 1–13, 1993; audience high attention score = 52%
Discussions were held about the wisdom of retaining U.S. troops in Somalia to provide famine relief to the country, which was engaged in civil war. A Congressman visiting marines was a target of rebel shooters but was not hurt.
Other news at the time: signing of the START II treaty; Iraq barred U.N. overflights; Bush planned to bomb military targets

Mogadishu, Somalia, March 3–25, 1993; audience high attention score = 28%
Discussion was held about turning U.S. relief efforts in Somalia over to the United Nations. Looters were targeting relief workers.

Other news at the time: The stand-off at Waco, Texas, between federal government agents and members of the Branch Davidian cult; the Rodney King trial

Table 11.2 presents a comparison of the amount of media attention the seven story groups received. It shows the differences within each group as well as between groups. The table confirms the normal assumption that greater exposure of the story leads to higher audience attention scores, but it also shows that there are important exceptions. Case 1, consisting of the shuttle disasters, is the most glaring exception. In that case an amply covered report about the *Columbia* explosion that started on the day of the event and continued for 11 days attracted a far smaller audience than a much briefer report reminiscing about the *Challenger* explosion that had occurred five months earlier. Cases 6 and 7 also violate the assumption with respect to story length, thanks to lengthy television specials. The implications of these data, including the exceptions, are discussed below.

We start our presentation of findings with a relatively detailed analysis of the school shooting cases that illustrates the nature of the analysis that we performed for each group. Obviously, there are too many cases for us to be able to report about each group in similar detail. Analysis and discussion of the differences between high- and low-potency cases in each of the seven groups follows, along with a report about how well these findings square with our five hypotheses. The chapter ends with some overall conclusions.

Table 11.3 provides a brief description of the kinds of arousing content elements that were coded for the Columbine High School case. The recapitulation makes it clear why this story was such a shocking event that it attracted a lot of attention from two-thirds of the viewers.

Table 11.4 displays the elements in the stories about each school shooting incident that social scientists have identified as potentially highly arousing. The table records the framing that was dominant in stories related to the incident, the manner of presentation in pictures and sounds, and the mentions of similar events that show that the story is more than a passing phenomenon. The table also reports the thrust of the surrounding stories, with stories that detract from the impact of the story subtracted from stories that enhance it. Surrounding stories were scored on a 6-point scale ranging from +3 for highly enhancing to −3 for highly distracting.

No single feature leaps out in table 11.4 to explain why the Colorado case garnered so much more attention than the others. Like the related stories, it led with regard to some arousal elements but lagged in others. Closer analysis of the facts behind the numbers shows that the most consequential factors in making the Colorado stories so highly arousing are

TABLE 11.2: Major coverage characteristics for high- and low-attention cases

Question group no.

	1	1	2	2	3	3	4	4	5	5	6	6	7	7
Audience (%)	46	80	46	70	39	68	5	60	24	62	23	60	28	52
No. of networks airing story	4	3	3	3	3	4	2	3	3	3	3	3	3	3
Days of coverage	11	4	4	6	6	9	3	8	7	8	8	5	6	6
Shortest story	0:30	1:40	2:10	1:00	2:00	3:10	2:00	2:40	3:00	1:00	2:10	2:00	2:00	2:00
Longest story	60:00	5:10	4:20	59:00	7:10	11:50	29:00	30:00	8:50	16:20	80:50	5:00	29:00	5:10
Action scenes	yes	no	yes	yes	yes	yes	yes	yes	yes	yes	yes	yes	yes	yes
Live scenes	no	no	no	no	no	yes	yes	yes	no	no	no	no	no	no
First segment	yes	yes	yes	yes	yes	yes	yes	yes	yes	no	yes	yes	yes	yes

Note: The shading identifies high-score cases in each group. Story length is listed in minutes and seconds. "First segment" is checked "yes" if the majority of stories appeared in the first segment of the broadcast. Case 1 = *Challenger* and *Columbia* disasters; 2 = Rodney King incident; 3 = school shooting cases; 4 = reactions to invasions abroad; 5 = Bosnia and Iraq intervention debates; 6 = Panama and Haiti dictator hunts; 7 = Somalia intervention cases.

TABLE 11.3: Content coding of Columbine High School case (abbreviated)

Category	Content
Human casualties and material damage	Fifteen dead, including the suicides of the 2 gunmen; at least 25 wounded; major material damage to school facilities.
Perpetrator demographics and psychographics	The two gunmen were identified as 17-year-old Dylan Klebold and 18-year-old Eric Harris. Both were seniors at Columbine High School and reportedly belonged to a group known as the "Trench Coat Mafia" because they wore black trench coats to school. The gunmen felt they were outcasts and supposedly opened fire on those who ridiculed them. The reasons for the attack have never been fully disclosed.
Victim demographics and psychographics	Thirteen dead and 25 wounded by gunfire. Most of the casualties were students but some teachers were hit as well, including teachers who had risked their lives to protect students.
Brutality of the event execution	The rampage began at about 11:30 A.M., when the two young men started throwing pipe bombs outside the school, then entered carrying multiple weapons and began firing at close range at students in the hallways, cafeteria, and library.
Relevant societal norms	Society is concerned with such gruesome, unusual events; people cannot believe that it happened in their low-crime community; they wonder when, and if, such crimes will stop. Officials and professionals feel that children need more guidance and security. Some students are scared to go back to Columbine; others feel they need to go back and continue life. The concern about troubled children is becoming greater, either because firearms are readily available or because of growing violence shown in entertainment and reported by the news media.
Situational complexity ambiguity	The story is confusing: unspeakable brutality, attack on humanity; people cannot make sense of it.

the magnitude of the event and the extent of coverage. The Columbine shootings had the greatest number victims and were covered by more network stories than were the related cases. Colorado's second-place position in terms of the percentage of frames using human interest must be weighed in light of the fact that the case was covered by 50 percent more

TABLE 11.4: High-arousal elements in school shooting stories (in percentages)

Location (attention score)	Colorado (68%)	Arkansas (49%)	Oregon (46%)	California (39%)
Frame: human interest	22	12	16	28
Presentation: close-up	27	13	9	34
Arousing visuals	40	60	56	28
Arousing sounds	6	6	6	6
Collective memory links	5	8	13	5
Number of stories with arousing features	9	6	2	6
Number of stories with reassuring news	—	—	—	—
First-section placement	76	77	67	100
Surrounding stories*	–3	–1	—	–1
Other news at the time*	—	–1	–1	–1

*Number of stories that strengthen impact minus the number of stories that weaken impact.

stories than its nearest competitor. Actual numbers tell the story. We counted 31 human interest frames for the Columbine case, 16 for California, 4 for Oregon, and 21 for Arkansas. The table omits other potentially arousing frames, such as the conflict frame, the powerlessness frame, and the morality frame, which were considered in the analysis. They present similar patterns. We also recorded specifics of arousing visuals and sounds and the substance of collective memory links, surrounding stories, and general conditions in the nation at the time. Because quantification inevitably distorts such data, we used qualitative methods for analyzing them and making comparisons.

Was the shooting spree at Columbine High School the first event of its kind? Was it a culmination of a series of closely spaced events? Did it receive an extraordinary amount of attention? The answer to the first two questions is no, and the answer to the third is yes. The Colorado shooting followed two earlier, closely spaced events in which attention did not mount for the subsequent event. Columbine was far enough removed from the prior events to make a "culmination effect" unlikely. But, as mentioned, it did gain substantially more media attention on the major networks than did the related events in terms of coverage time, numbers of stories, and the span of days over which these stories were broadcast. Table 11.5 tells that story.

Can we claim that table 11.5 reveals that massive attention to a story reflects how often and how long it is aired? Perhaps, but perhaps not. In the table, that rationale is contradicted by the Oregon case, which should rank well below the California shootings. Similarly, in three of the seven

TABLE 11.5: Network news offerings

Location (attention score)	Colorado (68%)	Arkansas (49%)	Oregon (46%)	California (39%)
Event dates	4/20/99	3/24/98	5/21/98	3/5/01
Number of stories about the event	17	13	3	7
Number of days of event coverage	9	6	1	6
ABC coverage time	35:00	11:20	1:30	4:50
CBS coverage time	26:40	19:20	1:30	8:50
NBC coverage time	36:10	18:00	—	15:20
CNN coverage time	35:00	39:40	7:30	—
Total	133:10	88:20	10:30	29:00

Note: Coverage time is given in minutes and seconds.

TABLE 11.6: Frequency of use of arousing words

Words	Colorado	Arkansas	Oregon	California
bloody	1	0	1	2
tragedy, tragic	5	1	0	1
horror, terror	5	1	0	0
violence, violent	20	8	1	2
war	5	0	0	0
threat, fear, nightmare	13	3	0	4
massacre, carnage	5	1	0	4
under fire, ambush	3	4	1	0
hate	8	0	0	2
rampage	1	0	0	4
Totals	66	18	3	19

comparisons shown in table 11.2, the lower-rated case in the group received substantially more exposure than the top-rated event. But closer examination revealed unusual circumstances in each case: repetition of coverage of an earlier, highly dramatic event in one case and coverage by television specials in two others. Such specials may have less impact than ordinary news stories.

The Colorado story reached a pinnacle of exposure in yet another category. When we compared stories vis-à-vis the use of an arousing vocabulary, Colorado was far ahead of related stories, as table 11.6 shows. It had more than three times as many such terms as did its nearest competitor, the lowest-ranked story in the group. Again, one group, the Bosnia/Iraq intervention cases, mars the effort to assign broad significance to the

TABLE 11.7: Characters shown on television news in emotional contexts

	State (attention score)			
Cast of characters	Colorado (68%)	Arkansas (49%)	Oregon (46%)	California (39%)
Perpetrators	—	5	—	4
Eyewitnesses	—	—	—	—
Victims	5	—	20	—
Victims' families	14	10	—	—
Involved onlookers	25	36	20	16
Police	11	2	—	20
Government officials	6	2	40	—
Others	39	45	20	60

Note: Figures represent the percentage of total characters shown in particular sets of stories (e.g., 5 percent of all characters shown in Colorado coverage were victims).

phenomenon. In that group, the top-rated story has less than half of the instances of arousing language than the bottom-rated story.

Many of our comparisons focus less on how often various story elements occur than on how powerfully they might stir the audience. For example, we compared how various types of people appearing in a story in an emotional context might affect the audience's attention level. The appearance of perpetrators of heinous crimes or the victims or the victims' kin, we thought, would be especially powerful (Aust and Zillmann 1996). A single victim or relative might arouse audience interest far more than seeing dozens of authoritative-sounding police officers or government officials.

Again these clues proved a bit disappointing in the school shootings. The Colorado case did show some strength in the expected directions, but it was not spectacular, as table 11.7 indicates. Only five percent of the emotion-arousing characters in stories about the Colorado attack were victims, a share exceeded in stories about the Oregon shooting. Yet the number of victims was the same in each case. Fourteen percent of the characters shown in the Colorado story were members of victims' families, which was the top score. That becomes impressive when one equates it to the images of fourteen grief-stricken faces appearing on the screen.

What Attracts Attention? Revisiting the Hypotheses

Overall, the findings presented in table 11.8 suggest that the cases that received the highest attention in each grouping featured a larger array

TABLE 11.8: Arousal elements that distinguish key cases from others

Case I.D.	1	2	3	4	5	6	7
Attention scores	80%	70%	68%	66%	62%	60%	52%
Arousing Story Elements							
A. More dramatic facts		XX	XX	XX	XX	XX	
B. Controversy among political elites featured	X				XX	XX	
C. More dramatic audiovisuals		X	XX		X		
D. More dramatic sounds	X						XX
E. Major norm violations			X	X		XX	XX
F. Substantially more appealing characters (e.g., children, seniors, friendly soldiers)		X	X				XX
G. Substantially more scary characters					X		XX
H. Substantially fewer reassuring characters				XX		XX	X
I. Substantially more human-interest frames				XX			
J. Substantially more conflict frames							XX
K. Substantially more powerlessness frames		X	X	XX			
L. Substantially more coverage time		X	XX	XX	X		
M. Substantially more stories		X	X	XX			
N. Substantially more coverage days			XX	XX			
O. Substantially more action scenes				XX			
P. More first-section placement	X	X					X
Q. Substantially more close-up views and nearby sounds		X				XX	X
R. More supporting surrounding stories				XX			X
S. More arousing collective memory links	XX	X		XX			
T. Fewer important distracting elements			X	X			
U. Major weaknesses in competing story in content or presentation		X			X	X	

Note: Items L–Q highlight the multiplication effect because they determine how often viewers had a chance to see the stories initially or see them repeated. Case 1 = shuttle disasters; 2 = Rodney King incident; 3 = school shootings; 4 = reactions to invasions abroad; 5 = Bosnia/Iraq intervention debates; 6 = Panama and Haiti dictator hunts; 7 = Somalia intervention cases.

of stronger arousal stimuli in various combinations than did less potent related cases. The cases that drew less notice featured similar arrays of threat elements, but these tended to be less menacing, and there were fewer factors overall. That holds true for all cases, regardless of the nature of the event, be it a shuttle explosion, teenagers engaged in a murderous rampage, or military operations involving foreign dictators. Single X marks in table 11.8 indicate the presence of the element. The double X marks identify story elements for which the difference in magnitude between the key case and related cases was particularly large. All cases are identified by numerals, and they appear in the order of their power to attract audience attention.

The first hypothesis—stories that move a high proportion of audience members from disposition to surveillance systems, as shown by high attention to news, have many more fear-arousing elements than their less potent counterparts—is confirmed if one grants that fear-arousing elements may prime horrid memories of events experienced several months earlier. That caveat is necessary to explain the prominence of the *Challenger* coverage, which occurred five months after the event but topped the timely coverage of the Columbine disaster by 37 percentage points. The earlier *Challenger* coverage had been highly dramatic, and many people had watched the event when first aired and in subsequent rebroadcasts. The double X mark in the collective memory category records that fact.

Otherwise, the evidence for confirmation of the first hypothesis is presented in table 11.8 in categories A through K, which deal with dramatic content features. The Somalia intervention cases (7), which were low-ranked in terms of drama (category A), compensate for this shortcoming with greater strength in other categories such as dramatic sounds, more scary characters, more conflict frames, and more major norm violations. Evidently, high rankings in emotional arousal can be achieved by multiplying elements as well as by showing exceptional strength in particular categories.

The second hypothesis—stories that move a high proportion of audience members from disposition to surveillance systems, as shown by high attention to news, have many more stimuli that suggest that grave harm is imminent for the self or significant others than their less potent counterparts—is confirmed if one accepts that memories of earlier highly dramatic coverage can be primed by subsequent coverage that occurs several months later. Content analysis of the most-watched stories reveals that, compared to related stories, they put more emphasis on the direct relevance of the various factual situations for the audience's welfare. Most such stories dwell on major violations of social norms which threaten the entire community (category E), as well as stressing how powerless the community is in coping with the serious situations under discussion (category K).

The third hypothesis—stories that move a high proportion of audience members from disposition to surveillance systems, as shown by high attention to news, have many more signals of journalistic importance than do their less potent counterparts—is also confirmed if one assumes that the memory of prior stories about the *Challenger* disaster was primed.

As noted above, when television specials are included in total coverage time, the Panama and Haiti dictator hunts (6) and the Somalia intervention cases (7) were exceptions. They follow normal patterns when these exceptional features are excluded. The evidence supporting the third hypothesis is presented in table 11.8 in categories L through Q.

The fourth hypothesis—stories that move a high proportion of audience members from disposition to surveillance systems, as shown by high attention to news, are embedded in a far more supportive context of political and social events including news than is the case for their less potent counterparts—is only weakly confirmed. The evidence is presented in categories R through U of table 11.8. Apparently, aside from the unique role played by links to collective memory in several stories, the enhancing effects of contextual factors played minor roles in triggering surveillance systems. It is also interesting to note that the serious weaknesses in some of the related stories recorded in category U often were matters of flawed reporting. Without these flaws, audience figures for the related stories would most likely have been much higher.

The fifth hypothesis—arousing fear reactions in large heterogeneous audiences requires combinations of interacting fear-producing stimuli occurring at the individual and the societal levels—is confirmed, although the influence is mixed. Some societal factors played only small roles. Examples are news reports about other events that occurred at the same time as our key stories and reports about the general political environment. But other societal factors were crucial in boosting the impact of a story. They include norm violations, controversy among political elites, and the impact of collective memories.

Further confirmation of the hypotheses comes from a comparison of the cases that aroused the highest attention with those that were lower on the scale. For example, when we compare the King case (2), which aroused high concern among 70 percent of the audience, with the Somalia intervention (7), which aroused 52 percent, we find that the King case excelled in two especially powerful categories: more dramatic facts and more coverage time and stories. It also aroused more collective memories. The comparison also suggests that stories lacking strength in the most powerful categories invariably compensate for the deficiency by achieving high scores on several other elements.

CONCLUSIONS

The most important conclusion from this study is the fact that stories that have many or powerful fear-arousing elements are potent enough to arouse the surveillance system of large numbers of viewers, inducing them to pay close attention to political news. This is consistent with the theory of affective intelligence. It means that the development of highly complex modern democracies can function satisfactorily if citizens play the monitorial role. Of course, the effectiveness of monitorial citizenship requires that the news media and other dispensers of crucial political information use their powers of arousal for the appropriate array of stories.

In terms of arousal factors, there are some real surprises. Overall, the magnitude of the danger as related in the story, rather than its visual and vocal aspects, seems to be the most important aspect of arousal. That fits well with the idea that arousal of the surveillance mechanism leads to involvement of the cognitive skills of television audiences. They think about the effects of a story even when the presentation is not spectacular. Of course, spectacular presentation features do help. In a similar vein, the impact of norm violations and reports about controversies among elites—matters that require thinking—appears to be highly arousing.

Another significant factor is the extent of coverage time. The key stories very often received substantially more minutes' worth of television coverage than did related stories. Lengthier coverage allows for presentation of larger numbers of arousing factors over a longer period of time, as well as for repetition of the same story, which facilitates the formation of deeper memory tracks. In addition, lengthier, more frequently repeated presentations also increase the possibility that more people are exposed to the story, thereby increasing the opportunity for higher attention scores.

Overall, if one gives double weight to elements that carry double X marks in table 11.8, the numbers of elements noted for each story are very close, aside from the *Challenger* case. The average is 13 elements, which is considerably higher than the average for the related stories. It is interesting that the Kuwait-Yugoslavia comparison, reported in column 4, which has the highest number of elements for the key case, also displays the biggest gap in attention scores—61 percentage points. This suggests that multiplying the arousal elements raises the arousal level.

From a methodological perspective, the greatest difficulty in doing these types of comparisons is the need to compare apples and oranges and decide how the evaluations of their features match up. For example, in the Rodney King cases, it was difficult to determine whether showing the fuzzy tape of the beating six times should be considered more or less arousing than a single showing of the beating plus multiple scenes of riot damage in Los Angeles, funerals of victims, pictures of their grieving relatives, and interviews with people who had lost their livelihood. It took multiple viewings of the tapes of the news stories to come to uncertain conclusions about whether there was a substantial difference in arousal power. Using multiple coders helped with such difficult decisions. Still, it does not allay all concerns about measurement errors. We hope that experiments that test the arousal potential of combinations of the various elements that we have identified will shed further light on the findings reported here. But, as any sports buff can attest, nothing can take the place of the real thing. Laboratories inevitably dampen the unique atmosphere of excitement that only real-world experiences can generate.

CHAPTER TWELVE

Meaning, Cultural Symbols, and Campaign Strategies

DAVID C. LEEGE AND KENNETH D. WALD

In a *New York Times* article published midway during the 2004 presidential campaign, Katharine Seelye (2004) argued that nominee John Kerry's appearances were aimed at reclaiming the endangered Democratic advantage among women voters. On *Live with Regis and Kelly*, Senator Kerry described his handling of a rape case during his first political position as a prosecutor. The following day he championed his health care proposals in Florida, a state loaded with seniors, disproportionately women. Then he met with an audience of women in Iowa to discuss national security. Polls had shown that security, personal and national, had become a major concern, especially among women.

For his part, President George W. Bush had effectively linked images of 9/11 with the anguish of mothers in southern Russia who had lost family members in a terrorist hostage and bombing catastrophe at a school. He had looked consistent and strong throughout the summer, while Kerry had failed to defend himself for weeks from scurrilous attacks by a campaign front organization called Swift Boat Veterans and POWS for Truth. Seelye implied that Kerry had reminded women of another Massachusetts nominee, Governor Michael Dukakis, who, responding during a nationally televised debate to a hypothetical question about the rape of his wife, icily framed it as a constitutional issue rather than showing masculine outrage.

There is little question that voters expect to know presidential candidates as humans and that, as Dan Schnur (chapter 15 in this volume) emphasizes from the perspective of a campaign manager, candidate biography is critical to message credibility. Voters like to see emotion where emotion would normally occur. They like to know that candidates are like them. Bush's father, born into a family of Connecticut Yankees and Wall

Street money, re-created himself as a Texas roughneck who devoured pork rinds and detested broccoli. Young Bush could make light of his difficulties with the English language and his Texas swagger—"In Texas, we call it walkin'," he told the 2004 Republican National Convention. He was an ordinary guy, a C– student, a booster, not a sophisticated patrician who skis with the jet set in Switzerland and speaks French. Linking Saddam Hussein to 9/11 in the week following the tragedy, Bush could say, "I wouldn't put it past him." And two years later, after Bush himself admitted there was no evidence of such a linkage, 44 percent of the public still embraced his first frame.

Emotions run deep in politics. Fears are readily transferred. Hatred is easily stoked. Scapegoating and other transfer mechanisms are there for the choosing. Once the image is shaped, it is hard to recover any other reality. In his novelized version of a Nixon-like politician in California, *The Ninth Wave*, Eugene Burdick creates the central figure, a political handler, who reduces all politics to two emotions, fear and hatred. We are not so reductionist. Emotions of pride, a feeling of security, or simple disappointment are also sufficient to affect outcomes in presidential races.

This chapter addresses a dominant strategy that has gained steam since the demise of the New Deal: the politics of cultural differences. First we develop a theory of cultural politics, then we discuss the dynamics of political campaigns, and finally we illustrate how emotions are used to mobilize or demobilize target groups within rival political coalitions. Campaign professionals try to foster a political climate in which they can use emotional appeals to structure the electorate in their favor. The theory of affective intelligence helps explain why this strategy seems to work so well. The larger message of the chapter is that emotions play a key role in long-term electoral transitions.

EMOTION IN A THEORY OF CULTURAL POLITICS

Culture can be thought of as a template for perceiving the world and for determining behavior. It has three functions: (1) to establish *identity*, (2) to define *norms* for behavior, and (3) to set *boundaries* on appropriate relationships (see Wildavsky 1987). Culture is allied with many ways of knowing: science, intuition, myth, and religion. Generally since the Enlightenment, Western peoples have sought to move knowledge into that which is verified by scientific procedures. But in many areas science does not yet give convincing answers, or the answers may threaten an established moral order. Under these circumstances societies may rely on founding myths surrounding their establishment or on religious beliefs to make social hierarchies legitimate.

For example, Americans have relied on two founding myths: (1) covenant theology, drawing on the Pilgrims' social contract, written up on the *Mayflower,* and (2) the "chosen nation" as embodied in the Puritan impulse to bring the blessings of Christian civilization to the wilderness of North America (Wald 2003, chap. 3). Covenant theology specified that ruler and ruled were in a sacred covenant relationship, with reciprocal duties under a watchful God; when one party broke them, the other was obligated to invoke sanctions. This became the rationale for the break with the king of England as embodied in the Declaration of Independence and ever after has justified both popular sovereignty and civil disobedience. Chosen nation doctrine rationalized the subjugation of indigenous peoples, slavery as an instrument for Christianizing Africans, and later the emancipation of slaves and the civil rights movement, anticommunism, economic reform, and opposition to abortion. Political convention speeches are replete with discourse about the "city on a hill." Chosen nation doctrine became the now-definitive rationale used by President Bush to invade Iraq and establish a Middle Eastern beachhead for democracy, enterprise, and, in the supportive statements of the religious Right, Christianity instead of Islam.

Culture is not monolithic for a nation-state. Those who have the same national identity often embrace conflicting norms and set boundaries differently. Because some values matter more than others to specific primary groups and secondary associations based on race, ethnicity, religious denomination, economic interest, locale, and region, people espouse different priorities for collectively binding (governmental) decisions. For some, a just society is based on power, wealth, social standing, rectitude, wisdom, health, respect for the natural environment, or some other value (see Lasswell and Kaplan 1950). Their preferred value has prior claim to governmental action. In a democratic society in particular, they compete with people who embrace a different value priority. Yet all of these can be characterized as cultures or at least subcultures. Swidler (1986) notes that people are seldom located in a monolithic cultural environment, yet they want their cherished values to dominate. Under such circumstances they select from a wide array—her term is "toolkit"—of cultural options. Thus, there is fluidity in the prior claims of a culture, and these become instruments for political action.

This is an important distinction in our understanding of cultural politics. "Culture wars" theorists (see Neuhaus 1984; Wuthnow 1988; Hunter 1991) assume a teleology: behind public policies are political actions, behind political actions are cultural differences, but behind them all are religious differences, particularly concerning the nature of authority. Like Weber and Niebuhr, we see more autonomy for politics. That is, an ambitious politician (is this a "repetitive redundancy," to use John T. McCutcheon's delicious play on words?) can choose or discard religious values or use none at all to justify his actions. As California's governor, Ronald Reagan signed into law the most liberal abortion policy known to the states, but as presidential candidate in the 1980 primaries he became devoutly pro-life. In the same primaries George H. W. Bush pushed the pro-choice option but, once Reagan's vice-president and heir apparent, he became pro-life. Al Gore voted against abortion funding and procedures while in the Senate, consistent with the values of his socially conservative Tennessee constituents, but became unabashedly pro-choice when he ran for president. George W. Bush treated gay marriage as a state-level option in 2000 but in 2004 called for a constitutional amendment to ban it. Far from being straitjacketed by teleology, as naïve culture war theory has it, public policy, cultural values, and religious rationales are linked to political ambition. Although cultural values sometimes appear fixed and predict political outcomes, just as frequently they are malleable and become the means for politicians or regimes to achieve a goal. In a remarkably candid interview, Republican House Majority Leader Tom Delay chastised his Senate counterpart for bringing up discussion of the gay marriage ban too early in 2004; the party needed it to shame Democrats in October, when voters would notice it, rather than in April, when voters would forget it (Babbington 2004).

Unlike the culture war theorists, we do not simply assume that cultural cleavages spontaneously generate electoral dislocations. Rather than embrace the implied black-box syllogism that says religion → culture → political change, we argue that a defensible model of cultural politics requires understanding both how elites politicize cultural appeals and the manner in which voters process these appeals. For the latter problem, it is crucial to understand the way voters respond to strong emotional appeals, the province of the theory of affective intelligence.

Our approach to cultural politics starts from the assumption that politics is collectively binding action to affirm values and achieve goals for a society. Political parties are coalitions of groups and individuals who mobilize in common to realize personal ambitions, set binding policies, and gain economic or value advantage within a nation-state. Parties sometimes unite their members with an ideology, a vision of the good society and the principal means of achieving it. More likely, parties are better known by the issues they own: for example, attention to the needs of the less well off via public systems for welfare, retirement, and health care; attention to the interests of corporations and entrepreneurs through favorable taxation or absence of regulation; or willingness to use multilateral negotiation to maintain world order or dispense with threats to the national interest or to act unilaterally through decisive military action. At a minimum, the electorate—the people whose votes or failures to vote are needed for political elites to hold office—will associate the parties with either their dominant ideology or their issue shorthand. That simplifies the vote choice and establishes a certain kind of campaign rationality for both party and voter (compare Downs 1957).

Over time, however, one party may become the permanent minority party in the affections of voters and must develop a strategy to make elections competitive. It either moves closer to the successful stances of the permanent majority party (Downs 1957) or it occupies more extreme positions outside the current consensus in hopes of mobilizing new voters, disassembling part of the majority party's coalition, or redefining the public agenda. With regard to race (Carmines and Stimson 1989), religious and family values (Layman 2001), and patriotism, gender, and religion (Leege, Wald, Krueger, and Mueller 2002), researchers have shown how the Republican Party has moved from permanent minority status to partisan parity by manipulating cultural differences in campaigns from the 1960s to the present.[1]

This approach to cultural politics recognizes, as suggested above, that people are embedded in primary groups, secondary associations, and local and regional networks. Sometimes they simply use the group as a frame of reference, a *social identification*. Sometimes they interact regularly with other members of the group and form a bond of *social cohesion* (for definitions of these terms see Turner 1982). Examining Catholics in

---

1. Because of the success of the GOP in waging cultural politics since the 1960s, a majority of our examples come from Republican sources. This is certainly not meant to suggest that Republicans alone use cultural appeals. As our book makes clear, cultural-style campaigning is used by both parties and the Democrats have not hesitated to invoke cultural themes when it was politically advantageous to do so. In some cases, this involves attempts to "invade" Republican-owned issue space such as President Bill Clinton's decision to embrace welfare reform or Senator Hillary Clinton's adroit emphasis on faith and family in the run-up to the 2008 presidential campaign. Beyond neutralizing the grounds for Republican cultural appeals, Democrats also use symbols to raise fear and anxiety among Republicans. For example, Democrats frame President George W. Bush's Supreme Court nominees as "radical" judges who are far outside the mainstream and may threaten cherished individual freedoms. This is clearly an effort to sow dissension among moderate and pro-choice Republicans and, in particular, women.

the 1960 election, Converse (1966b) showed that simple social identi-fication exerted a stronger pulling force toward Kennedy, the Catholic, than did regular attendance at Mass, a social cohesion measure. Other studies (for example, Huckfeldt, Plutzer, and Sprague 1993; Wald, Owen, and Hill 1988; Green, Guth, Smidt, and Kellstedt 1996) have shown that greater integration into the church community through regular interac-tion with co-religionists promotes common political choices. The impor-tant point is that the candidate must be seen as "one of us" and that this perception is best reinforced by fellow group members. Commenting on the earliest voting studies, Parsons observed, "the individual seems to vote, other things being equal, with the people whom he most directly identifies to be his own kind. . . . The question is not so much *for what* he is voting as it is *with whom* he is associating himself in voting" (Parsons 1959, 96).

Vote choice is a product of *meaning* and hence the province of cultural analysis. Wuthnow (1987, 37) argues that meaning is "an attribute of sym-bolism" and is "a function of the context in which a symbol, or the indi-vidual himself, was located." The most powerful symbols are found not in complicated theories of taxation and economic growth or in efficient structures for health care delivery or in strategies for fighting terrorists or winning a war. They are found in pictures and in sounds that tap into primary group experiences of things that promote pride or satisfaction or tap into reservoirs of fear or revulsion. Opening the envelope with the $600 tax rebate by the kitchen counter with one's spouse is far more pow-erful than an explanation of economic priming via government subsidies. The claim of victory in Iraq is best demonstrated by the staged toppling of a massive statue of a dictator before jubilant onlookers or by film of the victorious commander in chief emerging from a jet fighter in a flight suit. Pictures of flag-draped coffins carry more weight than sober Pentagon reports of the numbers of troops killed in a firefight. A naked male pris-oner humiliated at the end of a leash by a female National Guard member does more damage to the policy of finishing the war in Iraq than word of more insurgencies. An exposed breast during a half-time extravaganza at the Super Bowl dramatizes the moral corruption of Hollywood and leads to FCC penalties for CBS. (No one seems to have taken similar umbrage at the scantily clad cheerleaders on the sidelines of every NFL game or the incessant advertisements for Mike Ditka's erections—but he is a blue-collar coach and one of us, not Hollywood.) The pictures of a be-fuddled president reading an upside-down book in a classroom and then taking lengthy flights to here and there while his vice-president becomes the oracle to the nation after the 9/11 attacks are quickly and permanently banished in favor of a resolute president speaking defiantly at Ground Zero, in the presence of courageous cops and faithful firemen (see Jamieson and Waldman, chap. 6). Police, firefighters, and a confident mayor become symbols of patriotism and recovery; it is quickly forgotten that at the time of the attack the mayor was living with his mistress in adultery in the mayoral mansion in the presence of his wife and young children. Symbols meet the need for meaning in specific personal and historical contexts, and value priorities change as a result of the need for meaning.

Meaning is invested with emotion. It is far distant from cool rationality. When analysts ask, "Who is hurt by gay marriage?" the agenda swiftly changes to the lessons our children will learn or to the invocation of biblical injunctions. In the wake of CIA assessments that the United States has entered a quagmire in Iraq, the president reassures the nation and the world of the rightness of our position by referring to a mother whose son was saved but whose nephew was killed in the schoolhouse terror in southern Russia. This approach to policy rationalization locates the symbol in the treasured life experiences and worries of American mothers. Supporters of embryonic stem cell research seized on the death of the beloved Ronald Reagan after the long night of Alzheimer's; his son Ron Reagan, who was seldom close to his father, became an instant celebrity at the 2004 Democratic National Convention because of symbol, social context, and transfer of affection.

Modern campaign industries make cultural politics powerful. These industries include television, where the picture is the message and sounds set the mood (see Graber, chapter 11 in this volume, for compelling evidence of the power of symbols because of visual and aural cues), unlimited budgets for polling and market testing, focus group interviewing that comes closer to the dynamics of primary groups than do surveys of isolated respondents, and the identification of targets to be mobilized or demobilized through customized symbols. Political campaigns build on the emotions attached to social location and value position. They quickly turn on the salience of group identification and turn it off again. They permit agenda control and problem definition via both advertising and free media response to advertisements. They facilitate the sense of relative deprivation, as unworthy people are shown in advantaged situations. They generate enormous pride through national symbols and quasi-religious rituals. They stimulate sinister specters that mobilize our fear responses. If a regime loses its enemies, it must create new ones to remain in power. Thus the permanent campaign with the perpetual use of these tools characterizes the modern presidency. As candidates once waved a metaphorical bloody shirt to recall the righteous anger of northern voters, they now deploy pictures and sound to evoke the same sentiments. Politicians need the culturally *other* to fulfill their political ambitions.

Threats to the moral order, encapsulated in efficient symbols, are every bit as powerful as influencers of electoral choice as are the personal security concerns explored by other scholars of emotion in politics (see Nardulli and Kuklinski, chapter 13 in this volume). Indeed, factors such as fear of crime, military conflict, and even economic decline can be framed as cultural threats by means of symbolic appeals. Opposition to higher taxes becomes politically more salient when it is attached to anger about unworthy beneficiaries of public largesse (Sears and Citrin 1982), and war fever can be stoked to new levels by suggesting that the enemy is an opponent of our God, not merely of our interests (Caldwell 2004). The diffuse fear of crime was rendered concrete by the menacing face of Willie Horton and thus associated in the public mind with a presidential candidate who was held responsible for unleashing Horton on the vulnerable public. In the theory of affective intelligence, emphasizing threats, arousing anxiety, and inducing emotion are means for activating the audience's surveillance system and motivating action. By moving into the venue of cultural politics, showing how politicians deploy efficient symbols to alert voters to danger to their cherished social values, this chapter thus expands the rather limited conception of threats in the literature about political emotions.

CAMPAIGN DYNAMICS

We have adapted a model of campaign dynamics first outlined by Marcus, Neuman, MacKuen, and Sullivan (1996) but also sketched in pieces by Marcus and other collaborators. It is based on the emotions of enthusiasm, anxiety, and disappointment. It helps explain not only voter choice but also levels of turnout within target groups. It depends on powerful emotional symbols deployed among vote market segments after careful research and continuous monitoring by campaign organizations.

Although by the 1960s the New Deal was long past, and despite the presumed rise of independents, most voters continued to perceive political objects through partisan schemata. In fact, Miller and Shanks (1996) have demonstrated that the disproportionate number of baby boomers could account for the rising proportion of independents. Once they had sufficient experience with adult responsibilities and perceived their own political interests, they aligned with a party, as had their parents. Throughout the past half-century, then, most of the campaign action continued to revolve around partisan coalitions.

It was also based on what appeared to be a permanent Democratic majority. With a couple of exceptions, the House—the popular branch of government—had continuous Democratic majorities until the Republican breakthrough in 1994. Initially, it took a popular nonpartisan general, Dwight D. Eisenhower, to challenge the Democratic stranglehold on the White House. If Republicans were to win and could not do so in the foreseeable future by gaining the affections of the electorate, they would have to whittle down the size of the electorate. Rather than stimulating turnout among Republicans or converting Independents, strategies that were more appropriate for the long run, their short-term priority target was Democratic partisans. This strategy was consistent with the core operating principles of campaign strategists: first divide the electorate into segments and only then develop emotional messages appropriate to the targeted audience segment (Schnur, chapter 15 in this volume).

Why target partisan voters, who, conventional wisdom tells us, are the most resistant to persuasive communication designed to challenge their presuppositions? As MacKuen et al. (chapter 6 in this volume) contend, seemingly intransigent partisan voters are in fact quite malleable and may be detached from their habitual electoral choices by arousing anxiety and fear. Campaign professionals often assume, in Schnur's words (chapter 15), that "fear is the most effective way of discouraging the most virulent opposition (the sinners) from turning out at the polls." To heighten fear among Democratic voters, Republican campaigns deployed cultural appeals that stressed the threat posed to the moral order by Democratic policies and politicians. We extend the argument of MacKuen et al. by emphasizing that disaffected partisans reached by these powerful symbols are at least as likely to demobilize (stay home on Election Day) as to defect to the opposition.

Republican strategists chose a wide range of cultural symbols to create a sense of disillusionment among selected sectors of the Democratic coalition. Those who had taken over the leadership of the Democratic Party were painted as disloyal communist sympathizers, as elitists who did not have to deal with the daily consequences of racial desegregation, as big spenders who bought the votes of freeloaders, as morally degraded people who failed to respect God's design for keeping women in certain roles or ignored God's judgment concerning sexual permissiveness. These elitists even tried to take God out of American civic rituals. The message became, why would you want to support a party that no longer represents your values? Sit it out. Or, if angry enough, join us. Defect. Turnout declined and defection increased, particularly within Democratic groups.

The strategy helped break up the majority coalition not only by discouraging voting but also by creating anxiety sufficient for troubled Democrats to engage in an information search about the negatives of Democratic candidates and the positives of Republican candidates. The short-range purpose was to attract crossover voters based on specific wedge issues or on candidates' images. The long-range goal was to break the habit of voting Democratic and teach a new habit of voting Republican. Once the habit was formed, the voter would realign himself or herself with the Republicans.

Finally, when long-term Republicans could see on a regular basis that an election was close, they could become enthusiastic and translate their brighter hopes into political evangelizing. The converts showed the zeal characteristic of their new understanding of the world and became highly mobilized. The taste of success led many to see politics as an honorable cause, as a way to replace stupidity and evil with intelligence and righteousness. Thus, campaign dynamics revolved around strategies of mobilization, demobilization, and conversion.

Our research has traced campaign dynamics from the 1950s to the 2000 election (Leege, Wald, Krueger, and Mueller 2002). Masterful politicians and their entourages—Nixon, Reagan, and. we would now add, the Bushes—devised ways to define the opponent in culturally unacceptable ways and to fashion themselves as incorporating the hopes and fears of honorable middle Americans. As Edsall (1991) has noted, Democrats have been slow to understand that contemporary politics revolves around cultural values and have conducted elections as though economic policy and administrative competence were all that mattered. In the elections where Democrats did learn how to exploit cultural differences by painting the opposition as extremist—in 1964 and 1992 in particular—they were able to attract defectors and reduce turnout among Republican groups.

Via content analysis, we have examined the principal campaign themes in all presidential elections from 1960 to 2000, looked at the target groups, and assessed the nature of the affective appeals. Campaigns have centered on four cultural domains: patriotism, race, gender, and religion. At times, more blatant appeals—such as race-based appeals to relative deprivation among southern white Democrats—were cleaned up and turned into a culturally acceptable ideology of egalitarian individualism. More recently, when the fear of communism waned with the end of the cold war, a new reality, fear of terrorism after 9/11—could anchor patriotism. It could rationalize a wide range of policies from tax cuts for the well-to-do to invasion of Iraq to national energy and environmental policy to restrictions on movement by watch-listed political opponents.

We have examined the political histories of a dozen and a half target groups drawn from party coalitions. We devised a "politician's calculus of the vote." For a sequence of eleven to thirteen presidential elections, we took into consideration the party identifications, party loyalty or disloyalty, and turnout of these target groups, which include, for example, southern whites, white housewives, business and professional women, working-class ethnic whites outside the South, somewhat educated whites, and African American Christians. Then we developed factor scores that re-duced information from National Election Survey variables about issues and group affect. Finally, we used multinomial logit models to explain changes in loyalty, turnout, and defection within each group over the time series. (For the techniques employed see Leege et al. 2002, chap. 6.) In-terestingly enough, in about sixteen hundred equations, we found far less than half of the anomalous patterns that would have been expected to oc-cur by chance. In short, the models were strikingly successful in linking campaign themes, voters' feelings about issues and groups, and continuity and change in voting behavior within target groups.

In general, imagery that connected the parties' images to condensed feelings about racial groups and actors, use of the federal government to ensure equality of opportunity, and social welfare policies accounted for most of the perturbations in partisan patterns from 1964 to 1992 for most target groups. Another factor, what we have called "moral restorationism," started to appear in the 1980s but became very powerful among certain groups in the 1990s and 2000, especially for white evangelical Protes-tants and white southerners. Both race-based party ideology and moral restorationism ("family values") led certain groups—for example, white mainline Protestants and white business and professional women—to move away from their historic Republicanism and to respond to Demo-cratic cultural appeals based on values of tolerance, opportunity, and de-sirable social change. On occasion, a patriotism factor was important in accounting for party disablement, but this occurred mostly among south-ern white Democrats; rarely did it affect white, non-Latino Catholics, who were the initial subjects of this appeal in the Eisenhower days. In the 1972 election, virtually every wedge issue and negative outgroup feeling had an impact on the groups at play. Crystallization of party images was particularly strong in 1972, 1980, 1984, and 2000. We now illustrate the ways in which meaning, cultural symbols, and campaign strategies affect a couple of target groups over time.

CONTRASTING TARGETS: EVANGELICALS AND BUSINESS AND PROFESSIONAL WOMEN

Beginning about 1990, two groups—white evangelical Protestants and white business and professional women—have played key roles in the realignment and mobilization of the political parties. Each group was persuaded to change partisanship by the attraction or revulsion of the same set of themes, contained in the concept of moral restorationism. And earlier in the time series, other cultural themes resonated more prominently with each. Because the two groups are so intimately connected as endpoints on a continuum, it makes sense to treat their stories as interrelated.

In the 1920s, H. L. Mencken and Clarence Darrow could describe evangelicals as poorly educated southern country bumpkins. Lienesch (1993) has shown, however, that evangelicals, far from consisting only of Southern Baptists, Pentecostals, and fundamentalists, always had wings in mainline Protestant churches, were evident in northern cities, and had early developed networks of colleges, Bible colleges, publishing houses, and broadcasting stations. Average levels of education for those classified as evangelicals have increased over the past half-century. Further, when drugs, serial sex, and alcohol no longer provided meaning, many in the baby boom generation who had practiced the excesses of the 1960s at elite private and state universities had converted to a form of evangelical Christianity. This led to substantial growth in the suburban nondenominational megachurches.

George W. Bush is himself a model for this prodigal generation and has lost no opportunity to present himself to voters using these symbols. Evangelicals practice a *conversionist* theology (with an emphasis on a personal act of will to accept Christ into their lives), study the Bible for authoritative statements about how to live, witness to others, and in the face of national threat have reasserted "chosen nation" doctrine to justify the "war on terrorism," which translates as the war against Muslin extremists. Many evangelicals see Bush not only as "one of us" but as God's chosen vessel for these times of trial before the second coming of Christ to rule the earth (Rich 2004). Their changing demographic profile and their syncretistic beliefs, which merge Christianity and American patriotism, left them far more mobilizable than evangelicals had been earlier in the nineteenth century, when politics was an evil to be shunned.

Republicans first realized the ripeness of this group for partisan transformation in the struggle over the Equal Rights Amendment during the

1970s. Republicans' support for equal opportunity for women had had a long pedigree: they had inserted an ERA plank into the platform at the 1940 nominating convention. In fact, this was a tactic to mobilize a new base of support among women during the dark days of the New Deal. After all, educated Republican women and the mainline Protestant churches (Presbyterian, Congregationalist, Episcopal, and Methodist) had been at the forefront of many reform movements following emancipation of slaves, not the least of which was women's suffrage. But voting turnout of women still lagged. President Dwight Eisenhower appointed women to visible administrative posts and in fact generated the first measurable gender gap in voting, with women favoring Republicans. Democrats in turn recognized that Republicans were gaining an electoral advantage among women. President John F. Kennedy created the influential Commission on the Status of Women. Democratic congressional leaders added "sex" to the prohibited categories of discrimination in Title VII of the Civil Rights Act of 1964. By that point leaders in both parties had sponsored equal rights amendments to the Constitution.

In 1964 GOP presidential nominee Barry Goldwater said he could not support further civil rights legislation, claiming that it violated states' rights. In reaction, other leaders stepped up efforts to ban both racial and gender discrimination. In the 1960s and 1970s race-based and gender-based reform movements flourished, and white business and professional women came to the forefront of the latter. In politics, however, every action toward reform generates a reaction because someone's advantage is likely to be diminished. When President Richard Nixon received the Equal Rights Amendment from Congress and signed it, the Eagle Forum, headed by lawyer and conservative Catholic activist Phyllis Schlafly, and other conservative parachurch organizations leapt into action.

The conduct of Concerned Women of America in opposing the ratification of the ERA in several states, especially in the South but also in the North, convinced Republicans that support for the amendment should be dropped (see Mansbridge 1986; Matthews and DeHart 1990). Here was a remarkable network of evangelical women who could be mobilized at a moment's notice to bring the zeal of their faith to political action. The GOP had lagged behind the Democrats in precinct organization and lacked such mass-based mobilizing structures as organized labor. Evangelical churches and parachurch organizations could be the new precinct organizations. The intensity of religious commitment that had previously diverted evangelicals from political action could, when harnessed to a religious cause in politics, be used precisely as a mobilizing tool (Campbell 2004).

The symbols used by ERA opponents to describe the goals of the women's movement were particularly emotive. In North Carolina, amendment advocates were characterized as "stumpy, pushy Jews from New York." In turn, anti-ERA women, locals all, baked cakes and cookies for the legislators. The implication was that local women knew their proper place in the moral orders of society and family and would fight to preserve their traditional status (Matthews and DeHart 1990). The International Women's Year commission was castigated for seeking to build alliances with "our lesbian sisters." A GOP congressman characterized those at the 1976 IWY convention in Houston as "sick, anti-God, and unpatriotic," and a group of GOP leaders described them as "a gaggle of outcasts, misfits, and rejects." The counterfeminist movement picked up on Senator Sam Ervin's characterization of the ERA as "desexegragation," tying together negative symbols of elitist federal courts, race, and gender. Questions about combat roles for military women generated the pejorative term "women warriors," and the vision of same-sex bathrooms was deployed and deplored (Leege et al. 2002, 209–10, 15).

This process hinged on a sophisticated understanding of threat manipulation consistent with the assumption that negative emotion activates the individual's surveillance system and so stimulates learning (see Redlawsk, Civettini, and Lau, chapter 7 in this volume). The task of the ERA's critics was to convert a policy framed in terms of equality, arguably a natural sell for politically engaged women, into a danger. As if following the affective intelligence script, they used terms linking the amendment to stigmatized minorities, an especially effective way to generate anxiety (Brader, Valentino, and Shubay 2004), hoping that the tactic would raise anxiety about the legislation and prompt women to seek additional information from critical sources. Several of the conservative activists profiled by Kristi Andersen (1988) reported that their doubts about the ERA, first raised by the claims mentioned in the previous paragraph, crystallized only after they engaged in conversations with mentors from antifeminist organizations. These conversations, conducted within a biblical framework, enabled the women to perceive that a policy that once seemed benign was fraught with serious dangers for the entire social order. In time, they enlisted in the antifeminist movement.

The struggle over the ERA became coupled with the Supreme Court's decision in *Roe v. Wade* and later cases to extend the privacy doctrine to permit abortion. Leaders of the women's movement now made support for the pro-choice position a litmus test for political action. Catholics, who had historically claimed state protection for the unborn, were now drawn into the cultural political arena. Catholic women, who had a longer history of working outside the home than did Protestant women and who were attracted to the ERA's pay equity arguments, were now targets for negative social attribution appeals. How can you join hands with women's movement leaders who have so little respect for your beliefs about human life? Once again, women who might have been attracted to the ERA on other grounds learned that the legislation posed a severe danger to their cherished, God-given role as producers and nurturers of life (Luker 1984). Against such symbolic framing of the issues it became increasingly difficult for religious leaders of all types to claim that the amendment and the pro-choice position were central to the prophetic emancipation of women.

Republican political strategists who had served in the Nixon White House and were part of the Reagan movement henceforth coordinated their efforts with evangelical leaders, some members of the Catholic hierarchy, televangelists, and traditionalist women's organizations (Crawford 1980). Initially the name Moral Majority was given to the emerging Religious Right. When its leadership faltered under the Reverend Jerry Falwell, a new organization, the Christian Coalition, emerged under the direction of rival televangelist Pat Robertson. This group organized at the local church and precinct levels, contested control over GOP county and state central committees, recruited candidates, and compromised on some issues to build bridges to traditional Main Street and country club Republicans. By the late 1990s, forces allied to the Religious Right had taken over more than half of the state party organizations (Conger and Green 2002). No Republican politician seeking higher office could survive their overt hostility, as Senator John McCain discovered in 2000 after attacking them during the South Carolina primary. Even George W. Bush was forced to discard some of his top vice presidential choices after opposition from Christian Rightists who refused to accept pro-choice Republicans as legitimate in their adopted party.

Democrats, on the other hand, saw opportunity in attracting displaced business and professional women and mainline Protestants, groups that had been at the core of the traditional Republican leadership. They added the ERA to the party platform, nominated Representative Geraldine Ferraro to the presidential ticket, and passed a series of laws furthering the advancement of women in educational institutions and corporations. In alliance with sectors of the women's movement, they used "the behavior of fifteen white males" during the confirmation hearings of Supreme Court Justice Clarence Thomas as a stimulus to recruit women for the U.S. Senate and succeeded in many elections (Leege et al. 2002, 74). Freedom of choice about abortion continued to be a defining issue as many well-educated young women entered the corporate and professional labor markets. These women wanted to be free to decide whether and when they would interrupt their careers to have a baby. At the same time sexual norms were changing, and an active, satisfying sexual life became a goal for women as much as for men. Probably the most dramatic demographic change was in the proportion of women who remained housewives and those who entered business and the professions. The turning point coincided with the oil shocks and the inflationary spiral in the latter half of the 1970s. At the time of Kennedy's election in 1960, 60 percent of all women responding to NES surveys called themselves housewives; 9 percent were employed in business or professional occupations. By the time of Bill Clinton's reelection in 1996, the proportion of housewives had shrunk to 12 percent and the share of business and professional women had grown to 33 percent. Because the GOP was customizing its messages to appeal to the former and the Democrats were courting the latter, the GOP would have to find additional symbols to compete for the votes of business and professional women. Generally they have done this by using language that acknowledges these women's needs as responsible mothers (education), people who respect the traditional family (family values), and educated, successful members of the economy (tax cuts, smaller government). They have also featured women as senators, presidential nominees, and cabinet officials. In the 1990s and 2000, "soccer moms" came to symbolize the new target group. In 2004, as indicated above, personal and national security in the face of terrorist attacks became major themes.

Democrats have stayed pretty much with a formula that stresses reproductive rights ("a woman's right to choose") and policies that ensure the advancement of women on a leveled playing field (affirmative action, sexual harassment prosecution, and job training assistance). On occasion, when Republicans became too strident about righteousness— for example, with the "culture wars" language at the 1992 nominating convention—Democrats spoke of theocrats who would control people's bedrooms from the Capitol and the White House. They have made enduring negative symbols of Jerry Falwell and Pat Robertson. The specter of the religious Right's making appointments to the federal courts is always raised in Democratic campaigns. And because their base includes more of the economically deprived and single moms, they have stressed economic policies and social respect "for all types of families." They have also reminded the traditional civic leadership among mainline Protestants that people with less tolerant values now control the Republican Party that they once controlled. Republican leadership in Washington speaks with a southern accent and views policy through evangelical frames, pejorative language to the eastern mainline Protestant establishment that once controlled the Republican Party, the party of the main faith.

These trends came together in 1992 in the persons of the presidential candidates' wives. Republicans tried to portray Hillary Rodham Clinton as a symbol of what had gone wrong with feminism. An ambitious professional woman who seemingly showed contempt for housewives who baked cookies, she was implicitly held responsible for the disarray in her marriage. By contrast, the GOP deployed the grandmotherly Barbara Bush as the kind of wife who was suitable for a president. Perhaps the GOP effort garnered the diminishing homemaker, vote but it may well have backfired among the business and professional women who were more likely to see Mrs. Clinton as a role model.

Thus the parties have launched cultural symbols intended for these contrasting groups in the manner our theory has predicted, intending to dismantle a component of the opposite party's coalition. And much of that discourse is at a level of meaning that resonates with primary group considerations.

We now examine the electoral histories of each, noting first when the changes occurred and second the factors that accounted for change. Figure 12.1 portrays the massive changes in the voting behavior of white evangelical Protestants.

When the time series began, this group's makeup was 60 to 65 percent Democratic; by the end it was more than 50 percent Republican. More important is the manner in which white evangelicals have either failed to vote or defected. Only in 1964 did the Democratic candidate emerge from the election with a positive margin of support from white evangelicals. In 1960 massive defections and low turnout—both related to the candidacy of an Irish Catholic from Massachusetts who was decidedly not "one of us"—led to a Republican margin. Turnout was always low among evangelicals—in part because of socioeconomic status and in part because politics was the devil's business. Late in the time series, however, the most distinctive thing other than the massive movement to Republican identification is the high rate of turnout within both parties. Republican presidential candidates were always able to generate high defection rates among white evangelical Democrats, reflecting the initial southern strategy of both Barry Goldwater and Kevin Phillips and the growth of moral restorationist symbols. Democrats gained some Republican defectors in the 1990s. Clinton played to affinity themes—as a sunny Southern Baptist choirboy who sometimes couldn't resist the devil's temptation—and

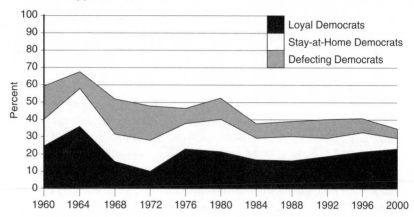

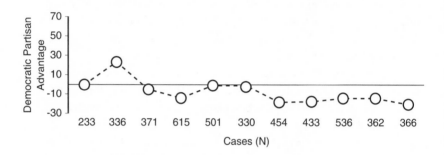

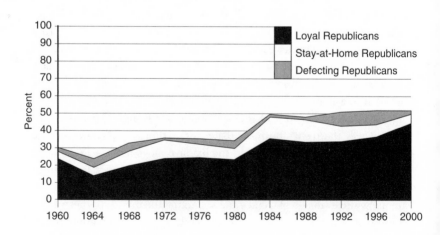

to economic issues. Otherwise, few target groups in our study betray such high responsiveness to cultural campaigning.

Table 12.1 indicates the reasons why white evangelical Democrats either failed to turn out or actually defected. Both are often good predictors of eventual realignment or alignment as Republicans.

As table 12.1 shows, race-based party ideology or its assumption into broader labels was the dominant reason for white evangelical Republicans to be attracted to Republican candidates from 1964 to 1988. (We have not included samples of campaign appeals based on race because that is not the central illustration in this chapter, but they are well documented in chapter 9 of Leege et al. 2002.) As early as the 1972 race, in which George McGovern was the Democratic nominee, moral restorationism was implicated in the social change factor. Although not statistically significant, it never quite left the campaigns in succeeding years. But by the 1990s, moral restorationism grew to be the dominant reason for evangelicals to leave the Democratic Party. In the 1960s, forms of patriotism that stressed military strength and anticommunism also appeared, although they were significant only in 1964. Yet in 1988 they reappeared significantly in the factor that captures George Bush's appeal to patriotism in defining Michael Dukakis's weakness on national defense. (Remember the flag salutes and Snoopy in the tank?) Thus, white evangelical Democrats have been responsive to many Republican cultural appeals, especially race, but as the agenda and contexts change, the defining themes change. As an aside, it is interesting that in 1992 and 1996 and especially in 2000 (analysis not shown on this table), items involving race loaded on the moral restorationism factor. In short, a similar definition of blacks as morally inferior people transfers to others "who do not live according to God's design."

Figure 12.2 portrays the electoral history of white business and professional women. Although in the earlier elections these women were not responding with as much sensitivity to the same campaign symbolism as did evangelicals, by the 1990s the Republican women became the mirror opposites, but not to the same extent. Business and professional women always have high turnout. They are educated and involved. But they respond to negative appeals not by disengaging but by defecting. The party loyalty and the defection figures for both Democrats and Republicans are high. These defectors are party affiliates who have indeed established a pattern of independent behavior. The partisan advantage favored Republicans in all years except the 1990s. Party identification favored Republicans only in 1984 and 1988. In the last three elections shown, all the movement in party identification, Democratic loyalty, and Republican defection favored the Democratic candidate. Our other data also show that young business

TABLE 12.1: White, non-Latino evangelical Protestant Democrats, 1960–96

Factors	Disengagement	Defection	Controls	Disengagement	Defection
		1960			
Government role/social spending	.788***	.784****	Education	−1.154	−.917*
			Gender	.760	.907*
Cynicism/trust in government	.583****	−.068	Income	−.431	.293
			Cohort	1.556***	−.463
Strength of United States	.462	.305	Southern location	−1.510**	.032
Isolationism/ internationalism	.005	−.162			
			Constant	−.904	−.415
Race/civil rights	.370	.060	$LR_{\chi^2}[20]$	50.94	
N	136				
		1964			
Old social cleavages	.044	−.085	Education	−.015	.633
Party ideology	.455*	1.139****	Gender	.561*	.196
Cynicism/ Anticommunism	.459***	.710***	Income	.008	.263
			Cohort	.208	−.361
			Southern location	−.211	.685
			Constant	−1.544	−2.994*
N	202		$LR_{\chi^2}[16]$	42.33	
		1968			
Race-based party ideology	.451	.989****	Education	.599	.947**
			Gender	.537	.348
Cynicism/trust in government	.769****	.734****	Income	−.866****	−.410*
			Cohort	1.826****	.888*
Anti-communism/law and order	−.050	−.195	Southern location	.571	.221
Anti-nativism/ Pro-minorities	.061	.035	Constant	−2.956**	−2.217*
N	162		$LR_{\chi^2}[18]$	61.84	
		1972			
Conservative reaction to social change	.087	.691**	Education	−.401	.204
			Gender	.569	−.265
Cultural populism	.283	−.011	Income	.097	.327*
Elite religious liberals	.066	.389*	Cohort	−.018	−.839***
			Southern location	.195	.480
			Constant	−.221	1.143
N	242		$LR_{\chi^2}[16]$	53.08	

Factors	Disengagement	Defection	Controls	Disengagement	Defection
		1976			
Opposition to racial or social change	.086	.331	Education	−.472	.295
			Gender	.278	−.282
Cynical isolationism/ moral restorationism	.368*	−.298	Income	−.176	−.401*
			Cohort	.200	−.261
Cultural populism	.115	.285	Southern location	.358	.486
Race-based party ideology	−.082	.754***			
			Constant	−.552	.216
N	185		$LR_{\chi^2}[18]$	37.01	
		1980			
Race-based party ideology	.779**	1.371****	Education	−.604	.402
			Gender	.257	−.019
Retreatist racial populism	−.705***	−.119	Income	−.407*	−.114
			Cohort	.616	.626
Moral restorationism	.232	−.040	Southern location	−.626	−.382
			Constant	.248	−1.954
N	132		$LR_{\chi^2}[16]$	34.65	
		1984			
Race-based party ideology	.628*	3.016****	Education	−.671	.361
			Gender	.325	2.215****
Race, rights, taxes	−.123	.020	Income	−.778****	−.203
Moral restorationism	−.147	−.167	Cohort	1.460****	.431
			Constant	.077	−.227
			Southern location	−1.002	−5.185****
N	133		$LR_{\chi^2}[16]$	80.06	
		1988			
Race-based party ideology	.238	1.511****	Education	−.940***	−.037
			Gender	.147	.576
Cynical isolationism	.791****	.984****	Income	−.391*	−.106
Moral restorationism	.464**	.313	Cohort	.717*	.3444
Racial interests	.099	−.047	Southern location	1.090**	.848
			Constant	−.449	−2.605
N	146		$LR_{\chi^2}[18]$	56.34	

TABLE 12.1: *continued*

Factors	Disengagement	Defection	Controls	Disengagement	Defection
		1992			
Race/Class/International order-based party	−.527	.165	Education	.244	1.052****
			Gender	−.277	.086
Cynicism/trust in government	−.158	.210	Income	−.497**	.018
			Cohort	1.426****	1.189****
Millennial Hopes	.338	.006	Southern location	.608	−.661
Morally restorationist party	1.182****	1.183****			
			Constant	−3.273***	−4.930****
N	175		$LR_{\chi^2}[18]$	65.85	
		1996			
Morally restorationist party	.706*	1.713****	Education	−1.169****	−.175
			Gender	.721	−.780
Embrace of internationalism	−.132	.092	Income	−.468*	.439
			Cohort	1.126**	.439
Antagonism toward outgroup	−.485*	−.342	Southern location	.389	−.255
			Constant	−1.843	−1.475
N	127		$LR_{\chi^2}[18]$	51.49	

Source: American National Election Studies, 1960–96. Reprinted with permission from Leege et al. 2002.

Note: Multinomial-Logit regression estimated via maximum likelihood, with voting Democratic as the base category. The $LR_{\chi^2}[df]$ statistic is the difference between likelihood ratios of a model estimated simply with a constant and the models reported above. This is similar to the joint F test of OLS regression.

* p < .1 (two-tail); ** p < .05 (two-tail); *** p < .025 (two-tail); **** p < .01 (two-tail).

and professional women aligning as Democrats can account for much of this massive increase. White business and professional women have become a new base of the Democratic Party. Elections in the next decade will be won or lost by the extent to which Democratic candidates can fashion appeals to keep them in their new partisan home.

Like most other groups, Democratic business and professional women defected in 1972 and from 1984 to 1992 because of race-based party ideology. In 1996, their party's stance on moral restorationism depressed turnout and also had a slight impact on defection. But it is quite the opposite for Republican business and professional women. Prior to 1980, with the

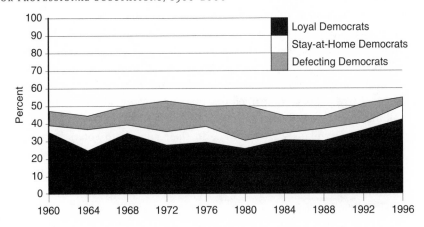

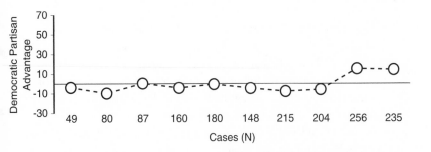

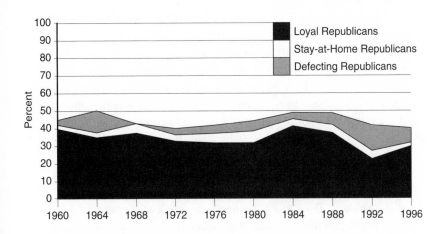

exception of 1964, they appear unfazed by cultural campaigning and remain loyal. In 1964, 1980, 1988, 1992, however, they took umbrage at the Republican candidates' use of racial code words and their party's racial policies. They were also the first to notice GOP candidates' appeals to moral restorationism—and defected. In 1984, 1992, 1996, and 2000 their defections were heavily accounted for by the GOP's appeals concerning gender, family lifestyle, sexuality, and the visibility given to evangelical leaders. They was accompanied by others who had made the transition all the way to identification with the Democratic Party.

Cultural symbols wax and wane in their appeals to voters because (1) contexts change and (2) candidates find new, more effective ways to package themselves and their opponents. The constant, however, is that the discourse will be at a level of meaning that is close to the voter's affective life.

IMPLICATIONS

This chapter has argued that theories of electoral transitions at the macro level will be improved by the explicit adoption of a micro-level theory of emotions. Although this study pursues research concerning cultural politics by incorporating inferences derived from theories of emotions in politics, the former also suggests areas for developing the latter. In particular, we note that prior collective work regarding emotions and the vote has not considered abstention as a political option. Rather, these works (see, for example, MacKuen et al., chapter 6 in this volume, and Nardulli and Kuklinski, chapter 13) document the impact of emotions on whether partisans vote for or against their party's candidate. The crucial assumption of affective intelligence theory—that anxiety about one's initially preferred candidate generates active information-seeking—implies that the voter is faced with a binary decision. But voters have a third option, abstention, which they often exercise when faced with unpalatable alternatives. In the classic accounts of cross-pressure theory, abstention is the rational response to an unpleasant set of alternatives. Does affective intelligence help us understand when anxiety promotes a change of normal behavior—moving, say, from the Democratic to the Republican checkbox on the ballot—and when it stimulates the decision to opt out of the electoral process altogether? Is it simply a matter of the magnitude of the anxiety? Does it occur when *both* candidates engender anxiety? Does the distinction between anger and anxiety, one stimulating action and the other encouraging avoidance (see Huddy, Feldman, and Cassese, chapter 9 in this volume), help us gain a purchase on whether anxious voters opt to defect rather than to demobilize? Given the centrality of defection to our understanding of partisan transformations, it is important to understand the psychological mechanisms that produce demobilization rather than defection. Extending the theory of affective intelligence to the problem of turnout will help close the inference gap between individual-level and collective models of electoral change.

CHAPTER THIRTEEN

Testing Some Implications of Affective Intelligence Theory at the Aggregate Level

PETER F. NARDULLI AND JAMES H. KUKLINSKI

Psychologists study emotions for their own sake. Political scientists care about emotions only if they further understanding of politics. Accordingly, this chapter begins with a conception of democratic governance and only then asks how incorporating emotions might enhance it. Three core desires—the desires for economic prosperity, individual physical safety, and collective physical security—serve as the conception's foundation. The conception predicts that when threats to these core desires arise and politicians fail to address them, an electorate that normally might not be watching voices its discontent at the ballot box.

Initially, we borrow from affective intelligence theory devised by Marcus and colleagues (Marcus, Neuman, and MacKuen 2000; MacKuen, Marcus, Neuman, and Keele, chapter 6 in this volume) and assume anxiety to be the triggering mechanism: threats to core desires increase anxiety, in turn evoking intense surveillance and departures from routine voting behavior.[1] We derive aggregate-level implications from this assumption and find some empirical support for them. When deriving the implications, however, we find affective intelligence theory to be lacking. It is silent as to the long-term dynamics between threats and anxiety or between

---

1. We skirt one key matter in this chapter: determining when an increasingly bad condition becomes a threat. Different people will see the same condition differently; some will interpret it as a threat, others will not. In fact, the complexity is greater than this. People might not see a bad condition as a threat until they feel anxiety. We adopt a frankly loose posture in this chapter and assume that a condition or a change in condition objectively becomes a threat once it reaches a certain threshold, which we do not specify. At that point, some people feel threatened, others do not. As the condition worsens further, additional people feel threatened.

anxiety and political decision making. The propositions thus represent our best guesses, but they are guesses, and their confirmation hardly represents indisputable support for the theory.

We then turn to two topics that in one form or another pervade many of the chapters in this volume: affective intelligence's singular focus on anxiety and the value gained from including emotions in the study of decision making. Whereas other authors address them from the perspective of individual-level mental processes, our aggregate-level perspective puts considerable distance between the workings of the human mind and the broad contours of (American) politics. From this perspective, some of the finer distinctions that motivate political psychology (between types of emotions, for example) look unimportant, at least given the current and still immature state of research in neuroscience and psychology.

A CONCEPTION OF REPRESENTATIVE DEMOCRACY, ANXIETY INCLUDED

Most studies of democratic governance adopt one of two perspectives. Beginning with Miller and Stokes (1963) and continuing through the 1970s, scholars used (typically cross-sectional) survey data to consider whether the actions of political elites, primarily legislators, correspond to the ideological leanings and policy preferences of their constituents. This bottom-up perspective, which views legislators' responsiveness as the key to effective democratic representation, found little to modest evidence of it, despite the strong assumption that causal influence flows completely from constituencies' preferences to legislators' roll-call behavior. Later, scholars turned to survey and laboratory experiments to demonstrate that elites shape the ways in which citizens think about issues. This work showed, for example, that people express more support for affirmative action when encouraged to view it as a remedy for past discrimination against African Americans than when encouraged to view it as reverse discrimination (Kinder and Sanders 1990; but see Druckman 2001; Druckman and Nelson 2003; Sniderman and Theriault 2004). In the vein of Schattschneider (1960), this top-down perspective places political elites in the driver's seat. Taken together, the two research traditions offer a minimal role for ordinary citizens; if politicians aren't ignoring them, they are telling them how and what to think.

The conception we offer immediately below differs from either of the two principal perspectives. Its key elements are a shared set of core political desires and the rise and fall of threats to those desires. It predicts that the rise of such threats, especially when they become severe, will cause citizens to react politically.

McCubbins and Schwartz's distinction (1984) between how police and fire departments function captures the essence of our conception. Just as members of fire departments do not constantly monitor their communities for fires, so citizens do not constantly monitor politics for purposes of evaluating their political agents' performances. Rather, fire alarms—conditions that threaten core political desires—draw citizens' attention. Especially when severe, multiple, and enduring, these fire alarms generate collective electoral jolts that affect politicians' electoral fortunes.

Core Political Desires

Whereas most studies of democratic governance focus heavily on citizens' preferences regarding current issues, ranging from race and abortion to size of the military, we begin with something more fundamental: core political desires. In Western societies, these core desires include general yearnings—for liberty, democracy, and happiness—as well as a set of derivative and more specific yearnings—for safety and security, economic prosperity, and equal treatment under the law. This set of yearnings falls second on Maslow's hierarchy of needs (1968) after physiological needs such as sex, food, and sleep, and citizens in developed nations expect them to be met. Indeed, their fulfillment constitutes the very definition of well-being in such societies.

In the United States and elsewhere, ordinary citizens look to politicians and other democratic stewards to ensure safety, security, and economic prosperity. They expect policymakers to keep their streets and neighborhoods safe, to prevent and protect them from outside aggression, and to keep inflation and unemployment within reasonable bounds. That these themes dominate political rhetoric underlines the importance of core desires to democratic governance.

Threats to Core Values

Threats to core values constitute the other key component in our conception of democratic governance. We assume that most people recognize such threats when they exist. The threats, after all, take well-known forms, such as rising crime rates, rising unemployment levels, and looming prospects of war. Moreover, the media cover such threats widely and intensely, especially as their seriousness grows. Partisan politicians who stand to gain from the threats' existence dramatize the bad and worsening state of affairs. For all these reasons, serious threats to core desires will appear on people's perceptual screens.

Threats come and go. If the country is at peace but the economy shows dramatic signs of faltering, the economy, not war, will grab most people's attention. In the absence of threats to any core value, that is, during times of peace, prosperity, and collective safety, partisan politics as usual will rule the day.

Note the importance of change, of ebb and flow, to the definition of a threat. A 10 percent unemployment rate represents a threat only because it is much higher than the 3 or 4 percent rate that preceded it. The identification of a condition as a threat, then, requires continuous comparisons to other conditions. Whether the current state of affairs represents a threat depends on how it stacks up vis-à-vis prior states, especially when citizens view relatively good conditions of the past as the norm.

But why do threats to core values, with their potentially damaging political consequences, occur at all? Why don't politicians always keep crime and unemployment rates at relatively low levels? One answer is that these phenomena ebb and flow independent of politics and policymaking. According to this view, politicians lack the capacity to preempt most potential threats. Alternatively, although politicians might possess the capacity to stop potential threats from becoming real, other demands take center court until potential turns to reality. Politicians, like citizens, respond to fire alarms. Because our interest is the citizenry's response to changing conditions, we do not adjudicate between these two explanations (Nardulli 2005 presents a fuller discussion). In any event, some combination of the two explanations probably comes closest to the truth.

Anxiety

According to the research program in affective intelligence (Marcus and MacKuen 1993; Marcus, Neuman, and MacKuen 2000), ominous-looking changes in the political environment initially gain citizens' attention. These out-of-the-ordinary changes activate the so-called surveillance system, which in turn produces anxiety. Heightened anxiety decreases reliance on habit and leads to a reconsideration of choices for purposes of changing the situation that evoked the emotion. Simply, and in the political context, anxious citizens begin to consider alternative political choices.[2]

---

2. Affective intelligence theory also identifies a key role for heightened enthusiasm, which occurs under positive conditions. Given the focus on threats to core values, this chapter does not consider the impact of enthusiasm.

Although this core idea has great intuitive appeal, the limits of affective intelligence theory become immediately obvious on trying to derive implications about the dynamics between environmental changes and anxiety, on one hand, and anxiety and behavioral changes, on the other. For example, do higher levels of threat lead linearly to higher levels of anxiety, or does the relationship take a different form? Do sustained, long-lasting threats increase anxiety more than short-lived ones? Do two severe threats create more anxiety than one threat, or does one severe threat alone push anxiety to its limit?

As a theory, affective intelligence offers no answers and, in fact, fails to raise the questions. Neuroscience's current inability to offer guidance and the authors' reliance on cross-sectional data explain the void. In our view, these are the very sorts of questions that political psychologists must pose and try to answer.

Accordingly, we posit the following propositions. Although we offer a rationale for each, we emphasize, again, the lack of theoretical and empirical guidance from affective intelligence theory. Our conception of democratic governance emphasizes change and dynamics; affective intelligence predicts only that surveillance will occur under high but not low anxiety.

All of the propositions we offer below stem from the same set of assumptions. Common to all are the following:

- Threats to common desires are potential sources of anxiety.
- People differ as to the level of threat that creates anxiety.
- People differ as to the level of anxiety that causes surveillance.
- People differ as to the level at which surveillance causes them to change voting behavior.

These assumptions recognize, first, that threats to common desires can change behavior and, second, that the threat → anxiety → surveillance → change-in-behavior chain will reach completion more quickly and with greater effects among some people than others.

Three propositions follow directly from the assumptions.

THE MAGNITUDE PROPOSITION

Prediction: The greater an external threat to core desires at any moment in time, the greater the change in aggregate voting behavior.

Rationale: Bigger threats cause more people to monitor their environments and change their behavior than do smaller threats.

THE ENDURANCE PROPOSITION

Prediction: The longer an external threat to core desires endures, the greater the change in aggregate voting behavior.

Rationale: Persistent threats produce anxiety and thus behavioral change among voters who did not become anxious earlier.

THE CONFLUENCE PROPOSITION

Prediction: The greater the number of core desires that are threatened at any moment in time, the greater the change in aggregate voting behavior.

Rationale: Simultaneous threats to two or more core values induce anxiety even among those with relatively high anxiety thresholds.

Figure 13.1 illustrates the logic of the magnitude, endurance, and confluence propositions using two domains: crime and unemployment. The horizontal axis represents time. Higher values on the vertical axis indicate greater threat and thus, presumably, a higher level of anxiety.

Note, first, that conditions in either domain can be better or worse at any particular point in time. So, for example, at time 3, the crime rate has gone up, increasing anxiety among some citizens who now see threats to their physical security. The unemployment rate, on the other hand, is too low to be a source of anxiety. Conversely, at times 6 and 7, deteriorating economic conditions induce anxiety by threatening some people's sense of economic security but the now-low crime rate does not. Second, bad conditions can endure for a long or a short time in either domain. Economic conditions, for example, deteriorate at three different times in the hypothetical example. Distinguishing the third time from the prior two is the enduring peak, which continues unabated for three years. In the real world, conditions that threaten people's core political desires vary considerably in their duration.

Finally, bad conditions in different domains can occur simultaneously, creating particularly serious threats to core political desires. In figure 13.1, crime and unemployment rates both peak at time 5. In the United States, civil unrest and crime rates both jumped markedly during the 1960s, much as inflation, unemployment, and international threats all did in the late 1970s. Such periods presumably generate especially high and widely shared levels of anxiety.

Rationality and deliberation also hold a place in affective intelligence theory. In their most widely cited work, Marcus and MacKuen (1993) show

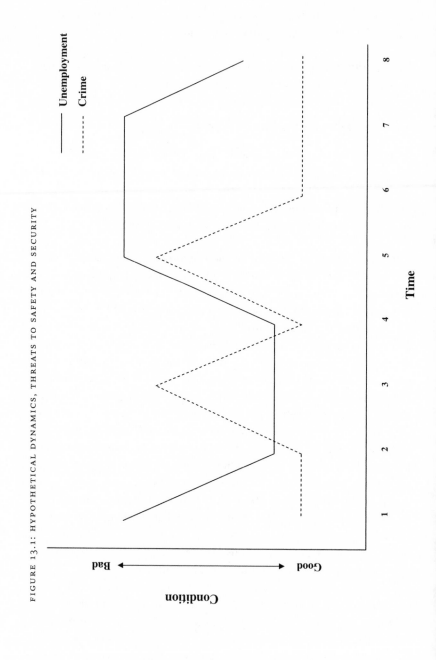

that voters who report relatively high levels of anxiety about a presidential candidate tend to rely more heavily on issues than on the candidates' partisanship. That is, they make more carefully considered judgments. The authors' most recent statement goes further and states, strongly, that increased anxiety[3] induces rational decision making. It tells individual that they are entering a situation of uncertainty, which leads them to rely on learning of alternatives and consideration of available choices as depicted by the rational choice approach (see chapter 6 in this volume).

The assumption that high anxiety leads to rational decision making suggests two additional propositions that predict how rationally acting voters should behave, collectively, in the face of threats to core desires. They are as follows:

THE PROSPECTIVE EVALUATION PROPOSITION

Prediction: Aggregate voting patterns, as responses to threats to core desires, depend on predictions of future conditions.

Rationale: Highly anxious and thus rationally calculating voters successfully predict future conditions at election time (Downs 1957; MacKuen, Erikson, and Stimson 1992).

THE PARTY REPUTATION PROPOSITION

Prediction: Aggregate voting patterns, as responses to threats to core desires, depend on the two parties' reputations in a policy domain.

Rationale: If the party with the stronger reputation in a policy domain holds office when a threat in that domain arises, it benefits from that reputation because voters do not see a good alternative.

AN AGGREGATE-LEVEL TEST OF AFFECTIVE INTELLIGENCE

We analyze the relationship between real-world conditions in three policy domains and voting returns, all measured at the county level.[4] In between

---

3. Proponents of affective intelligence still have not precisely defined high anxiety or provided a good empirical measure. We agree with Spezio and Adolphs (chapter 4 in this volume) that, intuitively, very high levels of anxiety should impair performance.

4. In terms of level analysis, at least, our study is the polar opposite of that by Redlawsk, Civettini, and Lau (chapter 7 in this volume).

the aggregated conditions and voting returns are assumptions about un-observed individual-level mental processes, assumptions that we take initially from affective intelligence theory. The causal chain is as follows:

$$\text{Rise of threatening condition} \to \text{Increase in anxiety} \to \text{Increase in cognition} \to \text{Reassessment of normal vote choice}$$

The chain's complexity is even greater than this, for there are also aggregation processes: from individual perceptions of threat to collective perceived threat, from individual anxiety to collective anxiety, and from individual votes to collective votes. Luskin (2002a, 2002b; also see MacKuen 2002) has documented the complexities of such aggregation processes. We simplified them by assuming that each of the collective relationships represented by the symbol $\to$ maps as a monotonic function. In support of this assumption, we do not expect worsening conditions to reduce collective perceived threat; nor do we expect collective anxiety to decline when collective perceived threat increases or deviations from the normal vote to fall as collective anxiety rises.

Data

To test the propositions, we used data about voting in presidential elections that derived from a comprehensive data archive. The primary unit of analysis in this data archive is the local electorate (counties and major cities).[5] The data archive includes election returns for all presidential contests from 1828 to 2000. Unfortunately, the unavailability of some variables restricted this analysis to elections between 1976 and 2000 (about 21,903 cases are available for analysis). We tested only the magnitude, confluence, prospective evaluation, and party reputation propositions; work in progress will address the endurance proposition.

Variables

Deviation from the incumbent party's normal vote (incumbent$_{DEV}$) serves as the dependent variable. It compares the actual presidential vote in any given election to an estimated vote based on the assumption that citizens' habitual voting patterns (voting Democratic, voting Republican, abstain-

---

5. For more information about the data collected for this project see (Nardulli 2005, appendix I, available at www.pol.uiuc.edu/faculty/nardulliresearch.html).

ing) solely determine their choices. We scaled incumbent$_{DEV}$ so that positive values represent greater-than-expected returns for the incumbent party.

We identified three core desires: physical safety, economic security, and safety from external harm. Five primary variables—current rate and one-year change in crime rate, current rate and two-year change in unemployment rate, and years of international peace—measure threats to the core desires. The national inflation rate and party of the incumbent serve as control variables.

"Years of international peace," by definition, is a national-level variable.[6] Although crime and unemployment rate data exist at all three levels—nation, state, and county—we selected the local-level measures. For one thing, one-year crime and two-year unemployment rates vary considerably across space and time at the local level. When the rates soar, the local media cover the problems extensively. Moreover, bad local conditions more directly threaten citizens' core political desires than do national ones. This is particularly true with respect to crime rates. Crime in local communities and neighborhoods poses a direct and immediate threat to residents' physical well-being; when it increases, people presumably take notice and become anxious. Finally, the local measures offer a good test of the confluence thesis, which posits that overlapping threats will create the highest levels of anxiety among the largest number of voters.

Using the local-level measures entailed making tradeoffs, not the least of which is a reduction in the number of years available for analysis. The U.S. Bureau of Labor Statistics began to publish local monthly unemployment rates in 1974, which is two years earlier than the Federal Bureau of Investigation began to publish local crime rates. National crime and unemployment figures go back much further. Moreover, the county-level data are noisy, a problem that arises because minor fluctuations in the number of jobs or crimes within small counties can cause deceptively large proportional increases.[7] We tried to identify all such cases and make proper adjustments, but this alone does not fully overcome the problem. Removing these cases from the analysis does not change the conclusions.

---

6. We are indebted to Scott Gartner for providing the data necessary to construct the variable for years of peace. He provided us with a data set for the correlates of war that lists the beginning and ending of all major military conflicts in U.S. history. The variable for years of peace ranged from 1 to 15 in our analysis pool.

7. For theoretical reasons noted above, we needed to test the interactive effects of these variables. This required multiplying "noisy" first-order terms, which only compounds the problem.

Moving from proposition to empirical test requires proper specification of the statistical models. For purposes of testing the magnitude proposition, we included the primary variables introduced above: local crime rate, change in local crime rate, local unemployment rate, change in local unemployment rate, and years of peace. We also included two interactions—local crime rate * change in local crime rate and local unemployment rate * change in local unemployment rate. These interactions allow for the possibility that changes in crime and unemployment rates most strongly affect normal votes when current rates are high. We hypothesize that the main and interactive terms will all linearly and positively affect incumbent$_{DEV}$ (see column 4 in table 13.1).

We added a series of interaction terms to test the confluence proposition. These include three two-way interactions: change in local crime rate * change in local unemployment rate, change in local crime rate * years of peace, and change in local unemployment rate * years of peace. Each interaction accounts for the possible compounding effects of two increasingly bad conditions. To be complete, we also included three- and four-way interactions that include, for crime and unemployment, both the rate and the change in rate (see table 13.1).

Testing the prospective evaluation proposition entailed adding a measure that captures the change in local unemployment rates for the three-month period immediately following the election (change in local unemployment rate$_{3\text{-MONTH FORWARD LAG}}$). A statistically significant relationship between it and incumbent$_{DEV}$ suggests that voters accurately project economic trends affecting their economic well-being and, more generally, that they make sophisticated judgments of political stewardship.

In evaluating the party reputation proposition, we take advantage of the fact that the two major U.S. parties enjoy different performance reputations in two of the domains examined in this analysis: crime and unemployment. Republicans have gained a reputation as a law-and-order party, and Democrats have not. At least since the New Deal, Democrats have held a reputation as supporters of unions and the working class and thus as proponents of full employment. In contrast, most observers see Republicans as generally favoring low interest rates rather than low unemployment rates.

Suppose crime rates jump while Republicans hold office. They should absorb fewer electoral losses than Democrats would under the same conditions. Rationally thinking voters will not expect the Democratic challenger to give higher priority to the crime problem than the Republican incumbent did. Reputation effects with respect to unemployment should work similarly, although, of course, they should favor Democrats.

TABLE 13.1: Summary of measures and predicted effects on deviations from the normal vote

Measure	Predicted effect
Magnitude effects:	
Local crime rate	−
Local unemployment rate	−
Δ local crime rate	−
Δ local unemployment rate	−
Local crime rate × Δ local crime rate	−
Local unemployment rate × Δ local unemployment rate	−
Years without war	−
Confluence effects:	
Δ local crime rate × Δ local unemployment rate	−
Δ local crime rate × years without peace	−
Δ local unemployment rate × years without peace	−
Local crime rate × Δ local crime rate × local unemployment rate × Δ local unemployment rate	−
Local crime rate × Δ local crime rate × years without peace	−
Local unemployment rate × Δ local unemployment rate × years without peace	−
Rationality effects:	
Δ unemployment rate three months after an election	−
Δ local crime rate × Republican incumbent	+
Δ local unemployment rate × Republican incumbent	−
Local crime rate × Δ local crime rate × Republican incumbent	+
Local unemployment rate × Δ local unemployment rate × Republican incumbent	−

Note: All measures are coded in the same direction, so that each measure is expected to be negatively associated with deviations from the normal vote. The two exceptions are the crime × Republican incumbent interactions.

We tested the party reputation hypothesis with two two-way interaction terms (change in local crime rate * Republican incumbent and change in local unemployment rate * Republican incumbent) and two three-way interaction terms—local crime rate * change in local crime rate * Republican incumbent and local unemployment rate* change in local unemployment rate * Republican incumbent.[8]

8. To expedite interpretation of the results, we changed the coding of the party incumbency in the unemployment interaction terms so that 1 equals Democrat and 0 equals Republican.

TABLE 13.2: Tests of propositions

Variable	Model 1	Model 2	Model 3
Intercept	.012	.065**	.012*
National inflation rate	−.009***	−.009***	−.009*
Republican incumbent	−.073***	−.070***	−.073*
Local crime rate	.003***	.004***	.004*
Local unemployment rate	.009***	−.038***	−.039*
Δ Local crime rate	−.003**	.005*	.001*
Δ Local unemployment rate	−.014***	−.025**	−.016*
Local unemployment rate × Δ local crime rate	−.000	−.000	−.001*
Local crime rate × Δ local unemployment rate	.000	.009*	−.012*
Years without war	−.010***	−.007***	−.004*
Δ local crime rate × Δ local unemployment rate		.000	.002*
Δ local crime rate × years without peace		−.001*	−.001*
Δ local unemployment rate × years without peace		−.002*	−.003*
Local crime rate × Δ local crime rate × local unemployment rate × Δ local unemployment rate		.000	−.001*
Local crime rate × Δ local crime rate × years without peace		−.001*	−.001*
Local unemployment rate × Δ local unemployment rate × years without peace		−.001***	.000*
Δ Unemployment rate three months after an election			−.006*
Δ Local crime rate × Republican incumbent			.007*
Δ Local unemployment rate × Republican incumbent			−.009*
Local crime rate × Δ local crime rate × Republican incumbent			.001*
Local unemployment rate × Δ local unemployment rate × Republican incumbent			−.005*
N	21,884	21,884	21,884
Adjusted R²	.35	.32	.31

* p < .05; ** p < .01; *** p < .001.

Results

To facilitate the discussion, we have presented a progression of multiple regression analyses. Table 13.2 reports the results for each model. The first model tests only the magnitude proposition, the second adds terms to test the confluence hypothesis, and the third adds yet more terms to test the rationality propositions.

The first column in table 13.2 reports the findings for Model 1. Magnitude effects explain about one-third of the variance in incumbent$_{DEV}$ (adjusted R^2 = .31). Although some of the estimated coefficients confirmed the proposition that locally based threats shape people's evaluations of incumbents, others did not. Changes in local crime and unemployment rates worked as hypothesized; increases in either one caused the incumbent to receive less electoral support than expected. On the other hand, existing rates had the opposite effects; the higher the crime rate during the year preceding the election or, in the case of unemployment, the two years before the election, the better the incumbent fared at the polls. Moreover, neither of the interactions between rate and change in rate significantly affected aggregate vote outcomes. As expected, the number of years without peace positively and strongly affected incumbent$_{DEV.}$ These first aggregate results, then, offer mixed support for the first proposition derived from affective intelligence theory's central idea that increased anxiety arising from threatening situations leads people to monitor their environments and rethink their normal partisan choices.

The confluence proposition predicts that the confluence of threatening events evokes emotional reactions from larger numbers of people and thus causes greater aggregate vote changes than any one isolated event. To test it (which, to our knowledge, has not been done before), we added interaction terms that measure the effects of simultaneous conditions in any two or all three domains. The estimated parameters in Model 2 tell a compelling story: bad conditions in two or three domains consistently cause greater deviations from the normal vote than bad conditions in one domain.

The third column in table 13.2 reports the statistical estimates of Model 3, which adds variables to test the two rationality propositions. The prospective evaluation proposition predicts that voters will accurately assess future conditions and use those assessments when choosing between the incumbent president and a challenger. Earlier, we used the twenty-four-month change in local unemployment rate to test the magnitude proposition. For Model 3 we used the rate for the three months immediately following the election. Economic prospects appear to cause deviations from habitual voting patterns; improved unemployment conditions three months after the election help the incumbent, and declining ones hurt him. The party reputation proposition predicts that threatening crime conditions will hurt incumbent Democrats more than incumbent Republicans, whereas threatening unemployment conditions will hurt incumbent Republicans more. The last four terms in Model 3 all support the proposition.

Consider crime. Increases in local crime rates adversely affect all incumbents' electoral fortunes, but, as predicted, they negatively affect Republican incumbents' electoral margins less than Democrats'. This holds true in general and also when prevailing crime rates are already high. When existing crime conditions look bleak and appear to be getting bleaker, rationally calculating voters conclude that replacing a Republican incumbent with a Democrat will not improve the situation. Behavior in the unemployment domain looks similar, although Democrats benefit. Bad performance on unemployment does not adversely affect Democratic incumbents' electoral fortunes as much as it affects Republican incumbents'.

Overall, then, the estimates support both of the rationality propositions and suggest that the increased anxiety evoked by bad or worsening conditions does not produce irrational, unthinking reactions. To the contrary, and in line with affective intelligence theory, emotions and rational evaluation appear to go hand-in-hand. At the least, the aggregate patterns support the implications that we correctly or incorrectly derived from the theory.

AFFECTIVE INTELLIGENCE THEORY AND THE STUDY OF POLITICS

We began with a particular conception of democratic governance, assumed anxiety to be the key mental mechanism, and then derived some implications. The operative term, again, is assumed; our data did not allow us to identify levels of anxiety among individual voters. The findings supported most but not all of the propositions we tested.[9] Score a point for affective intelligence theory.

The theory's central notion—that heightened anxiety increases attentiveness to one's external environment and thus causes more considered evaluation of that environment—has justifiably gained considerable status and acceptance in the discipline. Marcus and colleagues have documented the empirical veracity of this notion on numerous occasions and in a variety of ways. In formulating our own propositions, however, we uncovered some limits of affective intelligence theory, at least as we understand it. Most crucially and perhaps ironically, the theory focuses on

---

9. Unfortunately, the large number of cases almost ensures statistical significance of the estimated coefficients. Fortunately, nearly all of the parameters represent substantively meaningful relationships.

change (in environmental conditions, in levels of anxiety, in behavior) yet offers little guidance for dynamic conceptions of politics. It does not predict how anxiety will ebb and flow as a function of changes in real-world conditions, nor does it predict how political behavior will change as conditions change, except in the most general way.

Take, as a concrete illustration, the endurance proposition (which we did not test): the longer a threat exists, the more widespread anxiety will become. It assumes that a persistently bad condition will create anxiety among people who did not become anxious at the condition's outset. Alternatively, such a condition might reduce anxiety over time because more and more people come to accept it as part of their lives. In its current form, affective intelligence theory offers no help in choosing between these two very different predictions.

In short, we derived our propositions with minimal guidance from affective intelligence theory. We cannot say without qualification, therefore, that the predictions represent proper extensions of the theory. They make sense to us, but that alone does not justify them.

Perhaps we ask too much of affective intelligence theory. Marcus and colleagues build effectively on the study of emotions in psychology and neuroscience, but this research remains in considerable flux. In their companion chapters, Spezio and Adolphs (chapter 4 in this volume) and Huddy, Feldman, and Cassese (chapter 9 in this volume) document and summarize the competing theories and rapidly changing empirical results that characterize both fields. Most fundamentally, this research lacks the requisite theoretic foundations from which to make precise predictions about the dynamics of environment, anxiety, and behavior.

In fact, some of the current literature challenges the exalted status that Marcus and colleagues accord anxiety in their affective intelligence theory, raising two questions for this chapter. First, was anxiety necessary to derive our predictions? Would substituting fear or anger, for example, have generated similar predictions? Second, if anxiety is not necessary, is there reason nevertheless to give it top billing? We begin with substitutability.

In one of the first scientific studies of emotions and political choice, Conover and Feldman (1986) coined the effective phrase, "I'm mad as hell and I'm not going to take it anymore." They show that bad economic conditions make people angry, and then they vote incumbents out of office. Suppose we had taken this study as our point of departure for deriving implications. Would we have reached the same implications when substituting anger for anxiety? We think so. Conversely, had Conover and Feldman begun with anxiety rather than anger, they might have derived the same set of hypotheses.

Huddy, Feldman, and Cassese (chapter 9; also see Brader and Valentino, chapter 8) do not accept the substitutability thesis, however. Drawing on recent neuroscientific and psychological research that challenges the two-dimensional, positive-versus-negative-affect perspective on which Marcus and colleagues (and thus we) draw, they hypothesize that different negative reactions to real-world events produce different evaluations of those events. Their empirical analysis of a three-wave national panel shows that heightened anger and heightened anxiety similarly increased attention to news about the Iraq war. However, the two negative emotions shaped perceptions of the risk of and support for the Iraq war in different ways. Anger reduced estimates of risk and thus promoted support of the war; anxiety worked in the opposite way. In other words, one negative emotion, anger, led to approach, the other, anxiety, to avoidance.

These findings imply that substituting anger for anxiety should change our predictions. What those changed predictions might be, however, we cannot say. For whereas the Conover and Feldman findings readily transfer to our work, the findings of Huddy et al. do not. We can imagine anger and anxiety differentially affecting voter turnout, with anger increasing it and anxiety decreasing it, but the conception we adopted takes change in the direction of the vote, not change in turnout, as its central focus. This suggests that whether different specific emotions differentially affect evaluations and behavior depends heavily on the task citizens are performing.

Fear is another plausible substitute for anxiety. Evolved from the survival demands of our Stone Age ancestors (Barkow, Cosmides, and Tooby 1992; Damasio 1994, 1999; Hauser 1996; Le Doux 1996; Pinker 1997), it is among the most basic of all emotions, and it pervades human life. Would identifying fear as the triggering emotion in our conception of democratic governance have led to different predictions? Again, we see no reason to believe so.[10] But we might reach a different conclusion if the task of interest were turning out to vote.

Let us assume that the three negative emotions—fear, anger, and anxiety—produce similar predictions about aggregate changes in partisan voting patterns. Is there a compelling reason, nevertheless and for our specific purposes, to prefer anxiety as the triggering mechanism? If there is, we do not see it, at least from the perspective we adopted in this chapter Adopting fear or anger would work just as effectively as adopting anxiety. In fact, colloquial and far less precise terms such as *getting upset* or *feeling uptight* would serve the purpose as well as any of these terms.

---

10. Marcus (2002) himself has argued that fear and anxiety are largely one and the same.

This does not minimize the importance of the distinctions that neuro-science and political psychology seek to make; it underlines the long distance social scientists have yet to travel to connect mental processes and aggregate political patterns.

Until now the discussion reflects the central premise of this volume: without attention to emotions, political scientists cannot fully understand politics. This premise has focused authors' attention on questions such as, What are emotions? Should scholars construe emotions in terms of a single approach-avoidance continuum or as discrete and distinct entities? How and when do emotions affect political decision making? We, too, have adopted the premise, first by incorporating anxiety into our conception of democratic governance and, second, by asking whether only one emotion, anxiety, explains the reported aggregate patterns.

We conclude by questioning the premise itself: is reference to emotions essential to predicting the aggregate patterns we identified and, more generally, to the study of politics? To answer it requires that scholars not be blinded by momentary disciplinary emphases. In both psychology and political science, the emphasis on emotions has waxed and waned. Prior to the 1960s, the two disciplines, psychology especially, placed emotions (and feelings and motivations) at the center of their theories. As other contributors to this volume know, in the ensuing 25 years researchers lost sight of emotions and emphasized cognition and information processing instead. Psychologists, and thus political scientists, have now rediscovered them. This book reflects that rediscovery.

Suppose we had presented our conception of democratic governance 20 years ago. There would have been no references to emotions, and other scholars would not have questioned their absence. Yet our predictions would have mirrored those we offered above. One plausible conclusion: macro-conceptions of politics, or at the very least, ours, work well without reference to emotions.[11] We believe this to be a valid conclusion if taken literally.

It fails to recognize, however, that incorporation of emotions enriched the theoretical foundation of our work. Thinking in terms of emotions led to a fuller explication of the causal chain than we otherwise would have made. Moreover, it fails to acknowledge the value of and the need for continual interplay between individual- and aggregate-level studies. Assessing the relative values of appraisal theory and the somatic marker

---

11. Note that this conclusion is itself time-bound; if neuroscience and psychology advance such that precise predictions about the effects of different emotions can be made, it might no longer hold.

hypothesis (Spezio and Adolphs, chapter 4 in this volume) or the differential effects of anger and anxiety (Huddy, Feldman, and Cassese, chapter 9 in this volume) requires analysis at the level of the individual brain or lower. The crucial debates will and should occur at these levels. Political scientists would be remiss, however, if they did not continually try to determine whether the micro-level findings are consistent with higher-level political patterns. This is one of the most formidable challenges students of public opinion and political psychology face. It is tempting, therefore, for researchers to work solely at one or the other level of analysis. Unfortunately, this singular focus limits the discipline's capacity to understand politics and, in particular, the roles of citizens in it.

PART IV

Next Steps in Research and Outreach

The three chapters in the final part all adopt an integrative perspective on the arguments raised thus far but do so from three different perspectives.

First up are Lupia and Menning, who take a global view of affective politics from the perspective of game theory. They posit that many readers might be initially skeptical that game theorists and political psychologists would have much to say to one another because they would seem to define two poles on a continuum from conscious and calculated goal-oriented cognition to subconscious emotionality. But they make a convincing case, reminding us that most definitions of emotion derive from notions of the frustration of or success at goal-oriented behavior. Indeed, in chapter 1 we introduced a definition of *affect* as the evolved cognitive and physiological response to the detection of personal significance. So, setting aside the cultural stereotypes of affect as impulsive irrationality, the two traditions do not appear to be so distant. Alas, Lupia and Menning point out, scholars in these fields very seldom cite one another. But this chapter makes a strong and persuasive case that they should.

Think of game theory as more of a method of inquiry than a body of theory, they suggest. The tradition of game theoretic modeling requires clarity about both assumptions and ramifications that permit replication, which in turn "can reduce misunderstanding, increase the efficiency of scholarly debates, and hasten the accumulation of knowledge." It is hard to argue with those aspirations. As game theory expands into much more sophisticated modeling in which agents no longer are assumed to have perfect information, the relevance for political science in general and political psychology in particular becomes increasingly evident.

Next up is Dan Schnur, who, as a teacher of campaign politics and an active practitioner of the black art of campaign consulting, bridges two very different universes, or as he puts it, two planets, the proverbial Mars and Venus. Because he is the only contributor who is active among campaign practitioners, we asked him to emphasize that perspective and address the ways in which the research and analysis compiled in this volume would be interpreted by those in the field and, in turn, what questions the practitioners might ask that research should fruitfully address. A major theme of this chapter is a distinction among political variables that practitioners think about every day but that simply would not occur to academics: the distinction between the variables you as a strategist can do something about and those you can't. Schnur uses the example of candidate John Kerry's military record. The record itself, like most candidate attributes, is a given that the strategist inherits—what one can control is the way the record is contextualized as a campaign issue. Because academics are quick to preach about how campaigns ought to be run, given their theories of affect and cognition in mass political behavior, it is useful to be reminded that if practitioners may not do what they should, it may be because, naturally enough, they only do what they can.

Finally, Rose McDermott concludes the volume with a summative and forward-looking review. She has chosen to emphasize cognitive neuroscience in her title, but her purview is much broader. Her sense, which is shared by many contributors and in particular by Schreiber, Spezio, and Adolphs, is that we should actively leverage the dramatic technical developments in neuroscience to better understand the dynamic complexities of the interaction of cognition and affect. But McDermott, like the other contributors, warns that this is not a call to abandon traditional methods in political psychology. Quite the contrary, it should be, she argues, a stimulus to further research.

She reminds us that theory and method are inextricably intertwined and that a self-conscious convergence or triangulation of multiple methods has served us well before and should be defining character of the next generation of research concerning the affect effect.

CHAPTER FOURTEEN

Politics and the Equilibrium of Fear: Can Strategies and Emotions Interact?

ARTHUR LUPIA AND JESSE O. MENNING

Political scientists seek improved explanations of political behaviors and outcomes. Improvement comes not only from the promulgation of new concepts for thinking about politics but also from refined understandings of the conditions under which more established concepts apply. Political psychologists engage in such explorations. So do game theorists. We argue that these two groups have something to offer one another, something that can improve explanations of some of the social behaviors on which these groups focus. To set the stage for this offering, we begin with a brief description of what each group of scholars does.

Political psychologists use research concerning human thought and perception from other disciplines to inform and motivate their work. In this field there are no widely accepted guidelines for what it means to engage in the practice. Some political psychologists follow standard social psychological practices, designing research from a laboratory-based stimulus-response paradigm and running experiments whose relation to specific scientific questions is simple and clear. Others follow practices that are common to the study of public opinion and voting behavior. They draw inferences from regressions conducted on answers to multipurpose questions placed on large surveys. Still, political psychologists embed experiments in surveys. So instead of being defined by use of a single method, political psychology is defined by the use of an expanding range of methods.

Game theorists seek precise explanations of the causes of individual behaviors and collective outcomes. They use mathematized premises and conclusions to draw logically coherent inferences about when and why

We thank Adam Seth Levine for research and the volume editors, Ted Brader, and Elizabeth Suhay for helpful advice.

people behave as they do. Since the 1980s and 1990s, when an increasing number of scholars learned to design and solve games of incomplete information, game theorists have expanded their inquiries into questions of how thoughts, perception, cognition, and learning affect social phenomena. To date, however, political psychology and game theory have had very limited interaction.

Can these two endeavors converge in a constructive way? Yes, they can. Integrating aspects of game theory and political psychology can create valuable knowledge that neither approach can generate alone. In this chapter, we support this conclusion by focusing on the part of political psychology that focuses on emotions. With the publication of studies by Kinder (1994), Lodge and Taber (2000), Rahn (2000), Marcus, Neuman, and MacKuen (2000), and Brader (2005) has come greater interest in the emotional basis of political interactions (see also Lerner and Keltner 2002). We build on these efforts.

We work against the null hypothesis that game theory and the study of emotions are completely irrelevant to one another. This null hypothesis is no straw man. To see a rationale for believing it, consider the following statement by LeDoux (1996, 19): "[E]motions are things that happen to us rather than things we will to occur . . . external events are simply arranged so that the stimuli that automatically trigger emotions will be present. We have little direct control over our emotional reactions."

It is hard to disagree with the claim that emotional responses have a strong subconscious component. It may even seem reasonable to conclude that game theory—with its focus on incentives, strategic decision making, and goal-oriented learning—cannot clarify emotional aspects of politics. Such ideas are consistent with Elster's (2000, 692) conclusion: "The social sciences today, however, cannot offer a formal model of the interaction between rational and non-rational concerns that would allow us to deduce specific implications for behavior. As mentioned earlier, the idea of modeling emotions . . . is jejune and superficial. The fact that emotion can cloud thinking to the detriment of an agent's interests is enough to refute this idea."

Although there is much to disagree with in this claim, such as the separation of emotion and reason and the tendency to confound game theory as a method with very narrow notions of rationality, a critique of such ideas is not our focus. Instead, we offer a constructive attempt to yield improved inferences about important political phenomena.

It is not helpful to claim improvement without a standard against which to measure it. We choose applicability and argue that insights from game-theoretic studies of strategic decision making can clarify the conditions under which empirical claims about emotions in politics apply to particular situations. At the same time, we contend that replacing standard game-theoretic assumptions about how people react to particular stimuli with premises that are more realistic empirically can clarify the conditions under which important ideas about strategic behavior apply to politics.

A basic version of our argument is as follows: emotional responses have subconscious aspects. These aspects are beyond the purview of strategic decision making, incentives, goal-oriented learning, and other phenomena for which game theory is an effective explanation. But there is more to emotions and politics than what happens at the subconscious level. In thinking about the extent to which a game-theoretic logic of emotion in politics is possible, we find Damasio's distinction between primary and secondary emotions useful: "Primary emotions (read: innate, preorganized, Jamesian) depend on limbic system circuitry, the amygdala and anterior cingulate being the prime players. . . . But the mechanism of primary emotions does not describe the full range of emotional behaviors . . . they are followed by mechanisms of secondary emotions, which occur once we begin experiencing feelings and forming *systematic connections between categories of objects and situations, on the one hand, and primary emotions, on the other*" (Damasio 1994, 134, emphasis in original).

Unlike primary emotions, secondary emotions can be learned and inhibited. For questions of applicability, the question is "How?" An answer comes from research concerning emotions at the level of the neural substrate. It reveals important connections between emotional responses and goal orientation. As Kandel, Schwartz, and Jessell (1995, 610) describe it: "[T]he amygdala is required for the conditioning of an organism to the environment (or context) in which it lives. The survival of an organism depends on behaviors that maximize contact with biologically safe environments and minimize contact with dangerous environments. Many of these dangers are subject to modification through experience." Because many of the emotions that are relevant to political contexts are of the secondary variety (after all, it is hard to imagine someone fearing Bill Clinton from the womb) and because some political actors may attempt to evoke emotions as part of a persuasive strategy, the conditions under which political phenomena will induce or be affected by emotional responses will be a function of goal-oriented decision making (for example, directed learning), at least in part. In this sense, we follow Damasio (1995, 124), who argues:

> Culture and civilization could not have arisen from single individuals and thus cannot be reduced to biological mechanisms and, even less, can they

be reduced to a subset of genetic specifications. Their comprehension demands not just general biology and neurobiology but the methodologies of the social sciences as well. In human societies there are social conventions and ethical rules over and above those that biology already provides. Those additional layers of control shape instinctual behavior so that it can be adapted flexibly to a complex and rapidly changing environment and ensure survival for the individual . . . in circumstances in which a preset response from the natural repertoire would be immediately or eventually counterproductive.

Our argument continues with the premise that the kind of goal-oriented learning that Kandel et al. and Damasio describe can be affected by incentives and strategic decision making. As a result, incentives and strategy can affect the conditions under which emotions affect politics—and vice versa. Because game theory has proved to be an effective way to understand how incentives and strategies affect behaviors and outcomes in other contexts, we conclude that it can help researchers clarify the conditional relationship between emotional responses and political circumstances.

In the rest of this chapter we present the longer form of the argument, proceeding as follows. First, we focus on what the study of emotion can bring to game-theoretic analyses of politics. We do so by first breaking down what game theorists do and then showing where findings about emotion can make constructive contributions. Second, we reverse the question, examining what game-theoretic practices can bring to the study of emotion. We argue that the relevance of emotional phenomena to a given political situation is likely to depend on strategic factors. We then describe an example of new research in which game-theoretic and emotional considerations are integrated to constructive scientific ends.

CAN THE STUDY OF EMOTIONS IMPROVE POLITICAL GAME THEORY?

In this section we have two objectives. First, we debunk two widely held views of game-theoretic political science that, if true, would limit the value of attempts to integrate insights from the study of emotions. Second, we offer a framework for such integration. To accomplish both objectives, we begin with a brief description of what game theorists do.

Noncooperative game theory, the dominant form of game theory in use today, is a method of representing and explaining behaviors and outcomes in contexts where participants can act strategically. In this context, *strategy* means "plan of action." Game theory generates insights by allowing researchers to evaluate the extent to which one player's plan of action is a best response to the plans of others. If all players in a game perceive their plan of action as a best response to others' plans, then the game reaches a steady state—not one person has an incentive to change his or her plan of action at any point in the game. Such steady states are called equilibria.

Equilibria are focal in game theory because they constitute more reliable representations of social decision dynamics than do situations in which at least one player would want to change a plan of action. In other words, if we have described the game correctly and we offer every player in the game a prediction of what everyone in the game will do and every player truthfully responds "Yes, you have described my plan correctly," then the situation is in equilibrium and the prediction will be accurate. If, by contrast, one or more players were to say, "Now that I know what you have told me, I am going to change my plans," then the situation is out of equilibrium and the prediction will be inaccurate. In game-theoretic contexts, and all else constant, equilibrium means more reliable inference.

The credibility of equilibrium statements in noncooperative games depends in large part on a set of practices that game theorists follow when developing their models. A principal goal for game theorists is to offer logical clarity and precision regarding the topic of study. This goal induces scholars to state premises and conclusions in explicit terms and to make their relations transparent. Indeed, such transparency is required in the sense that when a game theorist draws a nonobvious conclusion from a set of premises, he or she is expected to prove (in the literal sense) that the conclusion is a direct logical implication of the premises. Merely waving one's hands at the relationship tends not to be credible. Moreover, for those who have sufficient mathematical background, such practices make the logic of game theoretic arguments replicable—which can reduce misunderstanding, increase the efficiency of scholarly debates, and hasten the accumulation of knowledge.

The same properties of game theory that increase the effectiveness of some efforts cause problems in others. For example, making models precise and analytically tractable usually requires the use of simplifying assumptions. Critics of game theory are quick to point out that some of these assumptions are unrealistic. Such criticisms are often fair and sometimes constructive. In two of these critiques, we see an opportunity for the empirical study of emotion to improve the applicability of political game theory. In one critique, game theory is criticized for imposing rationality. In the second, it is criticized for the way it treats information and perception. In what follows, we demonstrate that understanding the validity of these critiques provides a useful way to see how the introduction of emotion-related concepts can improve a model's applicability.

Much Ado about Rational Choice

Many game-theoretic efforts in political science are criticized for the minimal way in which they represent how people think. Game theorists respond to such criticisms by saying that people may not actually do the kinds of mathematical calculations attributed to actors in the model, but they act "as if" they think about the world in that way (see, for example, Satz and Ferejohn 1994). To judge the extent to which game-theoretic approaches satisfy "as if" standards, it is important to understand that theorists model individual psychologies in different ways.

Models vary in their assumptions. Some famous models such as the prisoner's dilemma or the median voter theorem are games of complete information, where all players are assumed to know everything about every aspect of the game. In recent decades, theorists have become facile with the mathematics of games of incomplete information. In these games, players may not know everything and may act on the basis of their beliefs. As a result, theorists now model a growing range of psychological processes (see, for example, Lupia, Zharinova, and Levine 2007).

That game theorists can model phenomena such as attention, perception, and learning is interesting because it runs counter to a common belief, namely, that game theory as an analytical method and the phenomenon known as rational choice theory are one and the same. This belief is mistaken.

Game theory is, above all, a method. Across all existing models, the intersection of assumptions is quite minimal; actors with all kinds of worldviews and psyches are allowed. What the modelers do share are basic rules for drawing inferences—those described above.

Rational choice theory, by contrast, means something less useful because extant definitions of rationality vary widely. By *rationality* some people mean wealth maximization, others mean selfishness (which may be nonmonetary), some mean omniscient decision making, and others mean something completely different (see Lupia, McCubbins, and Popkin 2000, 5–9 for a longer list). Therefore, many of our discipline's debates about whether people are rational are as much about failure to coordinate on semantics as they are about the substance of human decision making. Henceforth, we follow this advice on how to think about how people think.

> If we can distill these many definitions of rationality into one that is sensible empirically and widely applicable, we can avoid much of the confusion currently associated with the concept of rationality and, as a result, craft better explanations of why people do what they do. We will now argue for such a definition. The basis of our argument is that there is at least one issue on which these many definitions of rationality agree. The issue is that people have reasons for the choices they make. That is, regardless of people's genetics or socialization, if they are able to make choices, then reasons will precede these choices. Therefore, we conclude that *a rational choice is one that is based on reasons, irrespective of what these reasons may be.* (Lupia, McCubbins, and Popkin 2000, 7 emphasis in original)

Most psychologists focus on reason rather than rationality, where reason is nothing more than the normal functioning of the mind. Behavioral economists are moving toward a similar focus. The segment of political science that concerns itself with offering improved explanations of individual behavior and collective choice should do the same. As the game theorists who reside within this segment focus on reason instead of rationality, a productive joint venture with scholars of emotions becomes increasingly possible.

So if narrow notions of rationality and all ways of representing individual psychology in game theory were equivalent, and if emotion and reason were antithetical, then a constructive integration of game-theoretic methods and substantive insights about emotion would be impossible. Above, we explained why the first antecedent (equivalence) is false. We now do the same for the second antecedent (antithesis).

Many scholars, particularly since the wide dissemination of Damasio's *Descartes' Error: Emotion, Reason, and the Human Brain*, have shown that emotions can enhance information processing and improve decision quality. The correspondence between emotions and reason runs deep. As Kandel et al. (1995, 600) report, "An animal whose sympathetic nervous system is experimentally eliminated can survive as long as it sheltered, kept warm, and not exposed to stress. Such an animal cannot, however, carry out strenuous work or fend for itself." Emotions and what many people regard as reason are not antithetical. Indeed, as Phelps (2006, 46–47) concludes in her recent review of neuropsychological research, "[t]he mechanisms of emotion and cognition appear to be intertwined at all stages of stimulus processing. . . . Examining cognitive functions without an appreciation for the social, emotional, and motivational context will result in an understanding that may be limited in its applicability." Therefore, a joint venture between game theory and emotions in politics is potentially instructive. To realize this potential, however, we need to be more specific about how to incorporate emotional phenomena into a game-theoretic model.

Utility and Information as Entry Points for Emotions

The second criticism of game theory concerns its psychological adequacy. Consider, for example, the common practice of assuming that players have quadratic utility functions (for example, in a model where preferences and outcomes are represented by points in a space, utility declines in the distance between a player's ideal point and the outcome of the game—squared) or the assumption that players have uniform prior beliefs (that is, they believe that every possible state of nature is equally probable). We know that such assumptions are chosen for mathematical convenience (that is, uniform priors often allow universal inferences about game attributes without the use of complex derivations). We know that both practices make it easier for scholars to solve the models they construct. We also know that such assumptions are rarely, if ever, based on even a cursory examination of the decision makers' psychology.

Given what we know, it is worth stating that universal rejections of game theory on the basis of blanket critiques about the method's psychological inadequacy are of limited value, especially if the alternative is either unstated theory or brands of theorizing in which premises, conclusions, and their logical relations are stated imprecisely. Indeed, oversimplified assumptions about cognition in political science are not unique to game theory. Many attempts to explain political behavior, including those grounded in case studies or regression analysis, are based on premises with no apparent connection to concrete empirical findings from fields such as psychology. For example, when people use OLS or Probit to draw an inference about political psychology from survey data, they incorporate into their argument implicit assumptions about allowable relations between the included variables. When some of these variables are meant to represent behavioral phenomena and others are meant to represent psychological phenomena, the choice of a particular estimator implies concrete assumptions about the mechanics of reason whose relation to well-documented psychological insights are rarely, if ever, clearly established. As a result, one way to characterize the difference between game theorists' assumptions about psychological phenomena and those of many other scholars is that game theorists are more likely to state their assumptions clearly enough to be scrutinized. Put another way, for many descriptions of political behavior other than game theory, assumptions about peoples' mental states are less controversial only because they are less clearly articulated.

The challenge for us, then, is to clearly present in game-theoretic terms some of the emotion-relevant phenomena that are increasingly prevalent in political psychology. Such a task is made easier by the fact that all noncooperative games are built from a common list of conceptual elements. A brief review of this list reveals the places where emotions can be brought in.

Many game theory textbooks define the components of a game as follows: players, actions, strategies (plans of action), information (what people perceive and believe about various aspects of the game), outcomes (the consequence of their actions—games are most interesting when the outcome depends on multiple players' actions), payoffs (how people feel about various outcomes), and the equilibrium concept (the manner by which equilibria are determined). Of these, three are obvious candidates for introducing emotions: payoffs, information, and equilibrium concepts. We explain each in turn.

Payoffs are measured in terms of utility functions. A utility function represents how a person feels about a particular outcome. From the literature about emotions we can adopt the idea that a person's feeling about a situation can depend on whether emotional subsystems are activated. For example, if we hold the stimulus constant but vary whether the stimulus induces fear (where the variance may be due to differences in previous experiences with the stimulus), then we can expect a difference in how the person feels about outcomes that are associated with the stimulus.

What a player in a game knows is typically modeled as a probability distribution across important aspects of the game. A voter who is uncertain about a candidate, for example, is modeled as thinking about the candidate as if she assigns probabilities to various kinds of personality attributes or policy preferences that the candidate might have. We can use a similar representation to incorporate emotion. Consider, for example, that fear can be evoked by a conscious or subconscious association between an object and a painful outcome (one that provides sufficiently low utility). As Kandel et al. (1995, 608) describes it, "In fear conditioning, an initially neutral stimulus that does not evoke automatic responses can be paired with an electric shock such that, eventually, just the neutral stimulus will produce autonomic responses associated with fear." Therefore, if a player were to assign a particular object a sufficiently high probability of corresponding to a bad outcome, then it would be reasonable to expect that player to react as a fearful person would. By contrast, a player who viewed exactly the same object but assigned it a lower probability of leading to bad outcomes might not react fearfully. In other words, the object provides the players with information about the potential outcomes of the game, but players' experiences with the object lead them to react to it in different ways.

A third game component, equilibrium concepts, can also serve as a channel for introducing emotional phenomena into game-theoretic models. An equilibrium concept entails assumptions about how people react to the strategies and beliefs of others. We contend that variations in emotional responses can affect these aspects of a person's decision calculus. If fear motivates people to pay greater attention to a particular aspect of their environment, as Marcus, Neuman, and MacKuen (2000) conclude, then it may also lead them to generate different counterfactual assessments of their own behavior or that of others than would be the case if they were not fearful. This, in turn, may affect the extent to which they are willing to maintain a particular strategy in the presence of other strategies. It may be that a behavior that an actor perceives to be her best response given a particular set of facts about the strategies and beliefs of others may not be her best response if she receives the same facts in a fearful state. Varying equilibrium concepts, from, say, the Nash equilibrium concept to one that allows greater variations in counterfactual reasoning, such as the self-confirming equilibrium concept, can allow us to integrate a wider range of emotional content into game-theoretic models (for a detailed discussion of this topic, see Lupia and Zharinova 2004).

In sum, research concerning emotion conducted over the course of the past decade reinforces the idea that emotions are necessary for goal-oriented behavior. As scholars such as Rahn (2000), Marcus, Neuman, and MacKuen (2000), and Brader (2005) argue, emotions can affect the kinds of environmental stimuli to which people attend, the manner in which they react to what they see, and what they recall. Game-theoretic methods, if properly developed, can help us understand the logical consequences of such variations. Therefore, being more explicit about the integration of emotional content can improve the extent to which game-theoretic models provide reliable descriptions of strategic political interactions.

CAN GAME THEORY IMPROVE EMOTION-FOCUSED POLITICAL RESEARCH?

Contributors to this book are among those who have helped establish that emotion need not be the antithesis of reason. Such findings were helpful in explaining why research concerning emotions can improve the applicability of political game theory. Now we turn the tables and ask, "How can the use of game theory possibly improve the applicability of existing research regarding emotions and politics?" The answer, in short, is that previous work regarding emotions is largely silent about the topic of strategic interaction and about its implications for the conditions under which we should expect emotional phenomena to be relevant to political contexts.

In many studies, for example, a fear-relevant political variable is presented. Few scholars question the conditions under which the stimulus becomes fearful or the conditions under which it can cease to be so. And yet we know that people vary in the feelings they have about political phenomena and that these feelings can change over time. We also know that some people stake their political careers on the likely presence or absence of fear in political contexts. We know that creating a sense of fear can change the amount of discretion that citizens are willing to give to their political leaders or the concessions that one country or political faction will make to others. Some political leaders may perceive a personal benefit in creating fear. If the potential targets of such fear also know this, then they may have an incentive to be skeptical of stimuli that are meant to induce fear. Situations such as those described above are endemic in politics. They also have gamelike attributes such that the outcome depends on the beliefs and strategies of multiple players.

The presence of such attributes in politics is the reason why it is important to build on previous work by focusing on the extent to which aspects of goal-oriented learning and other strategic behaviors affect the political relevance of emotional phenomena. If it seems incorrect to discuss strategy, incentives, and emotions in the same sentence and to present their relationship as endogenous, we ask you to consider the following facts. To be certain, emotional responses have a strong subconscious element. There are aspects of emotional response over which we have no control. So we can agree that some aspects of emotional response are beyond the domain of goal-oriented learning. We can also agree that emotions are not applied entirely at random. Were this true, we could not accurately anticipate the emotional responses of others. But we can anticipate others' emotions—in their presence and in their absence—precisely because we come to learn that emotional responses have a contingent element. For example, what we fear depends in part on what we have experienced in the past and in part on where we are at the moment. Two manifestations of this contingency are that we learn to fear some things in our environment and that we can learn to suppress other fears. As Damasio

(1994, 130) states. "In many circumstances in our life as social beings, however, we know that our emotions are triggered only after an evaluative, voluntary, nonautomatic mental process. Because of the nature of our experience, a broad range of stimuli and situations has become associated with those stimuli which are innately set to cause emotions. The reaction to that broad range of stimuli and situations can be filtered by an interposed mindful evaluation."

Learning, in turn, can be affected by goal orientation. We are more likely to pay attention to and remember certain stimuli if we believe or observe that such attention correlates highly with our ability to achieve a particular goal. As Cacioppo and Gardner (1999, 199) state, "motivational strength increases as the distance from a desired or undesired endstate decreases." As a result, the conditions under which emotions affect some political interactions will be a function of incentives. Responses to such incentives, in turn, will be governed by a mix of conscious and subconscious phenomena. In some situations, the stimuli, incentives, learning algorithms, and subconscious activities will settle into a steady state—by which we mean that the relations between these phenomena will be predictable. Such steady states are what game theorists call equilibria, and they use these equilibria to characterize conditions under which some factors affect others. Therefore, the applicability of research concerning emotions and politics can be improved by examining the conditions under which emotional phenomena play particular roles in such steady-state relations.

The difference between our approach and that of current scholars of emotion can be seen with respect to the following conclusion (Marcus et al. 2000, 63–64): "Anxious voters will, in most instances, act very much like the rational voters as depicted by theories of public choice. However, when complacent, voters will in most instances look very much like the value protecting voters depicted by the theory of symbolic politics." We believe that this conclusion is true but only under certain conditions—conditions that are affected by strategic phenomena. Our point of departure is the premise that there is anything approaching a one-to-one correspondence between strategic, goal-oriented behavior and heightened anxiety. We consider such a relation very unlikely for the following reasons.

We know that emotions such as anxiety can cause a range of reactions. Anxiety can make some voters very attentive to environmental stimuli. It can, as Marcus and his colleagues describe, induce people to commit substantial mental energy to surveillance of their surroundings. We also know, however, that there are people for whom anxiety triggers withdrawal. If improved applicability is the standard against which we want to measure scientific progress, then game theory can be a powerful ally because it can help us understand the conditions under which each kind of outcome occurs.

But can research that integrates game-theoretic and emotion-based insights provide unique insights? We now address that point directly. Above, we built an argument about how attention can improve game theory by working from several criticisms of the ways in which game theorists draw inferences. The point was not to diminish the game theorists' effort but to point out places in the method where insights from the study of emotions can be most useful. We now construct the reverse argument. We offer a critique of the methods by which recent insights about emotions and politics have been generated—a kind of critique that is more likely to be offered by people who are not political psychologists—as a way of detailing how and why game-theoretic insights can help emotion-oriented scholars better achieve some of their primary objectives.

We can all agree that the post-Damasio literature in political science has been insightful. We can also agree that the insights come primarily from three kinds of studies: laboratory experiments, survey experiments, and general election surveys. The extent to which findings from such methods provide reliable inferences about the role of emotions in particular political situations can be questioned.

The main critique of laboratory experiments is well known: most are run using convenience samples of undergraduates or of residents of the communities in which political psychologists' primary employers are located. Questions arise about the extent to which student responses to focal stimuli accurately represent how others in the population would react.[1] Questions also arise about the extent to which stimuli presented in the laboratory environment evoke the same kinds of reactions that they would evoke in the same subjects in the field.

Because survey experiments are used less frequently in the study of emotions, the critiques against it are less familiar. These experiments are

---

1. We refrain from using the term *external validity* in this context. Like *rationality*, it is a term that means very different things to different people. For us, a claim about validation is most useful when it is anchored on a well-defined standard. Such a standard allows transparent and replicable comparisons. Our experience, however, is that many claims of external validity are of not of this kind. Instead, they are offered without clear reference and as the basis for a blanket rejection of experimental methods. Such critics may indeed have in mind a concrete standard that many experimental studies do not surpass, but the standard is seldom stated explicitly, which means that the validity claims themselves are difficult or impossible to validate.

typically housed within large surveys. Subjects in many prominent survey experiments are recruited via a process called random-digit dialing, a technique that leading survey houses use to acquire nationally representative subject pools in a cost-effective manner. When a survey house succeeds in acquiring a representative sample, survey experiments do not face the "convenience sample" critique. But because such experiments are usually conducted over the telephone or via the Internet, concerns about the extent to which reactions parallel those that researchers would see in less contrived circumstances remain.

Important insights about emotions in politics have also been drawn from nonexperimental components of national surveys. Such studies sample the perspectives of a broader range of people than do most laboratory experiments and, thus, provide shelter from the convenience sample critiques. The book *Affective Intelligence and Political Judgment*, for example, makes extensive use of the American National Election Studies (ANES). The ANES is valuable in many ways and has been used to refine the scientific understanding of numerous concepts and relationships. Yet several attributes of such studies stack the deck against their ability to serve as the basis for strong causal claims about emotions. Unlike experiments, the survey is designed and questions are written to serve many purposes. To date, few if any questions on these general-purpose surveys have been written to obtain the best possible measures of emotion-related concepts or with a specific emotion-related hypothesis in mind. Moreover, of the survey questions used in emotion-related research, most are based on self-reports of mental states. Across the scientific community, there is a general agreement that such reports are of questionable reliability, as Churchland (1995, 22) explains: "Humans are famously bad at describing their sensations—of tastes, of aromas, of feelings—but we are famously good at discriminating, enjoying, and suffering them. . . . And yet, while we all participate in the richness of sensory life, we struggle to communicate to others all but its coarsest features. Our capacity for verbal description comes nowhere near our capacity for sensory discrimination." Davidson (2003, 131) draws a similar conclusion, though in a different way:

> Much of the psychological literature on emotion implicitly assumes that emotions are conscious feeling states. A vast number of studies depend upon self-report measures to make inferences about the presence of emotional states. Such self-report measures are often outcome variables in studies on emotion and they often serve as "manipulation checks" to confirm the presence of an intended emotional manipulation. Failure to

find detectable change on self-report measures is sometimes offered as evidence that emotion was not elicited, and more frequently, the presence of self-reported emotion is taken as evidence that emotion has been activated. While the experiential side of emotion is unquestionably important and provides useful information to an individual that can be harnessed for adaptive functioning (e.g., Damasio 1994), it is also clear that much of the affect that we generate is likely to be non-conscious.

Such skepticism is shared in ongoing research about the kinds of personal attributes about which people can report reliably in a survey (see, for example, Tourangeau et al. 2000, chaps. 3, 6, 11.3) and work concerning the ways in which conventional survey interviewing techniques sometimes produce atypical and unrepresentative responses (Schwarz 1994).

Game theory does not solve these potential problems of experimentation or survey-based research, but if applied effectively, it can limit the critiques' impact. Scholars can use game theory to clarify the conditions under which empirical findings are robust to other circumstances—at least circumstances that can be represented in theoretical terms. Although many kinds of theorizing can play this role for scholars who want to generalize from empirical observations, game theory is particularly helpful when asking questions about the robustness of such observations to contexts in which strategic interaction matters.[2]

In most cases, when scholars conduct experiments, use surveys, or build theories, simplifying assumptions are required to produce findings that can be analyzed compactly. As a result, scholars who want their work to be broadly relevant are forced to make an "inductive leap" that projects their findings from a particular scientific context to a larger social domain. Different kinds of inference require different kinds of leaps (for example, a theorist needs to project in ways that an experimentalist does not). An advantage of research designs that integrate theoretical and empirical methods is that, in some cases, the inferential advantages of one approach can be used to counter the known limitations of other approaches. In political contexts where strategic behavior is not only possible but is witnessed with regularity, game theory can serve a supporting role for those performing studies of emotions and politics, whether experimental or survey-based. If properly developed, it permits strong,

---

2. Lupia and McCubbins (1998, chap. 6), for example, draw one-to-one comparisons between attributes of their formal models and attributes of their laboratory experiments to clarify what parts of the theory can be used to evaluate the generalizability of their empirical findings.

transparent, and logically coherent statements about the conditions that determine how and when potentially important emotional phenomena apply to politics.

CAN AN INTEGRATED APPROACH WORK? AN EXAMPLE

The link between emotions and game theory is just beginning to be explored. These initial explorations reveal important variations in emotional responses to different strategies. They also show how strategies depend on emotions.

A particularly promising set of activities can be found in economic-style experiments. Like experiments in psychology and other social sciences, these experiments gain their inferential power from the combination of experimental control and random assignment. They differ from other kinds of social science experiments, however, in that subjects are typically compensated on the basis of their performance during the experiment. In some cases, they are simply paid for choices they make. In other cases, and particularly in experiments motivated by game theory, subjects' compensation depends on the outcome of a game—their pay depends not only on what they do but also on the actions of others. Though promising in many respects, economic experiments do not provide a panacea when it comes to the study of emotions. Attempts to draw inferences from self-reports of emotional states or observed behaviors entail many of the same problems that vex other empirical researchers (as described above). Recently, innovative experimental designs, offered in the name of neuroeconomics, shed new light on the interaction between emotions and strategic behavior. They did so by getting around the self-reporting problem in a clever way.

Sanfey et al. (2003) use functional magnetic response imaging to track reactions of ultimatum game players at the level of the neural substrate. Ultimatum games are of interest to game theorists because early experiments showed that subjects play them in ways that the standard Nash equilibrium concept would not predict (see also McKelvey and Palfrey 1992, 1995 for a parallel demonstration on the centipede game). An ultimatum game involves two players and a finite sum of money, say, $10. One player is given the responsibility of proposing a division of the money. The other player can only accept or reject the offer. If the second player accepts the first player's offer, the players are paid accordingly. If the second player rejects the offer, both players get nothing. Using the Nash equilibrium concept, the prediction of the game is that the first player will propose to keep almost all of the money and that the second player, faced with a choice between being paid a small amount and being paid nothing, will accept. In laboratory experiments, however, the game is played differently. Many subjects propose a split closer to 50-50 than to the "almost everything for me" proposal predicted by Nash equilibrium concept. Moreover, subjects who are asked to play the role of the second player often reject offers that deviate from 50-50 although, strictly speaking, the rejection leaves them worse off financially (see, for example, Frohlich and Oppenheimer 2000).

Although many alternative explanations have been offered for such behaviors, Sanfey (2003, 1756) and his colleagues hypothesize that unfair offers (that is, those diverging from a 50-50 split) "would engage neural structures involved in both emotional and cognitive processing, and that the magnitude of activation in these structures might explain variance in the subsequent decision to accept or reject these offers." To test this hypothesis, they had subjects play identical versions of an ultimatum game against human and computer partners. In their experiment, "[p]articipants accepted all fair offers, with decreasing acceptance rates as the offers became less fair" (ibid.; their null hypothesis was rejected at the 0.03 level or smaller). More interesting, however, were the underlying neuronal patterns. They found that "[a]mong the areas showing greater activation for fair compared with unfair offers from human partners were bilateral anterior insula[, which is] particularly interesting in light of this region's oft-noted association with negative emotional states."

An important part of this finding is its distinction from subject reactions when the computer rather than the human player made exactly the same offers. Sanfey and colleagues find that "[t]he magnitude of activation was also significantly greater for unfair offers from human partners as compared to . . . unfair offers from computer partners" (2003, 1756; the null hypothesis was rejected at the 0.03 level or smaller). This result shows that subjects' emotional reactions to the play of the game were a function not of the payoff, because subjects did not respond *emotionally* when the computer made an unfair proposal. The extreme emotional reactions only followed unfair proposals from other players.

Moreover, the converse was also true—subjects' play was a function of their emotional responses. This relation is demonstrated by the fact that even after accounting for variations in the size of unfair offers, "participants with strong anterior insula activation to unfair offers rejected a higher proportion of these offers" (Sanfey 2003, 1756–57; the null hypothesis was rejected at the .05 level or smaller). Studies such as this inform game theory, improving our understanding of the conditions under which the well-known Nash equilibrium solution applies. These experiments, in other words, improve the applicability of the theoretical result. They also demonstrate that the relevance of subjects' emotional responses are conditional on strategic factors, including the extent to which the offer is perceived as unfair, and on whether they believe that such offers come from humans or from computer programs. In sum, in the Sanfey research agenda the empirical study of emotions and a game-theoretic representation of a social situation combine to provide superior insights about the relation between emotion and strategic behavior.

CAN AN INTEGRATED APPROACH WORK?
POSSIBILITIES FOR THE FUTURE

If a future generation of emotion-rich game-theoretic models comes to pass, their effectiveness will depend on the connection between the model's assumptions and the physical basis and mechanics of human cognition. Several of the contributions to *The Affect Effect* address the topic of emotions at this level and, in our view, provide potentially innovative starting points for scholars who want to better understand the conditions under which particular emotional phenomena apply to politics.

Consider, for example, Darren Schreiber's "Political Cognition as Social Cognition: Are We All Political Sophisticates?" (chapter 3 in this volume). Schreiber builds an argument about how political actors think about politics from empirical research on the properties of "mirror neurons." Mirror neurons facilitate mental representations of how other people think. They allow us to imagine how other people will respond. They also affect the extent to which we experience particular emotional responses simply by watching others have those responses. In game theory, premises about what people think about other people and how they expect them to respond play important roles. Once more is learned about the properties of mirror neurons, in particular the kinds of interpersonal attributes that these neurons are most likely to record and subsequently reduce in searches of memory, they could serve as a basis for analyses of strategic interaction that are more cognitively realistic. To this end, some game theorists have questioned the use of popular solutions concepts such as the Nash and the Bayesian-Nash concepts because of the rather severe assumptions they can imply about the quality of counterfactual reasoning. As mentioned above, alternative equilibrium concepts such as the self-confirming equilibrium concept have been proposed. A limitation of the concepts, however, is that they tend not to be psychologically rich. The self-confirming equilibrium concept, for example, allows for an expanded range of counterfactual assessments to be introduced into game-theoretic reasoning, but it does not provide a standard for choosing among the counterfactuals people can and do run. Understanding more about the properties of structures such as mirror neurons may provide a more credible basis for such models in the future.

Another constructive possibility is apparent in the contribution of Spezio and Adolphs (chapter 4 in this volume). One of our chief concerns in this chapter has been to improve the applicability of empirical research about emotions. A key step in achieving such progress is a better understanding of the conditions under which emotions affect politics. Spezio and Adolphs provide a helpful way to construct such arguments through their use of the Yerkes-Dodson law. This law portrays goal-oriented decision makers as more effective when experiencing moderate levels of emotion than when very emotional or not emotional at all. This view is obviously helpful when thinking about a decision theoretic task in which the consequence of a person's decision depends only on that decision. We contend that it can also be helpful in more strategic situations. We can imagine cases where players vary in the extent to which they are affected by emotions. In a game featuring multiple players, the impact of emotions would depend on the distribution of emotions among the players. Two low-emotion players playing a game with one another could produce a different collective outcome than would occur if one low-emotion played the same game with a moderately emotional or highly emotional player. In such a case, we would expect the political consequence of emotions to be determined not only by the emotional status of any one person but also by interactions between the goal orientations and emotional states of multiple players.

CONCLUSION

Some scholars believe that emotions and reason are independent. Others believe that emotions and strategic decision making are mutually irrelevant. Both beliefs may have had credibility at one point, but now that studies of the brain at several levels of analysis reveal deep connections among emotion, reason, and strategic thinking, such hypotheses are no longer credible.

Emotions play a significant role in the outcome of our political processes. But so does strategic interaction between various political actors. Researchers who focus solely on one of these aspects can teach us many things. But researchers who integrate both kinds of insights can teach us much more. By endogenizing and strategizing emotional reactions to politics, a game-theoretic approach can clarify the conditions under which politicians should seek to evoke fear among voters and the conditions under which people will respond to emotional appeals. To the extent that this approach increases our ability to connect our knowledge about the underpinnings of emotional life to real-world political phenomena, this union of game-theoretic principles and emotional research is beneficial.

CHAPTER FIFTEEN

The Affect Effect in the Very Real World of Political Campaigns

DAN SCHNUR

In the solar system of campaign politics, practitioners are from Mars. Academics are from Venus.

Although campaign professionals and academic researchers devote huge amounts of time and energy to developing a better understanding of this mutually fascinating field of study, deep-seated suspicions based on background, methods, and ideology have kept these two communities unnecessarily separated from each other. More problematic is the disparity between the goals set forth by the two groups: a researcher wants to learn, and a practitioner wants to win. The fact that these two goals are not mutually exclusive and actually contain significant areas of overlap is rarely noticed.

Even more problematic is the barely concealed disdain that the two groups hold for one another. Campaign managers and strategists tend to dismiss those who study politics as an academic pursuit as little more than ivory-tower idealists whose attitude toward political campaigns is obscured by unrealistic idealism and excessive distance. Academic researchers and theorists, for their part, are just as likely to look down on campaign practitioners as poorly educated vocational workers more likely to make decisions based on tradition and superstition than on empirical evidence.

All in all, this is not a promising landscape in which collaborative effort and mutual learning can occur. This mutual misunderstanding invariably leads to a cultural gap that has historically blocked the ability of these two communities to work together, to learn from each other, and ultimately to create a better political product. But as someone who has devoted portions of my professional career to pursuits on both sides of this unnecessary barrier, I firmly believe that both professions can benefit greatly from some effort toward reconciliation and cooperation.

The biggest challenge for those who study and research politics is to understand the limitations offered by a vantage point outside the campaign structure and the perils of projecting assumptions onto a decision-making process that is often both more and less logical than it appears. Conversely, the perspective offered by outside observers and researchers has the potential to be of great benefit to practitioners, if those working on a campaign would be willing to believe that an academic expert can offer insight that is of practical value. Both groups must be willing to concede that they have something to learn from the other before any reasonable expectation for progress can exist.

But the first step toward rapprochement is acknowledging the gap, and the political scientists and neuropsychologists who have contributed to this volume are making an admirable effort toward bridging this divide. But in order for the academic community to have its work applied in the realm of practical politics, more than good intentions and initial efforts are required. Rather, for campaign strategists and political scientists to join forces, a number of additional steps are necessary. Over the course of this chapter, I discuss the practicalities of these next steps and offer guidance to those looking to move their findings from the halls of academia to the rough and tumble of the campaign trail.

The answer to the broader question of the impact of emotion on political communication seems to be self-evident. As is the case with most forms of communication to a mass audience, an emotional appeal will almost always outweigh a message that relies solely on statistical or clinical evidence. But the usefulness of the preceding chapters comes not in the general but in the specific. The authors whose work composes this volume have given the field of practical politics an extremely valuable tool with which to delve more deeply into the effectiveness and impact of the use of emotion as a means of communication and persuasion. Their efforts provide a larger and deeper pool of information and analysis than is usually available to our profession from traditional public opinion research.

Although their findings provide a good first step in more closely allying our two disciplines, a level of insight that comes from hands-on experience is the next necessary component in that effort. Almost every chapter in this book raises questions that can form the basis of a critical self-examination on the part of political practitioners. But before the contributors' findings can be of practical use to campaign strategists and messaging specialists, the researchers must also take into account a variety of factors that are more easily seen from inside the campaign structure. These research efforts are extremely important, however, and practition-

ers would be making a serious mistake by ignoring this body of work because it lacks certain practical applications.

My contribution to this effort is outlined in a series of lessons that I
have accumulated throughout a career in campaign politics. I hope that
these lessons will assist the other contributors (and readers) in building
further on the initial good work compiled in these chapters by helping
them further develop their original theses into work products that also
account for factors most easily seen along the campaign trail.

LESSON ONE: IDENTIFYING THE TARGET AUDIENCE(S)

Begin by dividing the electorate into three broad categories: "saints," "sinners," and "salvageables" (in a construction borrowed from campaign professional Catherine Shaw's book *The Campaign Manager*).

Knowing that a candidate's saints (most loyal supporters) will respond
to an emotional appeal in a much different way than would the same
candidate's sinners (most virulent opponents) makes it much easier to
understand the relative effectiveness of different messaging options. Just
as important, the means by which a salvageable (undecided or loosely
aligned) voter approaches an election are very different from those by
which a voter with clear partisan tendencies in either direction approaches
it. Once this division has been accomplished, most of the messaging decisions discussed in this section become easier to apply in a real-world
setting.

The work in this volume centers around questions relating to the motivations of political consumers, most notably their reaction to different
types of verbal and visual emotive appeals. The findings offer great insight into the reasons why voters respond to various appeals in different
manners, but the studies tend to assume that members of the electorate
are essentially interchangeable. In order for these findings to have more
significant impact among campaign professionals, it is necessary to realize that distinct sectors of the electorate will react to similar appeals in
radically different ways.

In their work, Marion Just, Ann Crigler, and Todd Belt (chapter 10 in
this volume) have produced excellent research in identifying the factors
that cause individual voters to respond to appeals differently because of
their past and present life experiences. Similarly, Ted Brader and Nicholas
Valentino (chapter 8 in this volume) examine the emotional impact of
issues related to immigration on various subgroups of voters. And David
Leege and Kenneth Wald's examination of the affect of culturally based
political dialogue on elections (chapter 14, this volume) includes an

excellent discussion of that factor's influence on two very different groups of voters.

But the linkage between different life experiences on the part of voters and different types of messaging appeals is at the center of most campaign strategy decisions. Rather than developing and delivering a campaign message and then watching to see as that message impacts different voter groups in different ways, we begin our process by identifying the various communities within the electorate and then shaping a message (or messages) that can reach each of those groups in the most beneficial manner. In other words, a political practitioner examines the electorate first and then develops a message designed for maximum emotional appeal. The most useful research in this area, therefore, would reverse its starting and ending points, beginning with the identification of various voter groups and then examining the affect of messaging appeals.

For example, in the examination of the political effects of anger and anxiety, Leonie Huddy, Stanley Feldman, and Erin Cassese (chapter 9 in this volume) do extraordinary work in analyzing the ways in which voters respond differently to two very different types of negative emotional appeals. Understanding the motivational impact of anger and the more debilitating result of an anxiety-based appeal is something that political practitioners would find to be of great value in our work.

The next step, though, in order to maximize the usefulness of these findings, is to apply them to a more targeted overview of the electorate. If we know that a certain percentage of voters in an election will not cross party lines under any circumstances, we can develop an emotive appeal based on anxiety that will discourage those "sinners" from turning out on Election Day. By contrast, these findings reinforce our belief that loyal partisan voters (or saints) can be motivated to go to the polls with a message that elicits feelings of anger. Armed with a practitioner's understanding of targeting electoral segments, this chapter could address the more difficult question of tailoring messages to undecided voters. Can a salvageable voter be motivated by anger? Or is the risk-taking tendency that accompanies anger counterproductive in an appeal to that target audience?

Similarly, Doris Graber's research on breeching attention thresholds (chapter 11 in this volume) includes valuable lessons for candidates and officeholders engaged in an increasingly desperate effort to engage the electorate's attention at any cost. Her findings regarding the types of motivators that are more likely to attract the interest of the voters and the news media has real practical benefit, especially for campaign workers whose responsibilities include arranging news coverage for public events.

But increasingly, voters are turning to ideologically driven media sources for their information, forcing campaigns to narrowcast their messages to select groups of voters through specialized media outlets. As mainstream media continue to lose audience share, Graber's work becomes even more valuable if the appeal factors she catalogues are cross-referenced by the ideological disposition of the target audience and that audience sector's preferred media sources.

For example, the challenge for a Republican candidate to attract favorable coverage from Rush Limbaugh or for a Democrat to attract equally favorable attention from the Daily Kos Web site holds a much different set of requirements than if the two campaigns reversed their media goals. Consequently, their efforts to reach their respective sets of saintly voters proceeds on parallel tracks. Online political communication makes this calculus even more challenging than it is for traditional broadcast venues because the variables involved in sending a message via a conservative or liberal Web site, blog, or email tree allow candidates to attract attention from a much more narrowly targeted audience.

The discussion of swing voters and partisan loyalties undertaken by Michael MacKuen, George E. Marcus, W. Russell Neuman, and Luke Keele (chapter 6 in this volume) lays a direct predicate for strategies employed by both major national parties in the past presidential election. For years, conventional political wisdom held that persuading the middle swath of the electorate was the key to a winning campaign effort. But from opposite ends of the political spectrum, Karl Rove and Howard Dean both used the 2004 election to demonstrate the value in targeting a campaign's resources toward the motivation and mobilization of the party's core loyalists at the expense of targeting centrists. (Although the 2006 midterm elections suggested that the base motivation approach had both limitations and unanticipated consequences, evolutions in communications technology ensure that it will remain a viable strategic approach to voter targeting.)

That chapter provides an empirical underpinning for these strategic decisions, which could cause this research to be of significant importance to political operatives on both sides of the aisle attempting to learn the lessons of the preceding campaign. The growing relevance of ideological literacy at the expense of partisan loyalty is an argument in support of these base-motivating strategies as well. But unlike the authors, most campaign strategists no longer identify partisan defectors and independent voters as two separate and distinct cohorts. Advances in technology and targeted communication allow these voters to be approached through much more specific issue and policy appeals than this chapter would suggest is relevant. The greater practical value of this chapter lies in the ability of its authors to make their case while adapting it for the changing and increasing capabilities of crafting individual messages for individuals in addition to the broader ideological outreach they correctly identify.

Another area where the importance of voter targeting can be helpful is the debate about whether a valence-based appeal is more or less effective than one based in more particularistic emotional grounding. This discussion holds more relevance for a practitioner than most. But here, too, the type of audience to whom the message is targeted is likely to be more important in determining the most valuable course for designing messages.

Instinctually, most practitioners have come to believe that undecided or loosely aligned voters are won with an appeal based on more universal values, whereas the two parties feel that most reliable core supporters can be attracted with issues and emotions regarding which differing values are debated. Voters who cluster toward the center of the political spectrum tend to be less likely to believe that a candidate of one party or the other lacks core values or has wildly different goals for society than they do. So a more effective approach with this portion of the electorate is to convince them that one candidate is more likely to help society reach those goals than the other.

For example, there were precious few swing voters in the 2004 presidential election who doubted either George Bush's or John Kerry's desire to win the war against terrorism. Wisely, neither campaign attempted to make that case against its opponent. Both campaigns instead attempted to convince this targeted audience that their respective candidates had developed a strategy that was more likely to achieve that goal and that their candidate would be more proficient in doing so. Similarly, candidate Bill Clinton never tried to convince voters that either of his opponents was opposed to economic growth and job creation but, rather, told them that he was more likely to make that happen. In each of these cases, voters decided between two candidates whom they perceived to hold values similar to their own (and to the opponent's values).

On the other hand, the loyal base of both major parties is usually more amenable to a particularistic approach. Committed partisans are less likely to believe that the opposing candidate shares their values and tend to be less likely to seek out information sources that would convince them otherwise. The work of Huddy, Feldman, and Cassese (chapter 9 in this volume) is instructive in this discussion, because it suggests the ability of anger-inducing appeals to motivate audience reaction. Voters who are told (and who are willing to believe) that the opposition does not share their values are likely to become agitated, which increases their motivation to participate in the campaign in any number of ways.

Again, examples from the 2004 presidential campaign are instructive. Although the candidates tended to distance themselves from the most egregious of these messaging efforts, supporters of both campaigns made sustained appeals to their most loyal supporters that argued that the opposing candidate did not share their values. Whether the source was Bush supporters suggesting that John Kerry did not serve honorably during his time in Vietnam or Kerry backers hinting that President Bush would reinstitute the draft if reelected, both sides devoted great amounts of time and energy to questioning the values of the other candidate. But these appeals had their greatest impact on voters who were already most strongly committed to their preferred candidate.

Thus a voter's predisposition is as important as the message, and the nature and strength of the voters' loyalties make up the critical component in most emotion-based messaging decisions.

LESSON TWO: CANDIDATE BIOGRAPHY REINFORCES MESSAGE CREDIBILITY

When it comes to a candidate's ability to deliver a message to the voters, biography is destiny. What that candidate has accomplished in his or her personal, professional, and political life is the clearest (and sometimes the only) indicator that voters will have in judging the validity of the candidate's message. So in this section as well, the valuable research about message effectiveness is incomplete without examination of the context in which that message is delivered. If there is anything more important to the context of that message than the voting environment, it is the biographical credibility that comes with the candidate.

In a chapter titled "Meaning, Cultural Symbols, and Campaign Strategies," David Leege and Kenneth Wald (chapter 12) briefly touch on the efforts of John Kerry and George Bush to utilize their respective political biographies to establish credibility and an emotional connection with women voters. Similarly, Ann Crigler, Marion Just and Todd Belt (chapter 10 in this volume) address the relevance of candidates' personal traits in their discussion of hope and fear as emotional motivators. But for the most part, the principle addition to this volume's research would be a greater recognition of the candidate's role in the message delivery process.

Because any candidate can make any possible assertion to the electorate over the course of a campaign, the only means by which voters can judge the likelihood that a promise will be kept is that candidate's past behavior patterns. A politician who promises to cut taxes but has a history of supporting tax increases is unlikely to be judged as credible. A candidate who has consistently supported increased salaries for teachers over the course of a career is much more likely to have a similar proposal accepted by the voters. Although there is no guarantee that either candidate will behave in a manner that is consistent with past political behavior, the electorate will usually tend to rely on past action as the most reliable indicator for the future.

A candidate's voting record represents only a small fraction of his or her biography. In fact, a candidate's biography is the sum total of personal, professional, and political experience. As Leege and Wald relate, Kerry pointed to his professional biography as a prosecutor of rape cases to provide credibility to his appeal for support among women voters. More problematic was Kerry's emphasis on the military aspects of his professional biography. Although his record in Vietnam provided Kerry with important credentials for a challenger running in wartime, it also led to a prolonged debate with supporters of his opponent about the more controversial aspects of his service.

But the lesson to be learned from the brawl over Kerry's Vietnam record is not that he should have avoided the issue. Just the opposite: his military service was an important and exemplary part of his biography. (For the Monday morning quarterbacks reading this chapter, I suggest that the mistake was not responding to the charges against his military biography more quickly and forcefully.) His campaign's use of Kerry's professional-military biography did create another problem for his candidacy, though, in that this aspect of his life history all but overshadowed his personal and political biographies.

After a four-day Democratic National Convention that addressed his military service at great length and in greater detail, voters were extremely familiar with this aspect of Kerry's biography. But his life story since Vietnam was all but ignored, leaving the electorate with little familiarity with the credible career of public service that comprised his political biography. Not surprisingly, the Bush campaign was happy to fill in the blanks in a much less flattering manner. (This is not a partisan tendency, by the way. The Kerry campaign's overreliance on his military experience was foreshadowed by Bob Dole's identical decision in his own presidential campaign eight years earlier.)

Kerry's personal biography created an even greater challenge for his campaign. In a political environment in which the most likely path to a Democratic victory relied on a populist economic message, Kerry's affluent upbringing and current life situation left him ill-suited to carry that message of economic equality and fairness. Ironically, Kerry's personal story was not of significantly greater privilege than the incumbent's, but Bush's reelection did not rely on the same type pf message. Dick Gephardt, whose father drove a milk truck, or John Edwards, whose parents were textile mill workers, may have brought the credibility from their respective personal biographies to attack Bush for economic injustice. Kerry did not.

But Democratic primary voters understood the importance of their nominee's having credibility with regard to military and national security issues while the country was at war in Iraq. Kerry's military credentials were critical to his gaining his party's nomination. And though that professional biography should have been an important part of his overall biographical presentation, it obscured his campaign's ability to present a fuller picture of his life history.

Four years earlier, Bush had leaned almost as heavily on his personal biography for credibility with the voters under much different circumstances. Just as the fight against terrorism and the war in Iraq were the defining issues of the 2004 presidential campaign, the 2000 election was shaped by the legacy of the departing president, Bill Clinton. Bush's political biography was relatively brief, and his professional experience outside of politics provided little grist for his campaign. But with voters conflicted between support for Clinton's policy achievements and discomfort with his personal behavior, the Bush campaign was able to shine a spotlight on its candidate's personal, religious, and moral beliefs in a way that would have been far more difficult under other circumstances.

This emphasis on Bush's personal biography carried great risk. Although Bush had admitted in very general terms to a good deal of irresponsible behavior in his younger days, he had been very careful not to discuss any specifics that might offend voters attracted to his emphasis on morals and values. So when it was reported only a few days before the election that he had been arrested several years earlier for driving under the influence of alcohol, the revelation almost cost him the White House. Bush campaign advisors believe that this news story and its discouraging impact on socially conservative voters cost him a clear-cut victory and led instead to the controversy of the Florida recount.

The lesson from Bush's and Kerry's respective experiences is not that emphasizing a particular aspect of the candidate's biography is a bad idea but rather that such emphasis carries with it certain risks. Just as a candidate's biography can provide him with the credibility necessary to successfully persuade voters, that same information can also set a level of expectation for that candidate's future behavior. It doesn't matter whether those expectations have to do with military prowess or moral rectitude. Once the voters have reached a conclusion about a man or woman seeking office, they respond angrily when they find out they have been misled.

Biographical differences between candidates can have an enormous effect on the way a message is received by the voters. (Imagine the negligible impact of news of a drunk driving charge having been leveled against a young Bill Clinton or a twenty-something John McCain.)

An emotional appeal to voters, no matter how well designed, is only as credible as its source. Accounting for distinctions in the personal, professional, and political biographies of the politicians is another necessary variable that must be factored into the messaging equation. But the research presented in this volume, with only a few exceptions, assumes by implication that the candidate's role in the message delivery process is not nearly as important as are factors relating to the construction of the message itself.

In their otherwise excellent study of the factors that contribute to voters' emotions regarding the volatile issue of immigration, Brader and Valentino (chapter 8 in this volume) discuss in great detail the role that voters' identities play in their assessment of this issue. Although it would have been unreasonable to expect the authors to complete a comprehensive study of voter *and* candidate identities, the lack of significant examination of the biographical credentials of the candidates and officeholders charged with carrying these messages to the voters detracts from their overall conclusions.

The personal biography of a politician who immigrated to this country, the professional biography of a candidate who worked as a border patrol officer or immigration advocate, the political biography of an officeholder who has supported or opposed various types of immigration reform legislation—each of these factors would have a profound impact on the way messages about this issue would be received by voters. The authors are correct in their analysis of the role played in the cognitive process by a voter's partisanship, group identity, and ideology. But the biographical credentials and accompanying credibility are determinative as well.

LESSON THREE: THE VIEW IS ALWAYS DIFFERENT FOR A FRONTRUNNER AND AN UNDERDOG

The greatest advantage of empirical research about political campaigns is that it examines an emotionally volatile subject with perspective that is often missing from inside the campaign. The greatest limitation is accounting for the necessity of adjusting to changing circumstances over the course of a contested election cycle. Not to put too fine a point on it, it is a much different world for winners than for losers. In other words, candidates who are running ahead of their opponent approach their communications challenges much differently than those attempting to close a deficit.

It has been said that no military battle plan survives first contact with the enemy. Similarly, the most effective political strategies are constantly revised, adjusted, and updated as a campaign winds its way toward Election Day. So while preparation is the first step toward electing a candidate, the question immediately arises whether work performed outside the field of battle can be of use once the campaign has been engaged.

The answer to this question is an affirmative one. More difficult is identifying the limitations of research performed under circumstances that no longer exist. Brilliant research about the benefits and detriments of participating in candidate debates may be available, for example. But the calculation of whether to participate and under what circumstances is much different for a candidate with a ten-point lead in the polls who is trying to avoid a damaging mistake than it is for an opponent who is beginning to realize the importance of taking some risks.

These circumstances lend themselves most naturally to a discussion of positive and negative campaigning. There are legitimate discussions to be had about both approaches, from the often-substanceless content of purely positive advertisements to the discouraging impact on voter turnout of an overly negative approach. But these discussions are largely theoretical to a campaign that has just seen a double-digit lead in the polls evaporate or to a candidate who has just surged ahead of his opponent in the last weeks before an election.

The temptation for a candidate who is trailing badly in the polls to resort to an attack on his opponent grows in proportion to the deficit he faces, no matter how committed he once was to increasing voter turnout and to selling a positive agenda to the voters. Conversely, the most cynical adherent of attack advertising will suddenly learn the value of a positive message when presented with a comfortable lead in the polls two weeks before an election. Neither candidate is a hypocrite or a flip-flopper; rather, he or she is a realistic assessor of the circumstances.

Just, Crigler, and Belt (chapter 10 in this volume) devote their chapter to a penetrating examination of the role that emotional appeals based on hope and fear can shape an election outcome. In particular, practitioners can greatly benefit from their work on the topics of compensatory emotional appeal, the relation between candidate traits and emotional appraisal, and the self-selection of information sources that emerges along with these emotional states.

But the additional variable that would have made their research even more valuable is that of candidate status in relation to the opposition. The authors begin their study with an inspirational quotation from Bill Clinton's 1996 reelection campaign in which he speaks of "a choice between hope and fear, between unity and division." Without the benefit of polling data from the day on which that statement was uttered, it is reasonable to assume (given Clinton's comfortable victory over Dole in that year's election) that Clinton was the front-runner in the race at that point in time.

By substituting the practices of positive and negative campaigning for the concepts of hope and fear, one can assume that most candidates with leads over their opponents are more likely to appeal to voters on the basis of hope. Similarly, a campaign that is running behind is a good bet to discover the strategic advantages of emphasizing fear. An examination of Clinton's primary campaign against Paul Tsongas in 1992, when Clinton was fighting to catch his opponent, may bear out this supposition.

This point does not detract from the value of this research in the slightest. Rather, my goal is merely to add context that may help Just, Crigler, and Belt to take their work to the next level of practical application. By examining the relative merits of hope- and fear-based messaging based on a candidate's standing in the campaign, we may be able to learn more about how these two types of emotional appeals affect the voters in question. The authors are correct when they say that "hope is the most important emotion in the campaign, becoming crucial at the end of the campaign when citizens vote for a candidate." But it would be interesting to know what levels of fear are helpful in getting the candidate to that threshold of victory.

The discussion above about targeting voters is relevant to the discussion of hope and fear as well. I suspect that hope is the preferred means of communicating to a campaign's most loyal supporters (the saints) and that fear is the most effective way of discouraging the most virulent opposition (the sinners) from turning out at the polls. But the calibration of these two types of emotional appeals on salvageable voters would be fascinating. Here's hoping that it is included as part of the follow-up study.

LESSON FOUR: VOTERS' PRIMARY LOYALTY IS TO THEIR OWN INTERESTS

The most interesting discussion in contemporary politics is the role of culture and values in the voters' decision-making process. In the past generation, the two major political parties have accomplished one of the most extraordinary trades in American political history, each sending a critical segment of its respective support base to the opposition in exchange for an equally valuable bloc. Leege and Wald (chapter 12 in this volume) categorize the two groups as white business and professional women and white evangelical Protestants. In more casual political circles, we refer to them as soccer moms and Nascar dads.

Regardless of the language used to describe these two once-salvageable voter groups, the premise of the trade-off is the same. In both cases, groups of loyal party supporters developed their allegiances on the basis of economic affinity to their respective party ideologies. Women from economically upscale households tended to vote in large numbers for Republicans for reasons primarily related to personal finances, and working-class populist voters remained strong Democrats for similar reasons.

But over the course of the past two to three decades (depending on where you mark the trend's beginning), both of these voter groups began to cast their ballots with less regard for economic matters than for social and cultural issues. Leege and Wald have done an excellent overview of this dual loyalty shift, correctly noting that political appeals based on such cultural matters are much more likely to rely on emotion for their resonance with the targeted voting audience. Their assumption that "politics is collectively binding action to affirm values and achieve goals for a society" is the logical starting point for this discussion because it suggests that voters' basing their decisions on cultural rather than financial matters is a natural tendency rather than the aberration that political observers frequently consider it to be.

Their history of Republican outreach to working-class voters is very thorough, albeit laced with a certain hint of disapproval toward the GOP's tactics or beliefs. It provides a useful chronology of the various issues that led to the realignment of working-class voters during the Nixon, Reagan, and Bush presidencies. In their effort to concentrate on policy items related to religious beliefs and national security, the authors overlook the critical role of policy debates about such issues as crime, welfare reform, and judicial reform, each of which emerged as a key motivator for blue collar-voters in this period. Indeed, it was Clinton's support for the death penalty and his embrace of welfare reform that allowed him to successfully cast himself as a New Democrat in his 1992 campaign. His decision to sign a Republican welfare reform bill in 1995 proved to be a key component of his ability to move back to the center of the political spectrum in the aftermath of his administration's health care reform proposal, in time for his successful reelection campaign.

The authors' description of the corresponding Democratic outreach to professional women is valuable as well, although it may overestimate its relation to a backlash against increased Republican reliance on social and cultural conservatism. Although large numbers of economically successful, socially moderate voters of both genders reacted with suspicion to the GOP's move rightward, strong Democratic emphasis on abortion rights, environmental protection, and workplace equality played a significant role in attracting these voters before the influx of religious conservative voters into the GOP gathered force. (For many years, the issue of gun control was considered part of this framing as well, until changing tides of public opinion reduced its effectiveness for Democrats to one of motivating loyal supporters rather than persuading salvageable voters. The photo opportunity of John Kerry returning from a duck hunting expedition in the swing state of Ohio the week before the 2004 election effectively signaled the changing and diminished status of gun control as a persuasive issue for Democratic candidates.)

Because party identification tends to be a lagging indicator of voting behavior, Republican outreach to working-class voters had its roots in the Nixon campaigns of 1968 and 1972. The advantage that Republicans had traditionally enjoyed regarding national security issues had been lessened by mixed public opinion about the Vietnam War, so Nixon's emphasis on public safety proved to be the first step toward a realignment of this voting bloc. This trend accelerated during Reagan's campaigns of 1980 and 1984, whose emphasis on military and foreign policy strength restored the GOP's long-term advantage concerning these issues as well. Although the overtures to evangelical voters cited by Leege and Wald had begun at this point, they had not yet become central to Republican political strategy.

Yet it was at this point that issues such as abortion and the environment began to tug professional women and other economically successful voters away from the GOP and toward the Democrats. The size and scope of Reagan's victories masked the beginnings of this countertrend, which did not reach full fruition until Clinton's campaigns in the 1990s. Whereas Reagan had been able to paper over the emerging differences between Republican factions by stressing the disparities between his opponents' positions and his own economic and national defense policy agendas, Clinton was able to deemphasize these differences to the point where economically upscale voters felt comfortable basing their votes on social and cultural issues as well.

Leege and Wald's examination of the value of symbols in reaching out to these voter groups is very well done. It contains astute analysis that is of potentially significant benefit to practitioners in both parties. Once again, a great deal of additional benefit could be realized by taking this research to the next level of detail, specifically as it relates to the afore-mentioned practice of targeting specific voter groups. The examples of symbolism and imagery that they cite inarguably had dramatic impact on the news audience at the time they were made public. But it is equally in-disputable that these images had very different types of effects on various voter groups within that larger electorate. Images of Michael Dukakis in a tank or George W. Bush in a flight suit carried strong emotional impact, but did supporters of these two politicians respond in the same manner as did virulent opponents? The answer is almost certainly no, but a more thorough investigation of audience reaction broken down by voter groups and their past allegiances would constitute a breakthrough of great im-port and equally great application.

The photograph of John Kerry returning from a duck-hunting expedi-tion serves as an excellent template for furthering this discussion. Did Kerry's efforts at strengthening a cultural connection to gun owners and other social conservatives lessen their level of animosity toward him? Did the image persuade salvageable voters to support Kerry, either on the basis of this particular matter of public policy or as a result of a broader level of comfort and shared value assignation? Did the footage cause Kerry's saints, to either increase or decrease their motivation to support his candidacy?

Similar questions addressing Bush's "Mission Accomplished" speech could be answered by more targeted research as well. Did his appearance on the flight deck serve to motivate Bush's saints or to persuade salvage-ables? Did it have a discouraging effect on Kerry's strongest supporters? More important, how did the changing circumstances of the war in Iraq impact the voters' impressions of this imagery? At the time of the speech, it was widely assumed that Bush's reelection campaign would highlight footage from this event in television commercials. But several months later, it was Democratic campaign commercials that featured this image, obviously making a much different point in a radically different political environment. Additional research broken down by voter affiliation could help us better understand whether both campaigns made the correct de-cisions about use of the flight deck footage.

The shift in voters' priorities from economic to cultural issues raises another set of questions that would undoubtedly benefit from further re-search. Logic would suggest that compromise and conciliation are much more likely in the context of fiscal and economic debate than in an ex-change over matters that voters consider to be based in values and mo-rality. Two opponents arguing the details of tax reform, for example, can agree to a tax rate halfway between one proposal and the other. But middle ground is much more difficult to identify for such emotionally volatile issues as abortion, same-sex marriage, or religion in the public square.

In this discussion, any number of questions arise that would benefit from additional research. Is legislative compromise less frequently accomplished regarding cultural matters than economic policy? If so, does the emotive power of imagery and symbolism serve primarily to motivate supporters of a particular policy position, or can it serve as a persuasive tool for undecided voters? Can emotion-based appeal lay the groundwork for negotiation and cooperation, or does it serve to harden partisan positions?

LESSON FIVE: NEVER UNDERESTIMATE A CLINTON

One side note on Leege and Wald's chapter that may be of interest to political observers is their passing reference to Hillary Rodham Clinton's role in the 1992 presidential election. They correctly note that Clinton's emergence as a polarizing figure was based largely on the way different segments of the electorate viewed her professional and political accomplishments. In explaining her decision not to "stay home and bake cookies," Clinton simultaneously became either a touchstone or a lightning rod for millions of voters whose primary political motivations were based on social and cultural issues.

Perhaps the best way to trace the changing tides of cultural and social issues in the political arena is to observe the public statements Clinton made during her 2000 campaign for U.S. Senate and in the aftermath of John Kerry's defeat in the 2004 presidential election. Senator Clinton has adeptly addressed a range of social and cultural matters, from abortion rights to immigration policy. The firebrand of the early 1990s who rallied the support of professional women during her husband's campaign has demonstrated a deft touch for broadening her base of support among voters who had demonstrated significant antagonism toward her during earlier times.

During her Senate campaign, Clinton quickly recognized the hostility that existed toward her in the more conservative areas of upstate New York. Although the news media focused on the symbolic value of the amount of time she spent in the northern and western part of the state as part of a "listening tour," the substance of the remarks Clinton made during these forays showed a keen interest in alleviating the suspicions of her audiences by seeking out common ground on a variety of social issues. By the time Kerry was defeated four years later, Clinton was ready to build on this message and take it to a national audience.

In January 2005, Clinton made national headlines by urging supporters of abortion rights to seek common ground with their pro-life opponents. Though clearly not altering her long-time support for legal abortion, Clinton spoke about what she believed was a "tragic choice" and outlined her views on preventing unplanned pregnancies, promoting adoption, and recognizing the influence of religion in abstinence. In previous months, she had staked out more hard-line positions than had many in her party on immigration, border protection, and homeland security matters as well.

Clinton recognized that a strong base of support from the white business and professional women that Wald and Leege catalogue in their chapter is only one element of a winning coalition. As demonstrated by Democrats such as Kennedy, Carter, and her husband, Clinton began to reach out to culturally conservative voters on issues that serve as their primary political motivation. Her goal may have been to convince those Nascar dads to support her or simply to dampen the level of antipathy that had existed for her in the past. But her efforts were a clear signal that the ascendancy of social issues over economic concerns is a long-term phenomenon that successful politicians, practitioners, and researchers would do well to recognize.

SOME FINAL THOUGHTS ON THE SUBJECT OF PARTISANSHIP

The increasing tendency for voters to prioritize social and cultural issues is a logical point from which to address one final point: the ideological makeup of the academic research community and the impact of those preferences on the practical application of its findings in political campaigns. It is not particularly newsworthy that the world of higher education tends to skew toward the Democratic side of the political spectrum. Conservative and liberal analysts alike have offered a dizzying range of theories as to why this is the case. But for the purposes of this discussion, it may make more sense to simply agree to the existence of this reality than to attempt to ascertain the reasons for its existence. (In the interest of disclosure, I am a registered Republican.)

But my own partisan loyalties or ideological leanings aside, I argue strongly that a purveyor of academic research has an obligation to ignore his or her own political preferences in the conduct and dissemination of his or her work. The most successful scientific research takes place when the scientist sets aside his own opinions in order to approach the subject with a mind open to all possible outcomes. So I urge my new friends in this emerging partnership to leave their own opinions of the politicians they are studying out of their work. Their research deserves to be taken seriously by Republicans and Democrats alike, not only by practitioners whose partisan leanings happen to match those of the researchers.

Even if the nation's university faculties lean heavily toward one party instead of the other, the electorate is almost evenly split. The number of candidates appearing on ballots for local, state, and national offices reflects an equal division between the two major parties. In order for the research presented in this volume to have its maximum practical impact, it must be viewed by those on both sides of the aisle as valuable and serious work. The prospect of academic research being put to practical use has great benefit for both the researcher and practitioner. But it is understandable that researchers with strong ideological and partisan preferences have some reluctance to see their work used to elect a politician other than those who would normally enjoy their support. This is known in other circles as the "Oppenheimer effect," based on the regret expressed by the scientist Robert Oppenheimer as to the destruction caused by the nuclear weapons he helped create.

I have reconciled myself with the idea that Democratic students in my classes will probably apply the lessons I have taught toward the advancement of political goals of which I am a dedicated opponent. But I have come to believe that the benefits of sharing knowledge far outweigh the downside of that knowledge's use on behalf of a candidate or cause of which I disapprove. I strongly urge my colleagues to put aside their own concerns and prioritize the spread of their knowledge over the achievement of their own political preferences.

Knowledge exists for the good and the bad. The fact that hackers use sophisticated computer techniques to perpetrate crime and theft against others is not a logical argument against the invention of the Internet. Bank robbers use automobiles to travel to and from the scene of their crimes. Kidnappers may communicate by telephone to coordinate their activities and to contact the families of those abducted. But it is unlikely that Henry Ford and Alexander Graham Bell would rethink their inventions because of their occasional misuse.

Political scientists must reach the same conclusion. If scientific breakthroughs can advance the work of criminals, then we can come to terms with the idea that our research may someday benefit a politician whose election we would oppose. That is a small price to pay for the service this work can do for political practitioners, candidates, and citizens.

CHAPTER SIXTEEN

Cognitive Neuroscience and Politics: Next Steps

ROSE MCDERMOTT

Recent advances in the cognitive neurosciences have generated widespread interest across a number of disciplines in the inner workings of the human brain and their impact on important features of human behavior. In particular, this work has focused new attention and energy on the impact of emotion on various aspects of human psychology, including attention, motivation, memory, perception, language, learning, judgment, and decision making. This volume reflects the reconsideration of how emotion and thought intertwine in political contexts. Much of this work has emphasized the ways in which emotion influences political judgment and decision making. At first, this focus may appear unduly restrictive. Yet it is hoped that these applications represent merely the beginning of a larger enterprise that will spark many more investigations of the ways in which affect can influence important political outcomes through processes that go beyond judgment and decision making into the realms of motivation, learning, memory, and perception.

The goal in much of this work is to provide a richer understanding of the ways in which individual emotional reactions can be aggregated into collective political enterprises, as well as how political events and actions can provide feedback that in turn can affect individual feelings. Research in this area also seeks to bridge the theoretical and methodological gaps between the real micro experience of instant emotional response and the real macro world of political behavior.

This chapter begins with a discussion of some of the larger issues raised by the study of emotion and politics. This overview reasserts the importance of incorporating emotion into the study of politics and political science. The second section of this chapter focuses on the preceding chapters of this volume, noting points of agreement and disagreement

and analyzing the significance of these differences. The chapter concludes with some areas of opportunity for future steps in the study of
emotion and its application to politics.

HAS THE STUDY OF EMOTION IN POLITICS BEEN IGNORED?

Much of the research presented in this volume has concentrated on the
importance of emotion in accurately understanding political reality. The
implicit argument seems to assume that such inquiry has been ignored
or neglected in the past. And yet this is not entirely true. Early models of
American voting behavior, in particular, pointed to the critical influence
of psychological and affective factors in explaining electoral outcomes
(Adorno et al. 1950; Campbell et al. 1960; Converse 1964, 1975). Such
models were, however, based on older theoretical models of emotion in
psychology that have largely fallen out of fashion in the wake of methodological and technical advances in the empirical study of the brain and human behavior. This recent technological progress in the area of brain imaging has allowed scholars previously unimagined access to the specifics of
brain functioning. And this new wealth of information can, it is hoped, be
used to fashion more accurate models of decision making, with previously
unheard-of levels of empirical grounding and specificity. Moreover, these
advances in cognitive neurosciences are not limited to the study of emotion, as the chapter by Schreiber (chapter 3) carefully documents.[1] Further, recent technological innovations in biology and genetics also allow
previously unprecedented insight into these bases of behavior as well.

These advances serve to highlight the contributions that the study of
emotion can bring to our understanding of politics and political science.
In particular, the investigation of emotion can help pinpoint the source of
preferences on which models of rational choice depend (Bueno de Mesquita and McDermott 2004; Lupia and Manning, chapter 14). As most
of the chapters in this volume attest, emotion exerts a profound and in
many cases predictable impact on judgment, decision making, and information processing. Indeed, the theory of affective intelligence (Marcus,
Neuman, and MacKuen 2000; MacKuen et al., chapter 6) rests on the
fundamental importance of anxiety, aversion, and enthusiasm in understanding and predicting the various cycles of American voting behavior
(Marcus 2002). Much of the recent work in psychology, for example,
points to the way in which anxiety in particular can mediate the dynam-

---

1. All references to individual chapters are to those in this volume.

ics of human attention (Gray 1987; Damasio 1995). Specifically, anxiety works to draw a person's attention to the source of the fear. Individuals become hypervigilant in searching their environment for information and evidence relating to the perceived threat or source of anxiety. Such a strategy holds clear evolutionary advantages, since the ability to deter and respond to threats early aids survival prospects for those who react quickly to physical challenges. Finally, a more nuanced study of emotion allows for increased understanding of the importance of motivation in linking the attitudes and behavior of actors. Leege and Wald (chapter 12), for example, point at least indirectly to the importance of motivation in understanding voter abstention.

Yet important challenges exist in the study of emotion and its application to important political considerations. First, emotion is often discussed as though it were only one concept, and yet clearly emotion represents a class of phenomena. Whether one thinks about emotion in terms of valence, levels of arousal, a circumplex model, or various specific dimensions, work presented here and elsewhere (Lerner and Keltner 2000, 2001; Huddy, Feldman, and Cassese, chapter 9; Just, Crigler, and Belt, chapter 11; Brader and Valentino, chapter 8) demonstrates that specific emotions can exert specific effects. Lumping all emotions together, even all negative emotions, may obscure rather than clarify the precise effects that specific emotions exert on various behaviors. Keeping this specificity in mind in designing future studies may prove critical to uncovering the multidimensional effects of specific emotions on behavior.

This caution points directly to another. Careful use of terminology remains essential to the efficient progress of a unified research agenda. Part of the reason that rational choice made such quick inroads into political science in general, and international relations in particular, came from the consensus that its practitioners shared about what terms mean and how to use them. Spezio and Adolphs (chapter 4) provide a model of such specificity not only by carefully enumerating their use of specific terms such as *emotion* and *affect* but also by pointing to the different ways in which such terms may be used or misused by neuroscientists and political scientists. Most important, researchers need to agree on the proper place of physiological measures in defining emotion. Whereas many neuroscientists see these features as critical dependent variables in the definition of emotion, many political scientists measure emotion by self-report scales that come close to Damasio's (1994) understanding of *feeling* as opposed to *affect*. This measurement issue remains crucial at least in part because of the importance of making commensurate comparisons. Those who study emotion with skin conductance and heart rate may in fact be measuring something other than what is measured by those who ask people how they feel about, say, a candidate several minutes after viewing a videotape of a political advertisement or speech. Indeed, the difference in measurement also reflects difference in timing; those who examine physiological measurements may be tapping into an entirely different psychological process than are those who study self-report measures in which an element of memory and semantics necessarily intercede. Since self-reports are always mediated though semantics, how does this inevitable contamination affect our theories of emotion in social science? Differences between measures may be hard to interpret for a variety of reasons. Attempts to integrate or at least map physiological measures to self-report scales may help in this regard.

Such differences also point to the importance of specificity and standardization in other forms of measurement. If political scientists are going to continue to use self-report measures for purposes of cost, convenience, access, or similarity to large-scale public opinion polling, more attention will need to be paid to the way in which people use specific words for emotions. Do they mean the same thing when they talk about feelings and attitudes or when we ask them about either? How do we know that when one person says an event makes him or her anxious that another person would not refer to that same physiological experience by another name such as fear, anger, or hunger? Are they the same? Again, integration of physiological with self-report measures can aid in clarifying these measurement challenges. Marcus et al. (2006) address some of these challenges in recent work on the measurement of emotion. After noting the importance of identifying which emotions are most significant in political processes, they offer several useful recommendations for improving the political measurement of emotion. For current purposes, the most relevant of these suggestions include the importance of including measures of aversion as well as anxiety and a warning to avoid Likert-type scales in emotion research.

One of the interesting research questions that emerge from this quandary concerns the issue of where physiological signals for emotion originate. Just as rational choice models may see preference as the uncaused cause of decision making and prospect theory may find such an instigator in framing effects, we must take care not to relegate physiological measures to such an unexamined category. Regardless of the kind of genetic predisposition for some attitudes and temperaments pointed to by Schreiber (chapter 3), Brader and Valentino (chapter 8), and Spezio and Adolphs (chapter 4) and others (Alford and Hibbing 2004; Alford, Funk, and Hibbing 2005), culture and socialization can influence such expression. Damasio (1994) points to the essential role that learning plays in developing skin conductance responses and hunches in his famous Iowa gambling task. In his somatic marker hypothesis, Damasio argues that associations between certain activities and behaviors and positive and negative reinforcement help teach children to anticipate the hedonic nature of outcomes based on prior learning and on association between bodily signals and various payoffs. So the important question for social scientists revolves around the way in which physiological responses are mediated through various and specific cultural systems. What causes physiological responses? Can the expression of such responses be conditioned by particular social and political values or cultures? In short, social scientists should strive toward a more recursive understanding of the relations between physiology and different political, social, and cultural expressions of emotion. Specifically, how do current emotions become part of the deliberative reflection in which individuals engage when next they encounter similar individuals or experiences? How does past learning affect future physiological feedback in ways that encourage individuals to either approach or avoid particular political systems, leaders, or events? In chapter 12, Leege and Wald examine two particular cultures, Protestant evangelicals and white business and professional women, as Dan Schnur (chapter 15) does in his discussion of soccer moms and Nascar dads. But it is easy to imagine ways in which such cultural investigations can be broadened to examine more diverse political cultures and the way in which the expression of emotion in terms such as *trust, hope,* and *fear,* might manifest under, for example, various regime types, as Neblo suggests in chapter 2.

Regardless of these concerns, the study of emotion poses some important benefits as well. Earlier models in political science and economics traditionally understood emotion as only working to impede proper, rational reasoning. In other words, emotion could only cause problems. The work in this volume and elsewhere poses a devastating challenge to such a single-minded understanding. Emotions may, under certain conditions, prompt pejorative problems for normative decision making, as Cassino and Lodge argue in this volume (chapter 5), but emotion can just as easily aid the speed and efficiency of good decision making as well. Indeed, Spezio and Adolphs' (chapter 4) useful reminder of the Yerkes-Dodson curve poses a helpful suggestion for reconciling such apparent discrepancies, in a manner similar to the way the theory of affective intelligence appears to reconcile the competing models of the normal and rational voter (MacKuen et al., chapter 6). Specifically, too much emotion or too little may interfere with optimal decision making, but a moderate amount can

serve to facilitate decision making in effective ways. With this realization, we can begin to develop a more sophisticated, contextualized view
of how emotion can serve as both a virtue and a vice, depending on the
context and conditions. One goal of research, then, is to begin to distinguish the times when it will prove destructive from the times when it will
serve a helpful function.

Toward a Comprehensive Theory of Emotion

It is all well and good to discuss the ways in which specific findings in the
cognitive neurosciences can help advance our understanding of specific
processes, but such piecemeal application may suffer from an inability to
compete with more comprehensive understandings of political behavior.
So what might a theory of the role of emotion in politics that is consistent
with neuroscientific findings look like?

The most reasonable starting point for a model of emotion in politics
derives from evolutionary theories of biology and psychology. Such models, far from demanding the rigidly deterministic predictions often associated with early and inappropriate renderings, offers the critical insight that
behavior can be understood as a function of genetics interacting with the
environment. Further, genetics has encoded a rich array of evolutionary
adaptations that allow humans to respond in advantageous and efficient
ways to a whole host of recurrent problems that occurred in the past. For
many traditional psychologists, the reality of humans as political as well as
social animals remains surprising. Yet evolutionary models provide the obvious explanation that because reproduction is sexual, kinship mating produces deformities, and paternity before DNA analysis was not necessarily
obvious, selection pressures generate and sustain large social and political
groupings, which provide rich opportunities for associative mating.

As with many other facets of human behavior, evolutionary insights
can provide a comprehensive model of emotion, which can then be applied to political activities in provocative ways. From this perspective,
emotions evolved for functional reasons that operated to solve repeated
challenges and problems that humans have faced over time. As such, specific emotions engender, constrain, and otherwise control a wide variety of physiological and psychological forces, from sensory perception to
memory, communication, expression, motivation, attention, and learning. Because evolutionary pressures function by means of a combination
of chance and selection, emotional strategies and designs that operate
most successfully over time are retained and passed along to succeeding
generations, whereas those that fail are not reproduced. In this way, real

but individually unobservable patterns in the environment become recognized and exploited in a statistical way to create, sustain, and improve on the best structural designs, in the arena of emotion and elsewhere.

An evolutionary approach to the study of emotion and its integration into political life offers several advantages. First, it can easily account for the way in which emotion influence as wide variety of other physical and psychological phenomena. Similarly, it eradicates the need to artificially distinguish between cognition and affect as though such entities were separable, when in fact all evidence points to the way in which various brain functions are inextricably linked and work together in harmony. As Cosmides and Tooby write, "If the brain evolved as a system of information-processing relations, then emotions are, in an evolutionary sense, best understood as information-processing relations (i.e., programs) with naturally selected functions" (2000, 98).

Second, such an understanding provides a critical perspective on the meaning and function of discrete emotions as well as emotional processing more generally. Knowing the recurrent problems and challenges that humans faced in the past and presumably will confront in the future provides useful cures and information concerning how and why certain emotions function as they do, for good and ill, in the modern context.

Third, and perhaps most relevant for this volume, such a perspective provides a more comprehensive way to begin to examine the relation between individual predispositions, or personality, and emotions. Most of the earlier work on the theory of affective intelligence, such as that provided by the Big Five theories of personality (Loehlin et al. 1998), does not address this issue of stable responses by individuals across situations. Although some of the Big Five models have taken hold in personality and clinical psychology, most cognitive, social, and experimental psychologists tend not to believe in the existence of personality as colloquially defined and understood. Instead, most stress a more interactionist perspective that takes into account situational and biological pressures. Yet in this volume (chapter 8), Brader and Valentino note individual differences in predispositions. And there is nothing in the theory of affective intelligence or other extant models such as the somatic marker hypothesis (Damasio 1994) that occludes the possibility or existence of reciprocal feedback mechanisms between emotional experience and predispositions. An evolutionary approach allows an obvious mechanism by which individuals begin with some individual genetic orientations, which may include characteristics such as ideology or religiosity (Alford et al. 2005), that interact with the environment in ways that led to continual updating in reaction to circumstance and environmental cues. In this way, as

Cosmides and Tooby note, evolutionary psychology is both "environment-oriented and past-oriented in its functionalist orientation" (2000, 97).

Finally, an evolutionary approach offers a mechanism by which to incorporate the important yet divergent impact of culture on particular behavioral outcomes, including political outcomes. For example, facial expression of basic emotion appears universal, but different cultures may find it more or less adaptive for individuals to visually express specific emotions, such as fear or anger, in public.

How can an evolutionary interpretation of emotion provide a more enlightened view of politics? Analyzing emotions for the functions they serve in solving repeated problems sheds new lights on various political problems such as coalition formation, competition, violence and aggression, and dominance and status hierarchies, Understanding the origin and function of particular emotions can illuminate various aspects of their ability to entrain other physiological mechanisms and behaviors. This approach provides novel strategies for intervention concerning such facets of political life as cooperation, equality, and aggression.

This invocation of an evolutionary orientation is necessarily too brief, but perhaps it can begin to recalibrate more diverse approaches into a more organic whole. Clearly, as Schreiber (chapter 3) and Spezio and Adolphs (chapter 4) argue and demonstrate, any comprehensive theory of emotion in politics must draw on significant research in a variety of related disciplines, including evolutionary, social, and cognitive psychology, cognitive neuroscience, and biological anthropology. The key to undertaking effective interdisciplinary and multimethod work lies in honoring the people who do work that is not your own. The development of effective theoretical structures cannot depend on the use of a single method. Developing interinstitutional and collaborative enterprises to study emotion-related research can potentiate the discovery of new knowledge. As E. O. Wilson (1998) writes in his influential work *Consilience*, "The full understanding of utility will come from biology and psychology by reduction to the elements of human behavior followed by a bottom-up synthesis, not from the social sciences by top-down inference and guesswork based on intuitive knowledge. It is in biology and psychology that economists and social scientists will find the premises they need to fashion more predictive models" (206).

Measurement and Methodology

As mentioned above, theory and measurement remain inextricably intertwined. Each level of measurement, whether the micro level of individual action or the macro level of collective action, presents its own complications and difficulties. Indeed, the goal of a multilevel, multi-method investigation into the impact of emotion on politics, as has been attempted within the confines of this volume, lies in finding appropriate tests and generating suitable stimuli that can be used with various methods, and at different levels of analysis, in order to further refine our theoretical notions of specific political processes. Although it may prove necessary to use different theoretical concepts to investigate and explain concepts at different levels of analysis, consistent measurement of central variables such as affect remains essential to the successful accumulation of knowledge. Otherwise, investigators may talk across each other or obscure real findings in what appears to be measurement error.

As noted above, Marcus et al. (2006) present several recommendations for improvement in the measurement of politically relevant emotions. They argue that the traditional understanding of emotion imported from psychology actually distorts a proper examination of how emotion affects politics. They note that seemingly trivial shifts in the measurement of emotion can produce enormous differences in the way subjects respond, as can the more well-known framing effects in cognitive biases. As a result, some forms of measurement, such as orthogonal restriction in exploring emotional dimensionality, unnecessarily constrain findings while other disparate forms may reveal similar outcomes. They suggest, for example, that measuring the frequency and the intensity of a given emotion essentially elicits identical measures, as do certain phrases used to identify certain emotions, and therefore such questions and phrases can be used interchangeably without concern about reliability or validity in responses.

The key to successful measurement lies in its effective manipulation. Investigators must be able to systematically and efficiently induce and shift key emotions in ways that will allow observers to see whether subjects' behavior is related to prior theoretical expectations. Scholars need to know which emotion is being elicited and how it is being measured. The goal is to achieve clear results that can be replicated by others. In emotion research, one of the key confounds, which Cassino and Lodge (chapter 5) point out effectively, lies in how semantics may be related to on-line emotional processing at the time of judgment or decision. In other words, given that we know that episodic memory decays quickly, how do we know what we are getting when we ask a subject what she is feeling even relatively soon after an intervention? Can we elicit an on-line, accurate emotional memory at that time, or are we instead merely tapping into semantic memory processes? And, further, if we rely on self-report, how do we trust what subjects tell us about what they feel? It is not only that people lie about such things; they often honestly remain unaware of their own motives and feelings (Nisbett and Wilson 1977). Are they reporting subjective feelings? Clearly such reports are not as reliable or replicable as the emotional physiological measures that some neuroscientists use in assessing on-line emotional processing using skin conductance, heart rate, and other biological measures. Other nonintrusive measures used to assess on-line processes include reaction time and implicit association measures such as those employed by Cassino and Lodge (chapter 5). These types of measures are not as susceptible to the inherent limitations of semantics and introspection, but they may pose other research challenges related to the ability to map hedonic experience with behavioral outcomes.

These questions confirm the central importance of experimental research in investigating the impact of emotion on political judgment and decision making. And mood induction is likely to prove critical in the successful pursuit of this research. To achieve reliable and accurate measurement of some of the major emotional effects that political scientists are interested in, we need to create a solid experimental foundation. Once consensus in the measurement of particular emotional states has been accomplished, survey research can then build on this foundation to document particular effects.

Such research may require greater use of physiological measures of particular emotions. Of course, problems can arise in the use of such measures. Although facial expression of the seven basic emotions appears to be universal, it may prove difficult to distinguish one high-arousal, high-valence emotion from another on the basis of heart rate alone (think of the difficulty of distinguishing extreme anger from extreme sexual arousal in this way, for example). There is value in integrating some physiological measures into research about emotion because of their ability to show affective processing at the actual time of decision, judgment, assessment, or evaluation. The goal for social scientists, then, lies in going beyond the mere definition of a particular emotion to map its political importance. It may not mean much to know that a leader makes a person feel disgusted. How does this emotion serve as a measure of how trustworthy the person believes the politician to be? If a politician disgusts someone, would that voter then prove unwilling to support a particular policy that the leader advocates, even if the voter might like the idea on its merits? Think of Republicans so disgusted by Bill Clinton's sexual behavior that they found it difficult to support any of his domestic policies or of Democrats so disgusting by George W. Bush's arrogance and lies that they cannot support his war on terror.

Policy Effects

The last set of questions leads to the very real world of policy effects and the ways in which professional politicians may want to use emotional cues and signals to manipulate public opinion for electoral advantage. The current relevance of these issues is easily apparent when one observes the war on terrorism. The goal of terrorism itself, at least in part, is to instill fear in a population. Part of the goal of a responsive government is to try to deflect and manage this fear. The challenge for any government lies in how to keep its population alert to the threat without paralyzing the society.

In examining the impact of emotion on politics, real-world applications thus lie very close to the surface. Political campaigning remains rife with negative messages even as all parties decry its use. Politicians and political consultants target particular audiences based on their understanding of various groups' concerns. Indeed, Nardulli and Kuklinski's chapter (13) tests the theory of affective intelligence by examining the ways in which threats to economic prosperity, individual safety, and collective physical security predict electoral turnout at the aggregate level. Similarly, Huddy et al.'s chapter (9) examines the specific impact of anxiety and anger on support for the war in Iraq. And Brader and Valentino (chapter 8) examine the effects of anger, fear, and enthusiasm on attitudes toward immigration.

Emotional appeals in politics can take one of at least two different forms. The first focuses on personal attacks and criticisms, such as those by the front group Swift Boat Veterans against Senator John Kerry's Vietnam War record during the 2004 presidential election. Alternatively, such emotional appeals can challenge particular policy positions, such as the value and rectitude of national health care, prescription drug reform, welfare policy, environmental safeguards, or Social Security reform. Emotional appeals often devolve into messages that resort to trying to make individuals fearful or angry about a particular person or policy. And such appeals often appear to be designed not only to change attitudes but also to affect behavior by motivating viewers. When a candidate whom a voter supports comes under legitimate attack or demonstrates a divergence in policy preference from that of the voter, the person may feel less motivated to vote for that person. Indeed, the chapter by Redlawsk et al. (7) attempted to test the theory of affective intelligence in individual choice by manipulating the extent to which particular candidates agreed with the subject in terms of various policies.

One very important factor in the real world of politics and emotions is the media. Technology in the form of television and the Internet clearly exerts an enormous effect on the creating and manipulation of emotional symbols and ideas. Graber's careful chapter proves particularly instructive in this regard by drawing attention to the relations between emotion and both attentiveness to and attractiveness of various media stories. She demonstrates how fear in particular generates and stimulates audience attention to news. Indeed, she finds that the magnitude of danger remains the most important determinant of viewer arousal. She also finds that the time the media devote to a story also affects attentiveness. Just, Crigler, and Belt (chapter 10) similarly point to the way in which hope and enthusiasm can stimulate individuals to seek out political news and information. Yet given what we know about the lack of correspondence between actual and perceived judgment in the probability of lethal events (Litchenstein et al. 1977), it seems safe to assume that one of the problems raised by the relation demonstrated by Graber (chapter 11) lies in the way people draw inferences about frequency and likelihood of threat based on media coverage. When so many all-news networks need to fill so much time, a clear relation between actual and reported threat may not be likely, and yet peoples' perception of threat may be manipulated upwards nonetheless.

The Internet exacerbates this problem by allowing negative and emotional messages to become more self-selected and thus both more targeted and less amenable to correction. Such mechanisms of communication may spark motivation, but they also weaken opportunities for reasoned political debate and persuasion. As a result, many people are never exposed to another point of view. Further, casting political messages in narrow personal and emotional terms can eliminate the potential for common ground and lead to vehement disagreement. This process can help turn mere political adversaries into personal enemies and make governance by compromise increasingly difficult.

CONTRIBUTIONS TO THIS VOLUME

This volume presents an array of important contributions to the study of emotion in politics. Although they address different topics, these papers show some important similarities—and display some significant differences. Because this chapter is not intended as a mere summary, this section concentrates on some of the important divergences and why they matter. Although each paper is mentioned in this chapter, not every paper is discussed in this section because not every author entered into debates with others. The following focus on these debates is not intended to dismiss the importance of the other chapters. I offer suggestions about how to address some of these discrepancies in the final section of this chapter.

Similarities

The first similarity among the contributions is that almost all of them focus on some aspect of judgment and decision making. Few concentrate on other areas in which the cognitive neurosciences have made advances in our understanding of emotional processing. In particular, processes related to memory, learning (and how it informs processes of political socialization), and perception appear ripe for future investigation. Yet this concentration offers benefits as well as challenges. The focus on judgment and decision making arises not only because it presents an obvious area in which to apply work on emotion to politics but also because it remains an important one. To the extent that the authors attempt to debunk traditional assumptions concerning the ways in which emotion inevitably leads to problematic decision making, such investigation can aid in our understanding of how emotion specifically can influence our judgment for ill or good depending on context and circumstances. The challenge of such a restrictive emphasis lies in the implicit truncation of emotional processing to decision making, without a full understanding or appreciation of the way it can mediate other influential processes such as perception, memory, and learning.

The second striking similarity in most but not all of the papers involves their focus on American voting behavior. Although this attention may reflect a larger bias in the field of political science, surely the application of emotion to politics deserves a much wider and less ethnocentric treatment. This is not to say that such applications do not have their place and merit, or that people should not start from their strengths, but rather to encourage greater attention to areas and arenas of application outside the realm of American political behavior. Neblo (chapter 2) provides a provocative contrast when he argues for research into "the differential function of political emotion across different regime types and between rulers and ruled." Similarly, Lupia and Menning (chapter 14) advocate an examination of fear in other political contexts, including international conflict and political advertisement.

Differences

Some of the differences in the chapters in this volume simply reflect disciplinary background and emphasis. Spezio and Adolphs (chapter 4) and

Schreiber (chapter 3) focus on findings from the cognitive neurosciences, while Neblo (chapter 2) examines the historical insights provided by political philosophers in their various approaches to the interaction of emotion and politics. But some of the differences speak to broader theoretical discrepancies that deserve greater discussion.

Dual Process Model

The first difference that emerges, often implicitly, is directly addressed by Spezio and Adolphs in what they refer to as the dual process model of human cognition, a traditional dichotomy between automatic and controlled processing. Spezio and Adolphs note that to the degree to which dichotomies are not used as heuristics but are reified in theoretical distinctions, they are false. They go on to state that though there is clear experimental evidence for some distinction between behaviors that are influenced by conscious control and those that are not, it is unclear that postulating separate systems, one for controlled processing and one for automatic processing, aids in understanding the mechanisms behind the data. Dual process models can aid understanding because they deemphasize the fact that automatic processing is always involved in human activity, even during conscious control of decision making. They conclude that "postulating two distinct processing models obscures more than it reveals."

Although this discrepancy is not so evident in his chapter, Schreiber and colleagues (Liberman et al. 2003) posit this distinction in related past work on political sophistication in which they demonstrated that sophisticates relied on implicit associations and novices required more controlled processes in order to respond to political problems. In this volume Schreiber argues that this contrast emerges in the relation between explicit and implicit attitudes. Well-established judgmental heuristics represent the reflective, conscious, symbolic processes, whereas the reflexive system remains involved in the formation of automatic, implicit attitudes. Schreiber supports this argument by demonstrating the distinct neural substrates found for explicit and implicit attitudes, reflecting their functional differences. He notes that such attitudes can be in conflict.

Thus theoretical assumptions hold methodological implications. Whether this dichotomy remains important theoretically also poses measurement issues, as raised in the chapter (5) by Cassino and Lodge. They use a reaction time test to show that subjects evaluated candidates in line with automatic, affectively laden judgments, and they implicitly argue for the importance of the difference between automatic and controlled processing in the evaluation of candidates. Reaction time tests provide a different measurement of emotional processing than self-report measures, obviously, and such tests seem to get around the problems posed by semantic and memory confounds. Yet they also rely on the fact that automatic processing is faster than more controlled processing of information. In this chapter, Cassino and Lodge argue for the importance of affective, automatic processes in candidate evaluation. The significance of this insight emerges when they note that one consequence of this evaluative process is that the affect toward a social object may become decoupled from the facts about the object, potentially leading to serious errors in judgment.

As Spezio and Adolphs note, one of the potential problems with maintaining the distinction between automatic and controlled processing, when they find so many overlaps in the functional categories, is that it can yield theoretical constructs that make no room for the possibility that emotional processes also function in ways that are necessary and adaptive. This is similar in function, if different in language, from Lupia and Manning's (chapter 14) discussion about how some emotional reactions are subconscious while others remain conscious, and the latter can be, to some extent and at some times, strategically controlled and manipulated. This holds obvious benefits for survival of the organism so endowed. Cassino and Lodge (chapter 5), however, do note the way in which heavy reliance on automatic processes can lead to systematic deviations from normative theory. Thus whether scholars adopt a dual process model of decision making can affect not only the kinds of methods they might employ but also the kinds of conclusions that they reach.

Valence versus Dimensionality

The contributors adopt various theoretical assumptions concerning the appropriate underlying structure of emotion. In the introduction, the editors describe three different models for categorizing the structure of affect: discrete models centered on the study of specific emotions, valence models focused on a typically positive-to-negative dimensional array, and multidimensional models designed to extend valence models into structures such as the circumplex model. These implicit assumptions clearly affect the way in which emotion as such is investigated. Specifically, chapters that seek to delineate or test the theory of affective intelligence start from the assumption that emotion differs according to a basic positive or negative valence. This is operationalized in terms of enthusiasm or anxiety and, in some versions, aversion as well. Some models of emotion also tie this distinction to the basic approach-avoidance behavioral system, such that people approach positive stimuli and avoid negative ones. Chapters that adopt this perspective, at least as a starting point, include those by Redlawsk, Civettini, and Lau (chapter 7), Just, Crigler, and Belt (10), MacKuen et al. (6), Brader and Valentino (8), and Nardulli and Kuklinski (13).

Alternative approaches seek to uncover more specified dimensionality in the structure of emotion and its impact on political attitudes and actions. Huddy, Feldman, and Cassese (chapter 9) present the most self-conscious attempt to discuss the important ways in which specific negative emotions such as fear and anger may lead to significant and predictable differences in political beliefs. They argue for the importance of studying specific emotions so as to avoid the possibility of missing results that may wash out when all negative emotions, for example, are treated as equivalent.

Theory of Affective Intelligence

In many ways this volume serves as follow-up to Marcus, Neuman, and MacKuen's (2000) *Affective Intelligence and Political Judgment*. This theory argues for the central importance of enthusiasm and anxiety in political life. Specifically, anxious voters will seek out more information and use that information to make more fully considered political choices. In this regard the model appears similar to rational voting models except for the critical reliance on an emotional mechanism to spark the original information search. Similarly, if voters remain in a domain of happy complacency, or enthusiasm, they will rely disproportionately on well-established heuristic tools such as political party identification to determine vote choice. This side of the model remains reminiscent of normal voter models such as those presented by Campbell et al. (1960). This model can thus explain cyclical voting in American history and account for the variant findings of previous models. Indeed, many of the contributors sought to test, amplify, and expand this model in various individual and aggregate experimental and survey settings. In general, the results were mixed. While most tests demonstrated some support for the model, almost all tests also found important deviations from the major predictions of the model. These deviations appear to be systematic enough to merit consideration.

The chapter by Redlawsk, Civettini, and Lau (7) examined the theory of affective intelligence at the individual level. Using an experimental paradigm, the authors found the desired result for anxiety in the case

Cognitive Neuroscience and Politics 391

of the preferred candidate when the level of threat was high. The other results proved more disappointing for the theory. Subjects did not demonstrate the expected effects for rejected candidates at any level of threat or for the preferred candidate at lower levels of threat. In addition, the authors did not find the desired effects for anger or enthusiasm.

One of the reasons may lie in their experimental design, which confounds mood and threat. The manipulation shifts the extent to which the candidate agrees with the preferences of the subjects. It is not clear, however, that shifting information directly translates into mood effects, as assumed in the experimental design. It may do so, but it may not; observers cannot simply assume that such is the case. Information, but not mood, was manipulated. Mood induction experiments might be used in the future to more directly assess the impact of mood on evaluation in ways that retain a methodological distinction between mood and threat.

Just, Crigler, and Belt (chapter 10) examine hope as a special kind of enthusiasm in political life. Whereas some candidates may appeal to fear in their constituency, others appeal to hope. The question then becomes whether hope can serve as some kind of antidote to fear. Drawing on appraisal theory, they find that hope can generate increased information-seeking, albeit in a way which can bias that information. This finding would seem to run contrary to the assumption in the theory of affective intelligence that increased information-seeking is sparked differentially by anxiety.

Brader and Valentino (chapter 8) test whether the theory of affective intelligence can indeed subsume two alternative models of rational choice and symbolic politics when it comes to attitudes toward immigration. Using an analysis of national survey data, they find partial support for the model. Specifically, they find that fear of an economic downturn can help explain anxiety about immigration, and social identity can help explain enthusiasm. But they note that the most potent predictors of attitudes toward immigration derive from ethnic prejudice, a finding that would seem to support a symbolic politics approach. They find, in this regard, that anger looks more like fear. Their findings appear to be more consistent with a version of the theory of affective intelligence that incorporates aversion as a motivating feature independent of anxiety and enthusiasm.

Nardulli and Kuklinski (chapter 13) similarly tested the theory of affective intelligence at the aggregate level by predicting that threats to core values of economic prosperity and personal and collective safety could help explain electoral outcomes. Such threats were assumed to generate the anxiety that would lead to more information-seeking and subsequent electoral discontent. Their findings remain consistent with the theory's predictions, although they argue that emotion in the form of anxiety may be sufficient but not necessary as a triggering mechanism. If so, such a finding presumes a level of imitation among the population.

Finally, Huddy, Feldman, and Cassese (chapter 9) provide the most self-conscious departure from the theory of affective intelligence in posing differential effects for the impact of anger and anxiety, two distinct negative emotions, on significant political attitudes toward the war in Iraq. Consistent with findings reported elsewhere concerning the differential impact of anger and anxiety (Lerner and Keltner 2000, 2001), they find that although both emotions increase attention to the war, anger increases support and decreases the perceived sense of risk, and the opposite is found for anxiety. They find theoretical support for the importance of this distinction in cognitive theories of appraisal.

One additional theoretical point deserves mention at this juncture, in the context of chapter 9's call for increased specificity in our understanding and interpretation of emotional responses. Many authors treat anxiety and fear as synonymous, and this may be warranted much of the time. But sometimes they differ in important ways, as the following example illustrates. As Leege and Wald (chapter 12) point out in their discussion of the ways in which anxiety can demobilize people politically and behaviorally, anxiety can both motivate and interfere with information searches; this seeming tension is easily and quickly resolved within the context of the Yerkes-Dodson model advocated by Spezio and Adolphs (chapter 4). However, understood in the context of the differences between anger and anxiety broached by Huddy et al., it becomes clear that anger can serve as a precursor to action, particularly fighting, in a way that anxiety might not. Similarly, older work in social psychology indicated systematic differences in preferences for affiliation based on whether subjects were afraid or anxious (Sarnoff and Zimbardo 1961). Specifically, fear increases the desire for social affiliation, but the opposite is true for anxiety. Such a difference can pose profound political consequences for group behavior. Similarly, aversion and anger may present different political challenges and opportunities in ways that may make it important to separate them, theoretically as well as empirically.

Currently, the theory of affective intelligence subsumes anger. MacKuen et al. note (chapter 6) that anger is driven by the confrontation with familiar punishing stimuli and by the commitment of psychic and physical resources to learned defensive and aggressive behavioral routines. In this way, anger can prove to be an adaptive response. This is not so clear when it comes to enthusiasm, which, outside a reproductive context, holds much less of an adaptive advantage.

Some aspects of the theory of affective intelligence receive consistent support, including the seminal notion that increased anxiety generates more attention to information-seeking. Less support is found for the importance of enthusiasm, but this may simply reflect the well-known bias in psychophysics whereby organisms in general pay more attention to negative as opposed to positive feedback because of its differential import for purposes of survival (Kahneman and Tversky 1979). Anxiety can prove adaptive in an unsettling situation if the search for information presents a reasonable solution. If such a solution cannot be found, anxiety may prove maladaptive and counterproductive by generating long-term mood disorders.

FUTURE STEPS

There are at least three important ways in which the current work concerning emotion in politics can be extended in a productive manner. First, for such work to achieve wider acceptance and generalizability, applications must begin to move away from its almost exclusive attention to American voting behavior and public opinion research. Although previous research has demonstrated the universal existence and consistent facial expression of seven basic emotions (fear, anger, surprise, contempt, disgust, happiness, and sadness; Ekman and Friesen 1971, 1986; Izard 1971), much work remains to be done on the various ways in which specific emotions manifest themselves politically within the context of divergent social, political, and cultural structures. Do the same threats generate fear in Japan as in Britain? Do different populations respond to fear in predictably divergent ways politically, and might these differences explain why the Spanish threw their politicians out of office after the Madrid bombings but Bush was reelected after the 9/11 attacks? Even when people share an emotional experience in a universal way, cultural expression of such realities may differ. This appears to be true in primates. All monkeys can create tools from everyday objects, for example, but the specific objects they use differ according to function and culture. Monkeys that live near the water in Japan use rocks to crack open shellfish, whereas forest-dwelling monkeys use sticks and branches to dig fruits out of their skins. Monkeys transplanted from one venue to another cannot survive without the help of established members of the local culture to teach them how to get food. Similarly, people from different political cultures, say, democracy and authoritarianism, might express anger in different ways; one might become paralyzed while another might be energized into action.

Clearly, the impact of emotion on politics has widespread and manifest validity. Several of the authors point in this direction. Spezio and Adolphs (chapter 4) suggest four areas of promise for future research, none of which is inherently exclusive to American contexts. The first area is the way emotional processing is differentially related to consciously held beliefs and subliminal outcomes. Such research could productively take place in the arena of media studies, including international comparisons of various kinds of emotional and political appeals, as well as in the domain of leader evaluations. Second, they suggest attention to the interactions among emotion, its intensity, and stable individual political dispositions. One can imagine this kind of work focusing on various aspects of political socialization, again with the potential for cross-cultural comparisons. In the international realm, it might be interesting to see, for example, whether issues such as economic equality, gender, or other social justice concerns arouse greater emotional responses in some regime types than in others. Environmental concerns, especially those surrounding the introduction of genetically modified foods, appear to be much more contentious in welfare-oriented Westernized democracies, for example, than elsewhere. Third, they call for examining the relative roles of empathy and sympathy in assessing adversaries' political strategy. This research agenda seems like a perfect opportunity for a multimethod investigation of experimental studies of bargaining and negotiation combined with interview and case investigations, including the possibility of questioning real participants, in international trade and security organizations. Finally, they suggest inquiry into the relation between emotional processing and metaphor in political persuasion. Again, it is easy to see how experimental work might combine with large-scale surveys to examine the types of emotional messages and metaphors that appeal to particular constituencies with respect to different issues. Further attention to genetic determinants of political outcomes may prove illuminating as well.

Neblo similarly provides a model of the ways in which different research traditions can generate important and relevant insights into the place of emotion in politics via his invocation of classical political philosophers to inform our current theoretical understanding of the inherent interconnection between politics and psychology. Neblo calls for a very innovative comparative approach, based on Plato, to analyze the differential ways in which emotion functions across regime types. This kind of study could easily take on historical investigations as well as contemporary analysis of the ways in which various emotions such as trust, fear, and anger play out in the relations between leaders and followers as well as those between and among nations.

Finally, Lupia and Menning (chapter 14) discuss the way in which a game theoretic approach might illuminate the investigation of emotion in situations of international conflict, among others. Areas in which interpersonal communication offers the chance not only for strategic interaction but also for emotional manipulation and misperception offer rich opportunities for a combination of experimental, game theoretic, and historical case study analysis. After all, many people espouse the intuition that hatred in various forms can lead to war, or at least ethnic conflict and genocide, and yet few extant models in international relations explicitly acknowledge, much less account for, these personal factors in generating violence. And yet when leading military commanders argue in public that President Bush went to war in Iraq either to get revenge on Saddam Hussein for trying to kill his father or to try to compensate for what he saw as his father's failure to oust the Iraqi leader, emotional reality plays a prominent role in such explanations. Such a role may fall more on the derogatory side of our emotional model. But investigations that examine how leaders invoke historical analogies in quick and efficient ways to reach optimal solutions to current crises may present a more positive use of emotion-based pattern recognition.

Work on the impact of emotion in politics can move more in the direction of greater contextualization. Huddy, Feldman, and Cassese (chapter 9) find that anger and anxiety can yield consistent and predictable results, along with other findings about similarly reliable predictions concerning enthusiasm, aversion, and anxiety raised by the theory of affective intelligence; this points to the importance of greater specificity in our models of emotional impact. Different emotions may lead to different responses, and such specificity deserves consideration in research design. In this regard, one should note that the theory of affective intelligence has changed over time and represents, in some important ways, a moving target as it evolves in response to new findings and interpretations in brain science. Some reconciliation appears to be possible as the theory comes to incorporate notions of aversion, for example, that provide a more realistic comparison with the authors' notion of anger than either of the previous dimensions, anxiety and enthusiasm, offers. Further, the theory remains somewhat narrow in its application. It refers in particular to preconscious appraisals and thus has little to say about a more conscious and accessible theory of emotion. The theory of affective intelligence implies that such cognitive appraisals are of little consequence and thus can safely be ignored. This might be true, but it is more likely to be false because of the important ways in which emotion is likely to have evolved to provide recognizable signals of various internal states in order to trigger and allow conscious recalibration of experience (Cosmides and Tooby 2000).[2]

In this vein, current research has focused on anxiety, enthusiasm, fear, and anger. It might prove interesting to expand the repertoire of emotions that are considered worthy of study in political contexts. We know, for example, that sadness can mediate the effect of mood on memory; we know that it can influence the way information is processed. Happy people demonstrate more creative and optimistic decision making, and sad people display the opposite tendencies (Schwartz 2000; Schwartz and Clore 1983). But we know little about the impact of sadness on political action. This appears particularly relevant given the relatively high rates of post-traumatic stress reported by members of the American public following the terrorist attacks of 9/11 (McDermott and Zimbardo 2005).

Finally, we should heed Lupia and Menning's (chapter 14) persuasive call for a broader consideration of the relevant methods for examining the relation between emotion and politics. Lupia and Menning issue a quite compelling and carefully reasoned argument for the wider use of game theory in studies of emotion. They propose that the methodological relation between game theory and emotion should hold equally well for the theoretical relation between emotion and politics writ large. It is clear from the papers presented in this volume, as well as the topics they address, that a multimethod approach to the study of emotional processing in political life is necessary if substantial progress is to be made in the appropriate application of work in the cognitive neurosciences to real-life political processes.

This methodological pluralism appears particularly essential for gaining purchase on two specific, important, and related areas. First, studies that focus on emotional processing that takes place below the level of conscious awareness require multimethod approaches because any one strategy is unlikely to yield unequivocal results. This is true even in the domain of neuroscientific research. As carefully articulated by Spezio and Adolphs (chapter 4) and as corroborated by Schreiber (chapter 3), functional MRIs alone may be difficult to interpret, as are lesion studies. Tradeoffs exist between the use of EEGs, which provide better temporal resolution, and MRIs, which offer more precise structural information, for example. Studies that examine skin conductance, heart rate, and other physiological measures can help clarify and unify the definition of variables and measurement but may not always help us understand the relation between a person's experience and his or her expressions of

---

2. I am grateful to George Marcus for helpful discussion of this point.

emotion or differences in such variables across individuals. Therefore, multiple methods that can help triangulate on a particular finding, confirm findings in a variety of ways, or serve to refine theory and allow for further testing (as experiments can do with the help of formal models) all serve to increase confidence in the reality, validity, and reliability of given results.

Second, the use of multiple methods can help uncover the linkage between real, on-line emotional processing and our memory of such events. In particular, further experimental work using mood inductions and appropriate controls could give special attention to the linkage between verbal reports and real emotional processing as it is experienced in the moment. Specifically, experimental tests that incorporate physiological and self-report measures can examine the effect of the recall of emotional experience at a later time, even if the intervening period is short in duration. For, in reality, people may experience real emotions in the moment as they grow up in a political world, but when pollsters and others seek to understand and manipulate those experiences, they are not in fact tapping into the real experience, but rather are given the individual's memory of that experience, which may be susceptible to all sorts of biases, emotional and otherwise. And that process of memory encoding and activation may be as important for understanding relevant political processes as accurately understanding the actual emotional experience.

CONCLUSION

Earlier political science scholars may have ignored or neglected the impact of emotion on politics at least in part because it was so difficult to study and measure. As methods in the cognitive neuroscience improve, our understanding of the functioning of the human brain improves in ways that make empirically grounded investigations more plausible and gratifying. Yet we are clearly at the very beginning of our understanding of the complex relations among the brain, behavior, and emotion. Humility is an appropriate emotion in the face of this realization. Recognition of such daunting challenge should not distract us, however, from our goal of seeking greater understanding of the myriad ways in which emotion can influence political thought and action. Using more sophisticated and multiple measures in the service of more specific theories can help advance our knowledge in important ways.

Abelson, Robert P. 1963. Computer simulation of "hot cognitions." In *Computer simulation of personality*, ed. S. Tomkins and S. Messick. New York: John Wiley.

Abelson, Robert P., Donald R. Kinder, Mark D. Peters, and Susan T. Fiske. 1982. Affective and semantic components in political person perception. *Journal of Personality and Social Psychology* 42 (4): 619–30.

Abelson, Robert P., and Milton J. Rosenberg. 1958. Symbolic psycho-logic: A model of attitudinal cognition. *Behavioral Science* 3:1–13.

Abramowitz, Alan I. 1983. Social determinism, rationality, and partisanship among college students. *Political Behavior* 5 (4): 353–62.

Achen, Christopher. 1975. Mass political attitudes and the survey response. *American Political Science Review* 69:1218–31.

Adolphs, R. 2001. The neurobiology of social cognition. *Current Opinion in Neurobiology* 11 (2): 231–39.

———. 2002. Neural systems for recognizing emotion. *Current Opinion in Neurobiology* 12 (2): 169–77.

———. 2003a. Cognitive neuroscience of human social behaviour. *National Review of Neuroscience* 4 (3): 165–78.

———. 2003b. Is the human amygdala specialized for processing social information? *Annals New York Academy of Science* 985:326–40.

Adolphs, R., H. Damasio, D. Tranel, G. Cooper, and A. Damasio. 2000. A role for somato-sensory cortices in the visual recognition of emotion as revealed by three-dimensional lesion mapping. *Journal of Neuroscience* 20 (7): 2683–90.

Adolphs, R., D. Tranel, and A. Damasio. 1998. The human amygdala in social judgment. *Nature* 393:470–74.

Adolphs, R., D. Tranel, H. Damasio, and A. Damasio. 1994. Impaired recognition of emotion in facial expressions following bilateral damage to the human amygdala. *Nature* 372 (6507): 669–72.

Adorno, T., E. Frenkel-Brunswik, Daniel Levinson, and R. Sanford. 1950. *The authoritarian personality*. New York: Harper.

Ajzen, I., and M. Fishbein. 1980. *Understanding attitudes and predicting social behavior.* Englewood Cliffs: Prentice-Hall.

Alesina, Alberto, John Londregan, and Howard Rosenthal. 1983. A model of the political economy. *American Political Science Review* 87 (1): 12–33.

Alford, John, Carolyn Funk, and John Hibbing. 2005. Are political orientations genetically transmitted? *American Political Science Review* 99 (2): 153–67.

Alford, John, and Hibbing, John. 2004. The origins of politics: An evolutionary theory of behavior. *Perspectives on Politics* 2 (4): 707–23.

Alvarez, R. Michael, and John Brehm. 2002. *Hard choices, easy answers: Values, information, and American public opinion.* Princeton: Princeton University Press.

Andersen, Kristi. 1988. Sources of pro-family belief. *Political Psychology* 9 (2): 229–43.

Anderson, N. 1981. *Foundations of information integration theory.* New York: Academic Press.

Anderson, Norman, and Stephen Hubert. 1963. Effects of concomitant verbal recall on order effects in personality impression formation. *Journal of Verbal Learning and Verbal Behavior* 2:379–91.

Anderson, S. W., A. Bechara, H. Damasio, D. Tranel, and A. Damasio. 1999. Impairment of social and moral behavior related to early damage in human prefrontal cortex. *National Neuroscience* 2 (11): 1032–37.

Anderson, S. W., H. Damasio, D. Tranel, and A. Damasio. 2000. Long-term sequelae of prefrontal cortex damage acquired in early childhood. *Developmental Neuropsychology* 18 (3): 281–96.

Andrews, T. J., S. D. Halpern, and D. Purves. 1997. Correlated size variations in human visual cortex, lateral geniculate nucleus, and optic tract. *Journal of Neuroscience* 17 (8): 2859–68.

Arbib, M., and M. Bota. 2003. Language evolution: Neural homologies and neuroinformatics. *Neural Networks* 16 (9): 1237–60.

Aristotle. 1996. *Aristotle: The* Politics *and the* Constitution of Athens. [350 B.C.] Rev. student ed. *Cambridge texts in the history of political thought*, ed. S. Everson. Cambridge: Cambridge University Press.

Arnold, M. B. 1960. *Emotion and personality.* New York: Columbia University Press.

Aust, Charles F., and Dolf Zillmann. 1996. Effects of victim exemplification in television news on viewer perception of social issues. *Journalism and Mass Communication Quarterly* 73:787–803.

Averill, J. R. 1980. A constructivist view of emotion. In *Emotions and beliefs: How feelings influence thoughts.* Vol. 1, *Theories of emotion*, ed. R. Plutchik and H. Kellerman, 305–39. New York: Academic Press.

Averill, J. R., G. Catlin, and K. K. Chon. 1990. *Rules of hope.* New York: Springer-Verlag.

Avery, James, and Ellen D. B. Riggle. 2000. The role of general versus political intelligence in political decision-making. Paper presented at the annual meeting of the Midwest Political Science Association, Chicago.

Ax, Albert. 1953. The physiological differentiation between fear and anger in humans. *Psychosomatic Medicine* 15 (5): 433–22.

Axelrod, Robert. 1973. Schema theory: An information processing model of perception and cognition. *American Political Science Review* 67 (4): 1248–66.

Babington, Charles. 2004. GOP playing politics on gay marriage, Democrats say. *Washington Post*, 24 March, A2 (accessed July 19, 2006).

Barber, James David. 1972. *The presidential character: Predicting performance in the White House*. Englewood Cliffs: Prentice-Hall.

Bargh, J. A. 1994. The four horsemen of automaticity: Awareness, efficiency, intention, and control in social cognition. In *Handbook of social cognition*, 2d ed., ed. R. S. Wyer Jr. and T. K. Srull, 1–40. Hillsdale, NJ: Erlbaum.

———. 1997. The automaticity of everyday life. In *The automaticity of everyday life: Advances in social cognition*, ed. R. S. Wyer Jr., 10:1–61. Mahwah, NJ: Erlbaum.

Bargh, J. A., S. Chaiken, R. Govender, and F. Pratto. 1992. The generality of the automatic attitude activation effect. *Journal of Personality and Social Psychology* 62 (6): 893–912.

Bargh, J. A., S. Chaiken, P. Raymond, and C. Hymes. 1996. The automatic evaluation effect: Unconditional automatic attitude activation with a pronunciation task. *Journal of Experimental Social Psychology* 32(1): 104–28.

Bargh, John A., and Tanya L. Chartrand. 1999. The unbearable automaticity of being. *American Psychologist* 54 (7): 462–79.

Bargh, John A., Peter M. Gollwitzer, Annette Lee-Chai, Kimberly Barndollar, and Roman Trötschel. 2001. The automated will: Nonconscious activation and pursuit of behavioral goals. *Journal of Personality and Social Psychology* 81 (6): 1014–27.

Barkow, Jerome, Leda Cosmides, and John Tooby, eds. 1992. *The adapted mind*. New York: Oxford University Press.

Bar-On, Reuven. 1997a. *The Bar-On Emotional Quotient Inventory (EQ-i):A test of emotional intelligence*. Toronto: Multi-Health Systems.

———. 1997b. *The Bar-On Emotional Quotient Inventory (EQ-i): Technical manual*. Toronto: Multi-Health Systems.

Bar-On, Reuven, Daniel Tranel, Natalie Denburg, and Antoine Bechara. 2003. Exploring the neurological substrate of emotional and social intelligence. *Brain* 126:1790–1800.

Baron-Cohen, S. 1997. *Mindblindness: An essay on autism and theory of mind*. Cambridge: MIT Press.

Baron-Cohen, S., H. A. Ring, E. T. Bullmore, S. Wheelwright, C. Ashwin, and S. C. Williams. 2000. The amygdala theory of autism. *Neuroscientific and Biobehavior Review* 24 (3): 355–64.

Bartels, A., and S. Zeki. 2000. The neural basis of romantic love. *Neuroreport* 11 (17): 3829–34.

Barton, Robert A., and Robin I. M. Dunbar. 1997. Evolution of the social brain. In *Machiavellian intelligence II: Extensions and evaluations*, ed. A. Whiten and R. W. Byrne. Cambridge: Cambridge University Press.

Baumeister, R. F., J. M. Twenge, and C. K. Nuss. 2002. Effects of social exclusion on cognitive processes: Anticipated aloneness reduces intelligent thought. *Journal of Personality and Social Psychology* 83 (4): 817–27.

Baumeister, R. F., Kathleen D. Vohs, and Dianne M. Tice. 2005. How emotion helps and hurts decision making. Paper read at the Sydney Symposium on Social Psychology, Sydney, Australia.

Bechara, A. 2001. Neurobiology of decision-making: Risk and reward. *Seminars in Clinical Neuropsychiatry* 6 (3): 205–16.

———. 2004. The role of emotion in decision-making: Evidence from neurological patients with orbitofrontal damage. *Brain Cognition* 55 (1): 30–40.

Bechara, A., A. Damasio, H. Damasio, and S. W. Anderson. 1994. Insensitivity to future consequences following damage to human prefrontal cortex. *Cognition* 50:7–12.

Bechara, A., H. Damasio, and A. Damasio. 2000. Emotion, decision making and the orbitofrontal cortex. *Cerebral Cortex* 10 (3): 295–307.

Bechara, A., S. Dolan, N. Denburg, A. Hindes, S. W. Anderson, and P. E. Nathan. 2001. Decision-making deficits, linked to a dysfunctional ventromedial prefrontal cortex, revealed in alcohol and stimulant abusers. *Neuropsychologia* 39 (4): 376–89.

Bechara, A., D. Tranel, and H. Damasio. 2000. Characterization of the decision-making deficit of patients with ventromedial prefrontal cortex lesions. *Brain* 123 (pt. 11): 2189–202.

Bechara, A., D. Tranel, H. Damasio, and A. Damasio. 1996. Failure to respond autonomically to anticipated future outcomes following damage to prefrontal cortex. *Cerebral Cortex* 6:215–25.

Belt, Todd, Marion Just, and Ann Crigler. 2005. Accentuating the positive in US Presidential elections. Paper presented at the annual meeting of the American Political Science Association, 1–4 September, Washington, DC.

Ben-Ze'ev, Aaron. 2000. *The subtlety of emotions.* Cambridge: MIT Press.

Berenbaum, Howard, Frank Fujita, and Joyce Pfenning. 1995. Consistency, specificity, and correlates of negative emotions. *Journal of Personality and Social Psychology* 68 (2): 342–52.

Berkowitz, L. 2003. Affect, aggression, and anti-social behavior. In *Handbook of affective sciences*, ed. R. J. Davidson, K. R. Scherer, and H. H. Goldsmith. New York: Oxford University Press.

Berkowitz, L., and E. Harmon-Jones. 2004. Towards an understanding of the determinants of anger. *Emotion* 4:107–30.

Biocca, Frank. 1991. The role of communication codes in political ads. In *Television and political advertising: Signs, codes, and images*, ed. Frank Biocca, 2:27–43. Hillsdale, NJ: Erlbaum.

Bird, C. M., F. Castelli, O. Malik, U. Frith, and M. Husain. 2004. The impact of extensive medial frontal lobe damage on "theory of mind" and cognition. *Brain* 127 (pt. 4): 914–28.

Blair, R. J., J. S. Morris, C. D. Frith, D. I. Perrett, and R. J. Dolan. 1999. Dissociable neural responses to facial expressions of sadness and anger. *Brain* 122 (pt. 5): 883–93.

Blakeslee, Sandra. 2006. Cells that read minds. *New York Times*, 10 January 2006, 1.

Bless, Herbert. 2001a. The consequences of mood on the processing of social information. In *Blackwell handbook of social psychology: Intraindividual processes*, ed. Abraham Tesser and Norbert Schwarz, 391–412. Malden, MA: Blackwell.

———. 2001b. Mood and the use of general knowledge structures. In *Theories of mood and cognition: A user's handbook*, ed. L. L. Martin and G. L. Clore. Mahwah, NJ: Erlbaum.

Bless, H., D. M. Mackie, and N. Schwarz. 1992. Mood effects on attitude judgments: Independent effects of mood before and after message elaboration. *Journal of Personality and Social Psychology* 63 (4): 585–95.

Blight, James G. 1990. *The shattered crystal ball: Fear and learning in the Cuban Missile Crisis.* Savage, MD: Rowman & Littlefield.

Bodenhausen, G., L. A. Sheppard, and G. P. Kramer. 1994. Negative affect and social judgment: The differential impact of anger and sadness. *European Journal of Social Psychology* 24:45–62.

Bower, David H. 1988. Anxiety and its disorders: The nature and treatment of anxiety and panic. New York: Guilford.

Bower, G. H. 1991. Mood congruity of social judgments. In *Emotion and social judgments*, ed. J. P. Forgas. Oxford: Pergamon.

Bower, G. H., and J. P. Forgas. 2001. Mood and social memory. In *Handbook of affect and social cognition*, ed. J. P. Forgas, 95–120. Mahwah, NJ: Erlbaum.

Boyd, R., H. Gintis, S. Bowles, and P. J. Richerson. 2003. The evolution of altruistic punishment. *Proceedings of the National Academy of Science USA* 100 (6): 3531–35.

Brader, Ted. 2005. Striking a responsive chord: How political ads motivate and persuade voters by appealing to emotions. *American Journal of Political Science* 49(2): 388–405.

———. 2006. *Campaigning for hearts and minds: How emotional appeals in political ads work*. Chicago: University of Chicago Press.

Brader, Ted, and Nicholas A. Valentino. 2005. Emotions, identities, and the activation of stereotypes in response to immigration threats. Paper presented at the annual meeting of the International Society of Political Psychology, Toronto.

Brader, Ted, Nicholas A. Valentino, and Elizabeth Suhay. 2004. Seeing threats versus feeling threats: Group cues, emotions, and activating opposition to immigration. Paper presented to the annual meeting of the American Political Science Association, Chicago.

Bradley, Margaret M. 2000. Emotion and motivation. In *Handbook of psychophysiology*, 2d ed., ed. John T. Cacioppo, Louis G. Tassinary, and Gary G. Berntson, 602–42. Cambridge: Cambridge University Press.

Bradley, Margaret, M. Codispoti, B. N. Cuthbert, and P. J. Lang. 2001. Emotion and motivation I: Defensive and appetitive reactions in picture processing. *Emotion* 1:276–98.

Bradley, Samuel D. 2004. Decoupling pacing and information: An embodied, dynamic account of visual perception and memory. Paper presented at the International Communication Association Convention.

Brady, Henry E., and Paul Sniderman. 1985. Attitude attribution: A group basis for political reasoning. *American Political Science Review* 79:1061–78.

Breiter, H. C., R. L. Gollub, R. M. Weisskoff, D. N. Kennedy, N. Makris, J. D. Berke, J. M. Goodman, H. L. Kantor, D. R. Gastfriend, J. P. Riorden, R. T. Mathew, B. R. Rosen, and S. E. Hyman. 1997. Acute effects of cocaine on human brain activity and emotion. *Neuron* 19 (3): 591–611.

Breznitz, Shlomo. 1986. The effect of hope on coping with stress. In *Dynamics of stress: Physiological and social perspectives*, ed. Mortimer Appley and Richard Trumbull, 295–306. New York: Plenum.

Broadbent, D. E. 1971. *Decision and stress*. London: Academic.

Broca, P. M. 1999/[1861]. [The discovery of cerebral localization]. *Review of Prat* 49 (16): 1725–27.

Brosnan, S. F., and F. B. De Waal. 2003. Monkeys reject unequal pay. *Nature* 425 (6955): 297–99.

Brothers, Leslie. 1999. Emotion and the human brain. In *MIT Encyclopedia of the cognitive sciences*, ed. Robert A. Wilson and Frank C. Kiel, 271–73. Cambridge: MIT Press.

Bruner, Jerome S., and L. Postman. 1947. Emotional selectivity in perception and reaction. *Journal of Personality* 16:69–77.

Brunet, E., Y. Sarfati, M. C. Hardy-Bayle, and J. Decety. 2000. A PET investigation of the attribution of intentions with a nonverbal task. *Neuroimage* 11 (2): 157–66.

Bueno de Mesquita, Bruce, and Rose McDermott. 2004. Crossing no man's land: Cooperation from the trenches. *Political Psychology* 25 (2): 271–87.

Burdick, Eugene. 1956. *The ninth wave.* Boston: Houghton Mifflin.

Burnham, Walter Dean. 1970. *Critical elections and the mainsprings of democracy.* New York: Norton.

———. 1980. The appearance and disappearance of the American voter. In *Electoral participation: A comparative analysis,* ed R. Rose. Beverly Hills, CA: Sage.

Burns, Peter, and James G. Gimpel. 2000. Economic insecurity, prejudicial stereotypes, and public opinion on immigration policy. *Political Science Quarterly* 115 (2): 201–25.

Butler, G., and A. Mathews. 1987. Anticipatory anxiety and risk perception. *Cognitive Therapy and Research* 11:551–55.

Byrne, R. W. 1995. *The thinking ape: Evolutionary origins of intelligence.* Oxford: Oxford University Press.

Byrne, R. W., P. J. Barnard, I. Davidson, V. M. Janik, W. C. McGrew, A. Miklosi, and P. Wiessner. 2004. Understanding culture across species. *Trends in Cognitive Science* 8 (8): 341–46.

Byrne, R. W., and A. Whiten. 1988. *Machiavellian intelligence: Social expertise and the evolution of intellect in monkeys, apes, and humans.* Oxford: Oxford University Press.

Cacioppo, John T., and Gary G. Berntson. 1994. Relationship between attitudes and evaluative space: A critical review with emphasis on the separability of positive and negative substrates. *Psychological Bulletin* 115:401–23.

Cacioppo, John T., Gary G. Berntson, Tyler S. Lorig, Catherine J. Norris, Edith Rickett, and Howard Nusbaum. 2003. Just because you're imaging the brain doesn't mean you can stop using your head: A primer and set of first principles. *Journal of Personality and Social Psychology* 85 (4): 650–61.

Cacioppo, John T., Gary G. Berntson, John F. Sheridan, and Martha M. McClintock. 2000. Multilevel integrative analyses of human behavior: Social neuroscience and the complementing nature of social and biological approaches. *Psychological Bulletin* 126 (6): 829–43.

Cacioppo, J. T., and Wendi L. Gardner. 1999. Emotion. *Annual Review of Psychology* 50:191–214.

Cacioppo, John T., Wendi Gardner, and Gary G. Berntson. 1997. Beyond bipolar conceptualizations and measures: The case of attitudes and evaluative space. *Personality and Social Psychology Review* 1 (1): 3–25.

———. 1999. The affect system has parallel and integrative processing components: Form follows function. *Journal of Personality and Social Psychology* 76 (5): 839–55.

Cacioppo , John T., and Penny S. Visser. 2003. Political psychology and social neuroscience: Strange bedfellows or comrades in arms? *Political Psychology* 24 (4): 647–56.

Caesar, K., K. Thomsen, and M. Lauritzen. 2003. Dissociation of spikes, synaptic activity, and activity-dependent increments in rat cerebellar blood flow by tonic synaptic inhibition. *Proceedings of the National Academy of Science USA* 100 (26): 16000–16005.

Cage, John. 1961. *Silence: Lectures and writings.* Middletown, CT: Wesleyan University Press.

Calder, A. J., J. Keane, F. Manes, N. Antoun, and A. W. Young. 2000. Impaired recognition and experience of disgust following brain injury. *National Neuroscience* 3 (11): 1077–8.

Caldwell, Deborah. 2004. Evangelical general apparently linked to Iraqi prison abuse. Religion News Service, 28 May. www.baptiststandard.com (accessed July 19, 2006).

Calhoun, C., and R. C. Solomon, eds. 1984. *What is emotion? Classic readings in philosophical psychology*. New York: Oxford University Press.

Camerer, C. F. 2003. Psychology and economics: Strategizing in the brain. *Science* 300 (5626): 1673–75.

Campbell, Angus, Philip Converse, Warren Miller, and Donald Stokes. 1960. *The American voter*. New York: John Wiley.

Campbell, David E. 2004. Acts of faith: Churches and political engagement. *Political Behavior* 26 (2): 155–80.

Carmines, Edward G., and James A. Stimson. 1989. *Issue evolution: Race and the transformation of American politics*. Princeton: Princeton University Press.

Carr, L., M. Iacoboni, M. C. Dubeau, J. C. Mazziotta, and G. L. Lenzi. 2003. Neural mechanisms of empathy in humans: A relay from neural systems for imitation to limbic areas. *Proceedings of the National Academy of Science USA* 100 (9): 5497–502.

Carver, Chalres S. 2004. Negative affects deriving from the behavioral approach system. *Emotion* 4 (1): 3–22.

Cassino, Dan. 2005. Standing water: The causes and consequences of affective intransitivity. PhD diss., Stony Brook University, Department of Political Science.

Chaiken, Shelly. 1980. Heuristic vs. systematic information processing and the use of source vs. message cues in persuasion. *Journal of Personality and Social Psychology* 39 (5): 752–66.

———. 1987. The heuristic model of persuasion. *Social influence: The Ontario symposium* 5:3–39. Hillsdale, NJ: Erlbaum.

Chaiken, Shelly, and Yaacov Trope. 1999. *Dual-process theories in social psychology*. New York: Guilford.

Chance, Michael R. A., and Allan P. Mead. 1953. Social behavior and primate evolution. Paper read at Symposia of the Society for Experimental Biology VII.

Churchland, Paul M. 1995. *The engine of reason, the seat of the soul: A philosophical journey into the brain*. Cambridge: MIT Press.

Cicero, Marcus Tullius. 2002. *Cicero on the emotions: Tusculan Disputations 3 and 4*. Trans. and with commentary by Margaret Graver. Chicago: University of Chicago Press.

Citrin, Jack, and Donald P. Green. 1990. The self-interest motive in American public opinion. *Research in Micropolitics* 3:1–27.

Citrin, Jack, Donald P. Green, Christopher Muste, and Cara Wong. 1997. Public opinion toward immigration reform: The role of economic motivations. *Journal of Politics* 59 (3): 858–81.

Clore, G., and Centerbar, D. 2004. Analyzing anger: How to make people mad. *Emotion* 4:139–44.

Clore, Gerald L., and Andrew Ortony. 2000. Cognition in emotion: Always, sometimes, or never? In *Cognitive neurosciences of emotion*, ed. Richard D. Lane and Lynn Nadal, 24–61. New York: Oxford University Press.

Clore, G. L., R. S. Wyer, B. Dienes, K. Gasper, C. Gohm, and L. Isabel. 2001. Affective feelings as feedback: Some cognitive consequences. In *Theories of Mood and Cognition: A User's Handbook*, ed. L. L. Martin and G. L. Clore. Mahwah, NJ: Erlbaum.

Collins, A., and E. Loftus, E. 1975. A spreading activation theory of semantic processing. *Psychological Review* 82:407–28.

Collins, A., and M. Quillian. 1969. Retrieval time from semantic memory. *Journal of Verbal Learning and Verbal Behavior* 8:240–47.

Collins, Randall. 1998. *The sociology of philosophies: A global theory of intellectual change.* Cambridge: Harvard University Press.

Conger, Kimberly H., and John C. Green. 2002. Spreading out and digging in: Christian conservatives and state Republican parties. *Campaigns and Elections* 23 (1): 58–65.

Conover, Pamela Johnston, and Stanley Feldman. 1984. How people organize the political world: A schematic world. *American Journal of Political Science* 28 (1): 95–126.

———. 1986. Emotional reactions to the economy: I'm mad as hell and I'm not going to take it anymore. *American Journal of Political Science* 30:50–78.

Converse, Philip E. 1964. The nature of belief systems in mass publics. In *Ideology and Discontent*, ed. D. Apter. New York: Free Press.

———. 1966a. The concept of the normal vote. In *Elections and the political order*, ed. A. Campbell, P. E. Converse, W. E. Miller, and D. E. Stokes. New York: Wiley.

———. 1966b. Religion and politics: The 1960 election. In *Elections and the political order*, ed. A. Campbell, P. E. Converse, W. E. Miller, and D. E. Stokes, 96–124. New York: Wiley.

———. 1970. Attitudes and non-attitudes: Continuation of a dialogue. In *The quantitative analysis of social problems*, ed. E. F. Tufte. Reading, MA: Addison-Wesley.

———. 1975. Public opinion and voting behavior. In *Handbook of political science*, ed. F. I. Greenstein and N. Polsby. Reading, MA: Addison-Wesley.

Cornelius, Randolf R. 1996. *The science of emotion: Research and tradition in the psychology of emotions.* Upper Saddle River, NJ: Prentice-Hall.

Cosmides, Leda, and John Tooby. 2000. Evolutionary psychology and the emotions. In *Handbook of emotions*, 2d ed., ed. M. Lewis and J. Haviland-Jones. New York: Guilford.

———. 2002. Unraveling the enigma of human intelligence: Evolutionary psychology and the multimodular mind. In *The evolution of intelligence*, ed. R. J. Sternberg and J. C. Kaufman. Mahwah, NJ: Erlbaum.

———. 2004. Evolutionary pychology and the emotions. In *Handbook of emotions*, ed. M. Lewis and J. M. Haviland-Jones, 91–115. New York: Guilford.

Cottrell, Catherine A., and Steven L. Neuberg. 2005. Different emotional reactions to different groups: A sociofunctional threat–based approach to "prejudice." *Journal of Personality and Social Psychology* 88 (5): 770–89.

Crawford, Alan. 1980. *Thunder on the right.* New York: Pantheon.

Crigler, Ann, Marion Just, and Todd Belt. 2006. The three faces of negative campaigning: The democratic implications of attack ads, cynical news and fear-arousing messages. In *Feeling politics: Emotion in political information processing*, ed. David P. Redlawsk, 135–63. New York: Palgrave Macmillan.

Critchley, Hugo D., Rebecca Elliott, Christopher J. Mathias, and Raymond J. Dolan. 2000. Neural activity relating to generation and representation of galvanic skin conductance responses: A functional magnetic resonance imaging study. *Journal of Neuroscience* 20 (8): 3033–40.

Crivello, F., T. Schormann, N. Tzourio-Mazoyer, P. E. Roland, K. Zilles, and B. M. Mazoyer. 2002. Comparison of spatial normalization procedures and their impact on functional maps. *Human Brain Mapping* 16 (4): 228–50.

Damasio, Antonio R. 1994. *Descartes' error.* New York: Putnam.

———. 1996. The somatic marker hypothesis and the possible functions of the prefrontal cortex. *Philosophical Transactions of the Royal Society of London Bulletin for the Biological Sciences* 351:1413–20.

———. 1999. *The feeling of what happens: Body and emotion in the making of consciousness.* New York: Harcourt Brace.

———. 2003. *Looking for Spinoza: Joy, sorrow and the feeling brain.* New York: Harcourt.

Damasio, Antonio R., Anne Harrington, Jerome Kagan, Bruce S. McEwen, Henry Moss, and Rashid Shaikh, eds. 2001. *Unity of knowledge: The convergence of natural and human science.* Annals of the New York Academy of Sciences no. 935. New York: New York Academy of Sciences.

Dapretto, M., M. S. Davies, J. H. Pfeifer, A. A. Scott, M. Sigman, S. Y. Bookheimer, and M. Iacoboni. 2006. Understanding emotions in others: Mirror neuron dysfunction in children with autism spectrum disorders. *National Neuroscience* 9 (1): 28–30.

Darwin, Charles. 1996/[1859]. *The origin of species.* Edited by G. Beer. Oxford: Oxford University Press.

Davidson, R. J. 1995. Cerebral asymmetry, emotion and affective style. In *Brain asymmetry*, ed. R. J. Davidson and K. Hugdahl, 361–87. Cambridge: MIT Press.

———. 2003. Seven sins in the study of emotion: Correctives from affective neuroscience. *Brain and Cognition* 51:129–32.

Davidson, Richard J., Darren C. Jackson, and Ned H. Kalin. 2000. Emotion, plasticity, context, and regulation: Perspectives from affective neuroscience. *Psychological Bulletin* 126 (6): 890–909.

de Quervain, D. J., U. Fischbacher, V. Treyer, M. Schellhammer, U. Schnyder, A. Buck, and E. Fehr. 2004. The neural basis of altruistic punishment. *Science* 305 (5688): 1254–58.

de Waal, F. B. M. 1998. *Chimpanzee politics: Power and sex among apes.* Rev. ed. Baltimore: Johns Hopkins University Press.

Deacon, Terrence William. 1997. *The symbolic species : The co-evolution of language and the brain.* New York: Norton.

Delli Carpini, M. X., and S. Keeter. 1993. Measuring political knowledge: Putting first things first. *American Journal of Political Science* 37:1179–1206.

———. 1996. *What Americans know about politics and why it matters.* New Haven: Yale University Press.

Dennett, Daniel Clement. 1987. *The intentional stance.* Cambridge: MIT Press.

———. 2003. *Freedom evolves.* New York: Viking.

Derryberry, D. 1991. The immediate effects of positive and negative feedback signals. *Journal of Personality and Social Psychology* 61:267–78.

Descartes, Rene. 1979. *Meditations on first philosophy: In which the existence of God and the distinction of the soul from the body are demonstrated.* Trans. Donald A. Cress. Indianapolis: Hackett.

———. 1983. *Principles of philosophy.* Trans. with explanatory notes by Valentine Rodger Miller and Reese P. Miller. Boston: Distributed by Kluwer Boston.

———. 1989/[1649]. *The passions of the soul.* Trans. Stephen Voss. Indianapolis: Hackett.

Deutsch, Morton, and Harold B. Gerard. 1955. A study of normative and informational social influences upon individual judgment. *Journal of Abnormal and Social Psychology* 51 (3): 629–36.

Devine, P. G. 1989. Stereotypes and prejudice: Their automatic and controlled components. *Journal of Personality and Social Psychology* 56:1–13.

Dillard, James Price, and Eugenia Peck. 2000. Affect and persuasion: Emotional responses to public service announcements. *Communication Research* 27(4): 461–91.

Dimberg, U., M. Thunberg, and K. Elmehed. 2000. Unconscious facial reactions to emotional facial expressions. *Psychological Science* 11 (1): 86–89.

Dolan, R. J. 2002. Emotion, cognition, and behavior. *Science* 298: 1191–94.

Dovidio, John F., Kerry Kawakami, Craig Johnson, Brenda Johnson, and Adaiah Howard. 1997. On the nature of prejudice: Automatic and controlled processes. *Journal of Experimental Social Psychology* 33 (5): 510–40.

Downs, Anthony. 1957. *An economic theory of democracy.* New York: Harper and Row.

Druckman, James. 2001. The implications of framing effects for citizen competence. *Political Behavior* 23:225–56.

Druckman, James, and Kjersten Nelson. 2003. Framing and deliberation: How citizens' conversations limit elite influence. *American Journal of Political Science* 47: 729–45.

Dumont, Muriel, Vincent Yzerbyt, Daniel Wigboldus, and Ernestine H. Gordijn. 2003. Social categorization and fear reactions to the September 11th terorist atacks. *Personality and Social Psychology Bulletin* 29 (12): 1509–20.

Dunbar, R. I. M. 1993. Co-evolution of neocortical size, group size and langugage in humans. *Behavioral and Brain Sciences* 16 (4): 681–735.

Easterbrook, J. A. 1959. The effect of emotion on cue utilization and the organization of behavior. *Psychological Review* 66 (3): 183–201.

Edelman, Murray. 1964. *The symbolic uses of politics.* Urbana: University of Illinois Press.

Edsall, Thomas B. 1991. *Chain reaction: The impact of race, rights, and taxes on American politics.* New York: Norton.

Ekman, Paul, ed. 1982. *Emotions in the human face.* 2d ed. New York: Cambridge University Press.

———. 1992. An argument for basic emotions. *Cognition and Emotion* 6:169–200.

Ekman, Paul, and Richard J. Davidson. 1994. *The nature of emotion: Fundamental questions.* New York: Oxford University Press.

Ekman, Paul, and Friesen, Walt. 1971. Constants across cultures in the face and emotion. *Journal of Personality and Social Psychology* 17:124–29.

——— 1986. A new pan-cultural facial expression of emotion. *Motivation and Emotion* 10:159–68.

Ekman, Paul, and Erika Rosenberg, eds. 2005. *What the face reveals: Basic and applied studies of spontaneous expression using the facial action coding system (FACS).* 2d ed. New York: Oxford University Press.

Ekman, Paul, and Klaus Scherer. 1984. *Approaches to emotion.* Mahwah, NJ: Erlbaum.

Elder, Charles D., and Roger W. Cobb. 1983. *The political uses of symbols.* Ed. J. B. Mannheim. New York: Longman.

Elias, Norbert. 1939. *The history of manners.* New York: Pantheon.

Ellsworth, Phoebe C., and Klaus R. Scherer. 2003. Appraisal processes in emotion. In *Handbook of Affective Sciences*, ed. Richard J. Davidson, Klaus R. Scherer, and H. Hill Goldsmith. Oxford: Oxford University Press.

Elster, Jon. 2000. "Rational Choice History: A Case of Excessive Ambition." *American Political Science Review* 94:685–95.

Entman, Robert M. 1993. Framing: Toward clarification of a fractured paradigm. *Journal of Communication.* 43 (4): 51–58.

Erdelyi, M. H. 1974. A new look at the new look: Perceptual defense and vigilance. *Psychological Review* 81 (1): 1–25.

Erikson, Robert S., Michael MacKuen, and James A. Stimson. 2002. *The macro polity.* New York: Cambridge University Press.

Eysenck, M. W. 1992. *Anxiety: The cognitive perspective.* London: Erlbaum.

Eysenck, M. W., K. Mogg, J. May, A. Richards, and A. Mathews. 1991. Bias in the interpretation of ambiguous sentences related to threat in anxiety. *Journal of Abnormal Psychology* 100:144–50.

Fazio, R. 2001. On the automatic activation of associated evaluations: An overview. *Cognition and Emotion* 15:115–41.

Fazio, R., and Michael A. Olson. 2003. Implicit measures in social cognition research: Their meaning and use. *Annual Review of Psychology* 54:297–27.

Fazio, R., D. Sanbonmatsu, M. Powell, and F. Kardes 1986. On the automatic activation of attitudes. *Journal of Personality and Social Psychology* 50:229–38.

Feldman, Stanley. 2003. Values, ideology, and the structure of political attitudes. In *Oxford handbook of political psychology*, ed. D. O. Sears, L. Huddy, and R. Jervis. New York: Oxford University Press.

Feldman, Stanley, and Huddy, Leonie. 2005. The paradoxical effects of anxiety on political learning. Paper presented at the annual meeting of the Midwest Political Science Association, Chicago.

Feldman, Stanley, and Karen Stenner. 1997. Perceived threat and authoritarianism. *Political Psychology* 18(4): 741–70.

Feldman Barrett, Lisa, Michele M. Tugage, and Randall W. Engle. 2004. Individual differences in working memory capacity and dual-process theories of the mind. *Psychological Bulletin* 130 (4): 553–73.

Ferrari, P. F., V. Gallese, G. Rizzolatti, and L. Fogassi. 2003. Mirror neurons responding to the observation of ingestive and communicative mouth actions in the monkey ventral premotor cortex. *European Journal of Neuroscience* 17 (8): 1703–14.

Festinger, L. 1957. *A theory of cognitive dissonance.* Stanford: Stanford University Press.

Fetzer, Joel S. 2000. *Public attitudes toward immigration in the United States, France, and Germany.* New York: Cambridge University Press.

Fiorina, Morris P. 1981. *Retrospective voting in American national elections.* New Haven: Yale University Press.

Fiske, S. 1981. Social cognition and affect. In *Cognition, social behavior, and the environment*, ed. James Harvey, 227–64. Hillsdale, NJ: Erlbaum.

Fiske, S., and M. Pavelchak. 1986. Category versus piecemeal-based affective responses: Developments in schema-triggered affect. In *Handbook of motivation and cognition*, ed. E. Higgins, 167–203. New York: Guilford.

Fiske, S., and S. E. Taylor. 1991. *Social cognition.* New York: McGraw-Hill.

Fletcher, P. C., F. Happe, U. Frith, S. C. Baker, R. J. Dolan, R. S. Frackowiak, and C. D. Frith. 1995. Other minds in the brain: A functional imaging study of "theory of mind" in story comprehension. *Cognition* 57 (2): 109–28.

Ford, J. K., N. Schmitt, S. L Schechtman, B. M. Hults, and M. L. Doherty. 1989. Process tracing methods: Contributions, problems, and neglected research questions. *Organizational Behavior and Human Decision Processes*, 43:75–117.

Forgas, J. P. 1994. The role of emotion in social judgment: An introductory review and an affect infusion model (AIM). *European Journal of Social Psychology* 24:1–24.

———. 1995. Mood and judgment: The affect infusion model (AIM). *Psychological Bulletin* 117:39–66.

———, ed. 2000. *Feeling and thinking: The role of affect in social cognition.* Cambridge: Cambridge University Press.

Forgas, J. P., and J. C. Forster. 1987. After the movies: Transient mood on social judgments. *Personality and Social Psychology Bulletin* 13:467–77.

Fox, E. 1993. Attentional bias in anxiety: Adaptive or not? *Behaviour Research and Therapy* 31:487–93.

Frank, Robert. 1989. *Passions within reason.* New York: Norton.

Fredrickson, Barbara L. 2003. The value of positive emotions. *American Scientist* 91:330–35.

Fredrickson, Barbara L., and Christine Branigan. 2001. Positive emotions. In *Emotions: Current issues and future directions*, ed. Tracy J. Mayne and George Bonanno, 123–51. New York: Guilford.

Fridman, E. A., T. Hanakawa, M. Chung, F. Hummel, R. C. Leiguarda, and L. G. Cohen. 2004. Reorganization of the human ipsilesional premotor cortex after stroke. *Brain* 127 (pt. 4): 747–58.

Frijda, Nico H. 2004. The psychologists' point of view. In *Handbook of emotions*, ed. M. Lewis and J. M. Haviland-Jones, 59–74. New York: Guilford.

Frijda, Nico H., Peter Kuipers, and Elisabeth ter Schure. 1989. Relations among emotion, appraisal, and emotional action readiness. *Journal of Personality and Social Psychology* 57:212–28.

Frith, C. 2002. Attention to action and awareness of other minds. *Conscious Cognition* 11 (4): 481–87.

———. 2003. What do imaging studies tell us about the neural basis of autism? *Novartis Foundation Symposia* 251:149–66; discussion 166–76, 281–97.

Frith, C., and U. Frith. 1999. Interacting minds—a biological basis. *Science* 286:1692–95.

Frohlich, Norman, and Joe Oppenheimer. 2000. How people reason about ethics. In *Elements of reason: Cognition, choice, and the bounds of rationality*, ed. Arthur Lupia, Samuel L. Popkin, and Mathew D. McCubbins, 85–107. New York: Cambridge University Press.

Fromm, Eric. 1968. *The revolution of hope: Toward a humanized technology.* New York: Harper and Row.

Gallagher, H. L., A. I. Jack, A. Roepstorff, and C. D. Frith. 2002. Imaging the intentional stance in a competitive game. *Neuroimage* 16 (3, pt. 1): 814–21.

Gallese, V., L. Fadiga, L. Fogassi, and G. Rizzolatti. 1996. Action recognition in the premotor cortex. *Brain* 119 (pt. 2): 593–609.

Gallese, V., and A. Goldman. 1998. Mirror neurons and the simulation theory of mind reading. *Trends in Cognitive Science* 2 (12): 493–501.

Gallese, V., C. Keysers, and G. Rizzolatti. 2004. A unifying view of the basis of social cognition. *Trends in Cognitive Science* 8 (9): 396–403.

Garramone, Gina. 1984. Voter response to negative political ads. *Journalism Quarterly* 61:250–59.

Gazzaniga, M. S. 1985. *The social brain: Discovering the networks of the mind.* New York: Basic.

———. 1992. *Nature's mind: The biological roots of thinking, emotions, sexuality, language and intelligence.* Harmondsworth: Penguin.

Gazzaniga, M. S., R. B. Ivry, and G. R. Mangun. 1998. *Cognitive neuroscience: The biology of the mind.* New York: Norton.

Gervey, B. M., C. Chiu, Y. Hong, and C. S. Dweck. 1999. Implicit theories: The impact of personal information on decision-making. *Personality and Social Psychology Bulletin* 25:17–27.

Gibson, Rhonda, and Dolf Zillmann. 1998. Effects of citation in exemplifying testimony on issue perception. *Journalism and Mass Communication Quarterly* 75:167–76.

Gigerenzer, G. 1994. Why the distinction between single-event probabilities and frequencies is important for psychology (and vice versa). In *Subjective probability,* ed. G. Wright and P. Ayton. New York: Wiley.

———. 1997. The modularity of social intelligence. In *Machiavellian intelligence II: Extensions and evaluations,* ed A. Whiten and R. W. Byrne. Cambridge: Cambridge University Press.

Gigerenzer, G., and R. Selten, eds. 2002. *Bounded rationality: The adaptive toolbox.* Cambridge: MIT Press.

Gintis, H. 2000. Strong reciprocity and human sociality. *Journal of Theoretical Biology* 206 (2): 169–79.

———. 2003. The hitchhiker's guide to altruism: Gene-culture coevolution and the internalization of norms. *Journal of Theoretical Biology* 220 (4): 407–18.

Gladwell, Malcolm. 2005. *Blink: The power of thinking without thinking.* New York: Little, Brown.

Glimcher, Paul W. 2003. *Decisions, uncertainty, and the brain.* Cambridge: MIT Press.

Goel, V., and R. J. Dolan. 2003. Reciprocal neural response within lateral and ventral medial prefrontal cortex during hot and cold reasoning. *Neuroimage* 20 (4): 2314–21.

Golding, J. M., S. B. Fowler, D. L. Long, and H. Latta. 1990. Instructions to disregard potentially useful information: The effects of pragmatics on evaluative judgments and recall. *Journal of Memory and Language* 29:212–27.

Goleman, Daniel. 1995. *Emotional intelligence.* New York: Bantam.

Graber, Doris A. 1993. *Processing the news: How people tame the information tide.* Lanham, MD: University Press of America.

———. 2001. *Processing politics: Learning from television in the internet age.* Chicago: University of Chicago Press.

Granberg, Donald, and Thad A. Brown. 1989. On affect and cognition in politics. *Social Psychology Quarterly* 52:171–82.

Gray, Jeffrey A. 1987a. Perspectives on anxiety and impulsivity: A commentary. *Journal of Research in Personality* 21: 493–509.

———. 1987b. *The psychology of fear and stress.* 2d ed. Cambridge: Cambridge University Press.

———. 1994. Three fundamental emotion systems. In *The nature of emotion: Fundamental questions,* ed. Paul Ekman and Richard J. Davidson, 243–47. New York: Oxford University Press.

Green, Donald Philip, Susan Lee Goldman, and Peter Salovey. 1993. Measurement error masks bipolarity in affect ratings. *Journal of Personality and Social Psychology* 64 (6): 1029–41.

Green, J. B. 2003. Brain reorganization after stroke. *Topics in Stroke Rehabilitation* 10 (3): 1–20.

Green, John C., James L. Guth, Corwin E. Smidt, and Lyman A. Kellstedt. 1996. *Religion and the culture wars: Dispatches from the front*. Lanham, MD: Rowman and Littlefield.

Greene, J. 2003. From neural "is" to moral "ought": What are the moral implications of neuroscientific moral psychology? *National Review of Neuroscience* 4 (10): 846–9.

Greene, J. D., R. B. Sommerville, L. E. Nystrom, J. M. Darley, and J. D. Cohen. 2001. An fMRI investigation of emotional engagement in moral judgment. *Science* 293 (5537): 2105–8.

Greenspan, Patricia S. 1988. *Emotions and reasons: An inquiry into emotional justification*. New York: Routledge.

Greicius, M. D., G. Srivastava, A. L. Reiss, and V. Menon. 2004. Default-mode network activity distinguishes Alzheimer's disease from healthy aging: Evidence from functional MRI. *Proceedings of the National Academy of Science USA* 101 (13): 4637–42.

Griffiths, Paul E. 1997. *What emotions really are*. Chicago: University of Chicago Press.

Groopman, Jerome. 2004. *The anatomy of hope: How people prevail in the face of illness*. New York: Random House.

Gunderson, Keith. 1985. *Mentality and machines*. 2d ed. Minneapolis: University of Minnesota.

Gusnard, D. A., E. Akbudak, G. L. Shulman, and M. E. Raichle. 2001. Medial prefrontal cortex and self-referential mental activity: Relation to a default mode of brain function. *Proceedings of the National Academy of Science USA* 98 (7): 4259–64.

Gusnard, D. A., and M. E. Raichle. 2001. Searching for a baseline: Functional imaging and the resting human brain. *National Review of Neuroscience* 2 (10): 685–94.

Hacking, Ian. 1999. *The social construction of what?* Cambridge: Harvard University Press.

Hamilton, Edith, and Huntingon Cairns, eds. 1963. *Plato: The collected dialogues*. Princeton: Princeton University Press.

Happe, F., S. Ehlers, P. Fletcher, U. Frith, M. Johansson, C. Gillberg, R. Dolan, R. Frackowiak, and C. Frith. 1996. "Theory of mind" in the brain: Evidence from a PET scan study of Asperger syndrome. *Neuroreport* 8 (1): 197–201.

Harmon-Jones, E., and J. J. B. Allen. 1998. Anger and frontal brain activity: Asymmetry consistent with approach motivation despite negative affective valence. *Journal of Personality and Social Psychology* 74:1310–16.

Harmon-Jones, E., and J. Sigelman. 2001. State anger and prefrontal brain activity: Evidence that insult-related relative left-prefrontal activation is associated with experienced anger and aggression. *Journal of Personality and Social Psychology* 80 (5): 797–803.

Harnad, Stevan. 1990. The symbol grounding problem. *Physica D* 42: 335–46.

Harré, Rom, ed. 1987. *The social construction of emotions*. Malden, MA: Blackwell.

Harré, Rom, and Grant Gillett. 1994. *The discursive mind*. Thousand Oaks, CA: Sage.

Hauser, Marc. 1996. *The evolution of communication*. Cambridge: MIT Press.

Heilman, K. M. 1997. The neurobiology of emotional experience. *Journal of Neuropsychiatry and Clinical Neuroscience* 9 (3): 439–48.

Heims, H. C., H. D. Critchley, R. Dolan, C. J. Mathias, and L. Cipolotti. 2004. Social and motivational functioning is not critically dependent on feedback of autonomic responses: Neuropsychological evidence from patients with pure autonomic failure. *Neuropsychologia* 42 (14): 1979–88.

Henrich, Joseph, Robert Boyd, Sam Bowles, Colin Camerer, Herbert Gintis, Richard McElreath, and Enst Ferh. 2001. In search of Homo economicus: Experiments in 15 small-scale societies. *American Economic Review* 91 (2): 73–79.

Hermans, D., J. De Houwer, and P. Eelen. 1994. The affective priming effect: Automatic activation of evaluative information in memory. *Cognition and Emotion* 8:515–33.

Herstein, J. A. 1981. Keeping the voter's limits in mind: A cognitive process analysis of decision making in voting. *Journal of Personality and Social Psychology* 40:843–61.

Hess Report. 2000. "Week 9" (October). http://www.brookings.org/GS/Projects/Hessreport/week10.htm.

Heyes, C. M. 1998. Theory of mind in nonhuman primates. *Behavioral and Brain Sciences* 21 (1): 101–14; discussion 115–48.

Hilgard, E. R. 1980. The trilogy of mind: Cognition, affection, and conation. *Journal of the History of the Behavioral Sciences* 16:107–17.

Hobbes, Thomas. 1991/[1651]. *Leviathan*. New York: Cambridge University Press.

Hochschild, Jennifer L. 1981. *What's fair? American beliefs about distributive justice*. Cambridge: Harvard University Press.

Holland, John H. 1995. *Hidden order: How adaptation builds complexity*. New York: Addison-Wesley.

———. 1998. *Emergence: From chaos to order*. Reading, MA: Perseus.

Holloway, M. 2003. The mutable brain. *Scientific American* 289 (3): 78–85.

Huang, Li-Ning. 2000. Examining candidate information search processes: The impact of processing goals and sophistication. *Journal of Communication* 50 (Winter): 93–114.

Huang, Li-Ning, and Vincent Price. 1998. Motivations, information search, and memory structure about political candidates. Paper presented at International Communication Association annual conference, Jerusalem.

Huckfeldt, Robert, P. E. Johnson, and John D. Sprague. 2004. *Political disagreement: The survival of diverse opinions within communication networks*. Cambridge: Cambridge University Press.

Huckfeldt, Robert, Eric Plutzer, and John C. Sprague. 1993. Alternative contexts of political behavior: Churches, neighborhoods, and individuals. *Journal of Politics* 55 (2): 365–81.

Huddy, Leonie, Stanley Feldman, Theresa Capelos, and Colin Provost. 2002. The consequences of terrorism: Disentangling the effects of personal and national threat. *Political Psychology* 23:485–509.

Huddy, Leonie, Stanley Feldman, Charles Taber, and Gallya Lahav. 2005. Threat, anxiety, and support of anti-terrorism policies. *American Journal of Political Science* 3:610–25.

Huddy, Leonie, and Anna H. Gunnthorsdottir. 2000. The persuasive effects of emotive visual imagery: Superficial manipulation or the product of passionate reason? *Political Psychology* 21 (4): 745–78.

Hume, David. 1993/[1776]. *Essays moral, political, and literary*. New York: Oxford University Press.

———. 1998/[1751]. *An enquiry concerning the principles of morals*. New York: Oxford University Press.

———. 2000/[1739]. *A treatise of human nature*. New York: Oxford University Press.

Humphrey, Nicolas K. 1976. The social function of intellect. In *Growing points in ethology*, ed. P. P. G. Bateson and R. A. Hinde. Cambridge: Cambridge University Press.

Hunter, James Davison. 1991. *Culture wars: The struggle to define America*. New York: Basic.

Hutchings, Vincent L., Nicholas A. Valentino, Tasha S. Philpot, and Ismail K. White. 2006. Racial cues in campaign news: The effects of candidate issue distance on emotional responses, political attentiveness, and vote choice. In *Feeling Politics*, ed. David Redlawsk, 165–86. New York: Palgrave Macmillan.

Iacoboni, Marco, Matthew D. Lieberman, Barbara J. Knowlton, Istvan Molnar-Szakacs, Mark Moritz, C. Jason Throop, and Alan Page Fiske. 2004. Watching social interactions produces dorsomedial prefrontal and medial parietal BOLD fMRI signal increases compared to a resting baseline. *Neuroimage* 21 (3): 1167–73.

Innes-Ker, Åse, and Paula M. Niedenthal. 2002. Emotion concepts and emotional states in social judgment and categorization. *Journal of Personality and Social Psychology* 83 (4): 804–16.

Isbell, Linda M., and Victor C. Ottati. 2002. The emotional voter: Effects of episodic affective reactions on candidate evaluations. In *The Social Psychology of Politics*, ed. Victor C. Ottati et al., 55–74. New York: Kluwer.

Isen, Alice 2000. Positive affect and decision making. In *Handbook of emotions*, 2d ed., ed. Michael Lewis and Jeannette M. Haveland-Jones, 417–35. New York: Guilford.

Iyengar, Shanto. 1991. *Is anyone responsible? How television frames political issues*. Chicago: University of Chicago Press.

Iyengar, Shanto, and Donald Kinder. 1987. *News that matters: Television and American public opinion*. Chicago: University of Chicago Press.

Izard, C. 1971. *The face of emotion*. New York: Appleton-Century-Crofts.

Izard, C., and S. Buechler. 1980. Aspects of consciousness and personality in terms of differential emotions theory. In *Emotion: Theory, research, and experience*, vol. 1, *Theories of emotion*, ed. R. Plutchik and H. Kellerman, 165–87. New York: Academic Press.

Jackson, James S., Kendrick T. Brown, Tony N. Brown, and Bryant Marks. 2001. Contemporary immigration policy orientations among dominant-group members in Western Europe. *Journal of Social Issues* 57(3): 431–56.

Jacoby, J., J. Jaccard, A. Kuss, T. Troutman, and D. Mazursky. 1987. New directions in behavioral process research: Implications for social psychology. *Journal of Experimental Social Psychology* 23:146–75.

Jacoby, William G. 1995. The structure of ideological thinking in the American electorate. *American Journal of Political Science* 39 (2): 314–35.

———. 2006. Value choices and American public opinion. *American Journal of Political Science* 50:706–23.

Jamieson, Kathleen Hall, and Paul Waldman. 2003. *The press effect: Politicians, journalists, and the stories that shape the political world*. New York: Oxford University Press.

Judd, C. M., and J. A. Krosnick. 1989. The structural bases of consistency among political attitudes: The effects of political expertise and attitude importance. In *Attitude structure and function*, ed. A. R. Pratkanis, S. J. Breckler, and A. G. Greenwald, 99–128. Mahwah, NJ: Erlbaum.

Just, Marion R., A. Crigler, D. Alger, T. Cook, M. Kern, and D. West. 1996. *Crosstalk: Citizens, candidates, and the media in a presidential campaign*. Chicago: University of Chicago Press.

Just, Marion, A. Crigler, and T. Buhr. 1999. Voice, substance, and cynicism in campaign media. *Political Communication* 16 (1): 25–44.

Kahneman, Daniel, Paul Slovic, and Amos Tversky. 1982. *Judgment under uncertainty: Heuristics and biases*. Cambridge: Cambridge University Press.

Kahneman, Daniel, and Amos. Tversky. 1973. On the psychology of prediction. *Psychological Review* 80:237–51.

———. 1979. Prospect theory: An analysis of decision under risk. *Econometrica* 47:263–91.

———. 1982. On the study of statistical intuitions. *Cognition* 11 (2): 123–41.

———. 1996. On the reality of cognitive illusions. *Psychology Review* 103 (3): 582–91; discussion 592–96.

Kandel, E. R., J. H. Schwartz, and T. M. Jessell. 1995. *Essentials of neural science and behavior*. Norwalk, CT: Appleton and Lange.

Karbe, H., A. Thiel, G. Weber-Luxenburger, K. Herholz, J. Kessler, and W. D. Heiss. 1998. Brain plasticity in poststroke aphasia: What is the contribution of the right hemisphere? *Brain and Language* 64 (2): 215–30.

Karpinski, A., R. B. Steinman, and J. L. Hilton. 2005. Attitude importance as a moderator of the relationship between implicit and explicit attitude measures. *Personality and Social Psychology Bulletin* 31 (7): 949–62.

Katz, Elihu, and Paul Felix Lazarsfeld. 1955. *Personal influence: The part played by people in the flow of mass communications*. Glencoe, IL: Free Press.

Keith, Bruce E., David B. Magleby, Candice Nelson, Elizabeth Orr, Mark C. Westlye, and Raymond Wolfinger. 1997. *The myth of the independent voter*. Berkeley: University of California Press.

Kelley, Harold H. 1967. Attribution in social psychology. *Nebraska Symposium on Motivation* 15:192–238.

Kelley, Stanley. 1983. *Interpreting elections*. Princeton: Princeton University Press.

Kelso, J. A. Scott. 1995. *Dynamic patterns: The self-organization of brain and behavior*. Cambridge: MIT Press.

Key, V. O. 1961. *Public opinion and American democracy*. New York: Knopf.

Key, V. O., and M. C. Cummings. 1966. *The responsible electorate: Rationality in presidential voting, 1936–1960*. New York: Vintage.

Kinder, Donald R. 1994. Reason and emotion in American political life. In *Beliefs, reasoning, and decision making*, ed. Roger Schank and Ellen Langer, 277–314. Mahwah, NJ: Erlbaum.

———. 1998. Opinion and action in the realm of politics. In *The handbook of social psychology*, 4th ed., ed. Daniel Gilbert, Susan Fiske, and Gardner Lindzey, 2:778–867. New York: McGraw-Hill.

———. 2003. Belief systems after Converse. In *Electoral democracy*, ed. Michael MacKuen and George Rabinowitz, 13–47. Ann Arbor: University of Michigan Press.

Kinder, Donald R., and Lisa D'Ambrosio. 2000. War, emotion, and public opinion. Unpublished manuscript, University of Michigan.

Kinder, Donald, and Lynn Sanders. 1990. Mimicking political debate with survey questions: The case of white opinion on affirmative action for blacks. *Social Cognition* 8:73–103.

———. 1996. *Divided by color*. Chicago: University of Chicago Press.

Knutson, B., C. M. Adams, G. W. Fong, and D. Hommer. 2001. Anticipation of increasing monetary reward selectively recruits nucleus accumbens. *Journal of Neuroscience* 21 (16): RC159.

Kohler, E., C. Keysers, M. A. Umilta, L. Fogassi, V. Gallese, and G. Rizzolatti. 2002. Hearing sounds, understanding actions: Action representation in mirror neurons. *Science* 297 (5582): 846–48.

Kosslyn, S. M., J. T. Cacioppo, R. J. Davidson, K. Hugdahl, W. R. Lovallo, D. Spiegel, and R. Rose. 2002. Bridging psychology and biology: The analysis of individuals in groups. *American Psychologiy* 57 (5): 341–51.

Kozhevnikov, M., and M. Hegarty. 2001. Impetus beliefs as default heuristics: Dissociation between explicit and implicit knowledge about motion. *Psychonomic Bulletin and Review* 8 (3): 439–53.

Krolak-Salmon, P., M. A. Henaff, J. Isnard, C. Tallon-Baudry, M. Guenot, A. Vighetto, O. Bertrand, and F. Mauguiere. 2003. An attention modulated response to disgust in human ventral anterior insula. *Annals of Neurology* 53 (4): 446–53.

Krosnick, J., and L. Brannon 1993. The media and the foundations of presidential support: George Bush and the Persian Gulf Conflict. *Journal of Social Issues* 49:167–82.

Krosnick, J., and D. Kinder. 1990. Altering the foundations of support for the president through priming. *American Political Science Review* 84:497–512.

Krosnick, J. A., et al. 1993. Attitude strength: One construct or many related constructs? *Journal of Personality and Social Psychology* 65 (6): 1132–51.

Kruglanski, A. W., and D. M. Webster. 1996. Motivated closing of the mind: Its cognitive and social effects. *Psychological Review* 103:263–83.

Kunda, Ziva. 1990. The case for motivated political reasoning. *Psychological Bulletin* 108(3): 480–98.

Kurzban, R., J. Tooby, and L. Cosmides. 2001. Can race be erased? Coalitional computation and social categorization. *Proceedings of the National Academy of Science USA* 98 (26): 15387–92.

Ladd, Everett C. 1978. *Where have all the voters gone?* New York: Norton.

Lakoff, George, and Mark Johnson. 1999. *Philosophy in the flesh: The Embodied mind and its challenge to Western thought.* New York: Basic.

Lanzetta, John T., D. Sullivan, R. Masters, and G. McHugo. 1985. Emotional and cognitive responses to televised images of political leaders." In *Mass media and political thought: An information-processing approach*, ed. Sidney Kraus and Richard M. Perloff, 85–116. Beverly Hills: Sage.

Larsen, J. T., C. J. Norris, and J. T. Cacioppo. 2003. Effects of positive and negative affect on electromyographic activity over *zygomaticus major* and *corrugator supercilii. Psychophysiology* 40 (5): 776–85.

Lasswell, Harold D., and Abraham Kaplan. 1950. *Power and society: A framework for political inquiry.* New Haven: Yale University Press.

Lau, Richard R. 1995. Information search during an election campaign: Introducing a process tracing methodology for political scientists. In *Political judgment: Structure and process*, ed. M. Lodge and K. McGraw, 179–206. Ann Arbor: University of Michigan Press.

Lau, Richard R., and David P. Redlawsk. 1997. Voting correctly. *American Political Science Review* 91 (September): 585–98.

———. 2001a. An experimental study of information search, memory, and decision-making during a political campaign. In *Citizens and politics: Perspectives from political psychology*, ed. James Kuklinski. New York: Cambridge University Press.

———. 2001b. Advantages and disadvantages of cognitive heuristics in political decision making. *American Journal of Political Science* 45 (October): 951–71.

———. 2006. *How voters decide: Information processing in a political campaign.* New York: Cambridge University Press.

Lauritzen, M. 2001. Relationship of spikes, synaptic activity, and local changes of cerebral blood flow. *Journal of Cerebral Blood Flow and Metabolism* 21 (12): 1367–83.

Layman, Geoffrey. 2001. *The great divide: Religious and cultural conflict in American party politics.* New York: Columbia University Press.

Lazarsfeld, Paul Felix, Bernard Berelson, and Hazel Gaudet. 1948. *The people's choice: How the voter makes up his mind in a presidential campaign.* [2d]. ed. New York: Columbia University Press.

Lazarus, C. E. 1993. Four systems for emotion activation: Cognitive and noncognitive processes. *Psychological Review* 100:68–90.

Lazarus, R. S. 1991a. Cognition and motivation in emotion. *American Psychology* 46 (4): 352–67.

———. 1991b. *Emotion and adaptation.* New York: Oxford University Press.

———. 1991c. Progress on a cognitive-motivational-relational theory of emotion. *American Psychology* 46 (8): 819–34.

———. 1999. The cognition-emotion debate: A bit of history. In *Handbook of cognition and emotion,* ed. Tim Dalgleish and Mick J. Power, 3–19. New York: Wiley.

———. 2001. Relational meaning and discrete emotions. In *Appraisal processes in emotion: Theory, methods, research,* ed. Klaus R. Scherer, Angela Schorr, and Tom Johnstone, 37–67. New York: Oxford University Press.

Lazarus, R., A. Kanner, and S. Folkman. 1980. Emotions: A cognitive-phenomenological analysis. In *Emotion: Theory, research, and experience,* vol. 1, *Theories of emotion,* ed. R. Plutchik and H. Kellerman, 189–217. New York: Academic.

Lazarus, Richard S., and Bernice N. Lazarus. 1994. *Passion and reason: Making sense of our emotions.* New York: Oxford University Press.

LeDoux, Joseph. 1996. *The emotional brain: The mysterious underpinnings of emotional life.* New York: Simon and Schuster.

LeDoux, Joseph, and Michael Rogan. 1999. Emotion and the animal brain. In *The MIT encyclopedia of the cognitive sciences,* ed. Robert A. Wilson and Frank C. Kiel, 269–71. Cambridge: MIT Press.

Leege, David C., Kenneth D. Wald, Brian S. Krueger, and Paul D. Mueller. 2002. *The politics of cultural differences: Social change and voter mobilization strategies in the post–New Deal Period.* Princeton: Princeton University Press.

Leohlin, John, Robert MacCrae, Paul Costa, and Oliver John. 1998. Heritabilities of common and measure-specific components of the big five personality factors. *Journal of Research in Personality* 32 (4): 431–53.

Lerner, Jennifer, and Dacher Keltner. 2000. Beyond valence: Toward a model of emotion-specific influences on judgment and choice. *Cognition and Emotion* 14 (4): 473–93.

———. 2001. Fear, anger, and risk. *Journal of Personality and Social Psychology* 81 (1): 146–59.

Lerner, Jennifer S., Julie H. Goldberg, and Philip E. Tetlock. 1998. Sober second thought: The effects of accountability, anger, and authoritarianism on attributions of responsibility. *Personality and Social Psychology Bulletin* 24 (6): 563–74.

Lerner, Jennifer S., Roxana M. Gonzalez, Deborah A. Small, and Baruch Fischhoff. 2003. Effects of fear and anger on perceived risks of terrorism: A national field experiment. *Psychological Science* 14 (2): 144–50.

Lerner, Jennifer, S. and Larissa Z. Tiedens. 2006. Portrait of the angry decision maker: How appraisal tendencies shape anger's influence on cognition. *Journal of Behavioral Decision Making* 19 (2): 115–37.

Lewis, M. 2004. The emergence of human emotions. In *Handbook of emotions*, ed. M. Lewis and J. M. Haviland-Jones, 265–80. New York: Guilford.

Lewis, Thomas, Fari Amini, and Richard Lannon. 2000. *A general theory of love*. New York: Random House.

Leventhal, H., and Klaus R. Scherer. 1987. The relationship of emotion to cognition: A functional approach to a semantic controversy. *Cognition and Emotion* 1:3–28.

Libet, B. 1985. Unconscious cerebral initiative and the role of conscious will in voluntary action. *Behavioral and Brain Sciences* 8:529–66.

———. 1993. Conscious subjective experience and unconscious mental functions: A theory of the cerebral processes involved. In *Models of Brain Function*, ed. R. Cotteril. Cambridge: Cambridge University Press.

———. 2004. *Mind time: The temporal factor in consciousness*. Cambridge: Harvard University Press.

Lieberman, M., Ruth Gaunt, Daniel T. Gilbert, and Yaacov Trope. 2002. Reflection and reflexion: A social cognitive neuroscience approach to attributional inference. *Advances in Experimental Social Psychology* 34:199–249.

Lieberman, M., J. M. Jarcho, and A. B. Satpute. 2004. Evidence-based and intuition-based self-knowledge. *Journal of Personality and Social Psychology* 87:421–35.

Lieberman, M., K. N. Ochsner, D. T. Gilber, and D. L. Schacter. 2001. Attitude change in amnesia and under cognitive load. *Psychological Science* 12:135–40.

Lieberman, M., Darren Schreiber, and Kevin Ochsner. 2003. Is political cognition like riding a bicycle? How cognitive neuroscience can inform research on political thinking. *Political Psychology* 24 (4): 681–704.

Lienesch, Michael. 1993. *Redeeming America: Piety and politics in the new Christian Right*. Chapel Hill: University of North Carolina Press.

Litchenstein, Sarah, Paul Slovic, Baruch Fischhoff, M. Layman, and B. Combs. 1978. Judged frequency of lethal events. *Journal of Experimental Psychology* 4:144–49.

Lodge, M. 1995. Toward a procedural model of candidate evaluation. In *Political judgment: Structure and process*, ed. Milton Lodge and Kathleen M. McGraw, 111–40. Ann Arbor: University of Michigan Press.

Lodge, M., David V. Cross, Bernard Tursky, and Joseph Tanenhaus. 1975. The psychophysical scaling and validation of a political support scale. *American Journal of Political Science* 19 (4): 611–49.

Lodge, M., K. M. McGraw, and P. Stroh. 1989. An impression-driven model of candidate evaluation. *American Political Science Review* 83:399–419.

Lodge, M., and C. Taber. 2000. Three steps toward a theory of motivated political reasoning. In *Elements of reason: Cognition, choice and the bounds of rationality*, ed. A. Lupia, M. McCubbins, and S. L. Popkin, 183–213. New York: Cambridge University Press.

Lodge, M., M. R. Steenbergen, and S. Brau. 1995. The responsive voter: Campaign information and the dynamics of candidate evaluation. *American Political Science Review* 89:309–26.

Lodge, M., and P. Stroh. 1993. Inside the mental voting booth: An impression-driven process model of candidate evaluation. In *Explorations in political psychology*, ed. Shanto Iyengar and James McGuire, 225–63. Durham, NC: Duke University Press.

Logothetis, N. K. 2002. The neural basis of the blood-oxygen-level-dependent functional magnetic resonance imaging signal. *Philosophical Transactions of the Royal Society of London, Bulletin of Biological Sciences* 357 (1424): 1003–37.

———. 2003. The underpinnings of the BOLD functional magnetic resonance imaging signal. *Journal of Neuroscience* 23 (10): 3963–71.

Logothetis, N. K., and B. A. Wandell. 2004. Interpreting the BOLD signal. *Annual Review of Physiology* 66:735–69.

Lowenstein, George F., Elke U. Weber, Christopher K. Hsee, and Ned Welch. 2001. Risk as feelings. *Psychological Bulletin* 127:267–86.

Lowery, Brian S., Curtis D. Hardin, and Stacey Sinclair. 2001. Social influence effects on automatic racial prejudice. *Journal of Personality and Social Psychology* 81 (5): 842–55.

Luker, Kristin. 1984. *Abortion and the politics of motherhood*. Berkeley: University of California Press.

Lupia, Arthur. 1994. Shortcuts versus encyclopedias: Information and voting behavior in California insurance reform elections. *American Political Science Review* 88:63–78.

Lupia, Arthur, and Mathew D. McCubbins. 1998. *The democratic dilemma: Can citizens learn what they need to know? Political economy of institutions and decisions*. Cambridge: Cambridge University Press.

Lupia, Arthur, Mathew D. McCubbins, and Samuel L. Popkin. 2000. Beyond rationality: Reason and the study of politics. In *Elements of reason: Cognition, choice and the bounds of rationality*, ed. Arthur Lupia, Mathew D. McCubbins, and Samuel L. Popkin, 1–20. New York: Cambridge University Press.

Lupia, Arthur, with Jesse O. Menning. 2006. When can politicians scare citizens into supporting bad policies: Strategy and emotion in an equilibrium of fear. http://mpra.ub.uni-muenchen.de/1048/.

Lupia, Arthur, and Natasha Zharinova. 2004. Do political actors have beautiful minds? Counterfactual variation and self-confirming equilibrium in game-theoretic political science. Unpublished manuscript, University of Michigan and Princeton University.

Lupia, Arthur and Natasha Zharinova, and Adam Seth Levine. 2007. Should political scientists use the self-confirming equilibrium concept? Explaining the choices of cognitively limited actors. http://mpra.ub.uni-muenchen.de/1618/.

Luskin, Robert. 2002a. Political psychology, political behavior, and politics: Questions of aggregation, causal distance, and taste. In *Thinking about political psychology*, ed. James Kuklinski. New York: Cambridge University Press.

———. 2002b. From denial to extenuation (and finally beyond): Political sophistication and citizen performance. In *Thinking about political psychology*. ed. James Kuklinski. New York: Cambridge University Press.

Luskin, Robert C., John P. McIver, and Edward G. Carmines. 1989. Issues and the transmission of partisanship. *American Journal of Political Science* 33 (2): 440–58.

Mackie, Diane M., Thierry Devos, and Eliot R. Smith. 2000. Intergroup emotions: Explaining offensive action tendencies in an intergroup context. *Journal of Personality and Social Psychology* 79:602–16.

Mackie, Diane M., and Eliot R. Smith, eds. 2002. *Beyond prejudice: From outgroup hostility to intergroup emotions*. Philadelphia: Psychology Press.

MacKuen, Michael. 1984. Exposure to information, belief integration and individual responsiveness to agenda change. *American Political Science Review* 78:372–91.

———. 2002. Political psychology and the micro-macro gap in politics. In *Thinking about political psychology*, ed. James Kuklinski. New York: Cambridge University Press.

MacKuen, Michael, Robert S. Erikson, and James A. Stimson. 1988. Elections and the dynamics of ideological representation. Paper presented at the annual meeting of the American Political Science Association, Boston.

MacKuen, Michael, Robert S. Erikson, and James A. Stimson. 1992. Peasants or bankers? The American electorate and the U.S. economy. *American Political Science Review* 85:597–611.

MacKuen, Michael, and George E. Marcus. 1994. Affective intelligence during a presidential campaign. Paper presented at the annual meeting of the American Political Science Association, New York.

MacKuen, Michael, George E. Marcus, W. Russell Neuman, Luke Keele, and Jennifer Wolak. 2001a. Emotional framing, information search, and the operation of affective intelligence in matters of public policy. Paper presented at the annual meeting of the Midwest Political Science Association, Chicago.

———. 2001b. Emotions, information, and political cooperation. Paper presented at the annual meeting of the American Political Science Association, San Francisco.

MacLeod, Colin, and Andrew Mathews. 1988. Anxiety and the allocation of attention to threat. *Quarterly Journal of Experimental Psychology* 38A: 659–70.

Maddock, R. J. 1999. The retrosplenial cortex and emotion: New insights from functional neuroimaging of the human brain. *Trends in Neuroscience* 22 (7): 310–16.

Mansbridge, Jane. 1986. *Why we lost the ERA*. Chicago: University of Chicago Press.

Manza, Jeff, and Clem Brooks. 1999. *Social cleavages and political change: Voter alignments and U.S. party coalitions*. Oxford: Oxford University Press.

Marcus, George E. 1988. The structure of emotional response: 1984 presidential candidates. *American Political Science Review* 82 (3): 737–61.

———. 2000. Emotions in politics. *Annual Review of Political Science* 3:221–50.

———. 2002. *The sentimental citizen: Emotions in democratic politics*. University Park: Pennsylvania State University Press.

———. 2003. The psychology of emotion and politics. In *Oxford handbook of political psychology*, ed. David O. Sears, Leonie Huddy, and Robert Jervis, 182–221. New York: Oxford University Press.

Marcus, George E., and M. B. MacKuen. 1993. Anxiety, enthusiasm, and the vote: The emotional underpinnings of learning and involvement during presidential campaigns. *American Political Science Review*, 87:672–85.

Marcus, George E., Michael MacKuen, Jennifer Wolak, and Luke Keele. 2006. The measure and mismeasure of emotion. In *Feeling politics*, ed. David Redlawsk. New York: Palgrave Macmillan.

Marcus, George E., W. Russell Neuman, and Michael Mackuen. 2000. *Affective intelligence and political judgment*. Chicago: University of Chicago Press.

Marcus, George E., W. Russell Neuman, Michael B. MacKuen, and John L. Sullivan. 1996. Dynamic models of emotional response: The multiple roles of affect in politics. In *Research in micropolitics*, ed. Robert Y. Shapiro, Michael Delli Carpini, and Leonie Huddy, 33–59. Greenwich, CT: JAI.

Marcus, George E., John L. Sullivan, Elizabeth Theiss-Morse, and Sandra L. Wood. 1995. *With malice toward some: How people make civil liberties judgments.* Cambridge: Cambridge University Press.

Martin, L. L., T. Abend, C. Sedikides, and J. D. Green. 1997. How would I feel if . . . ? Mood as input to a role fulfillment evaluation process. *Journal of Personality and Social Psychology* 73:242–53.

Martin, L. L., and Abraham Tesser. 1996. *Striving and feeling: Interaction among goals, affect, and self-regulation.* Mahwah, NJ: Erlbaum.

Martin, L. L., D. W. Ward, J. W. Achee, and R. S. Wyer. 1993. Mood as input: People have to interpret the motivational implications of their moods. *Journal of Personality and Social Psychology* 64:317–26.

Maslow, Abraham. 1968. *Toward a psychology of being.* New York: Van Nostrand.

Masters, Roger D., and Denis G. Sullivan, 1993. Nonverbal behavior and leadership: Emotion and cognition in political attitudes. In *Explorations in political psychology,* ed. Shanto Iyengar and William McGuire, 150–82. Durham, NC: Duke University Press.

Mathews, A., and C. MacLeod 1986. Discrimination of threat cues without awareness in anxiety states. *Journal of Abnormal Psychology* 95: 131–38.

Mathiesen, C., K. Caesar, N. Akgoren, and M. Lauritzen. 1998. Modification of activity-dependent increases of cerebral blood flow by excitatory synaptic activity and spikes in rat cerebellar cortex. *Journal of Physiology* 512 (pt. 2): 555–66.

Matthews, Donald G., and Jane S. DeHart. 1990. *Sex, gender, and the politics of ERA.* New York: Oxford University Press.

Mayer, J. D., and Y. N. Gaschke. 1988. The experience and meta-experience of mood. *Journal of Personality and Social Psychology* 55:102–11.

McCabe, K., D. Houser, L. Ryan, V. Smith, and T. Trouard. 2001. A functional imaging study of cooperation in two-person reciprocal exchange. *Proceedings of the National Academy of Science USA* 98 (20): 11832–35.

McCabe, K., and V. L. Smith. 2000. A comparison of naive and sophisticated subject behavior with game theoretic predictions. *Proceedings of the National Academy of Science USA* 97 (7): 3777–81.

McCann, J. A. 1997. Electoral choices and core value change. *American Journal of Political Science* 41:564–83.

McCombs, M., and D. Shaw. 1972. The agenda-setting function of the mass media. *Public Opinion Quarterly* 36:176–87.

McCubbins, Mathew, and Thomas Schwartz. 1984. Congressional oversight overlooked: Police patrols versus fire alarms. *American Journal of Political Science* 28:165–79.

McDermott, Rose. 2004. The feeling of rationality: The meaning of neuroscience for political science. *Perspectives on Politics* 2 (4): 691–706.

McDermott, Rose, and Philip Zimbardo. 2005. The psychology of terrorist alarms. In *The psychology of terrorism,* ed. B. Bonger, L. Beutler, J. Breckenridge, and P. G. Zimbardo. New York: Oxford University Press.

McGraw, K. M., M. Lodge, and P. Stroh. 1990. On-line processing in candidate evaluation: The effects of issue order, issue importance and sophistication. *Political Behavior* 1:41–58.

McGuire, William J. 1990. *The poly-psy pelationship: Three phases of a long affair.* Washington, DC: International Society of Political Psychology.

McKelvey, Richard, and Thomas Palfrey. 1992. An experimental study of the centipede game. *Econometrica* 60:803–36.

———.1995. Quantal response equilibria in normal form games. *Games and Economic Behavior* 10:6–38.

McKeon, Richard, ed. 1941. *The basic works of Aristotle.* New York: Random House.

McQuail, Denis. 1997. *Audience analysis.* Thousand Oaks, CA: Sage.

Mellers, B. A. 2000. Choice and the relative pleasure of consequences. *Psychological Bulletin* 126 (6): 910–24.

Mellers, B. A., A. Schwartz, and A. D. Cooke. 1998. Judgment and decision making. *Annual Review of Psychology* 49:447–77.

Miller, George A. 1956. The magical number seven, plus or minus two: Some limits on our capacity for processing information. *Psychology Review* 63: 81–97.

Miller, M. B., J. D. Van Horn, G. L. Wolford, T. C. Handy, M. Valsangkar-Smyth, S. Inati, S. Grafton, and M. S. Gazzaniga. 2002. Extensive individual differences in brain activations associated with episodic retrieval are reliable over time. *Journal of Cognitive Neuroscience* 14 (8): 1200–1214.

Miller, Warren E., and J. Merrill Shanks. 1996. *The new American voter.* Cambridge: Harvard University Press.

Miller, Warren, and Donald Stokes. 1963. Constituency influence in Congress. *American Political Science Review* 57: 45–56.

Mogg, Karin, Andrew Mathews, Carol Bird, and Rosanne Macgregor-Morris. 1990. Effects of stress and anxiety on the processing of threat stimuli. *Journals of Personality and Social Psychology* 59: 1230–37.

Moore, D. R., V. Rothholtz, and A. J. King. 2001. Hearing: Cortical activation does matter. *Current Biology* 11 (19): R782–4.

Morgenstern, Oskar, and John von Neumann. [1944]/1980. *Theory of games and economic behavior.* Princeton: Princeton University Press.

Morris, J. P., Nancy K. Squires, Charles S. Taber, and Milton Lodge. 2003. Activation of political attitudes: A psychophysiological examination of the hot cognition hypothesis. *Political Psychology* 24 (4): 727–46.

Morris, J. S., C. D. Frith, D. I. Perrett, D. Rowland, A. W. Young, A. J. Calder, and R. J. Dolan. 1996. A differential neural response in the human amygdala to fearful and happy facial expressions. *Nature* 383 (6603): 812–15.

Mueller, John. 1999. *Capitalism, democracy and Ralph's Pretty Good Grocery.* Princeton: Princeton University Press.

Murphy, F. C., I. Nimmo-Smith, and A. D. Lawrence. 2003. Functional neuroanatomy of emotions: A meta-analysis. *Cognition and Affect in Behavioral Neuroscience* 3 (3): 207–33.

Muthen, Linda K., and Bengt O. Muthen. 2001. *Mplus: Statistical analysis with latent variables.* Los Angeles: Muthen and Muthen.

Mutz, Diana Carole. 1998. *Impersonal influence: How perceptions of mass collectives affect political attitudes.* Cambridge: Cambridge University Press.

———. 2002. The consequences of cross-cutting networks for political participation. *American Journal of Political Science* 46 (4): 838–55.

Nardulli, Peter. 2005. Popular efficacy in the democratic era: A re-examination of electoral accountability in the U.S., 1828–2000. Princeton: Princeton University Press.

Neely, J. H. 1976. Semantic priming and retrieval from lexical memory: Evidence for facilitatory and inhibitory processes. *Memory and Cognition* 4:648–54.

Nelson, John S., and G. Robert Boynton. 1997. *Video rhetorics: Televised advertising in American politics.* Urbana: University of Illinois Press.

Nelson, Thomas E., and Donald R. Kinder. 1996. Issue frames and group-centrism in American public opinion. *Journal of Politics* 58 (4): 1055–78.

Neuhaus, Richard John. 1984. *The naked public square: Religion and democracy in America.* Grand Rapids, MI: Eerdmans.

Neuman, W. Russell. 1986. *The paradox of mass politics: Knowledge and opinion in the American electorate.* Cambridge: Harvard University Press.

Neuman, W. Russell, Marion R. Just, and Ann N. Crigler, 1992. *Common knowledge: News and the construction of political meaning.* Chicago: University of Chicago Press.

Nimmo, Dan, and James Combs, 1985. *Nightly horrors: Crisis coverage in television network news.* Knoxville: University of Tennessee Press.

Nisbett, Richard, and Timothy Wilson. 1977. Telling more than we can know: Verbal reports on mental processes. *Psychological Review* 87: 231–59.

Norris, Pippa. 2000. *Virtuous circle: Political communications in postindustrial societies.* New York: Cambridge University Press.

Northoff, Georg, and Felix Bermpohl. 2004. Cortical midline structures and the self. *Trends in Cognitive Science* 8 (3): 102–7.

Nussbaum, Martha. 2001. *Upheavals of thought: The intelligence of emotions.* Cambridge: Cambridge University Press.

Oakley, Kenneth Page. 1964. *Man the tool-maker.* Chicago: University of Chicago Press.

Oatley, Keith. 1999. Emotions. In *The MIT encyclopedia of the cognitive sciences,* ed. Robert A. Wilson and Frank C. Kiel, 273–75. Cambridge: MIT Press.

———. 2000. The sentiments and beliefs of distributed cognition. In *Emotions and beliefs: How feelings influence thoughts,* ed. Nico H. Frijda, Antony S. R. Manstead, and Sacha Bem, 78–107. Cambridge: Cambridge University Press.

Öhman, Arne. 2000. Fear and anxiety: Evolutionary, cognitive, and clinical perspectives. In *Handbook of emotions,* ed. Michael Lewis and Jeanette M. Haviland-Jones, 573–93. New York: Guilford.

Olsen, R. A. 1997. Desirability bias among professional investment managers: Some evidence from experts. *Journal of Behavioral Decision Making* 10:65–72.

Orbell, J., T. Morikawa, J. Hartwig, J. Hanley, and N. Allen. 2004. "Machiavellian" intelligence as a basis for the evolution of cooperative dispositions. *American Political Science Review* 98 (1): 1–15.

Ortony, Andrew, Gerald L. Clore, and Allan Collins. 1988. *The cognitive structure of emotions.* New York: Cambridge University Press.

Osgood, Charles E., George J. Suci, and Percy H. Tannenbaum. 1957. *The measurement of meaning.* Urbana: University of Illinois Press.

Ottati, Victor C., and Robert S. Wyer Jr. 1993. Affect and political judgment. In *Explorations in political psychology,* ed. S. Iyengar and W. J. McGuire, 296–315. Durham, NC: Duke University Press.

Page, Benjamin, and Robert Y. Shapiro. 1992. *The rational public*. Chicago: University of Chicago Press.

Pantoja, Adrian D., and Gary M. Segura. 2003. Fear and loathing in California: Contextual threat and political sophistication among Latino voters. *Political Behavior* 25 (September): 265–86.

Park, J., and M. R. Banaji. 2000. Mood and heuristics: The influence of happy and sad states on sensitivity and bias in stereotyping. *Journal of Personality and Social Psychology* 78:1005–23.

Parsons, Talcott. 1959. "Voting" and the equilibrium of the American political system. In *American voting behavior*, ed. Eugene Burdick and Arthur Brodbeck, 80–120. Glencoe, IL: Free Press.

Petty, R. E., and J. T. Cacioppo. 1986. The elaboration likelihood model of persuasion. In *Advances in Experimental Social Psychology*, ed. L. Berkowitz. New York: Academic.

Phelps, Elizabeth A. 2006. Emotion and cognition: Insights from studies of the human amygdala. *Annual Review of Psychology* 57: 27–53.

Phelps, Elizabeth A., Kevin J. O'Connor, William Cunningham, E. Sumie Funayama, J. Christopher Gatenby, John C. Gore, and R. Banaji Mahzarin. 2000. Perfomance on indirect measures of race evaluation predicts amygdala activation. *Journal of Cognitive Neuroscience* 12 (5): 729–38.

Phillips, M. L., W. C. Drevets, S. L. Rauch, and R. Lane. 2003. Neurobiology of emotion perception I: The neural basis of normal emotion perception. *Biological Psychiatry* 54 (5): 504–14.

Phillips, M. L., A. W. Young, S. K. Scott, A. J. Calder, C. Andrew, V. Giampietro, S. C. Williams, E. T. Bullmore, M. Brammer, and J. A. Gray. 1998. Neural responses to facial and vocal expressions of fear and disgust. *Proceedings of the Royal Society of London, Bulletin in Biological Sciences* 265 (1408): 1809–17.

Pinker, Steven. 1994. *The language instinct*. New York: Morrow.

———. 1997. *How the mind works*. New York: Norton.

———. 1999. *Words and rules: The ingredients of language*. New York: Basic.

———. 2002. *The blank slate: The modern denial of human nature*. New York: Viking.

Plutchik, Robert. 1980. A general psychoevolutionary theory of emotion. In *Emotion: Theory, research, and experience*, vol. 1, *Theories of emotion*, ed. R. Plutchik and H. Kellerman, 3–33. New York: Academic.

Plutchik, Robert, and Hope R. Conte. 1997. *Circumplex models of personality and emotions*. Washington, DC: American Psychological Association.

Popkin, Samuel L. 1991. *The reasoning voter: Communication and persuasion in presidential campaigns*. Chicago: University of Chicago Press.

Pratto F., and O. P. John. 1991. Automatic vigilance: The attention-grabbing power of negative social information. *Journal of Personality and Social Psychology* 61:380–91.

Premack, D., and G. Woodruff. 1978. Does the chimpanzee have a theory of mind? *Behavioral and Brain Sciences* 4:515–26.

Price, C. J., and K. J. Friston. 2002. Degeneracy and cognitive anatomy. *Trends in the Cognitive Sciences* 6 (10): 416–21.

Quattrone, George A., and Amos Tversky. 1988. Contrasting rational and pyschological analyses of political choice. *American Political Science Review* 82 (3): 719–36.

Quillian, Lincoln. 1995. Prejudice as a response to perceived group threat: Population composition and anti-immigrant and racial prejudice in Europe. *American Sociological Review* 60 (4): 586–611.

Raghunathan, Rajagopal, and Pham, Michel Tuan. 1999. Negative moods are not equal: Motivational influences of anxiety and sadness on decision making. *Organizational Behavior and Human Decision Processes* 79:56–77.

Rahn, Wendy M. 2000. Affect as information: The role of public mood in political reasoning. In *Elements of reason: Cognition, choice and the bounds of rationality*, ed. Arthur Lupia, Mathew D. McCubbins, and Samuel L. Popkin, 130–50. New York: Cambridge University Press.

Rahn, Wendy M., John Aldrich, and Eugene Borgida. 1994. Individual and contextual variations in political candidate appraisal. *American Political Science Review* 88(1): 193–99.

Rahn, Wendy M., and Katherine Cramer. 1996. Activation and application of political party stereotypes: Specifying the effects of different communication media. *Political Communication* 13:195–212.

Raichle, M. E. 2003. Social neuroscience: A role for brain imaging. *Political Psychology* 24 (4): 759–64.

Raichle, M. E., A. M. MacLeod, A. Z. Snyder, W. J. Powers, D. A. Gusnard, and G. L. Shulman. 2001. A default mode of brain function. *Proceedings of the National Academy of Science USA* 98 (2): 676–82.

Redlawsk, David P. 2001. You must remember this: A test of the on-line model of voting. *Journal of Politics* 63 (February): 29–58.

———. 2002. Hot cognition or cool consideration? Testing the effects of motivated reasoning on political decision making. *Journal of Politics* 64 (November): 1021–44.

———. 2004. What voters do: Information search during election campaigns. *Political Psychology* 25:595–610.

RePass, David E. 1971. Issue salience and party choice. *American Political Science Review* 65 (2): 389–400.

Rich, Frank. 2004. The passion of the Bush. *New York Times*, 3 October.

Riggle, Ellen D. B., Mitzi M. S. Johnson, and Scot Hickey. 1996. Information monitoring of strategic decision making: A process tracing demonstration. Paper presented at the annual meeting of the Midwest Political Science Association, Chicago.

Rizzolatti, G., and M. A. Arbib. 1998. Language within our grasp. *Trends in Neuroscience* 21 (5): 188–94.

Rizzolatti, G., and L. Craighero. 2004. The mirror-neuron system. *Annual Review of Neuroscience* 27:169–92.

Rizzolatti, G., L. Fadiga, L. Fogassi, and V. Gallese. 1999. Resonance behaviors and mirror neurons. *Archives of Italian Biology* 137 (2–3): 85–100.

Rizzolatti, G., L. Fadiga, V. Gallese, and L. Fogassi. 1996. Premotor cortex and the recognition of motor actions. *Cognitive Brain Research* 3 (2): 131–41.

Robinson, M. D., and G. L. Clore. 2002. Episodic and semantic knowledge in emotional self-report: Evidence for two judgment processes. *Journal of Personality and Social Psychology* 83:198–215.

Rokeach, Milton. 1973. *The nature of human values*. New York: Free Press.

Roseman, I. 1984. Cognitive determinants of emotions: A structural theory. In *Review of personality and social psychology*, ed. P. Shaver, 11–36. Beverly Hills: Sage.

————. 1991. Appraisal determinants of discrete emotions. *Cognition and Emotion* 5 (3): 161–200.

Roseman, I., A. A. Antoniou, and P. E. Jose. 1996. Appraisal determinants of emotions: Constructing a more accurate and comprehensive theory. *Cognition and Emotion* 10:241–77.

Roseman, I., and Craig A. Smith. 2001. Appraisal theory. In *Appraisal processes in emotion: Theory, methods, research*, ed. K. R. Scherer, A. Schorr, and T. Johnstone, 3–19. Oxford: Oxford University Press.

Rosengren, Karl Erik, Lawrence A. Wenner, and Philip Palmgreen, eds. 1985. *Media gratifications research: Current perspectives*. Beverly Hills: Sage.

Rowe, A. D., P. R. Bullock, C. E. Polkey, and R. G. Morris. 2001. "Theory of mind" impairments and their relationship to executive functioning following frontal lobe excisions. *Brain* 124 (pt. 3):600–16.

Russell, J. A. 1980. A circumplex model of affect. *Journal of Personality and Social Psychology* 39:1161–78.

————. 2003. Core affect and the psychological construction of emotion. *Psychological Review* 110:145–72.

Russo, J. E., V. H. Medvec, and M. G. Meloy. 1996. The distortion of information during decisions. *Organizational Behavior and Human Decision Processes* 66:102–10.

Rutenberg, Jim. 2003. Suffering news burnout? Rest of America is, too. *New York Times*, 11 August.

Sanbonmatsu, D. M., and R. H. Fazio. 1990. The role of attitudes in memory-based decision making. *Journal of Personality and Social Psychology* 59:614–22.

Sanfey, Alan G., James K. Rilling, Jessica A. Aronson, Leigh E. Nystrom, and Jonathan D. Cohen. 2003. The neural basis of economic decision-making in the ultimatum game. *Science* 300:1755–1958.

Sarnoff, Irving, and Philip Zimbardo. 1961. Anxiety, fear, and social isolation. *Journal of Abnormal and Social Psychology* 62: 356–63.

Sato, W., S. Yoshikawa, T. Kochiyama, and M. Matsumura. 2004. The amygdala processes the emotional significance of facial expressions: An fMRI investigation using the interaction between expression and face direction. *Neuroimage* 22 (2): 1006–13.

Satz, Debra, and John Ferejohn. 1994. Rational choice and social theory. *Journal of Philosophy* 9102: 71–87.

Saxe, R., S. Carey, and N. Kanwisher. 2004. Understanding other minds: Linking developmental psychology and functional neuroimaging. *Annual Review of Psychology* 55:87–124.

Schattschneider, E. E. 1960. *The semi-sovereign people*. New York: Holt, Rinehart and Winston.

Scheler, Max. 1954. *The nature of sympathy*. Trans. P. Heath. London: Routledge and Kegan Paul.

Scherer, Klaus R. 1993. Plato's legacy: Relationships between cognition, emotion, and motivation. Paper read at Société Psychologique de Québec.

————. 2000. Emotions as episodes of subsystem synchronization driven by nonlinear appraisal processes. In *Emotion, development, and self-organization: Dynamic systems approaches to emotional development*, ed. M. D. Lewis and I. Granic. New York: Cambridge University Press.

———. 2003. Introduction: Cognitive components of emotion. In *Handbook of the affective sciences*, ed. R. J. Davidson, H. Goldsmith, and K. R. Scherer. New York: Oxford University Press.

———. 2005. Unconscious process in emotion: The bulk of the iceberg. In *Emotion and Consciousness*, ed. Barrett, Lisa Feldman, Paula M. Niedenthall, and Piotr Winkielman, 312–34. New York: Guilford.

Scherer, Klaus R., Angela Schorr, and Tom Johnstone. 2001. *Appraisal processes in emotion: Theory, methods, research*. Oxford: Oxford University Press.

Scheve, Kenneth F., and Matthew J. Slaughter. 2001. *Globalization and the perceptions of American workers*. Washington, DC: Institute for International Economics.

Schneider, W., and R. M. Shiffrin. 1977. Controlled and automatic human information processing: I. Detection, search, and attention. *Psychological Review* 84:1–66.

Schreiber, Darren, and Marco Iacoboni. 2004. Sophistication in evaluating political questions: Neural substrates and functional mechanisms. Paper read at the Political Methodology Annual Conference, Stanford and Palo Alto.

Schorr, Angela. 2001. The evolution of an idea. In *Appraisal processes in emotion: Theory, methods, research*, ed. K. R. Scherer, A. Schorr, and T. Johnstone, 20–34. Oxford: Oxford University Press.

Schroeder, U., A. Hennenlotter, P. Erhard, B. Haslinger, R. Stahl, K. W. Lange, and A. O. Ceballos-Baumann. 2004. Functional neuroanatomy of perceiving surprised faces. *Human Brain Mapping* 23 (4): 181–87.

Schudson, Michael, 1998. *The good citizen: A history of American public life*. New York: Free Press.

Schulkin, J. 2000. Theory of mind and mirroring neurons. *Trends in Cognitive Science* 4 (7): 252–54.

Schwartz, Norman, and Gerald Clore. 1983. Mood, misattribution and misjudgments of well-being: Informative and directive functions of affective states. *Journal of Personality and Social Psychology* 45 (3): 513–23.

———. 1988. How do I feel about it? The informative function of affective states. In *Affect, cognition and social behavior*, ed. K. Fiedler and J. Forgas. Toronto: Hogrefe International.

———. 2003. Mood as information: 20 years later. *Psychological Inquiry* 14 (3–4): 296–303.

Schwartz, Shalom. 1992. Universals in the content and structure of values. In *Advances in experimental social psychology*, ed. M. P. Zanna, 1–65. New York: Academic.

———. 1994. Are there universal aspects in the structure and content of human values? *Journal of Social Issues* 50:19–46.

Schwarz, Norbert. 1990. Feelings as information: Informational and motivational functions of affective states. In *Handbook of motivation and cognition*, ed. E. T. Higgins and R. M. Sorrentino, 2:527–61. New York: Guilford.

———. 1994. "Judgment in a social context: Biases, shortcomings, and the logic of conversation." *Advances in Experimental Social Psychology* 26:123–62.

———. 2000. Emotion, cognition, and decision making. *Cognition and Emotion* 14 (4): 433–40.

Schwarz, Norbert, and H. Bless. 1991. Happy and mindless, but sad and smart? The impact of affective states on analytic reasoning. In *Emotion and social judgments*, ed. J. P. Forgas, 55–71. Oxford: Pergamon.

Searle, John. 1980. Minds, brains, and programs. *Behavioral and Brain Sciences* 3:417–24.

Sears, D. O. 1983. The person positivity bias. *Journal of Personality and Social Psychology Public Opinion Quarterly* 44:233–49.

———. 1986. College sophomores in the laboratory—influences of a narrow database on social-psychology views of human nature. *Journal of Personality and Social Psychology* 51(3): 515–30.

———. 1993. Symbolic politics: A socio-psychological theory. In *Explorations in political psychology*, ed. Shanto Iyengar and William McGuire, 113–49. Durham, NC: Duke University Press.

———. 2001. The role of affect in symbolic politics. In *Citizens and politics: Perspectives from political psychology*, ed. James Kuklinski, 14–40. New York: Cambridge University Press.

Sears, D. O., and J. Citrin. 1982. *Tax revolt: Something for nothing in California.* Cambridge: Harvard University Press.

Sears, D. O., and J. L. Freedman. 1967. Selective exposure to information: A critical review. *Public Opinion Quarterly* 31(2): 194–213.

Sears, D. O., and C. L. Funk. 1991. The role of self-interest in social and political attitudes. *Advances in Experimental Social Psychology* 24:1–91.

Sears, D. O., and P. J. Henry. 2003. The origins of symbolic racism. *Journal of Personality and Social Psychology* 85:259–75.

Sears, D., C. Van Laar, M. Carrillo, and R. Kosterman. 1997. Is it really racism? The origins of white Americans' opposition to race-targeted policies. *Public Opinion Quarterly* 61:16–53.

Seelye, Katharine Q. 2004. Kerry in a struggle for a Democratic base: Women. *New York Times*, 22 September. www.nytimes.com.

Shafir, Eldar, and Robyn A. LeBoeuf. 2002. Rationality. *Annual Review of Psychology* 53:491–517.

Shamay-Tsoory, S. G., R. Tomer, B. D. Berger, and J. Aharon-Peretz. 2003. Characterization of empathy deficits following prefrontal brain damage: The role of the right ventromedial prefrontal cortex. *Journal of Cognitive Neuroscience* 15 (3): 324–37.

Shaver, P., J. Schwartz, D. Kirson, and C. O'Connor. 1987. Emotion knowledge: Further exploration of a prototype approach. *Journal of Personality and Social Psychology* 52:1061–86.

Shiffrin, R. M., and W. Schneider. 1977. Controlled and automatic human information processing: II. Perceptual learning, automatic attending, and a general theory. *Psychological Review* 84:127–90.

Sidanius, Jim, and Felicia Pratto. 1999. *Social dominance: An intergroup theory of social hierarchy and oppression.* Cambridge: Cambridge University Press.

Simon, Herbert A. 1967. Motivational and emotional controls of cognition. *Psychological Review* 74 (1): 29–39.

———. 1979. Information processing models of cognition. *Annual Review of Psychology* 30:365–96.

Sinclair, Stacey, Brian S. Lowery, Curtis D. Hardin, and Anna Colangelo. 2005. Social tuning of automatic ethnic attitudes. *Journal of Personality and Social Psychology* 89:583–92.

Skinner, B. F. 1938. *The behavior of organisms: An experimental analysis.* New York: Appleton-Century.

Skitka, Linda, Christopher W. Bauman, and Elizabeth Mullen 2004. Political tolerance and coming to psychological closure following the September 11, 2001 terrorist attacks: A model comparison approach. *Personality and Social Psychological Bulletin* 30:743–56.

Smith, C. A., and P. C. Ellsworth. 1985. Patterns of cognitive appraisal in emotion. *Journal of Personality and Social Psychology* 48:813–38.

Smith, C. A., and L. D. Kirby. 2001. Toward delivering on the promise of appraisal theory. In *Appraisal processes in emotion: Theory, methods, research*, ed. K. R. Scherer, A. Schorr, and T. Johnstone, 121–37. Oxford: Oxford University Press.

Smith, C. A., and R. S. Lazarus. 1990. Emotion and adoption. In *Handbook of personality: Theory and research*, ed. L. A. Pervin, 609–37. New York: Guilford.

Sniderman, Paul M., Pierangelo Peri, Rui J. P. de Figueiredo Jr., and Thomas Piazza. 2000. *The outsider: Prejudice and politics in Italy*. Princeton: Princeton University Press.

Sniderman, Paul, and Sean Theriault. 2004. The structure of political argument and the logic of issue framing. In *Studies in public opinion*, ed. William Saris and Paul Sniderman, 133–65. Princeton: Princeton University Press.

Snyder, C. R. 1994. *The psychology of hope*. New York: Free Press.

Snyder, C. R., J. Cheavens, and S. T. Michael. 1999. Hoping. In *Coping: The psychology of what works*, ed. C. R. Snyder, 205–32. New York: Oxford University Press.

Staats, Sara R., and Marjorie A. Stassen. 1985. Hope: An affective cognition. *Social Indicators Research* 17 (3): 235–42.

Stearns, Peter N. 2004. History of the emotions: Issues of change and impact. In *Handbook of Emotions*, ed. M. Lewis and J. M. Haviland-Jones, 91–115. New York: Guilford.

Steenbergen, Marco. 2001. The Reverend Bayes meets John Q. Public: Patterns of political belief updating in citizens. Presented at the annual meeting of the International Society of Political Psychology, Cuernavaca, Mexico.

Steenbergen, Marco, and Bradford S. Jones. 2002. Modeling multilevel data structures. *American Journal of Political Science* 46 (1): 218–37.

Steenbergen, Marco, Whitt Kilburn, and Jenny Wolak. 2001. Affective moderators of on-line and memory-based processing in candidate evaluation. Paper presented at the annual meeting of the Midwest Political Science Association, Chicago.

Stein, N. L, T. Trabasso, and M. D. Liwag. 2000. A goal appraisal theory of emotional understanding: Implications for development and learning. In *Handbook of emotions*, ed. M. Lewis and J. M. Haviland-Jones. New York: Guilford.

Sternberg, Robert J., and James C. Kaufman. 2002. *The evolution of intelligence*. Mahwah, NJ: Erlbaum.

Stimson, James A. 1991. *Public opinion in America: Moods, cycles and swings*. Boulder: Westview.

———. 2004. *Tides of consent: How opinion movements shape American politics*. New York: Cambridge University Press.

Stone, Valerie E., Simon Baron-Cohen, Andrew Calder, Jill Keane, and Andrew Young. 2003. Acquired theory of mind impairments in individuals with bilateral amygdala lesions. *Neuropsychologia* 41:209–20.

Sullivan, Denis G., and Roger D. Masters. 1988. Happy warriors: Leaders' facial displays, viewers' emotions and political support. *American Journal of Political Science* 32:345–68.

Sundar, S. Shyam. 2003. News features and learning. In *Communication and emotion*, ed. Jennings Bryant, David Roskos-Ewoldsen, and Joanne Cantor, 275–96. Mahwah, NJ: Erlbaum.

Sundquist, James L. 1983. *Dynamics of the party system: Alignment and realignment of political parties in the United States*. Rev. ed. Washington, DC: Brookings Institution.

Swidler, Ann. 1986. Culture in action: Symbols and strategies. *American Sociological Review* 51 (2): 273–86.

Taber, C. S. 2003. Information processing and public opinion. In *Oxford handbook of political psychology*, ed. D. O. Sears, L. Huddy, and R. Jervis. New York: Oxford University Press.

Taber, C., M. Lodge, and J. Glather. 2001. The motivated construction of political judgments. In *Citizens and politics: Perspectives from political psychology*, ed. James Kuklinski, 198–226. London: Cambridge University Press.

———. 2006. Motivated skepticism in the evaluation of political beliefs. *American Journal of Political Science* 50(3): 755–69.

Tajfel, Henri. 1982. Social psychology of intergroup relations. *Annual Review of Psychology* 33:1–39.

Takahashi, Hidehiko, Noriaki Yahata, Michihiko Koeda, Tetsuya Matsuda, Kunihiko Asai, and Yoshiro Okubo. 2004. Brain activation associated with evaluative processes of guilt and embarrassment: An fMRI study. *NeuroImage* 23 (3): 967–74.

Taylor, Shelley E., and Suzanne C. Thompson. 1982. Stalking the elusive "vividness effect." *Psychological Review* 2:155–81.

Teasdale, J. D. 1983. Negative thinking in depression: Cause, effect, or reciprocal relationship? *Advances in Behaviour Research and Therapy* 5:3–25.

Teidens, Larissa Z. 2001. The effect of anger on the hostile inferences of aggressive and nonaggressive people: Specific emotions, cognitive processing, and chronic accessibility. *Motivation and Emotion* 25:233–51.

Tellegen, Auke, David Watson, and Lee Anna Clark. 1999a. Further support for a hierarchical model of affect. *Psychological Science* 10 (4): 307–9.

———. 1999b. On the dimensional and hierarchical structure of affect. *Psychological Science* 10 (4): 297–303.

Thomas, David L., and Ed Diender. 1990. Memory accuracy in recall of emotions. *Journal of Personality and Social Psychology* 59:291–97.

Thorndike, Edward L. 1898. Animal intelligence: An experimental study of the associative process in animals. *Psychological Review Monographs* 2:551–53.

Thulborn, K. R., P. A. Carpenter, and M. A. Just. 1999. Plasticity of language-related brain function during recovery from stroke. *Stroke* 30 (4): 749–54.

Tiedens, Larissa Z., and Susan Linton. 2001. Judgment under emotional certainty and uncertainty: The effects of specific emotions on information processing. *Journal of Personality and Social Psychology* 81:973–88.

Todorov, A., A. N. Mandisodza, A. Goren, and C. C. Hall. 2005. Inferences of competence from faces predict election outcomes. *Science* 308 (5728): 1623–26.

Tooby, John, and Leda Cosmides. 1990. The past explains the present: Emotional adaptations and the structure of ancestral environments. *Ethology and Sociobiology* 11:375–424.

Tourangeau, Roger, Lance J. Rips, and Kenneth Rasinski. 2000. *The psychology of the survey response*. New York: Cambridge University Press.

Tranel, D., A. Bechara, and N. L. Denburg. 2002. Asymmetric functional roles of right and left ventromedial prefrontal cortices in social conduct, decision-making, and emotional processing. *Cortex* 38:589–612.

Tulving, Endel, Hans J. Markowitsch, Fergus I. M. Craik, Reza Habib, and Sylvain Houle. 1996. Novelty and familiarity activations in PET studies of memory encoding and retrieval. *Cerebral Cortex* 6:71–79.

Turing, Alan. 1950. Computing machinery and intelligence. *Mind* 59: 433–60.

Turner, John C. 1982. Toward a cognitive redefinition of the social group. In *Social identity and intergroup relations*, ed. Henri Tajfel, 15–40. New York: Cambridge University Press.

Twenge, J. M., K. R. Catanese, and R. F. Baumeister. 2002. Social exclusion causes self-defeating behavior. *Journal of Personality and Social Psychology* 83 (3): 606–15.

Umilta, M. A., E. Kohler, V. Gallese, L. Fogassi, L. Fadiga, C. Keysers, and G. Rizzolatti. 2001. I know what you are doing: A neurophysiological study. *Neuron* 31 (1): 155–65.

Visalberghi, E., and D. Fragaszy. 2001. Do monkeys ape? Ten years after. In *Imitation in Animals and Artifacts*, ed. K. Dautenhahn and C. Nehaniv. Cambridge: MIT Press.

Vogt, B. A., D. M. Finch, and C. R. Olson. 1992. Functional heterogeneity in cingulate cortex: The anterior executive and posterior evaluative regions. *Cerebral Cortex* 2 (6): 435–43.

Wacker, Jan, Marcus Heldmann, and Gerhard Stemmler. 2003. Separating emotion and motivational direction in fear and anger: Effects on frontal asymmetry. *Emotion* 3 (2): 167–93.

Wald, Kenneth D. 2003. *Religion and politics in the United States.* 4th ed. Lanham, MD: Rowman and Littlefield.

Wald, Kenneth D., Dennis E. Owen, and Samuel S. Hill Jr. 1988. Churches as political communities. *American Political Science Review* 82 (2): 531–48.

Watson, David. 1988. Intraindividual and interindividual analyses of positive and negative affect. *Journal of Personality and Social Psychology* 54 (6): 1020–30.

Watson, David, and Lee Anna Clark. 1992. Affects separable and inseparable: On the hierarchical arrangement of the negative affects. *Journal of Personality and Social Psychology* 62 (3): 489–505.

Watson, David, and Auke Tellegen. 1985. Toward a consensual structure of mood. *Psychological Bulletin* 98:219–35.

Watson, David, David Wiese, Jatin Vaidya, and Auke Tellegen. 1999. The two general activation systems of affect: Structural findings, evolutionary considerations, and psychobiological evidence. *Journal of Personality and Social Psychology* 76 (5): 820–38.

Watson, John B. 1913. Psychology as the behaviorist views it. *Psychological Review* 20:157–77.

Way, Baldwin, and Roger Masters. 1996. Political attitudes: Interactions of cognition and affect. *Motivation and Emotion* 20:205–36.

Wegner, Daniel M. 2002. *The illusion of conscious will.* Cambridge: MIT Press.

Weiss, H. M., K. Suckow, and R. Cropanzano. 1999. Effects of justice conditions on discrete emotion. *Journal of Applied Psychology* 84:786–94.

West, Darrell M. 2001. *Air wars:Television advertising in election campaigns, 1952–2000.* 3d ed. Washington: CQ Press.

Westholm, Anders. 1999. The perceptual pathway: Tracing the mechanisms of political value transfer across generations. *Political Psychology* 20 (3): 525–51.

White, Geoffrey. 1993. Emotions inside out: The anthropology of affect. In *Handbook of emotions*, ed. Michael Lewis and Jeannette M. Haviland-Jones, 29–39. New York: Guilford.

Whiten, A., and Richard W. Byrne. 1988. The Machiavellian intelligence hypotheses: Editorial. In *Machiavellian intelligence: Social expertise and the evolution of intellect in monkeys, apes, and humans*, ed R. W. Byrne and A. Whiten, 1–9. Oxford: Oxford University Press.

Whiten, A., and Richard W. Byrne. 1997. *Machiavellian intelligence II: Extensions and evaluations*. Cambridge: Cambridge University Press.

Whiten, A., and R. Ham. 1992. On the nature and evolution of imitation in the animal kingdom: Reappraisal of a century of research. In *Advances in the Study of Behavior*, ed. P. Slater, J. Rosenblatt, C. Beer, and M. Milinski, 239–83. San Diego: Academic.

Wicker, B., C. Keysers, J. Plailly, J. P. Royet, V. Gallese, and G. Rizzolatti. 2003. Both of us disgusted in my insula: The common neural basis of seeing and feeling disgust. *Neuron* 40 (3): 655–64.

Wierzbicka, Anna. 1999. *Emotions across languages and cultures: Diversity and universals*. Cambridge: Cambridge University Press.

Wildavsky, Aaron. 1987. Choosing preferences by constructing institutions: A cultural theory of preference formation. *American Political Science Review* 81 (1): 3–21.

Will, George F. 1983. *Statecraft as soulcraft: What government does*. New York: Simon and Schuster.

Williams, J. H., A. Whiten, T. Suddendorf, and D. I. Perrett. 2001. Imitation, mirror neurons and autism. *Neuroscience and Biobehavior Review* 25 (4): 287–95.

Williams, J. Mark G., Fraser N. Watts, Colin MacLeod, and Andrew Mathews. 1997. *Cognitive psychology and emotional disorders*. 2d ed. Chichester: Wiley.

Wilson, E. O. 1998. *Consilience*. New York: Knopf.

Wilson, Timothy D. 2002. *Strangers to ourselves: Discovering the adaptive unconscious*. Cambridge: Belknap Press of Harvard University Press.

Wilson, Timothy D., Dolores Kraft, and Dana S. Dunn. 1989. The disruptive effects of explaining attitudes: The moderating effects of knowledge about the attitude object. *Journal of Experimental Social Psychology* 25:379–400.

Wilson, Timothy D., and Jonathan W. Schooler. 1991. Thinking too much: Introspection can reduce the quality of preferences and decisions. *Journal of Personality and Social Psychology* 60 (2): 181–92.

Winkielman, Piotr, and Kend Berridge. 2003. Irrational wanting and subrational liking: How rudimentary motivational and affective processes shape preferences and choices. *Political Psychology* 24 (4): 657–80.

Winkielman, P., R. B. Zajonc, and N. Schwarz. 1997. Subliminal affective priming resists attributional interventions. *Cognition and Emotion* 11:433–65.

Winslow, J. T., N. Hastings, C. S. Carter, C. R. Harbaugh, and T. R. Insel. 1993. A role for central vasopressin in pair bonding in monogamous prairie voles. *Nature* 365 (6446): 545–48.

Witte, Kim, and Mike Allen. 2000. A meta-analysis of fear appeals: Implications for effective public health campaigns. *Health Education and Behavior* 27 (5): 591–615.

Wolak, Jennifer, Michael MacKuen, Luke Keele, George E. Marcus, and W. Russell Neuman. 2003. How the emotions of public policy affect citizen engagement, public deliberation, and the quality of electoral choice. Paper presented at the annual meeting of the American Political Science Association, Philadelphia.

Wuthnow, Robert. 1987. *Meaning and moral order: Explorations in cultural analysis.* Berkeley: University of California Press.

———. 1988. *The restructuring of American religion: Society and faith since World War II.* Princeton: Princeton University Press.

Wynne, C. D. 2004. Animal behaviour: Fair refusal by capuchin monkeys. *Nature* 428 (6979): 140; discussion 140.

Yavuz, H. S., and W. A. Bousfield. 1959. Recall of connotative meaning. *Psychological Reports* 5:319–20.

Yerkes, Robert M., and John D. Dodson. 1908. The relation of strength of stimulus to rapidity of habit-formation. *Journal of Comparative Neurology and Psychology* 18:459–82.

Yiend, Jenny, and Andrew Mathews. 2001. Anxiety and attention to threatening pictures. *Quarterly Journal of Experimental Psychology* 54A: 665–81.

Young, L. J., Z. Wang, and T. R. Insel. 1998. Neuroendocrine bases of monogamy. *Trends in Neuroscience* 21 (2): 71–75.

Young, L. J., J. T. Winslow, Z. Wang, B. Gingrich, Q. Guo, M. M. Matzuk, and T. R. Insel. 1997. Gene targeting approaches to neuroendocrinology: Oxytocin, maternal behavior, and affiliation. *Hormones and Behavior* 31 (3): 221–31.

Zajonc, R. B. 1968. Attitudinal effects of mere exposure. *Journal of Personality and Social Psychology* 9 (2):1–27.

———. 1980. Feeling and thinking: Preferences need no inferences. *American Psychologist* 35:151–75.

———. 1984. On the primacy of affect. *American Psychologist* 39:117–24.

———. 2000. Feeling and thinking. In *Feeling and thinking,* ed. J. P. Forgas, 31–58. New York: Cambridge University Press.

Zak, Paul, Rob Kurzban, and William Matzner. 2004. The neurobiology of trust. *Annals of the New York Academy of Science* 1032:224–27.

Zaller, John R. 1992. *The nature and origins of mass opinion.* Cambridge: Cambridge University Press.

———. 2001. Monica Lewinsky and the mainsprings of American politics. In *Mediated politics,* ed. W. Lance Bennett and Robert Entman, 252–78. New York: Cambridge University Press.

Zaller, J., and S. Feldman. 1992. A simple theory of the survey response: Answering questions versus revealing preferences. *American Journal of Political Science* 36:579–616.

Zillmann, Dolf, and Hans-Bernd Brosius. 2000. *Exemplification in communication: The influence of case reports on the perception of issues.* Mahwah, NJ: Erlbaum.

Zysset, S., O. Huber, E. Ferstl, and D. Y. von Cramon. 2002. The anterior frontomedian cortex and evaluative judgment: An fMRI study. *Neuroimage* 15 (4): 983–91.

Zysset, S., O. Huber, A. Samson, E. C. Ferstl, and D. Y. von Cramon. 2003. Functional specialization within the anterior medial prefrontal cortex: A functional magnetic resonance imaging study with human subjects. *Neuroscientific Letters* 335 (3): 183–86.

CONTRIBUTORS

Ralph Adolphs is the Bren Professor of Psychology and Neuroscience in the Division of the Humanities and Social Sciences at the California Institute of Technology, where he studies the neural and psychological basis of social behavior in humans, focusing on how humans recognize emotions from people's facial expressions and from other visual cues.

Todd Belt is an assistant professor of political science at the University of Hawai'i at Hilo. His teaching and research interests include political psychology, public opinion, mass media, and political behavior.

Ted A. Brader is an associate professor in political science and in the Center for Political Studies of the Institute for Social Research at the University of Michigan. His research focuses on political psychology, especially the role of emotion, the effects of political communication, and the formation of partisan identities. He is the author of *Campaigning for Hearts and Minds: How Emotional Appeals in Political Ads Work*.

Erin Cassese is an assistant professor in the Department of Political Science at West Virginia University. Her research interests lie in political behavior and public opinion, with an emphasis on political cognition, political identity, and gender.

Dan Cassino is currently on staff at the Department of Politics at Princeton University.

Andrew J. W. Civettini is an assistant professor of political science at Knox College. His research focuses on political decision making, women in American politics, and legislative behavior.

Ann N. Crigler is a professor in and chair of the Department of Political Science at the University of Southern California and for many years the director of the Jesse M. Unruh Institute of Politics. Recent publications include *Rethinking the Vote: The Politics and the Prospects of Election Reform* and *Common Knowledge: News and the Construction of Political Meaning.*

Stanley Feldman is a professor of political science at Stony Brook University. He is a past president of the methodology section of the American Political Science Association and a former member of the board of overseers of the American National Election Studies. He has published articles on public opinion, political psychology, and methodology.

Doris A. Graber is a professor of political science and communication at the University of Illinois at Chicago. Her books and writings have focused on processing political information, learning from audiovisuals in television news and entertainment, and the impact of political language. Recent publications include *The Power of Communication: Managing Information in Public Organizations* and *Processing Politics: Learning from Television News in the Internet Age*.

Leonie Huddy is a professor of political science and director of the Center for Survey Research at Stony Brook University. Her general field of interest is the psychological origins and dynamics of public opinion and intergroup relations.

Marion R. Just is a professor of political science at Wellesley College and a research associate of the Joan Shorenstein Center on Press, Politics, and Public Policy at the John F. Kennedy School of Government at Harvard University. She is a coauthor of *Crosstalk: Citizens, Candidates and the Media in a Presidential Campaign* and *Common Knowledge: News and the Construction of Political Meaning*. Her current projects concern political campaigns, psychological aspects of voting, local television news, and political uses of the Internet.

Luke Keele is an assistant professor in the Political Science Department at Ohio State University. His research interests are at the intersection of American politics and statistical research methods.

James H. Kuklinski is the Matthew T. McClure Professor of Political Science at the University of Illinois at Urbana-Champaign. His research interests include the nature and quality of citizen decision making.

Richard R. Lau is a professor of political science at Rutgers University, where he directed the Whitman Center for the Study of Democracy from 2003 to 2006. He is also affiliated with the Center for Health, Health Care Policy, and Aging Research at Rutgers and is currently the director of graduate studies in the Political Science Department.

David C. Leege is a professor emeritus of political science at the University of Notre Dame, author of articles and books on religion and politics and the uses of cultural themes in political campaigns, and former chair of the board of overseers of the American National Election Studies.

Milton Lodge is Distinguished Professor in the Department of Political Science at Stony Brook University and codirector of the Laboratory for Political Research, with research interests in information processing.

Arthur Lupia is the Hal R. Varian Collegiate Professor of Political Science at the University of Michigan and principal investigator of the American National Election Studies. He uses a multidisciplinary perspective to examine how information and incentives affect political behavior.

Michael MacKuen is the Burton Craige Professor of Political Science at the University of North Carolina, Chapel Hill, and the coauthor of *Affective Intelligence and Political Judgment* and *The Macro Polity*. His research has focused on the way that citizens gather and digest information about politics and the economy as well as on the ways that the broader macro polity connects citizens, politicians, and public policy in a systemic way.

George E. Marcus is a professor of political science at Williams College. He is president of the International Society of Political Psychology and chair of the board of directors of the Roper Center.

Rose McDermott is an associate professor of political science and is associated with the Sage Center for the Study of the Mind and the Center for Evolutionary Psychology at the University of California, Santa Barbara, and is a senior scholar at Stanford University's Center for Interdisciplinary Policy, Education, and Research on Terrorism. She has published extensively on political psychology in international relations and on the use of experimentation in political science.

Jesse O. Menning received a master's degree in political science from the University of Michigan in 2005. He is currently an information technology consultant.

Peter F. Nardulli is a professor of political science and law at the University of Illinois at Urbana-Champaign. He is the founding director of the Cline Center for Democracy. His research interests include law and politics, empirical democratic theory, and institutions and societal development.

Michael Neblo is an assistant professor of political science at Ohio State University and a faculty associate in the John Glenn School of Public Affairs and the Center for Interdisciplinary Law and Policy Studies. His research and teaching focus on democratic theory, political psychology, and their intersection.

W. Russell Neuman is the John Derby Evans Professor of Media Technology in Communication Studies at the University of Michigan and coauthor of *The Gordian Knot: Political Gridlock on the Information Highway, Affective Intelligence and Political Judgment,* and *Common Knowledge: News and the Construction of Political Meaning.*

David Redlawsk is an associate professor of political science at the University of Iowa. His research focuses on voter information processing and the role of emotions in voter decision making. He is coauthor of *How Voters Decide: Information Processing during Election Campaigns* and editor of *Feeling Politics.*

Dan Schnur is an adjunct instructor at the University of California, Berkeley, and the University of Southern California. He has worked on four presidential and three gubernatorial campaigns. He now advises nonprofit, foundation, and corporate clients on communications and media strategy.

Darren Schreiber is an assistant professor in the Department of Political Science at the University of California, San Diego. His research interests center on the integration of agent-based models of macro political dynamics and computational models of political cognition in individuals in an effort to illuminate the emergence of political ideology in mass publics. He also served as research director at the Center of Excellence in Cancer Communication Research at the Annenberg School of Communication at the University of Pennsylvania.

Michael L. Spezio is a postdoctoral scholar in affective and social neuroscience at the California Institute of Technology. His work focuses on the neuroscience of social gaze and of complex social decision making based on information from bodily cues.

Nicholas A. Valentino is an associate professor in communication studies and political science at the University of Michigan. His research interests focus on the impact of mass media during political campaigns on the attitudes and political behavior of citizens, with a focus on the impact of political advertising on the criteria citizens use during candidate evaluation.

Kenneth D. Wald is Distinguished Professor of Political Science at the University of Florida. He writes extensively on the political role of religion in advanced industrial societies.

Crustinie ←?

375° pre-heat

lightly Brushes Slices
w/ EVOO

Toast 8 minuts -
            golden Cool

(2) 1 large garlic glove

Store in air tight

(1) Mince garlic food processer / + Chickp (2) ADD 1 C

3 tbl son lemon (3) + 2Tbl wa (4)

½ tsp Salt (5)

½ tsp Pepper (6) — Process til smi

w/ machine running

(7) Till Smooth ¼ Cup Evoo   casly chop

Together (8) ¼ cup Sundried tomatoes

(9) 2 Tbl Basil

(10) 2 Tbl parsly

Blend until finely Chopped

Spoon tbsp
mixture
Garnish w/ chz
or zest